Powering
THE FUTURE

The electricity industry and Australia's energy future

Jan Luksled

Thankyou for you assistance
in making this work.

Jonelist Regards

Michael Johnson.

Edited by Michael Johnson and Stephen Rix

Powering THE FUTURE

The electricity industry and Australia's energy future

Pluto Press Australia in association with
the Public Sector Research Centre,
University of New South Wales

First published in 1991 by Pluto Press Australia Limited,
PO Box 199, Leichhardt, NSW 2040
in association with the Public Sector Research Centre,
University of New South Wales, Kensington, NSW 2033.

Book and cover design by Maqq Walker, Pluto Press Australia

Cover illustration: Kerrie Leishman

Printed and bound by Southwood Press, 80 Chapel Street,
Marrickville, NSW 2204

Australian Library Cataloguing in Publication Data

Powering the future.

Bibliography
ISBN 0 949138 67 3

1. Electric utilities - Australia. I. Johnson, Michael. II Rix, Stephen.
III. University of New South Wales. Public Sector Research Centre.
338. 47621310994

Contents

PREFACE

Powering the Future is the latest example of a development within the Australian trade union movement of commissioning the academic community to undertake major research projects designed to expand the unions' understanding of the motivations and mechanisms of challenges which they face. Such research reports also assist in the development of alternative and effective policies designed to avert the threats posed by those challenges.

The major trade unions in the electricity industry (with financial support from the major industry body) have taken the courageous step of commissioning this report, designed to examine, in some depth, all aspects of the electricity industry. And to do so on a national basis.

The industry is facing three important challenges which it has not previously had to confront.

First, the industry has to meet the challenge of restructuring and improved efficiency if it is to play an important part in meeting Australia's economic and social objectives.

Second is the direct challenge posed by the general retreat from the economic and political advances made over the last two centuries which have seen the rise of the involvement of the public sector in the provision of basic goods and services to a citizenry which has achieved a role in decision-making.

Third is the global challenge we face, in common with other species, resulting from two centuries of human exploitation of the planet's natural resources. For that reason the report examines the electricity industry in the energy sector.

The trade unions have commissioned this research on a national basis. That is indicative of the movement's awareness of the direction that the electricity industry must take in confronting the challenges it faces. The industry has, with few exceptions, been based in the States since the Second World War. Before that, much of the industry was even more fragmented and uncoordinated. It is this fragmentation that has resulted in many of the decisions and policy prescriptions which now bedevil the industry, and the trade unions advocate, as a minimum measure, that the industry become more nationally oriented and aware.

Nevertheless, it also true that the electricity industry while operating under this disadvantage has achieved for the Australian people an electricity service encompassing virtually the whole nation, which operates with high safety standards and which has an enviable record of reliability that compares with the best in the world.

This has been achieved by an industry which is, with very few exceptions, public sector owned and operated. It is this recognition which has led to the research project giving considerable attention to the issue of public sector "reform".

In this report the term "reform" is used honestly. The unions recognise that in many respects the public sector requires genuine reform. Issues of involvement by citizens and by employees are central to our perspective on reform. At a more detailed level — for example in accounting practices and pricing policy — we have also recognised that significant technical, public policy and political changes are required.

However, unlike the ideologues of the corporate sector, the conservative "think tanks" and the senior levels of the bureaucracy, the research team involved in the production of this report refuse to accept that simplistic solutions to complex problems will improve either the operation of public sector bodies or the standard of living of the Australian community. The perspective that the researchers offer on this issue is, unlike the simplicity of the ideologues, rooted firmly in an understanding of the role of the public sector and practical options for change.

The authors of *Powering the Future* have had little more than six months to prepare this report. It needs to be acknowledged that they have managed to produce the most farsighted and wide ranging work on the electricity industry in Australia. All who read it will become aware of the immensity of the task that they agreed to undertake and the quality of the finished result. In addition, the reader will note that the work has been undertaken by an interdisciplinary team who consulted and liaised with a wide range of other organisations. To our knowledge, it the first time that such a group has been brought together to produce a report on the electricity industry from a national perspective.

Finally, we should alert the reader to two salient facts.

What has been achieved is not a policy document. The democratic principles of the trade union movement do not allow policy to be developed independently of the structures which have evolved which embody democratic procedure. The report, therefore, will become an important input to that democratic policy making procedure.

Finally, the reader should be aware that, while the trade union representatives were involved in discussions with the authors regarding the content of the report, at no time did they attempt to restrict the honest and considered views of the authors.

Terry Johnson
Secretary
Electrical Trades Union

Jack Cambourn
Secretary
Federated Engine Drivers and Firemens Association of Australasia

Jack Merchant
President
Municipal Employees' Union

Steve Gibbs
Secretary (to 1 July 1991)
Municipal Officers' Association

For and on behalf of the commissioning unions.

The Commissioning Unions
The following unions commissioned the *Powering the Future* research project undertaken through the Public Sector Research Centre at the University of New South Wales:
Municipal Officers' Association
Electrical Trades Union
Federated Engine Drivers and Firemens Association
Municipal Employees' Union
Australian Institute of Marine and Power Engineers
Amalgamated Metal Workers Union/Association of Drafting, Supervisory and Technical Employees
Public Service Association of New South Wales
Public Sector Union
Association of Professional Engineers of Australia.

The Following Industry Bodies Provided Financial Support
Electricity Supply Association of Australia
State Electricity Commission of Victoria.

An Executive Committee made up representatives of the MOA (Leigh Hocking), ETU (Graeme Watson and Grahame Gosling) and the FEDFA (Chris Price until December 1990, and Roberta Moore since that time); a researcher (John Kaye), the Director of the Public Sector Research Centre (Michael Johnson) and the Project Manager (Stephen Rix) met frequently to discuss the progress of the project.

A Management Committee, to which other commissioning unions sent representatives also met regularly. The Committee was made up a representatives of the PSA of NSW (Richard Hickling); the PSU (Pat Ranald); the ACTU (Jenny Acton); the MEU (Greg McLean); the APEA (Geoff Symington); the AMWU/ADSTE (Peter Ewer and then Anne Donellan); and TUTA (Don Sutherland and then Kathy Galvin).

A representative of the ESAA and SECV (Neville Henderson) was also a member.

Leigh Hocking acted as Secretary to these Committees. He also worked untiringly to ensure the unions' continued involvement in the project process.

Stephen Rix, Project Manager, was responsible for the day-to-day organisation of the research, maintaining links between the research team and the unions, and consultation with members.

What is the Public Sector Research Centre

The Public Sector Research Centre is an inter-disciplinary research centre at the University of New South Wales committed to the production of high quality research and information about all aspects of the public sector. The research and information is disseminated through its publications, seminars and educational activities to governments, the trade union movement, the academic and general community. The Centre was established in 1989 as a joint initiative of the public sector trade unions and the University of New South Wales and is managed by committees, with their members drawn from the University, the trade unions and the community. For further information about the Centre and its activities contact the Secretary, the Public Sector Research Centre, University of New South Wales, PO Box 1, Kensington, NSW 2033.

The Authors

Bob Beatty, Editor *Electricity Week*

Claire Gerson, freelance environmental researcher and journalist, Sydney

Michael Johnson, Director, Public Sector Research Centre, and member of the Faculties of Arts and Social Science and Commerce, University of New South Wales.

John Kaye, Senior Lecturer in the School of Electrical Engineering and Computer Science, University of New South Wales

Colm Kearney, Professor of Economics and Director of The Centre for Product Innovation And Export Development, University of Western Sydney

Hugh Outhred, Senior Lecturer in the School of Electrical Engineering and Computer Science, University of New South Wales

Anthony Owen, Associate Professor of Economics and Director of the Centre for Applied Economic Research, University of New South

Wales

Stephen Rix, Project Manager (on leave from the NSW Treasury)

Leigh Snelling, workplace change consultant, Melbourne

Bob Walker, Professor of Accounting, University of New South Wales

Each chapter contains material from each of the authors and the responsibility for this book is that of the final editorial team.

EXECUTIVE SUMMARY

This book contains the results of a major research project which surveyed the changes taking place in the energy sector in Australia's economy and society; and which assessed the impact these changes would have on the electricity industry beyond the year 2000. The project's research team comprised specialists in public sector management, economics, accounting, the environment, industrial relations and the technical features and operations of the electricity supply industry (ESI).

The research program required an assessment of the state of the electricity industry, its prospects, and its capacity for reform. Out of this assessment came a range of insights into the way in which the electricity industry and the energy sector in which it is embedded, are changing. These insights enabled the development of a consistent strategy designed to equip the industry with the resources needed to confront its challenges. This strategy would provide long term benefits to the institutions, their workforces and the community.

In this executive summary we provide a select list of the research report's findings, and the major policy suggestions arising from them.

We commenced by outlining a set of fundamental industry objectives developed on the basis of workforce and community priorities. A wide disparity between this set of objectives and the industry's performance was found. We also discovered that many of the plans being developed by the electricity authorities (and other reviewers) were inadequate or misplaced. Their plans simply fail to deal with the scale of the changes likely to impact on the industry over the next decade.

The report's principle suggestion is the adoption by all industry participants of an industry strategy.

This strategy would incorporate:
• a program of national integration;
• institutional changes;
• operational reforms; and
• programs to address the industry's current objectives and its challenges over the next decade.

Privatisation is rejected because it would create obstacles to necessary and overdue reform. Rather, the strategy incorporates a range of microeconomic, and public policy, suggestions which would improve production, distribution and end-use efficiencies in the existing industry.

As part of that strategy, we suggest that a representative and accountable *National Electricity Industry Committee* be established which would replace the industry's existing peak body — the Electricity Supply Association of Australia — while absorbing some of its technical functions. Industry trade unions, governments, industry management, the community and environmentalists would be represented at the national and State level, while union representation at the workplace level would be guaranteed.

The National Industry Committee would be an advisory body, developing reform proposals which could engender wide support.

Chapter 1
The major issues confronting the electricity supply industry (ESI) in Australia are its orientation to growth; its lacklustre management performance; the environmental imperative; its State-based orientation resulting in a lack of co-ordination; and inadequate arrangements to ensure proper accountability.

The industry is required to improve its production, distribution and end-use efficiency; to meet customers needs at appropriate prices; to institute processes to ensure optimum returns from its primary energy inputs; and to meet its obligations to its employees and the wider community.

Chapter 2

The central role of the energy conversion industry in the energy sector is indicated. It is clear that, as a result of having this role, the industry needs to build a new set of relationships with its workforce, its customers and the community. The industry needs to incorporate new demand-side and supply-side options which are altering the profile of energy use.

Chapter 3

There is a diverse range of public and private energy sector institutions operating in each State. Each of these institutions is faced with a range of specific challenges, and each has features which tend to slow down its responsiveness to these challenges. The history and structure of the electricity industry, in particular its engineering "culture", are major barriers to reform.

Greater flexibility, enhanced responsiveness to consumers and recognition of the legitimate role of government in the industry were identified as a priorities in the industry.

Chapter 4

This chapter outlines the macroeconomic context in which the energy sector operates. It suggests that the emphasis given to fiscal austerity at the expense of infrastructure development has prejudiced Australia's international competitiveness and export performance. In the context of the challenges facing the electricity industry, the analysis suggests that appropriate levels of new investment in demand side initiatives, the development of the national grid, and the refurbishment of plant are required.

The development of a new system of national accounting which incorporates environmental degradation is likely to significantly alter assessments of the industry's contribution to the Australian economy.

In conventional economic terms, the monopolistic character of the industry, its externalities and the industry's long time horizons for investment (creating large uncertainties) mean that continuing significant levels of government involvement in the industry

are inevitable.

Chapter 5

In Chapter 5 the environmental impact of a traditionally profligate supply-side culture within the industry are outlined.

The development and enforcement of more rigorous environmental standards would contribute to the development of a more environmentally responsible ESI.

Renewable energy technologies, which are capable of linking directly with the transmission grid, are available now. It is clear, however, that a laissez faire approach to their utilisation would significantly slow the *rate* of utilisation.

Threats to occupational and community health and safety emerge from a variety of sources. The industry must undertake programs designed to minimise these threats.

Chapter 6

Energy forecasting methods are reviewed in Chapter 6. It is clear that each of the methods employed has significant deficiencies. Such methods have tended to underrate the importance of the demand-side.

The forecasts for energy consumption to the year 2000 presented in this chapter indicate Australia's consumption of electrical energy use in the economy and the residential sector are likely to rise 2.3 per cent to the year 2000 while consumption for manufacturing use will rise 1.6 per cent.

The increased demand can be met by improving the existing national grid. No expansion in generation capacity until, at the earliest, the mid-1990s is necessary. Greater emphasis on demand-side measures would probably delay the need even further. On the basis of these forecasts, the ESI's demand for black coal is expected to increase by 56 per cent and for brown coal by 9 per cent by 2005 unless an accelerated program of energy substitution is adopted. This is likely to have a range of significant consequences.

This chapter underscores the conclusion that an aggressive coordinated industry strategy is essential to help improve the efficiency of the industry, and to institute demand-side measures.

Chapter 7

Chapter 7 shows that the industry's poor planning decisions have resulted, in part, from a lack of consumer participation in the ESI's decision-making processes. Privatisation, with its consequent need for extensive regulation, offers no solution to this problems and would, in some respects, further aggravate the situation.

Incorporating environmental considerations; a broader, national energy sector perspective; and more open decision-making processes is essential if investment planning is to become more efficient.

Chapter 8

Chapter 8 reviews current industry pricing practices, and shows these are a major source of the industry's poor efficiency performance.

A range of reforms to price setting and tariff determination are discussed, including the adoption of socially optimal pricing practices. Privatisation would not resolve the pricing problem.

Price calculations must incorporate externalities. The socially negative effects of such incorporation must be balanced by strategies to minimise these effects.

Chapters 9 and 10

The evolution of the statutory authority form for public sector undertakings is outlined in Chapter 9. This history shows that current demands for a greater business orientation by authorities have historical antecedents. Demands for greater managerial autonomy are shown to be at odds with the principles of responsible government in a Westminster system.

Greater managerial autonomy and the adoption of private sector methodologies are shown to be fraught with risk for the ultimate owners of statutory authorities and public assets, the citizens. In addition, union and government initiated policies, such as Equal Employment Opportunity, would be prejudiced.

Chapter 10 examines the practical implication of reforms based on poorly understood private sector practices. Not surprisingly, the results are inimical to accountability.

Nevertheless, major deficiencies exist in the accounting practices of electricity (and other) authorities. The chapter concludes that immediate adoption of "Statements of Recommended Practice" would assist in rectifying these deficiencies.

Many electricity authorities' annual reports are deficient in both content and presentation. Originally intended as a major source of accountability, the standards of preparation must be improved immediately. The planning documents of some authorities are shown to be deficient.

While Chapter 10 is critical of the standard of reporting, the role played by Auditors-General result in a general level of public sector financial reporting superior to that in the private sector.

Corporatisation and privatisation are likely to result in reduced levels of accountability and openness. For instance, private sector auditors have less power over their clients' accounting standards than the Auditors-General have over statutory authorities.

Chapter 10 also indicates that reform arguments based on the "discipline of the market" are facile.

Chapter 11

This chapter begins with an analysis of measures which purport to produce accurate comparative efficiency figures. Measures of ESI Total Factor Productivity (TFP) produced by the Industry Commission (IC) are shown to be based on a deficient theory, and their application results in gross inaccuracies. The TFP and economy-wide gains which the IC claims would be available if "international best practices" were adopted are overstated.

The IC's recommendations should therefore be rejected due to their lack of factual basis. The report shows that gains can only be achieved through better management, and more participatory forms of decision-making.

The report did find, however, that while the industry has made significant efficiency gains over the last five years, overall levels are still deficient. In addition, techniques which ensure total, *overall* industry efficiency need to be developed.

Chapter 12

Chapter 12 outlines a National Electricity Industry Strategy.

The Strategy is based on an understanding of the benefits to be gained from genuine microeconomic reform. Such reform gives a central role to trade union participation at all levels of decision-making within the industry.

There are significant employment opportunities available in the industry. The industry requires significant reorientation to realise these opportunities. This reorientation comprises, in addition to the matters summarised above, a representative and national focus. The need for a proper register of the workforce's skills, its gender break-up, its location and the training and development opportunities which are available is urgent for an industry undergoing a radical transformation.

For that reason we have proposed the establishment of a representative *National Electricity Industry Committee*, which would play an advisory role in the industry. The representative nature of that Committee would be duplicated in its sub-committees which would assist in the development of national electricity industry recommendations.

The Committee would be serviced by a full-time secretariat, and would also have an attached research unit. Each of the authorities represented on the National Committee would need to guarantee access to their information bases.

The industry's recent industrial relations experience, as outlined in Appendix 1, indicates that the current management style is inimical to effective participation by the unions in decision-making. The range of matters on which the unions have attempted to achieve a positive policy influence indicates that their involvement would be to the ultimate advantage of the industry, its customers and the community.

ACKNOWLEDGEMENTS

Obviously, no book of this size is solely the result of the work of the authors. Many others have provided considerable assistance and advice.

First, we must thank the trade unionists from the sponsoring unions _ both officials and members — who have made their reflections and knowledge of the industry freely available to us and which has done so much to elucidate the central themes of the book. In particular, we would like to thank Leigh Hocking, John Walkley, Paul Burns and Tim Lee (MOA); Terry Johnson, Graeme Watson, Grahame Gosling and Arnold Sierink (ETU); Jack Cambourn, Chris Price and Roberta Moore (FEDFA); Peter Ewer, Pat Johnston and Alistair Machin (AMWU); and Abe David (BWIU/FEDFA). Laurie Carmichael, Peter Moylan and Jenny Acton (ACTU) provided us with invaluable comments and suggestions.

Neville Henderson (SECV and ESAA) has provided invaluable support.

Our colleagues at the Public Sector Research Centre (Jane Coulter, Barbara Reen, Michael Howard, Laura Mitchell and Ray Harty) were always prepared to discuss the content of the report and provide assistance. Their editorial assistance has made this publication possible. Yvette Stern prepared invaluable material for us as part of her Honours work at the University.

From within the University of New South Wales, the following people have provided support and encouragement: Randall Albury and Jane Morrison who made it possible for the Project Manager to sit, phone and word-process; Gavin McDonell who generously offered advice and assistance based on his own considerable knowledge; Professors Gilbert and Wicken, Pro-Vice Chancellors for helping us to get through the labyrinthine administrative structure of the University; Merrilee Robb, Office of Sponsored Research; the staff of the Printing Unit who performed wonders; the staff of the Menzies Library, amongst whom we must especially mention Richard D'Avigdor; and the University Travel Clerk, Annie Ayoub.

Mark Diesendorf (Australian Conservation Foundation) has always been willing to discuss the material as it was being produced.

Hugh Saddler and Grahame Larcombe took time out from their own heavy workload to discuss the project.

Don Sutherland and Kathy Galvin (Trade Union Training Authority) worked unstintingly to assist us in our consultations with members, and both brought a real depth of knowledge and experience to our work.

Peter Wilmshurst (Co-editor, Legal Service Bulletin) provided us with an unexpected forum in which to air our concerns with the direction of corporatisation.

Tony Aspromourgas spent considerable time providing detailed comments on sections of the research, as did Professor Roger Wettenhall, Peter Kriesler, Professor Ian Inkster, Trevor Stegman and David Richardson.

There are many other people whose assistance we would like to acknowledge — journalists, public servants, merchant bankers and others — but whom we cannot name. This is indicative of a society which is closing its doors to open and free debate. It is a disturbing development.

ABBREVIATIONS

AARF	Australian Accounting Research Foundation
ABARE	Australian Bureau of Agriculture and Resource Economics
ACA	Australian Coal Association
ACF	Australian Conservation Foundation
ACS	Australian Construction Services
ACT	Australian Capital Territory
ACTEW	ACT Electricity and Water Authority
ACTU	Australian Council of Trade Unions
AGA	Australian Gas Association
ALP	Australian Labor Party
AMC	Australian Manufacturing Council
AMWU	Amalgamated Metal Workers Union
APEA	Australian Petroleum Exploration Association Ltd
APEA	Association of Prefessional Engineers, Australia
ARU	Australian Railways Union
ATSIC	Aboriginal and Torres Strait Islanders Commission
BEIR	Biological Effects of Ionising Radiation
BHP	Broken Hill Proprietary Limited
BOMA	Building Owners and Managers Association
BOO	Build, Own and Operate
BWIU	Building Workers Industrial Union
CO_2	Carbon Dioxide
CEGB	Central Electricity Generation Board, UK
CHEIS	Community Home Energy Improvement Sheme
CHP	Combined Heat and Power (co-generation)
CPI-X	Price Cap System
CRA	Conzinc Rio-Tinto Australia Ltd
CSIRO	Commonwealth Scientific and Industrial Research Organisation
CSO	Community Service Obligation
DEN	Department of Energy, UK
DENDE	Department of National Development and Energy
DGES	Director General of Electricity, UK
DITR	Department of Industry Technology and Resources

DSM	Demand-Side Management
DSO	Demand-Side Option
ECNSW	Electricity Commission of New South Wales
EDF	Electricite de France
EEC	European Economic Commission
EIA	Environmental Impact Statement
Elcom	Electricity Commission of New South Wales
EMF	Electromagnetic Field
EPA	Environmental Protection Agency,
EPAC	Economic Planning and Advisory Council
ERA	Energy Resources Australia
ERDIC	Energy Research Development and Information Service
ESAA	Electricity Supply Association of Australia
ESD	Economically Sustainable Development
ESI	Electricity Supply Industry
ETSA	Electricity Trust of South Australia
ETSU	Energy Technology Support Unit, UK
ETU	Electrical Trades Union
FEDFA	Federated Engine Drivers and Firemen's Association of Australasia
FES	Fuel and Electricity Survey
GBE	Government Business Enterprise
GDP	Gross Domestic Product
GFCV	Gas and Fuel of Victoria
GTLC	Gippsland Trades and Labour Council
HEAS	Home Energy Advisory Service
HEC	Hydro Electric Commission
HZ	Hertz
IAEA	International Atomic Energy Agency
IEA	International Energy Agency
IC	Industry Commission
ICRP	International Commission for Radiological Protection
IMP	A Macroeconomic Model
IOU	Investor Owned Utilities
LCP	Least Cost Pricing
LPG	Liquid Petroleum Gas
LRMC	Long Run Marginal Cost Pricing
LRP	Long Run Pricing
MCC	Melbourne City Council
MOA	Municipal Officers Association
MTFU	Metal Trades Federation of Unions
MW	Megawatt
NCSC	National Companies and Securities Commission

NEED	Demand Side Intangibles
NGC	National Grid Company, UK
NIEIR	National Institute of Economic and Industrial Research
NIMBY	Not In My Backyard (Syndrome)
NSW	New South Wales
NTPWA	Northern Territory Power and Water Authority
OECD	Organisation for Economic Cooperation and Development
OPEC	Organisation of Petroleum Exporting Countries
ORANI	A Macroeconomic Model
PAWA	Northern Territory Power and Water Authority
Pj	Petajoules
PJT	Prices Justification Tribunal
PSRC	Public Sector Research Centre
PUC	Public Utilities Commission,US
PUR	Public Utilities Regulation Act,US
QEC	Queensland Electricity Commission
RAPS	Remote Area Power Supply
R & D	Research and Development
ROR	Rate of Return
RTA	Roads and Traffic Authority, New South Wales
SE	Sydney Electricity
SECV	State Electricity Commission of Victoria
SECWA	State Energy Commission of Western Australia
SGDP	Sustainable Gross Domestic Product
SMA	Snowy Mountain Hydro Electric Authority
SMHEA	Snowy Mountains Hydro Electric Authority
SNA	International Standard for Accounting
SO_2	Sulphur Dioxide
SOE	State Owned Enterprises
SOFC	Solid Oxide Fuel Cells
SPCC	State Pollution Control Commission
SRA	State Rail Authority
SRMC	Short Run Marginal Cost Pricing
SSCFPA	Senate Standing Committee on Finance and Public Administration
SSCIST	Senate Standing Committee on Industry, Science and Technology
STORPS	Statements of Recommended Practices
TOU	Time of Use
TPA	The Pipeline Authority
UMFA	United Mineworkers Federation of Australia
VTHC	Victorian Trades Hall Council
WCED	World Commission on Environmental Development

CHAPTER 1

POWERING THE FUTURE

1.1 Introduction

Powering the Future: The Electricity Industry and Australia's Energy Future is a report that shows that a national electricity industry strategy, which would incorporate national integration within an overall national energy policy has become a major economic, political and public administration priority. The urgency comes from the need for structural adjustment, from the impact of the current recession and the realisation of the environmental damage the industry has caused. All levels of government in Australia, the trade union movement, the private sector, and the community are putting the industry under minute scrutiny.

At present, many of the electricity authorities, the Industry Commission, the Commission for the Future, State and federal working parties, environmental groups, academics and other researchers are all developing ideas for the industry based on their own perspectives. Few (if any) of them have attempted to bring together an analysis of all the factors affecting the industry and develop an overall strategy for reform. The overall objective of all this research and policy development should be a programme for a more efficient, environmentally sound industry that can meet people's energy needs, and contribute to the economic and social objectives of Australia.

However only this project, commissioned by the employees in the industry, and financially supported by the Electricity Supply Association of Australia, has attempted to develop an integrated analytical and policy package that begins to address all these objectives. The reasons are the obvious ones: the employees in the industry and their trade unions are concerned more than anybody with what they do and how they do it; with its impact on the economy, society, the environment; and of course with the factors that determine their working life. *Powering the Future* sets out to outline an industry strategy that reflects these concerns.

Over time, the electricity industry, because of the flexibility and utility of its product, has taken a greater role in economic and social life. During the 1970s the electricity industry expanded rapidly (along with the energy sector in general). Electricity led the way in expanding its capacity to supply the increased demand for energy which, it was anticipated, would be needed for economic growth. Part of this growth was expected to occur in the form of a 'Resources Boom' that, ultimately, did not meet expectations. The result was stagnation in the industry in the 1980s.

In the face of this decline, the major trade unions representing and serving the employees in the industry decided to take the initiative and commission a review of the sector and the broader energy industry in which it is embedded. The objective was to identify the major changes likely to take place in the industry and their consequences, to equip all the people within the industry with this knowledge and to identify strategies that would help manage these changes. It was stipulated that the strategy would have to meet the needs of those inside and outside the industry.

1.2 The Trade Union Movement and Reform

The decision to commission the report is part of an ongoing commitment by the trade union movement to the principle that reform is necessary and urgent in respect to the electricity industry in particular, and the economy in general. This commitment began with the negotiation of the Australian Council of Trade Unions/Australian Labor Party (ACTU/ALP)

Prices and Incomes Accord in 1982, an agreement that marked a commitment of the trade unions to an industry development approach contained within industry policies, as we discuss in Chapter 12 of this report.

Through the ACTU, the electricity industry unions were party to this new perspective that has, most recently, informed award restructuring. A desire to ensure these reforms are backed up by an industry strategy has guided the unions' contribution to this report, which is part of the process needed to build an efficient and effective electricity industry within the energy sector beyond the year 2000.

1.3 Key Emerging Issues

There are a wide range of issues that are of concern in an electricity industry undergoing rapid change. These include:

Orientation to growth

There is a concern among many in the industry that despite broad government and community commitment to a drive for energy efficiency and a limit to carbon dioxide emissions, some parts of the electricity industry are still setting themselves unrealistic load-growth objectives. This is something that promotes wasteful energy use and will be harmful to the industry and its customers in the medium term. It also puts off the need to take decisions about revamping tariffs for an energy-efficiency dominated environment.

That such a perspective still guides many decision-makers in the industry was borne out at a conference in Sydney in 1989 which an energy minister opened with reassuring words about how the government was committed to reaching the Toronto goal on greenhouse, only to be followed on the platform by the chief executive of his generating authority who urged the industry to "get out there and sell more electricity" (Beatty, 1989b, p.2).

A few months later, when the minister announced approval to go ahead with a scheme that would connect 200 remotely situated property owners to the grid, doubtful landholders had their arms twisted by the knowledge that they would be denied access to a remote power subsidy if they declined to take part in the scheme. That meant subsidising a major grid connection

for very small load and high losses, in preference to sustaining a remote area power supply industry that was doing quite well in the area (Allison et al, 1990).

Efficiency

Efficiency is a high priority for management and unions. In the privately owned energy sectors, this scarcely rates a mention.

It is all too common that, when managements of both public and private utilities undertake efficiency drives without consultation, they seem to come up with schemes that focus on shedding jobs, rather than ways of expanding into related areas that develop the energy business.

Environment

Here the dominant concern is the greenhouse issue. Responses vary across the energy industries, but oil and coal interests are generally against taking any action. The position of the electricity industry varies between States, and management stances and government policies are as yet unclear in some States. There are also emerging concerns with the environmental consequences of the establishment and operation of electricity infrastructure.

National coordination or cooperation

Undoubtedly there are gains to be made from the interconnection of the State electricity systems but whether that should be preceded by corporatisation is a major question for the trade unions, and also has implications for the management of public sector assets. Electricity supply authority managements are in favour of a national grid, but they do not want it to be owned by a single entity, public or private, and this perspective is shared by the trade unions.

Decentralisation

In contrast to the recent past this is seen as a major way of increasing organisational and managerial efficiency. One of its major effects is that it dictates that union structures have to be localised. This can be a problem for highly centralised union structures, as the Public Service Association of New Zealand found during the restructuring of the industry in recent years.

Accountability of planning processes

The trade unions continue to advocate structures being set up, and decision making processes implemented, which are open to public scrutiny and which are accountable to the industry's ultimate owners, workers, and consumers. There are also many in the community concerned with the industry's lack of accountability on such issues as the environmental consequences of the industry's current operations.

Private sector participation

The momentum for privatisation — in a variety of forms — is building. This is a major concern as its necessity in most cases, has not been proven.

Electric and magnetic fields

This is a 'sleeper' issue that is beginning to waken. It has both community and occupational health and safety implications. Some consider the industry globally has been too emotional in its treatment of this issue (Brodeur, 1989). The recent inquiry for the New South Wales government by Sir Harry Gibbs reported that the industry should implement a policy of "prudent avoidance" in respect to fields (Gibbs,1991, p.60).

Risk management

Risks from a wide variety of sources (including plant and health and safety issues) are of continuing concern.

Revamping tariffs

This is considered an urgent necessity. The current tariff structure is a major reason for the slowness of energy efficiency initiatives to get off the ground. This subject is dealt with in detail in Chapters 7 and 8.

A viable power equipment manufacturing industry

It is thought that for many years now the Australian electrical manufacturing industry has been trying to engender some standardisation among supply authorities so that they can lengthen manufacturing runs and use the local market as a base from which to win export sales. Very little progress has been made, and a major cost-cutting opportunity has been foregone. In many cases the reason is ill-placed engineering pride, coupled with an "us-and-them" attitude on the part of the authorities.

1.4 The Scope for Change in Line with Strategic Objectives
Moving from supply-side to demand-side activities

An area of major job growth is seen in demand-side management (DSM). Such potential can be effectively utilised if the public sector becomes involved, whether through investment programs or direct participation in installing and maintaining demand-side options (DSOs).

At present, industry management is seen to be hesitating: the newness of the technology and lack of familiarity with managing means that its adoption has been slow. According to one distribution authority chief executive: "In some utilities, paralysis through analysis of possible benefits has replaced a real commitment to DSM as a significant alternative to generation expansion" (Hoffman, 1991, p.1).

Speaking in favour of the acceleration of demand side activities in Australian utilities at a power industry reform conference, he listed fifteen reasons why implementation has been so slow, including the narrow outlook of engineering staff, and the domination of utilities by generation interests. In addition, many utilities are taking the view that they need to bolster financial positions that have been considerably weakened by a combination of capacity surpluses and price restraint before they start investing in energy efficiency.

Other Australian supply industry leaders who have given their public backing to an accelerated demand management push are George Bates and Jim Smith of the State Electricity Commission of Victoria, and Graeme Longbottom of the Hydro-Electric Commission of Tasmania.

This move to demand-side activities will cut overall energy costs and, depending on how it is implemented, could boost employment on the distribution side of the power industry. It could form the focus for a campaign for power industry change that combines environmental, consumer and union interests, all of whom stand to benefit.

In addition to the impact on local industry, the potential for — not to mention the global environmental significance of — exporting demand-side technology means it can be an important contributor to the national economy in both the public and private sectors.

The drive for efficiency — a double edged sword

The pressure for the electricity supply industry to increase its efficiency and reduce costs poses a difficult challenge for unions: on the one hand it is in the interest of all workers to maintain a healthy economy and on the other hand pressure for greater efficiency often means pressure on staffing levels.

It is apparent from the employment trends in the industry that jobs in the industry have been disappearing over the past five years, so a new approach may be useful. Can the industry be steered in a direction that encompasses new jobs? That is a possibility. One of the options is demand management which is, apart from pilot activity by the State Electricity Commission of Victoria, an untried force in Australia. The move to demand side management is a major theme of this report and there is an emerging management commitment to the concept.

Labour force reductions

One of the major thrusts of the changes being implemented is towards greater labour productivity. Voluntary redundancy schemes are being used to achieve this goal, and there is little sign that this pressure will reduce.

For example the Strategic Plan for the New South Wales electricity industry targeted a 24 per cent increase in productivity between 1989/90 and 1994/95 (Electricity Supply Industry of New South Wales, 1991). The plan estimates that staff numbers in the distribution section of the industry will decline progressively from about 15,600 at 30 June 1990 "to a target level of 14,000 by June 1995". This downward pressure on staff numbers in NSW electricity distribution follows a strenuous campaign on redundancies that has seen a 30 per cent reduction in staff over two years in the generation and transmission side of the industry from about 10,500 in 1988 to 7,300 in 1990.

It is worth noting that savings from these cuts in the workforce do not appear to have been passed on to the consumer in the form of price cuts. For example, although the wages bill for the Electricity Commission of New South Wales went down from 1988 to 1990 due to the separations of some 3000 people, and labour and labour-related costs went down A$35m, the average price at which the Commission sold electricity over that period increased by more than 10.5 per cent to 5.85c/kWh.

In 1990 the Electricity Commission of New South Wales' (ECNSW) labour-cost reductions were more than offset by a $55M increase in its operating costs, which the Commission says was "mainly as a result of increased emphasis on plant maintenance at power stations" (ECNSW, 1990), an emphasis that is likely to grow as the proportion of new plant commissioned in the total activity of the ECNSW declines over the next few years.

Nevertheless, the New South Wales industry as a whole is bent on more staff cuts across the board. The first ever statewide electricity supply industry strategic plan was approved by the Electricity Council, a coordinating body, in 1990. That plan calls for a 24 per cent labour productivity increase within four years, during a time when sales are expected to grow at between 0.8 per cent and 4 per cent a year. Even if the highest sales level does transpire, that still means some 8 per cent of the industry's 22,900 staff have been targeted for departure, i.e. at the lowest estimate, some 500 jobs a year are targeted over the next four years.

New South Wales is not alone in this endeavour to increase its labour productivity: the State Energy Commission of Western Australia has targeted a 15 per cent increase in power station labour productivity to be achieved between 1991 and 1995, and recent history shows that the workforce in Australia's electricity supply industry as a whole declined from 80,400 in 1985 to 71,100 in 1989. These reductions are a major source of concern to the trade unions and the community as not only are jobs lost but, under the existing arrangements in the industry, the skills and experience of the people concerned are lost as well.

Organisational change as a medium of reform

One way reform is being introduced in the industry is corporatisation. Corporatisation has done the rounds of other public sector activities, such as airlines, broadcasting and telecommunications. An anticipated gain from this process is enhanced efficiency. For a range of reasons, this is a major area of examination by this report (Chapters 9 and 10).

One of the first organisations scheduled to be

corporatised is the Australian Capital Territory's Electricity and Water Authority. This medium-sized enterprise operates at the electricity distribution level, and has a turnover of about $200M, some 85 per cent of which is earned from electricity sales. It has been set a corporatisation target date of 1 July, 1991.

Although the New South Wales government has been talking about the corporatisation of the ECNSW for some time, it is now apparent that the initial target date of March 1991 has not been met and the latest indications at the time of publication were that the move was likely to be made before the end of 1991 (Pickard, 1991, p.10).

The Queensland electricity supply industry is being sized up for corporatisation. Early in 1991 a steering committee was set up to deal with the question, and was looking at models with a number of degrees of disaggregation. The Minister for Resource Industries, Ken Vaughan, said that privatisation was not a possibility (Vaughan, 1991).

Private sector participation

Private sector participation in the industry is already extensive through the provision of generating capacity and contracting out of services. Hundreds of megawatts are already installed in the Pilbara, at Mt Isa, at Anglesea in Victoria and new investment is under way at Gunnedah in New South Wales as well as on several small hydro schemes throughout the state. In addition the State Electricity Commission of Victoria is actively encouraging the development of co-generation in industry and hospitals throughout the State.

In the Northern Territory, a private company has been licensed to build and operate a 132kV transmission line, and to sell to customers nearby. The territory's public utility, the Power and Water Authority, sells power to the operator, NT Power Pty Ltd, at one end of the line and buys it back at the other (*Electricity Week*, 26 February, 1990).

Thus private sector participation in the power industry has already begun, and is likely to be extended in the coming decade to baseload stations. Schemes being considered in the short term include selling off Victoria's Loy Yang B and a privately owned and operated 600MW station at Collie in Western Australia.

The push for more gas-fired generation

Another impetus for change is the search for less labour-intensive and less CO_2-producing forms of generation. It should be noted that gas is more effective if sold directly to customers for use in heating, cooking and hot water systems than in turning it into electricity first. Further gas-fired generating plant is less expensive. The Australian Gas Association has been pushing this hard in recent years (AGA, 1990), while at the same time looking for new electricity utility customers.

1.5 Priorities for Action

In the present decade, the electricity industry will undergo a transformation, with the search for efficiency goals and increasing emphasis on the demand-side as the two major driving forces. Changes in industry structure and modes of production are likely to be substantial. Resistance from industry management is likely to be considerable given its slow reaction to the pressures that have been growing for some time.

The pressure on trade unions will be enormous as they not only have to deal with the general programme of reform undertaken with the other members of the ACTU, but with the changes taking place in their own industry as well.

As an example of what's happening in the industry, the power unions in Western Australia have been faced by demands from the employer and industrial tribunals for input to restructuring to the point where they have been unable to participate in the decision making about establishing a private power station in the State.

In the current climate, management is instituting cost-cutting designated as "politically necessary" with a speed that threatens to brush the unions aside. The unions are under pressure to develop a role for themselves, which ensures that changes being made reflect their members' interests.

It was as a result of these imperatives that the Public Sector Research Centre research team was called upon to undertake research into the industry and help develop strategies for change.

1.6 *Powering the Future's* Guiding Principles and Perspectives

To meet the demands of the project, an interdisciplinary team of researchers was drawn together with broad experience within and outside the industry. The project's work started out by identifying principles and issues which were considered important for the project to consider if the electricity industry was to continue to play an important role in the economy and society.

The research work took a strategic approach that focused on the electricity industry in its present and likely future contexts. Within this framework, project participants developed a range of overarching policy guidelines which would contribute to the achievement of enhanced industry efficiency and effectiveness to maximise the welfare of those inside and outside the industry. These included the objectives of:

- assuring consumers the right to enjoy energy services at a reasonable price;
- a recognition of both the key role of energy in the nation's economy, and of the electricity industry's contribution to this. To play its part in the energy sector there must be the development of an industry strategy which is aimed at the achievement of efficiency gains in a rational and planned manner; and
- maintaining the nation's equity in its resource base, and exploitation of these resources in an environmentally sound manner.

Guided by these objectives, the researchers, based on their industry experience and assessment of the future, identified specific factors requiring review which they considered were likely to be critical to the future of the energy sector and the electricity industry. Accepted wisdom has often been to ignore these factors.

The analysis of the electricity industry recognised its position as part of an overall energy sector. The commitment to the efficient operation of the sector, and the industry, led to consideration of all related issues. These included the fact that the greenhouse scenario should be considered as a probable reality, and that a move to more demand-side emphasis in the industry (and a long-term commitment to renewable sources of energy) was considered likely.

Arising from this consideration, and the pattern of past development of the industry, it was considered that there had probably been too great a reliance on supply-side analyses of energy issues which has distorted policy responses to energy related problems. The industry's effect on the environment had been mostly ignored.

The consequences of the supply-side emphasis was that most of the energy sector institutional arrangements in Australia concern suppliers. The consideration of effects of the industry on consumers was limited to safety issues. This pattern of development, as Chapter 3 shows, has been a major constraint on policy initiation and implementation. A result has been a general failure of accountability provisions. The project team considered that demand-side interest would accelerate in the future and would necessitate changes to these arrangements, including release of more market information.

Related to the focus of research there was thought to be a need for new research on monitoring technologies; for identifying consumer needs; for developing detailed indicators of efficiency and effectiveness; and developing new institutional models that reflect the demands of the industry and the community. This was necessary because, for example, current demand forecasting methodologies are inadequate to deal with emerging energy issues, while performance indicators and efficiency measures were poorly developed and inadequate.

These issues are taken up here in Chapters 6 to 12. Given this perspective the *Powering the Future* team examined the major aspects of the industry with a view to developing suggestions for strategies to meet the likely imperatives of the industry into the next century.

The electricity industry and an industry strategy

The greatest challenge in adapting and taking the leadership in a time of rapid change is that of changing the *culture* of an industry. This means everybody has to be involved in the process of change, most importantly, those employed in the industry. As part of any reorientation of the electricity industry there should therefore be a recognition of the right of trade unions to a role in decision-making, a role which they can only perform if they are given access to all relevant sector and industry information and are represented on industry bodies. This issue is a major theme of Chapters 9 to 12.

Change means the provision of the human skills and the organisation to undertake it and creating this capacity through industry retraining. This could be combined with demand-side service provision and application of environmentally sensitive extensions of activities to provide a realistic and financially responsible means of reallocating some of the electricity industry workforce to socially-useful activities and developing new job opportunities.

Breaking up the industry into a "core-periphery" model would destroy the capacity to restructure, and act as an obstacle to change. Dismantling an industry that has many characteristics of a natural monopoly (and privatising it) was found to be a severely limited option.

This issue is the subject of particular attention right throughout this report, especially Chapter 11. The historically necessary role that the public sector has played in the development of the electricity industry, and the deficiencies of the private sector in providing public goods is examined in Chapters 9 to 11. A search was made to see if there were any rational arguments for the disaggregation of the generation and transmission networks. Efficiency considerations also suggested that pricing policy should be examined to identify opportunities to enhance the achievement of the industry's goals. This and tariff setting is dealt with in Chapters 7 and 8.

National integration of the industry is a desirable and inevitable short-term development, but it was thought that the institutional arrangements need to reflect growing community and trade union concern with the operations of the existing State-based authorities. Both the State-based organisations and the peak organisation, the Electricity Supply Association of Australia (ESAA), presently direct the industry with little community or trade union participation. The reasons for this are outlined in Chapters 3 and 8 which reviews the sector's institutions, and shows that their development was conditioned by the "golden age" of the 1940s and 1950s. It is considered the State authorities should undergo fundamental reform to ensure that public scrutiny and participation in decision-making becomes possible; and that the ESAA should wind-up when the National Electricity Industry Committee is established.

Economic framework
Powering the Future also examines the economic role of the electricity industry. It was considered

that macroeconomic policy settings need to incorporate an emphasis on adequate provision of future necessary infrastructure, such as refurbishment and the creation of a national grid. In addition, the provision of demand-side facilities would bring substantial economic and social benefits. These matters are the subject of Chapters 4 and 5 of this report, which conclude that national accounting standards must change if they are to adequately incorporate environmental issues.

Finally, it was recognised that given the large role energy plays in some value-added, export industries, improvements in the efficiency of the energy sector can be expected to flow through to these industries and this must be examined. This is the subject of Chapter 11 which finds that the measures used to assess the industries efficiency are poor and badly used.

Nevertheless, there is evidence of efficiency gains over the last five years, a process which could be accelerated through a process of genuine consultation. For example, the SECV achieved a 50 per cent improvement in productivity between 1985 and 1989 (SECV Annual Report, 1990), although this is a partial measure and tells us nothing about other efficiency gains that may have been jeopardised (e.g. end-use efficiency).

Environmental policy
In respect of the environmental impact of the industry, a more rational balance between supply-side and demand-side policies needs to be developed is a theme running throughout the report, beginning in Chapter 2.

In this light, States' development policies need to be examined and amended to place less reliance on an expansionist electricity industry and a better focus on overall energy management. It was proposed there must be greater renewable energy research and development expenditure undertaken, and less emphasis given to nuclear energy research. These issues are the subject of Chapter 5. The environmental consequences of mining activity associated with electricity generation is also considered, and it is suggested that this concern should be incorporated into long-term planning. Associated with these questions was that of occupational, and community, health and safety issues which need to be incorporated into an energy strategy.

Public policy issues

It was considered that the greatest failure of the electricity industry as a whole over the last two decades has been the failure of management at the institutional and political level, failures that have been exposed through poor investment decisions, wasted resources and the resulting social and economic dislocation. Electricity authorities have, in many cases, been managed like political fiefdoms, hidden from proper public scrutiny and accountability and this is likely to remain a problem unless alternative governance models and strategies are adopted. This is a central focus of this report especially in Chapters 9, 10 and 12.

It is considered that a consistent rationale needs to be developed for the management of statutory authorities, which takes into account the concept of responsible government. This is the subject of Chapters 9 and 10. It was considered that it needs to be recognised that the total removal of statutory authority decision-making from the political realm will never be achieved, and that the history of the electricity industry indicates that many positive features actually flow from this.

Further, it was considered there are significant deficiencies in the private sector legal environment which should not be duplicated in the public sector. The New South Wales experience of corporatisation was examined. It was clear from this examination that it provided few good reasons for extending the application of such policies. For example, it is shown that the choice of accounting techniques and methods has a great capacity to create illusions. Accordingly, arguments based on the application of private sector accounting standards and methodologies to the public sector have little direct applicability. Nevertheless, it was thought that accounting practices in the public sector required development and continual monitoring. There should also be a standardisation of such practices and special attention should be paid to the role of auditors in the public sector, these matters being the subject of Chapter 10 and elsewhere in the report.

Privatisation was examined to see it would lead to the substitution of one form of regulation

(ownership) for another (legislation), and overseas experience was to reviewed to see what support there was for this policy prescription. Chapter 11 examines this matter.

Finally, no statutory authority (or any other business for that matter), is limited to having solely financial goals and in recognition of this, the application of concepts such as community services obligations are reappraised in the light of their role in the industry.

Community matters

Related to the community role of government business enterprises (GBEs) it was thought that sections of the Australian population might have been underserviced by the electricity industry, and that realistic policies and practices might need to be developed to deal with these inadequacies (e.g. extension of power to remote aboriginal communities, and services for people with disabilities).

The role of the unions

Finally, and perhaps most importantly it was thought more democratic and accountable forms of policy and decision making need to be developed, with a recognition of the rights of workers and consumers to information and involvement in institutionalised representative forums. The research was guided by the recognition that public sector managers need to recognise that they manage assets which are, ultimately, owned not by governments but by the citizens.

1.7 Conclusion

The research team has tried to present the material in as an accessible form as possible. It deals with complex theoretical and empirical issues in as simple a way possible recognising the need to deal with some issues in technical detail for reasons of exposition.

Powering the Future: The Electricity Industry in Australia's Energy Future was initiated as a result of a wide range of pressures on the electricity industry, its employees and their representative trade unions. These pressures come from general economic and environmental concerns, specific institutions, interest groups and a wide range of individuals inside and outside the industry, some with the interests of the industry at heart and others without.

In the following chapters of this report, we attempt to provide some information and ideas to facilitate the management of change that will benefit the industry and the community.

CHAPTER 2

ELECTRICITY: MAKING ENERGY WORK

2.1 Ways of Thinking about Energy

The electricity supply industry is one of Australia's major industries. It is a significant employer and makes an important contribution to the nation's Gross Domestic Product (GDP) and is a significant energy user and supplier. It is appropriate to think of electricity as one part of the energy sector; hence in this Chapter we provide an overview of that sector.

Energy is a critically important resource in modern Australia. It provides inputs for production in all sectors of the economy, and for vital functions in domestic and social settings. Its extraction, processing, transmission and use have major impacts on the environment, both local and global. The sector is a major employer in its own right — in several cases the dominant regional industrial activity — and the price of energy is an important factor in the economy generally and for the community's standard of living.

There are very few instances in which energy products are enjoyed for their own sake[1]. Gas is valued for its ability to provide heat through combustion and, ultimately, to help cook dinners, raise temperatures and provide motive force in industrial processes; petroleum, gas and electricity are inputs to transport.

One energy policy analyst put it well when he said:

> The use of energy is not an end in itself, either for society or for the individuals who make up society... Societies and individuals do not need or want energy, they need food, clothing, housing, transport, health, education and so on. Energy helps obtain these things, and that is why it is important for society (Saddler, 1981).

The veracity of this observation has important implications for the Australian electricity supply industry, which has traditionally concentrated its efforts on selling electrical energy, rather than on need and demand patterns in relation to its product.

The Australian government's most recent national energy policy paper, issued in 1988, elaborates a detailed perspective on the role of energy in society:

> Energy is fundamental to our living standards and to the conduct of economic activity. Its costs, including cost inputs to transport, are a significant factor in the costs of almost all goods and services traded in the domestic and international markets. Satisfactory energy supplies are fundamental to achieving our national objectives of economic growth and security, bearing in mind that, if energy supplies are inadequate or supplied inefficiently, this will represent a serious constraint on economic growth and on community living standards. Moreover, effective energy supply, including delivery to final consumers, usually requires substantial investment, the nature and scale of which can constitute a major demand on the community's capital resources. Such capital must be invested as efficiently as possible (Department of Primary Industries and Energy, 1988, p.1).

However, the final sentences in this passage approach energy from the supply-side. They indicate the continued domination of that approach. While the statement emphasises correctly that a major determinant of satisfactory outcomes from the use of energy is the cost at which the energy is sold, **it fails to recognise that the efficiency with which energy is used is often just as important as the cost of supply.**

The shift in thinking to placing a priority on end-use efficiency, which has gained legitimacy and respectability in many energy bodies in the United States and some European nations over the last decade, has only recently begun to surface in the mainstream of the Australian energy industry.

Although in other parts of the world financial efficiency and customer satisfaction appear to have been the prime motivations for this policy shift, in Australia these did not become salient factors in public utility thinking until concern over the impact of the greenhouse effect took hold in the community in the late 1980s. However late it was in reaching Australia, the change of focus has now occurred: in the Australia of the 1990s and beyond, energy will be thought about more in terms of who is using it and what they want from it. This does not mean that supply-side issues will not be important. Rather, it indicates a move to a more balanced perspective on the whole sector. That is the perspective from which we look at energy in this chapter.

2.2 Who Uses Energy in Australia?

In broad terms, the biggest users are the transport industry, and all other industry including agriculture, mining, iron and steel production and aluminium smelting. Residential use of energy accounts for about 12 per cent of the total, and commercial institutions 5 per cent. The remaining 2 per cent are petroleum products used as lubricants, greases, bitumen and solvents, i.e. although they are potential sources of energy, they are not used to provide energy. More details are provided below.

The current pattern of energy consumption in Australia²

Total energy consumption in Australia in 1990-91 was an estimated 4096 petajoules (PJ), an increase of 3.7 per cent on 1989-90 which reinforces the trend of relatively high rates of growth in energy consumption evident since the upturn in economic activity following the economic recession of the early 1980s. This is now likely to change, as we show in later in this report.

Within overall energy consumption, the share of various primary fuels has changed markedly since the 1960s, due to the discovery of significant quantities of indigenous natural gas and the price pressures of the 1970s. Of total consumption, coal (both black and brown) and crude oil/petroleum products currently account for 41 per

cent and 36 per cent respectively. Natural gas accounts for 17 per cent, while wood (2 per cent), bagasse (2 per cent), hydro (1 per cent) and solar (negligible) are of relatively minor importance. The trend away from oil is most noticeable if these figures are compared to comparable data for the early 1970s. In 1970-71 crude oil's share of total energy consumption peaked at 51.3 per cent. While conservation and substitution pressures within the energy sector have been most pronounced for crude oil and petroleum products, the rate of decline in oil's share of total consumption has slowed markedly in the past few years. This is probably attributable to the relatively low level of world oil prices between 1986 and 1989.

Petroleum products

The major end-use of crude oil and other petroleum fuels is in the transport sector, and particularly in road transport. The potential for economic substitution of other fuels for petroleum products in all transport applications remains limited, despite ongoing effort to develop alternatives. There has, however, been substantial substitution out of oil-based products in non-transport applications. The consumption of petroleum products in non-transport applications has fallen from 44 per cent of total petroleum products consumption in 1973-74 to 23 per cent in 1989-90. The declining share of non-transport uses is further evidenced by the changing shares of types of petroleum products within the total. Since the late 1970s sales of fuel oil, kerosene, heating oil and industrial diesel fuel have all fallen substantially. Over the same period consumption of the transport fuels (automotive gasoline, automotive diesel oil, aviation turbine fuel and LPG) has continued to increase.

Automotive gasoline is used almost exclusively as a fuel in road transport vehicles, with only very small amounts used in other applications. Rates of growth in consumption of automotive gasoline have declined sharply since the early 1960s. Consumption growth fell steadily to around 5 per cent a year in the early 1970s. Following the first oil price shock, growth fell to less than 4 per cent a year, and in 1979-80 the second oil price shock induced a fall in the level of consumption. Since that time, consumption growth has been irregular, but generally low. There were signs that this

situation had changed recently: growth of 3.5 per
cent in 1987-88 was the highest since 1977-78,
and was followed by a relatively strong 3.1 per
cent growth in 1988-89. However, the rate fell
back to 1.1 per cent in 1989-90. The proportion
of unleaded automotive gasoline reached 27 per
cent of the total in 1989-90, and is expected to
account for over half by 1993-94.

Automotive diesel oil is mostly used as a road
transport fuel, although small amounts (9 per
cent of total consumption in 1989-90) are used
in non-transport applications, 2 per cent is used
in water transport and 7 per cent is used for rail
transport, where it is the major fuel. Consumption growth has generally been much higher
than for automotive gasoline, and was a strong
7.3 per cent in 1988-89 and 3.4 per cent in 1989-
90.

Natural gas
Even more dramatic a change than oil's falling
share of total energy consumption has been the
emergence of natural gas as a major source of
energy in Australia. Since the exploitation of the
Bass Strait fields commencing in 1969, natural
gas use has increased from a negligible share of
total energy consumption to 17.4 per cent in
1989-90. The major end-uses of natural gas are
as a fuel for manufacturing industries (43.1 per
cent of total consumption in 1988-89) and electricity generation (23.4 per cent). Other
significant end-uses are in the residential sector
(12.2 per cent) and the mining industry (12.0
per cent). The fastest growing end-use sectors
have been electricity generation (particularly
with the utilisation of North-West Shelf gas for
this purpose in Western Australia from 1984
onwards) and the basic metal products sector,
where natural gas has been substituted for significant quantities of fuel oil.

Coal
Coal now accounts for the largest share of Australian total energy consumption, with black coal
representing an estimated 29.4 per cent and
brown coal 11.5 per cent in 1989-90. The share
of black coal in total energy consumption declined during the 1960s but has remained fairly
steady since. By contrast, brown coal's share
changed little until 1985-86, but has increased
sharply over the past three years.

Coal is used predominantly for electricity generation in Australia, 73.3 per cent of black coal
and 96.2 per cent of brown coal consumed in
1989-90 being used for this purpose. Other users of black coal include coke makers (16.7 per
cent) and manufacturing industry (9.1 per cent),
with small amounts also used in mining, commercial, sea transport and residential
applications. Other uses of brown coal include
briquetting and manufacturing.

Renewables
Renewable sources of energy made up an esti-
mated 6.7 per cent of total energy consumed in
Australia in 1989-90.

The major source of renewable energy is wood,
which contributed 2.5 per cent of total energy
consumption. Consumption of wood fell
throughout the 1960s to reach a low of 87.4 PJ in
1975-76. Since 1977-78, it has slowly increased,
but as a share of total energy consumption it has
fallen. Seventy-six per cent of fuel wood is used
in the residential sector. Most is consumed in
Victoria and New South Wales, although its proportion of total energy consumption is greatest
in Tasmania at 11.7 per cent.

The next largest source of renewable energy
(2 per cent) is bagasse, which is used as a source
of process heat in sugar mills in Queensland and
New South Wales. The third largest source, hydro-electricity, contributed only 1.4 per cent of
total energy consumption in 1989-90, and accounted for 12 per cent of total electricity
supplied to end-users. The total consumption of
hydro-electricity has not grown since the mid
1970s.

While use of solar energy is growing rapidly (at
an average rate of nearly 19 per cent a year over
the past decade), direct consumption of solar
energy still made up less than 0.1 per cent of total
energy consumption in 1989-90. Solar energy is
estimated to account for only around 3 per cent
of the total energy consumed for the purpose of
residential water heating.

It should be noted that the major source of
energy statistics, the Bureau of Agricultural and
Resource Economics (ABARE) statistics, are very
limited when it comes to assessing the importance of renewable sources of energy to the
Australian economy, in that they significantly
understate the role of solar energy. This statisti-

cal collection limits consideration of solar energy to the use of solar water heaters, and it estimates the contribution from this source by drawing on census data of the number of such appliances in service and multiplying this by the imputed quantity of electricity replaced by solar collectors.

This approach has at least two limitations. First, solar energy's fundamental contribution to the historical basis of the national economy is ignored. Radiant energy from the sun is the basis of all global food production, by which carbon dioxide from the atmosphere is transformed into simple sugars. This means that solar energy is a vital input to agriculture and so underpins Australia's important crop-based and livestock industries, such as forestry, wheat, sugar, meat and wool.

Second, it ignores the most popular form of domestic solar technology in Australia today, the solar clothes dryer (or clothes line as it is more popularly known), inclusion of which would no doubt multiply by many times the contribution of solar energy to the economy.

Energy conversion

The largest use of energy in Australia remains the conversion of one form of energy to another. In 1989-90 about 78 per cent of total primary energy made available in Australia was input to the conversion sector. Around 33 per cent of total energy consumption occurred in the conversion of these primary energy forms into higher valued secondary forms of energy, such as electricity and refined petroleum products. Around 14.8 per cent of that portion was direct energy use within the conversion industries. The remainder was energy loss — that is, energy which was not recovered in a usable form during the conversion process. The great majority of this energy loss is due to inefficiencies inherent in the conversion process; there are physical limits to the efficiency which can be achieved even in principle in these processes.

The major energy conversion industries are electricity generation, oil refining, coke production, town gas manufacture, and briquetting. The conversion sector is dominated by electricity generation. In 1989-90 a total of 1565.7 PJ of energy was used to make 483.0 PJ of electricity available to end-users — an overall conversion efficiency of about 31 per cent, compared with an OECD average of around 35 per cent (International Energy Agency, 1989). Much of the energy used in electricity generation is dissipated to the environment as low-grade waste heat, which in general it is not economic to use in Australia.

End-uses

After the conversion sector, the largest energy using sector is manufacturing (27.1 per cent of total energy consumption) followed by transport (25.7 per cent), residential (8.0 per cent), commercial (3.6 per cent), mining (4.2 per cent) and agriculture (1.5 per cent). The shares of the transport, mining and commercial sectors are slowly increasing, while that of manufacturing is slowly falling, reflecting Australia's changing industrial structure.

Of the energy provided to end-users in 1989-90, just under half (49.4 per cent) was in the form of petroleum products, 18.9 per cent natural gas, 17.8 per cent electricity, 7.2 per cent coal and its by-products and 6.7 per cent renewable. The shares of natural gas and electricity are slowly rising at the expense of the other forms of energy.

2.3 Energy imports and exports

Australia is a large exporter of energy resources. About 75 per cent of total primary energy production is exported. The consequences of this are considerable in that exports enable considerable economies of scale in the coal industry which benefit the electricity industry. Coal exports also contribute to greenhouse gas emissions with other effects downstream. The primary energy production statistics show that despite Australia's role as a significant producer on a world scale of both coal and uranium, it uses very little of these in end-use applications. The reasons for this are very different.

In the case of uranium, Australian governments have ruled against the domestic use of uranium as a source of energy, largely because of community concern over the safety issue. At the time of writing (March 1991) the federal government is considering further relaxing the conditions applying to uranium mining, primarily in order to take advantage of its possible contribution to export revenue.

In the case of coal, which was a fuel of major

importance — and also of major pollution impact — during the period of European industrialisation, its direct use has declined around the world and in Australia, and it is now used mostly to fuel generating stations, which convert it into electricity. About 65 per cent of coal extracted is exported, and about 28 per cent is used for electricity generation.

2.4 Prospects[3]

Prospective demand for energy in the Australian market has in the past been seen as a fairly predictable quantity. However, a severe recession in Australia in the early 1980s put a dip in the energy consumption curve that stands as a reminder that demand does not inexorably increase.

Energy consumption patterns in future decades will likely be affected by government action to curb emissions of greenhouse gases. Because government control over the energy sector is concentrated in electricity production and distribution, it is likely that the electricity will be a major site of government efforts to control emissions.

Already, the Victorian government has outlined plans for deferring the expansion of generating capacity through the utilisation of cheaper means of balancing electricity demand and supply (*Greenhouse: Meeting the Challenge*, the Victorian Government's Statement of Action October 1990). Other governments are beginning to take similar steps, albeit at a much slower rate.

A survey carried out for the Electricity Commission of New South Wales has shown that domestic electricity consumers are prepared to pay more for their electricity if the extra revenue is devoted to reducing the greenhouse impact of power generation by increasing the efficiency of existing electricity use (Morgan, 1989). These are much cheaper solutions to energy problems than the capacity expansions that have traditionally dominated thinking in the electricity industry. One study estimates that by 1996 the New South Wales industry could free up 2.9 terawatt-hours of electrical energy a year at a cost per kilowatt-hour of 1.0 cents or less (Greene, 1989). This amounts to 6 per cent of electricity sold by the ECNSW in 1989/90, for which the average selling price was 5.8c/kWh. Thus energy savings rep-

resent both a significant and potentially profitable opportunity for investment.

2.5 Conclusion

This chapter looked at the role and pattern of the use of energy in Australia. The industry has focused on supply rather than end-use efficiency but it is suggested here, and elsewhere in the report, that this emphasis must change to a more 'wholistic' approach to energy issues .

The source and use of energy in Australia has been changing rapidly over the last two decades - away from oil, especially for non-transport usage while gas use has risen to account for nearly 20 per cent of all energy consumed. Coal is the major energy source and for electricity it is also the major input. The use of renewables is rising fast, but from a very small base (not counting natural solar sources). The biggest users of converted energy from one form to another are the petroleum and electricity industries. It is therefore appropriate to analyse the electricity supply industry (ESI) as part of the energy industry as a whole.

This chapter has indicated some of the critical issues that will accelerate changes in the industry in the future. These changes will not be limited to the energy sector, as the discussion of the greenhouse issue indicates. More importantly, the community's attitude towards the energy sector is changing rapidly; it has shown it is not only willing to make sacrifices for positive change but is also likely to want more participation in the decisions of an industry that effects it so fundamentally.

Notes

1. Petrol sniffing is possibly the only such instance.

2. Data and projections in this section are based upon Australian Bureau of Agricultural and Resource Economics (1991).

3. Further discussion of these points occurs in Chapters 5 and 6.

CHAPTER 3

MAJOR INSTITUTIONAL ARRANGEMENTS

3.1 Introduction

The characteristics of the energy industry are, in part, a product of the nature of the institutions that operate in the industry. This chapter reviews them all, focusing in detail on those in the Electricity Supply Industry (ESI). The continuing problems of accountability and control in the ESI are a product of its historical development and this chapter examines that process. While authorities in the publicly owned ESI have responded to a lesser or greater extent over time to governments, they have been much less responsive to their employees, their customers and the community. The reasons for this lack of responsiveness can be found in the process of creation of, and the attempts to manage the authorities, since 1945.

3.2 Supply-side Structures — How the Industry Gets What It Wants

The electricity supply industry

Electricity supply is primarily a public sector function. The bulk of generation, transmission and distribution of electricity is handled similarly in all States and Territories of Australia: namely,

by statutory authorities responsible to a relevant government minister and reporting to the parliament.

There are, however, variations in the executive structure below the level of the Minister. Most State governments have vested responsibility for generation, transmission and distribution in a single authority: the Hydro-Electric Commission of Tasmania, the State Electricity Commission of Victoria, the Electricity Trust of South Australia, the State Energy Commission of Western Australia, and the Power and Water Authority in the Northern Territory. However, in Queensland and New South Wales, distribution has been placed under the responsibility of separate boards and county councils, respectively.

Table 3.1 provides a snapshot of the industry. More detail is provided in the following paragraphs.

Tasmania

In Tasmania, electricity is generated, transmitted and distributed by the Hydro-Electric Commission (HEC). Traditionally a construction authority as well as an operator, the HEC has in

Table 3.1
KEY ELECTRICITY STATISTICS 1989/90

	Tas	Qld	NSW	WA	SA	Vic	NT	Snowy Mnts	ACT
No. of customers (000)	219	1,169	2,400	597.6	660	1,874	46.9	3	107.3
Annual gigawatt hrs. sold	8303	21,497	44,800	8,810	8,030	30,592	972	4,306	2091
Staff numbers*	3729	8,553	22,900	5,109*	5,696	17,962‡	760	843	790
Annual revenue $m	381	1,807	3,800	1,033	793	2,469‡	128	158	184
Installed gen. capacity MW	2315	5,098	11,000	2,384	2,350	6,653‡	371	3,740	—

• Excluding gas   ‡ SECV only   * There have been further significant reductions in staff numbers since this data became available

Source: data supplied from *Electricity Week* collected from authorities' Annual Reports.

recent years reduced the rate at which it brings on new plant and is in the process of winding down the construction side of its operation.

A peculiar feature of the HEC's customer base is that a large proportion of its load (65 per cent in the year to June 1990) is taken by a small number of major industrial customers (21 at 31 December, 1989), which hold contracts for specified blocks of output from particular power stations. This has often been the source of friction in the State. In 1990 the government called an inquiry into Tasmanian electricity tariffs which cast doubt on the need for the secrecy of the contracts and on the way they have been structured in relation to the balance of Tasmania's electricity tariffs (Bartels, 1990).

During the 1970s the HEC's development plans became the centre of an environmental conflict as conservationists attempted unsuccessfully to prevent the flooding of Lake Pedder as part of the Gordon River stage one project. In the 1980s, however, conservationists were successful in saving the Franklin River from inundation in what would have been stage two of the Gordon development.

Since Gordon stage two was halted by federal government intervention in 1982, the HEC has gone on to develop other schemes to help meet its demand. However, the opportunities for further large-scale hydro developments have now been exhausted, and gas-fired generation is under consideration, along with the potential of energy efficiency to curb the growth in demand. As well, there is discussion of a possible link with the mainland taking place.

Low rainfall in the HEC's storages over recent years has spurred it to increase its demand management activities. In the year to 30 June 1990, it had to spend $30 million to operate its oil-fired power station at Bell Bay (HEC, 1990, p.3) and a similar amount is likely to be required in year to June 1991. In 1990 a consultant was commissioned to advise on the potential for energy efficiency measures in the State. He advised the Commission to adopt a policy of aggressively evaluating and pursuing energy efficiency and demand-side options, to make organisational changes to facilitate this, and to set itself a fifteen year target (Sioshansi, 1990, p.7).

There has recently been some controversy over whether the HEC is actually subject to ministerial direction or not. The conservative nature of the State's Legislative Council, which has opposed greater ministerial control, means this confusion is likely to continue for some time.

Queensland

In Queensland, the seven area boards are constituted by legislation and appointments to them are made by the responsible minister. The commissioner of the Queensland Electricity Commission (QEC) is a member ex-officio of each board. The QEC sees the role of the Boards as follows:

> The primary responsibility of an Electricity Board is to supply electricity to customers within its area and to plan, design, construct, maintain and manage works for this purpose. The Electricity Boards may also sell, hire and repair electrical articles, undertake research and development, provide technical advice, promote and encourage the efficient and economic use of electricity, set up training schools and conduct training courses for their employees and undertake programs to educate the public in electrical safety (Queensland Electricity Commission, 1990, p.10)

New South Wales

Excluding the Snowy Mountains scheme, which is under separate control, in New South Wales, the great bulk of generation and a significant proportion of transmission is the responsibility of the Electricity Commission of New South Wales (ECNSW). The Eraring Power Station is privately owned, but operated by ECNSW.

In all but three cases, distribution of electricity is the responsibility of County Councils which are formed by appointees of directly elected local government bodies throughout the State. The first exception is the Broken Hill area, where the electricity distribution is carried out by the Electricity Department of Broken Hill City Council. The second is Tenterfield Shire Council. The third, which came into being in January 1991, is Sydney Electricity, a statutory authority formed to take over the functions of Sydney County Council.

Western Australia

The State Electricity Commission of Western Australia (SECWA) carries out transmission and retailing of natural gas in addition to its (much larger) electricity business. This gives it a great flexibility to change the sales of its products, by manipulating the demand for each. SECWA purchases substantial quantities of electric power from private operators in the Pilbara iron ore province. It also leases and operates a privately owned transmission line between the Eastern Goldfields region, centred on Kalgoorlie, and the South East transmission grid.

SECWA is presently gearing up to install the State's first major combined cycle power plant, with a planned capacity of 300MW. As part of that decision, it has also put to the unions and the coal companies that in return for productivity improvements and fuel price reductions it will make a commitment to a 2x300MW coal-fired station at Collie to be running by 1996. The station is likely to be privately owned and operated. If the unions and the companies do not agree, SECWA will go ahead with a second 300MW combined cycle unit. At the time of writing (March 1991) it was unclear whether the companies would be prepared to reduce their prices sufficiently to make a deal possible.

The case is an interesting one, because it embodies a series of interrelated factors — the on-going viability of a country centre, the differing interests of mining and power generation institutions, and the priorities of government and management in achieving reductions in electricity prices. It shows clearly how decisions about the electricity industry are extremely closely intertwined with the performance of the economy in general.

South Australia

Electricity supply in South Australia is dominated by, but not totally in the hands of, the Electricity Trust of South Australia (ETSA). Local government bodies and private companies undertake electricity distribution in remote areas.

The South Australian government has released an energy discussion paper that canvasses a more active role for demand management in the State and points out that ETSA is moving away from a previous decision that the next baseload station would be a third 250MW unit at the existing

Northern Power Station (SA Government, 1991). ETSA is now canvassing the possibilities of alternative coalfields, a gas-fired combined cycle plant, and greater use of the interconnection. The report observes that a slowing down of the growth in demand could push the need for new capacity back beyond 1998, when it is presently scheduled, and provide further time for decisions to be made.

Victoria

Although the State Electricity Commission of Victoria (SECV) is the major electricity retailer in the state, 11 local government bodies have retained responsibility for reticulating electricity in parts of the Melbourne metropolitan area. Disagreements between the councils and the SECV over pricing and other aspects of the organisational structure led the Victorian government to commission a major review by the State's Grants Commission (NIEIR, 1989). The negotiations concerning the relationship between the municipal electricity undertakings and SECV are proceeding. The response by electricity trade unions to one of the Review's recommendations is outlined in Chapter 12. It is understood that the councils are considering consolidation.

The SECV has led the way on demand-side planning in the Australian electricity industry, announcing in 1989 that it would spend more than $50m over the succeeding three years on developing and piloting programs thought suitable for the Victorian market (SECV/DITR, 1989). Nevertheless, the program was taken to task for not being ambitious enough, when a United States expert was asked to evaluate it (Lovins, 1990) (see also Chapter 12).

Another issue of vital interest in Victoria is the move to alleviate the State's financial woes by undertaking piecemeal privatisation of SECV business units. The most spectacular of the proposals is for selling off the partly completed 2x500MW Loy Yang B station. The industrial relations aspects of this proposal are dealt with in Chapter 12.

Northern Territory

The Northern Territory Power and Water Authority (NTPWA) took over the functions of the Northern Territory Electricity Commission on June 30, 1987. It is the main generator and distributor of electricity in the Northern Territory and was the first power authority to introduce the combined cycle gas technology into service in Australia.

Snowy Mountains Scheme
This is run by the Snowy Mountains Hydro-electric Authority (SMA) in parallel with the Snowy Mountains Council. This duality of control has proven to be unwieldy and fraught with problems, and is under review at present. In the absence of immediate plans for expansion of this system, pricing does not include a component for capital works, other than refurbishment. The Snowy provides one of the points of power exchange for the New South Wales/Victoria/South Australia interconnection. More detail is provided in the discussion of national integration in Chapter 12.

As we indicate in the following chapters, hydro schemes can perform an important function as "storage points" for electricity. The proposal from the NSW government to purchase the Scheme could threaten its utility as a cross-over point for existing interconnection, and its potentially larger role in an eastern seaboard grid.

Australian Capital Territory
The ACT Electricity Authority, which had been administered by the federal government, was recently combined with the water and sewage authority to form ACT Electricity & Water (ACTEW). As part of the self-government arrangements, it has been transferred to the control of the ACT government. The ACT government is proceeding to transform the authority into a corporation, with the target for the new body to come into operation by 1 July 1991. The ACT generates negligible quantities of electricity.

3.3 Gas Industry
Distribution in the Australian gas industry is carried out by a mixture of public and private enterprises, which are heavily regulated. SECWA transmits and distributes natural gas as well as generating, transmitting and distributing electricity. The two natural gas reticulation networks serving Brisbane are privately owned, as is the transmission line from Roma. In New South Wales, natural gas is distributed by private op-

erators. A federal government authority (The Pipeline Authority) owns and operates the pipeline from Moomba to the Sydney hinterland, and its spur lines. This has been put up for sale. The Gas and Fuel Corporation of Victoria and the South Australian Gas Company have significant degrees of private ownership. Production, especially offshore, is dominated by the big international oil companies, but Australian expertise within BHP Limited would probably enable the development of new fields using purely local expertise.

3.4 Oil Industry
The oil industry is dominated by major transnational corporations which are largely vertically integrated. There is some interest in local investment in other energy industries, such as natural gas and coal. There is already some investment in these areas.

Little has changed since Saddler wrote in the late 1970s that the structure of the petroleum industry in Australia had been fashioned largely so as to benefit its private sector participants (Saddler, 1981). The main change has been that the industry has become more concentrated with the exit/absorption of the Golden Fleece and Total operations and the decision by Esso to quit as a small player in the distribution end of the business.

3.5 Coal Industry
The predominant markets for coal mined in Australia are overseas. Ownership of black coal is mainly in private hands, though control of the resource is vested in the Crown. The ECNSW mines are presently up for sale. In South Australia, and Victoria, low-quality coal is mined by the utilities for use in power stations. Two private companies mine low-quality coal in Western Australia near Collie, where it is sold to SECWA for use in power generation. As might be expected, the coal industry in Western Australia is a major participant in the current debate concerning the siting and type of a new baseload power station. In the industry the payment of royalties by coal producers is a matter of perennial dispute.

3.6 Characteristics of the Energy Sector and the Role of the State

The role of the public sector in the Australian energy sector has historically been one of facilitating private investment. On the development of the oil industry in Australia, a Royal Commission report said in 1976:

> The industry today represents not so much an indigenous industry which has evolved in response to the organic needs of the Australian people; rather it is an imposition upon the Australian people of a convenient marketing strategy exported by the international companies and utilised by them in Australia (quoted in Saddler, 1981, p.97)

Stark examples involving the electricity industry can be seen in more recent times with the direction to SECWA to provide a domestic market for gas from the North West Shelf project, so as to underpin the viability of the project's domestic phase, and from the installation of new generating capacity in New South Wales during the 1980s to meet the demands of prospective aluminium smelters. This was one cause of the overinvestment which occurred.

As we have noted above, present demands for greater efficiency in the electricity supply industry, combined with greater demand-side pressures and environmental constraints, makes the articulation of a clear set of objectives covering all these concerns a matter of priority.

3.7 The History of the Electricity Industry

In addition to its willingness to intervene in the industry, the state played the central role in putting together the present ESI. In the electricity sector the state historically played a rescuer's role. In New South Wales a large number of privately owned generating enterprises were combined to form the Electricity Commission of New South Wales in 1950. In Victoria, the SECV was formed after the war when Sir John Monash was given the government's backing to develop the brown coal resources of the Latrobe Valley and so remove the State's reliance on coal imports from New South Wales.

The Snowy Mountains Scheme is among the greatest of the state initiatives in the power industry. This began in 1949 as a major development project, propelled by post-war op-

timism. An economic analysis made of the scheme some years ago (McColl, 1976) suggested that the private sector still would not be interested in building this scheme, as it produced a negative net present value. The Snowy Scheme has the other purpose of supplying irrigation water to New South Wales, Victoria and South Australia. The Snowy highlights the importance of government planning and an overall energy vision for Australia. It is an interesting contrast to see private entrepreneurs now attempting to shoulder their way into the industry in the name of increasing efficiency. The reason is that the risk associated with the technology has been reduced, and the deregulation mood in all shades of government offers the hint of grand profits in the offing. But this report will show that given the challenges facing the industry the development of a large-scale private sector would be unwise.

In South Australia Rosenthal and Russ in their study *The Politics of Power* record the role played by a conservative government in establishing ETSA:

> The former Premier of South Australia... nationalised the State electricity supply in 1946...The Act remains essentially unchanged today and... the Trust is its own master. In June 1980 a confidential memo titled 'ETSA: Roping in the Trust' was prepared for the Liberal Minister for Mines and Energy... setting out ways of 'making the Trust subject to the control and direction of the Minister'. It made four complaints about the Trust's attitude, including the 'reluctance of ETSA to accept specific government policies, e.g. secondment schemes', and the 'reluctance of ETSA to work closely with the Energy Division of the Department of Mines and Energy with regard to energy management in South Australia's and thus avoid duplication (and lack of coordination) of effort.
>
> (In May 1983, the government instituted an Inquiry). By appointing the Inquiry the South Australian government hoped to solve the State's electricity problems and it also sought to make ETSA more accountable. However, in the longer term, its efforts could be ineffective without significant amendments to ETSA's Act (Rosenthal & Russ,

1988, pp.40–42).

The difficulties of governments in managing their electricity authorities is illustrated in another celebrated case, that of the HEC in Tasmania. Rosenthal and Russ, who have studied the authorities, record the problems when they combine with conservative allies to defeat reform:

> Like ETSA, the Hydro-Electric Commission (HEC) of Tasmania has greater autonomy than its Victorian and New South Wales counterparts.
>
> Until 1979 there was little ministerial control of the HEC. (In that year the Premier attempted to)… bring the organisation under greater government control and he proposed some broad-ranging amendments to the HEC's Act. However, the legislation met with stiff opposition from the Upper House, traditionally an ally of the HEC.
>
> The legislation was watered down and finally the Act was amended to bring the Commission under general Ministerial control by requiring it to respond to Ministerial directives and government policy decisions, but with certain qualifications. The Commission could object to a direction given by the Minister and appeal to the Governor, thus maintaining the lack of accountability to the elected government. The deficiencies in the Act go a long way in explaining the subsequent Franklin Dam environmental dispute (Rosenthal and Russ, 1988, p.42).

3.8 Political/Economic Forces that have Shaped the Industry

Although governments have been a driving force in the development of industry, and have seen the control of electricity prices as an important prerogative, the power industry bureaucracies, based on their monopoly of technical knowledge and expertise, have a high level control of the industry. This has only recently begun to be challenged in Australia.

The first serious challenge came in 1982, with the vigorous attempts by the new government in Victoria to make the State Electricity Commission (SECV) more accountable to government, and through the government, to the citizens. In great measure, the government's success was due to the fact that a number of senior managers were due to retire from the SECV at about the time the responsible Minister David White began to push for change. The initiatives at the time led to the institutionalisation of an industrial democracy process, and of community consultations over SECV plans and initiatives. This marked a major reform to the industry.

Less successful attempts came from the governments of New South Wales and Tasmania later in the decade. In the case of New South Wales the trigger was widespread power disruption; in that of Tasmania, the controversy over plans to dam the Franklin River for hydro power. Although the New South Wales government instituted some initiatives at the time, the degree of change it was able to introduce was quite limited, due for the most part to the tenacity of the ECNSW management structure.

A review of the organisation's structure by an internationally known management consultancy produced, at vast expense, a fairly limited range of suggestions as to how the Commission's performance might be altered. The report was weakened by the vagueness of its recommendations, and changed very little in the ECNSW's operations. It was not until several years later, when Peter Cox, a former Labor Minister for Transport, was shifted into the energy spot, that change began for the industry in New South Wales. He implemented a commission of inquiry into the ECNSW's plans for future generating capacity. The inquiry established that in drawing up its plans, the ECNSW had "forgotten" to allow for some 12,000MW of capacity which would be available through alternative means, such as extending the life of existing stations (Beatty, October 1986, p.32). As a result of the inquiry, Cox implemented a requirement that the ECNSW should prepare a 30–year generation plan every three years, to be tabled in parliament.

However, even before the first of these plans was tabled, it was apparent that the ECNSW management was prepared to avoid its responsibilities under the legislation and mislead the public about its plans: it failed to reveal the planned closure of Tallawarra power station in its draft plan. It also all but ignored the impact of the greenhouse effect on its planning (Beatty, 1989a, p.2). The ECNSW was able to behave like this for two reasons: because it was under the nominal control of a minister who relied on advice drawn largely from the ECNSW itself; and because a swift closure of a higher cost station was in the interests of the new Greiner Government, which was pursuing an agenda of financial reform in statutory authorities. In addition, the Minister had (perhaps inadvertently) overseen the dismantling of a formerly powerful source of alternative advice on electricity matters, the Department of Energy. Although there is some evidence that change is in the wind, top management in the ECNSW has still yet to demonstrate the commitment to demand management strategies that has been in evidence in other States.

In Tasmania, the position was largely the same. In the early 1980s the State's Premier, Doug Lowe, was deposed over his support for an alternative to the Franklin Dam, and his successor's government lost the subsequent election, largely because it failed to support the pro-dam position being espoused by the HEC. Then, as now, the Tasmanian government lacked any substantial alternative source of advice and was heavily reliant on single-minded HEC senior bureaucrats. The HEC was described by a government-sponsored report as having overstepped the role for which it was created:

> It would seem that the Hydro-Electric Commission has been permitted, in the absence of adequate policy guidance, to act as a de facto, and largely autonomous, economic planning agency... This is indisputably not its role. (Thompson, 1981, p.26)

Change is now (March 1991) on the way in Tasmania, sponsored by a shaky government comprising a minority Labor and a smaller complement of green independents.

It is this history of either an inadvertent overturning of the role of governments in a Westminster system, or its deliberate subversion, which informs our discussion of public sector reform in Chapters 9 and 10. The examples above reveal some of the power that has been wielded by the electricity industry in Australia. In summary the forces that have shaped the industry have included:

- the need for an electricity system in each State and territory as a backbone for industrial and social development;
- the need for a major investment in the capital intensive technology that emerged in the

1940s and 1950s which facilitated the development of large power generating centres remote from the centres of load demand;
- the development of an engineer-dominated culture within the industry that rose to meet the challenges of undertaking that task;
- failure by that culture to foresee the major changes in energy consumption that occurred in the 1980s or to react to it, largely because the engineer-led managements were still locked into the supply-side mind-set that had dominated their organisations for the past thirty years; and
- failure by governments, because of lack of sufficiently strong independent advice, to instil flexibility in the managements of the electricity organisations or to extract accountability for those planning errors and to change the development mind-set.

If the evidence above suggests the industry has been able to resist the influence of governments responsible it has been able to manage its consumers with even less regard, as we now outline.

3.9 Working out What the Consumer Wants

Most of the institutional arrangements covering the energy industries in Australia concern suppliers. The constraints in regard to consumers are limited to safety considerations and obligations to deal fairly with energy suppliers. There has been very little further thought to the interests and role of the consumer. That is beginning to change with greater emphasis being placed on demand-side matters.

Exceptions to this general rule are to be found in the Victorian government's community energy consultation program, advocacy work by the Australian Consumers' Association on energy efficiency, and the occasional opportunity for the public to be heard at inquiries relating to the energy industry. In general, public consultation programs conducted by energy agencies have had few resources, which has meant that input to them is dominated by the large producers and the largest customers, who can afford the time and effort to be involved. Their interests are more likely to be served in such a situation.

Australia's main energy industries are all dominated by the supply enterprises, which are in virtually all cases larger than their largest customers. As part of their sovereignty over customers they have maintained tight control of information elicited from market surveys. It is very rare, even in public sector energy enterprises, for the results of customer surveys to be used in open debates over the performance and direction of the industry.

While one might expect this type of attitude from managements of organisations in the private sector, which are set up to make profits for their shareholders, there would appear to be no compelling reason why this should be the case in public authorities, that operate in monopolistic markets and are largely owned by their consumers. One plausible explanation for the similarity of outlook between public and private sector energy enterprise managements in Australia turns on what has been called an "engineering culture". In a discussion of why it might be that the management of Australian electricity authorities behaves so similarly to their private sector counterparts in industrial and environmental disputes, Saddler had this to say:

> The origins of the various Electricity Commissions provide an interesting clue. Far from being conceived as a step on the road to socialism, the nationalisation of the electricity in three states (New South Wales, Victoria, South Australia) was actually initiated by conservative governments. Whether conservative or labor governments were responsible, business interests put up virtually no opposition to the nationalisations. There is a great contrast with the hysterical (but effective) opposition to Mr Rex Connor's rather modest proposals for government involvement in the petroleum industry. The reason for the difference is simply that electricity supply is not a very profitable undertaking, chiefly because of the massive amounts of capital it requires... thus by nationalising the electricity industry, State governments were acting not against capital, but for it, and there is no a priori reason to suppose that the industry itself will operate in a more socially responsive way simply because governments have taken on the burden of financing its development.
> The social and educational background of the people in managerial positions in the electricity authorities is also significant. They are mostly engineers and almost all men...

they hold the same sort of views and are part of the same social grouping as their colleagues employed in the private energy industry. Indeed, they consciously see themselves as part of the same social enterprise — engineering the supply of energy. It would be quite unrealistic to expect electricity authority managers to have distinctly different attitudes toward industrial relations, environmental protection or their responsibility to the public (Saddler, 1981, pp.115–116).

Since the late 1970s the profitability of the electricity industry has increased somewhat — witness the interest in privatisation in Australia and its occurrence in New Zealand and the United Kingdom. This, however, has only underscored the fact that utilisation of private sector methodologies is increasingly a feature of the supply authorities in Australia.

3.10 Conclusion

In this chapter, we have provided an overview of the Australian energy sector, and the Australian electricity industry. Within this overview, we have begun to elucidate some of the major themes of this report. These themes include the emergence of pressures to which the industry has not previously had to respond; the need to ensure that electricity industry management becomes more flexible and responsive to community concerns; and the need for governments, as elected representatives, to reassert authority in terms of priority setting and key decision-making. At the same time, given the domination by the private sector of other industries within the sector, there is a clear need for government to retain its role as a "player". This will not be achieved if governments succumb to the current pressure for privatisation.

CHAPTER 4

POWERING THE ECONOMY: FINANCING ELECTRICITY INFRASTRUCTURE

4.1 Introduction

The purpose of this chapter is to set the overall macroeconomic scene against which deliberations about the role of the electricity industry in the Australian economy over the next two decades can be made. The chapter is structured as follows. It begins by presenting an overview of Australia's economic performance over the last decade, presenting the main developments on the aggregate demand-side of the economy as well as describing developments on the supply-side of the economy. It points to the main problem which has occurred in the external trading situation.

The way in which the environment is included in economic considerations is important and Section 3 introduces the reader to recent developments which have occurred in incorporating environmental and resource issues into the national accounting framework which is used to measure national production and income — a new framework that will change the way in which the ESI is assessed.

There is a need to understand the macroeconomic settings and constraints within which policies to address the needs of the energy sector must must be placed. Section 4 points out that our current trading performance is unsustainable and that concerted policy action is required rather than allowing market forces to 'correct' the problem. It then proceeds to describe how tight fiscal, monetary and incomes policies have been implemented in order to curtail the growth in foreign indebtedness.

The role of infrastructure provision is critical and Section 5 addresses the issue of the optimal supply of electricity generation capacity. It begins by addressing the circumstances in which the public sector ought to be involved in the provision of infrastructure. It provides a general macroeconomic framework for considering the optimal supply of infrastructure based on comparing the benefits with the costs. It then looks in detail at government expenditure programs and argues that although the optimal provision of infrastructure is not related in a simple fashion to variations in the level of public investment, continued cutting on capital expenditure programs is without economic justification. It concludes that an integrated forward-looking infrastructure policy, including that relating to the supply of electricity generation capacity, is required in order to enhance Australia's economic performance into the next century.

The final section concludes that continued neglect of public capital investment programs due to pursuit of fiscal surpluses is without economic justification and risks adversely affecting the long run performance of the Australian economy. Rather, a national, public inquiry is needed with a particular attention to ESI, to ascertain the social and economic infrastructure needs requiring development. Two such needs have been identified elsewhere in this report: on the demand-side, investment in those technologies which would offset the traditional overemphasis on supply-side assets and techniques; and, on the supply-side, investment in a nationally coordinated transmission grid.

4.2. Macroeconomic Developments in the Last Decade

Tables 4.1 to 4.3 present an overview of the development of the Australian economy over the last decade. All tables and figures for this chapter are to be found in Appendix 2 at the end of the book.

Part A of Table 4.1 describes the components of aggregate demand and Part B of the Table describes the supply-side of the economy over the same time period. Tables 4.2 and 4.3 then focus on the external accounts. They provide details of the current and capital accounts of the balance of payments and the implications of these developments for the economy's international debt situation (both in levels as in Table 4.3A and in ratio form to GDP and exports as in Table 4.3B).

Looking first at the demand-side, consumption expenditures grew steadily over the decade at an average annual growth rate of 3.3 per cent in real terms. Business fixed investment exhibited its usual cyclical behaviour, averaging 5.3 per cent annual real growth over the first half of the decade and 7.6 per cent over the second half. The latter figure hides the investment boom of 1987–88 to 1988–89 in which real growth rates of 16.4 per cent and 14.5 per cent were recorded prior to the emergence of the slump with a real decline of 1.4 per cent during 1989–90. Government spending grew at an average annual real growth rate of 3 per cent during the first half of the decade before tighter fiscal stance curtailed this to 1.9 per cent during the latter 5 years. Modest export growth was superseded by strong import growth which resulted in an annual average net export performance of –$4,855m during the decade. This development has played a large part in Australia's current trading problems which will be dealt with in greater detail below. The upshot of these developments was an average annual real growth rate of GDP of 3.3 per cent, which was made up of 2.9 per cent during the first half and 3.7 per cent during the second half of the decade. This performance will not be matched in the early 1990s as the economy currently experiences recession.

The developments on the supply-side of the economy which produced this performance on GDP are summarised in part B of the Table 4.3. The population aged over 15 years grew by 1.47 millions from 1983–84 to 1989–90 and this was accompanied by rising participation rates in each of these years of the Hawke Labor Government. In spite of this, however, the government managed to generate 1.45 million new jobs during this period while the workforce grew by 1.29 millions. The net effect of these developments was a reduction in the unemployment rate from a high of 9.6 per cent in 1983–84 to 6.2 per cent in 1989–90. As pointed to in the preceding paragraph, this admirable achievement of the Hawke Government was made possible by strong

economic growth. It was also made possible, however, by strict discipline in real wage outcomes which is a recognised accomplishment of the Prices and Incomes Accord. After rising by 2.37 per cent on average from 1980–81 to 1982–83, real earnings declined by 0.8 per cent on average over the rest of the decade. The outlook for unemployment in the early 1990s is not good, however, as the effects of the recession are expected (as at March 1991) to result in unemployment rates of up to 9 per cent by the end of 1991. A fundamental question which arises, therefore, is the extent to which the real wage restraint will achieve much long-term employment growth.

The basic problem which has confronted the economy over recent decades has been that export revenues have grown too sluggishly. As a per centage of GDP, our exports rose by less than 6 per cent from the 1960s to the 1980s which compares unfavourably with growth rates ranging from 36 to 65 per cent in Britain, Canada, Germany, Japan, Sweden and the United States over the same period. The composition of our exports can be described in a number of ways. In 1987–88, our total exports of $49.1b comprised $40.9b (83 per cent) in merchandise trade and $8.2b (17 per cent) in services. With respect to our merchandise exports, $19.7b (48 per cent) were unprocessed primary produce, $5.9b (14 per cent) were processed minerals and fuel, $4.9b (12 per cent) were processed food, $4.6b (11 per cent) were simply transformed manufactures and $4.5b (11 per cent) were elaborately transformed. The overall picture which emerges is one of sluggish growth by international standards together with poor performance in adding value by manufacturing and processing to our abundant endowments.

This situation is highlighted by the presentation of the balance of payments accounts over the last decade in Table 4.2. Worsening performance on both merchandise trade and invisibles trade has resulted in the now well-known blow-out in the current account deficit. This has been financed by capital account surpluses which have become increasingly constituted by non-official portfolio investment by foreign residents in Australia. Table 4.3 illustrates the implications of this adverse trading performance for the build-up in foreign indebtedness. As part A of the Table illustrates, this build-up in indebtedness has been largely the result of private sector net borrowings. Of a total net external debt amounting to $108.2b in 1988–89, $12.394b (11.45 per cent) was the responsibility of the public sector, while the remainder of $95.851b (88.55 per cent) was the responsibility of the private sector. As part B of Table 4.3 illustrates, the economy's total net debt as a per centage of current price GDP amounted to 32.1 per cent in 1988–89. This figure entailed a debt service ratio of 20.4 in 1988–89 compared to 5.4 at the start of the decade. This development has raised questions about sustainability and has been at the forefront of concerns to tighten the stance of both fiscal and monetary policies in order to curtail the demand for imports by slowing down the rate of growth of the economy.

In addition to these trends, a number of other salient features of Australia's foreign indebtedness has been summarised by EPAC (1989) as follows. First, more than 60 per cent of Australia's gross foreign debt is denominated in foreign currencies and about 60 per cent of this is denominated in United States dollars. It is noteworthy that the former figure has declined since many Australian offshore borrowers were stung by the devaluation of the Australian dollar. Second, the debt-equity ratio of our foreign debt has risen sharply in recent years and this has been accompanied by a decline in the maturity of the debt which places greater strains on our ability to service the outstanding foreign debt.

4.3. Sustainable Development and National Accounting

Having outlined how the Australian economy has developed over the last decade, it is important in the current context to draw attention to recent developments in incorporating the environmental and resource affects of production in the national accounts. This issue has gained prominence in recent times due to growing concern about environmentally sustainable development over the medium to long term.

The Australian national accounts, from which much of the data presented in Section 2 are derived, are based upon the United Nations' international System of National Accounts (SNA) which was last revised in 1968. These ac-counts measure economic production as the process whereby natural resources, accumulated capital assets, labour and knowledge are applied to produce goods and services. Natural resources including the environment, however, play a passive role in assessing the production of national income — their exclusion being rationalised on the basis of conceptual and practical difficulties in valuing resource and environmental assets such as air and water quality, fish stocks, native flora and fauna etc. The depletion of natural resource assets therefore produces no debit charges against current national income to reflect the implied reduction in a nation's capacity to produce future income. The current SNA therefore implicitly assumes that natural resources are "gifts from nature" in unlimited supply and with a zero supply price. As Repetto et al (1989) have argued, under the current SNA, "…a country could erode its soil, extract its minerals, cut down its trees but measured income would appear unchanged as these resources disappeared".

A number of macroeconomists have recently begun working on the elimination of this weakness in the SNA. These economists have argued for the need to measure "sustainable income" which is defined as the maximum amount that can be consumed in a given period without reducing the amount of possible future income. For example, Lavin (1990) makes the point that the current SNA, by neglecting the consumption of resource assets in the production of current national income, overstates the amount of income that can be currently consumed without adversely affecting the capacity to produce future income. This international work has not been ignored by the Australian Bureau of Statistics (ABS, 1990, p.64) who have recently reported that "the conventional national accounts framework should be modified or extended to take into account such factors as the extent of renewability and the rate of depletion of natural resources, and of changes in the quality of the environment".

The current SNA is presently undergoing intensive revision by economists and statisticians from the Statistical Offices of the United Nations and the European Community, the Organisation for Economic Cooperation and Development, the International Monetary Fund and the World

Bank. Expert group meetings to date have resulted in the production of a redrafted SNA which acknowledges the existence of many shortcomings with respect to environmental and natural resource accounting. It has not been possible thus far, however, to replace the existing concepts of income with "sustainable income" until outstanding conceptual issues are resolved and empirical analyses performed. In spite of this, a consensus has emerged in attempts to link environmental accounting to the core of the SNA by means of "satellite accounts" which provide measures of defensive expenditures and of the use, depletion and degradation of natural resources. The "satellite accounts" also allow aggregate indicators of environmentally adjusted and/or "sustainable income" to be produced (further details of this are provided by the ABS, 1990).

More specifically, the current draft framework for the proposed set of "satellite accounts" focuses upon:

i) the use of natural resource assets in production and final demand with adjusted concepts of value added, consumption, capital formation and wealth accumulation;

ii) environmental degradation and pollution from the affects of production, consumption and natural events;

iii) the incorporation of environmental protective defensive expenditures; and

iv) the calculation of various environmentally adjusted indicators.

With regard to the latter, "*environmentally adjusted GDP*" is calculated by subtracting government and household environmental protective defensive expenditures from currently measured unadjusted GDP (such expenditures of industry are already included as intermediate consumption in unadjusted GDP). This reflects the fact that such expenditures are now viewed as the intermediate rather than the final consumption of the relevant sectors. Another indicator is "*sustainable GDP*" (SGDP) which is calculated as "*environmentally adjusted GDP*" minus environmental costs which result from the depletion of natural resources and environmental degradation due to economic activity and natural events. It is worth noting that additions to the natural resource base are not included in income but accounted for only when exploited.

These developments are likely to have major implications for an ESI which is not currently viewed in a framework that includes all its resource costs or the value of its externalities.

4.4. The Macroeconomic Policy Settings

The fundamental question remains, however, about whether our current external position ought to be a matter of concern for government policy, or whether the government should allow the market mechanism to deliver the required adjustment. The answer comes under two headings; namely, "consumption smoothing" and "sustainability".

Consumption smoothing

A number of economists have recently argued that Australia's level of international indebtedness should not be of concern to policy makers unless the debt is largely the liability of the public sector. Since this is not the case, and since some level of international indebtedness is obviously optimal for an economy which is open to trade in commodities, services and financial assets, it has been argued that the matter is a private sector concern and that governments should allow the market mechanism to deliver the required adjustment.

It is important to note here that the literature on international and public finance does not provide unambiguous guidelines for deciding upon optimal levels of indebtedness. The results which emanate from the traditional work on international finance a la Fleming (1962) and Mundell (1963) are not reliable because the model along with its subsequent extensions has been recently criticised for 'postulating' rather than deriving its fundamental aggregative equations from microeconomic optimising behaviour and for inadequately specifying the intertemporal framework of budget constraints and consumption/production decisions. Kearney (1990) and Kingston (1991) provide critical evaluations of this literature. The new intertemporal optimising models of, for example, Frenkel and Razin (1988) and Pitchford (1989), focus on the concept of "consumption smoothing" in explaining the determination of optimal foreign indebtedness. The basic idea here is that variations in the external environment (e.g. volatile terms of trade) which confront a small open economy like Australia will cause variations in the flow of national income, and this will lead to variations in savings behaviour by economic agents who desire a smooth pattern of consumption. Net foreign indebtedness will consequently rise when income is temporarily low and it will decline again when income is temporarily high. It is important to note, however, that if a terms of trade disturbance delivers a permanent reduction to domestic income, consumption behaviour must adjust. Dornbusch (1983) makes this point.

It will be abundantly clear from the preceding paragraph that the critical element of this argument concerns the extent to which any significant change in the terms of trade is *temporary* or *permanent* in nature. It is, however, impossible to be sure about which of these scenarios is correct until time has elapsed to pass judgement. The dangers of failing to adjust consumption patterns in response to a permanent decline in the terms of trade which is mistakenly perceived to be temporary are clear. Indeed the riskiness of this approach becomes even more clear when cognisance is paid to current views about the medium and long term prospects for Australia's terms of trade. The international evidence which exists indicates that the process of stabilising the external constraint of an indebted economy is more costly the longer the adjustment is delayed. The concern of minimising this adjustment cost belongs to government rather than to the private institutions who incur the foreign indebtedness. It is, therefore, appropriate for the government to monitor the economy's foreign debt situation and take steps to ensure that it does not become excessive.

Sustainability

In the light of the above remarks on the "consumption smoothing" concept, the question of sustainability of current account deficits becomes important. The idea of sustainability in the current context is directly analogous to that concerning the sustainability of government budget deficits, see for example, Trehan and Walsh (1988). The general principles of sustainability have been applied to the external constraint by *inter alia*, Sachs (1981), Pigott (1989) and Kearney (1990).

The conditions which determine sustainability

can be summarised by defining the current account deficit (CD) as the sum of the trade account deficit (TD) plus interest payments (r) on the stock of net external debt (D)

$$CD = TD + rD \ (1).$$

Sustainability implies a stable ratio of net external debt to GNP. This condition can be written algebraically as

$$DD/D = DY/Y = q \ (2)$$

which states that the proportional rate of growth of external debt (DD/D) is equal to that for GNP (DY/Y) and both are equal to q. If the current account deficit is related to income in a stable fashion (CD/Y), equation (2) implies that the country's external debt-to-income ratio will vary positively with the current account/income ratio and indirectly with the economy's growth rate. This can be seen by multiplying both sides of equation (1) by Y and reorganising while noting that DD = CAD

$$(D/Y) = (CAD/Y)/q \ (3).$$

The essential insight which emerges here is that the economy's long-run debt-to-income ratio varies directly with the long-run current account performance and indirectly with the growth of GNP. Another insight concerning the servicing obligations on the stock of net indebtedness can be obtained by combining equations (1) and (3) to obtain (4)

$$\begin{aligned} (TD/Y) &= (CAD/Y) - r(D/Y) \\ &= (1 - r/g)(CAD/Y) \ (4). \end{aligned}$$

This states that if the interest rate which is payable on the economy's net external debt is equal to the economy's growth rate, the trade account must balance in the long run so that the current account invisibles are sufficient to service the external debt. If the economy manages to grow faster than the relevant interest rate, the trade account can be in deficit in the long run. If, however, this condition is not met, the trade account must be in long run surplus. Table 4.4 documents the sustainability of Australia's external trading position in terms of equation (4) over the last two decades. Looking firstly at the decade from 1970–1980, it is clear that the economy did not have a sustainability problem because the growth rate of real output averaged 3.74 per cent while the ratio of the current account to output averaged 1.89. With a zero average real interest rate during this time, the situation would have been sustainable as long as the trade account deficit as a ratio to GDP did not exceed 1.89 on average. As note (1) to the Table points out, however, the trade account was in surplus on average by more than this amount.

This situation, however, has changed markedly in an adverse direction since then. During the decade from 1980 to 1990, the economy's real growth rate has declined to 3.27 per cent on average while the current account deficit has risen to 4.84 per cent of domestic output. This situation has been accompanied by a rise in the foreign real interest rate to an average of 5.77 per cent. The implications of these adverse developments for the sustainability of Australia's trading position are dramatic. Instead of achieving the required surplus on trade account of 3.7 per cent of output, Australia's actual trade account surplus has deteriorated to 0.73 per cent of output. In short, Australia's current trading performance is not sustainable and economic adjustment is unavoidable.

Do we have a choice about what kind of adjustment is implemented? The answer to this question is yes. The government can either take the initiative to correct the fundamental imbalances in our international payments accounts or it can choose to allow the market mechanism to correct the problem through substantial depreciation of the foreign exchange value of the Australian dollar. The Hawke Labor Government has opted for the former approach for reasons which are economically sensible. If no policy action is taken to alleviate Australia's current build-up of indebtedness, the country's foreign creditors will eventually cease to hold Australian dollar denominated assets at prevailing rates of return. The result of this will be either continued upwards pressure on domestic interest rates or substantial depreciation of the currency. Neither of these scenarios can be construed as being beneficial to Australia's long-term economic welfare.

The policy settings

The government has enacted a four-pronged policy approach to solve the country's trading problem. In addition to wage restraint and an extensive program of microeconomic reform, both fiscal and monetary policy settings have been tightened in order to slow down the growth of aggregate demand. Table 4.5 and Figure 4.1 illustrate developments in the stance of fiscal policy in terms of the economic transactions of the Commonwealth General Government, while Table 4.6 and Figure 4.2 illustrate how monetary policy settings have been altered during the last decade.

Looking firstly at the stance of fiscal policy, it is clear that it has tightened considerably during the latter part of the decade. More specifically, with revenues peaking at 28.7 per cent of GDP in 1986-87, outlays declined in real terms during each of the last four years. This has resulted in a dramatic turnaround in the fiscal stance from a budget deficit of over 4 per cent of GDP in 1983–84 to a surplus of over 2 per cent of GDP in 1989–90.

Looking next at the stance of monetary policy, Part A of Table 4.6 and part B of Figure 4.2 shows that in spite of fluctuating terms of trade, the trade weighted index of the Australian dollar on foreign exchange markets declined by 39 per cent between 1980/81 and 1985/86 before stabilising at around that level. It is a creditable feature of the Prices and Incomes Accord agreement that in spite of this depreciation, the rate of inflation of the domestic price level has been brought down to less than 7 per cent at present. This, together with high interest rates (both nominal and real as well as the foreign interest differential) has facilitated the stabilising of the trade weighted index over the past five years.

4.5 Assessing the Adequacy of Public Infrastructure: the Electricity Industry

In what circumstances ought the public sector be involved in the provision of infrastructure? In addition to historical and ideological reasons for involvement, the traditional answer to this question as given by Baumol, Blinder, Gunther and Hicks (1988) involves the main cases of market failure; namely, imperfect and monopolistic competition, externalities, public goods, distributional inequality, the existence of severe business cycles, and poor intertemporal allocation of resources. Groenewegen (1990) demonstrates how the current Treasury view, as documented by Borthwick (1990), neglects the latter three cases of market failure in its list of justifications for governmental involvement, and also seems to neglect private sector investment myopia which is important since much infrastructural investment is capital intensive with long time horizons prior to profitability.

A general macroeconomic framework for considering the optimal provision of infrastructure involves comparing the *benefits* of enhanced infrastructure provision with the *costs* of financing it. Indeed, as we shall see below, recent work on this topic has concurred about the relevance and importance of cost-benefit analysis.

The benefits from enhancing the level of infrastructure provision are:
  i)   increased output;
  ii) higher productivity growth; and
  iii) improved trading performance.

The main costs are mostly associated with the sources of finance:
  i)   lower expenditure on current programs;
  ii) higher taxation;
  iii) monetary creation;
  iv) issuing debt;
  v)   issuing equity;
  vi) raising efficiency; and
  vii) raising prices.

Some remarks on these are appropriate here. With regard to the benefits, Nevile (1987) describes how public investment expenditures raise output and employment in the short run in economies which are less than fully employed. He notes that the public sector in Australia plays a large role by international comparisons in adding to the capital stock, and that increases in the amount of capital per head have been more important in Australia than in most other countries in raising productivity growth. In addition, productivity growth is essential if Australia is to alleviate its foreign trading constraint over the medium to long term.

International studies of recent vintage provide supportive evidence of these findings. Aschauer (1989) demonstrates that in the United States, public non-military investment expenditures (particularly in key sectors such as energy and transportation), exert strong influence on private sector productivity and investment. Barro (1989) reports that the share of public investment in GDP in 72 post-war economies exerts a positive influence on economic growth, although the statistical significance of the estimates did not remain intact following sample and specification changes.

With regard to the costs of infrastructure pro-

vision, governments can either reduce outlays on current programs or raise taxes. Both of these are politically unpopular, although the latter may be hidden in the form of "bracket creep". We shall have more to say about this shortly. Monetary financing is not recommendable because of its inflationary consequences. Bond financing and equity financing are the more popular financing methods in recent times. With regard to the first of these, the "crowding out" hypothesis has received little empirical support. With regard to the latter, both partial and full privatisation is being implemented (although few large GBE proposals have yet gone beyond the policy stage) in Australia. In most overseas cases of privatisation, the public assets have been grossly undervalued, and taxation or other incentives have been required to sell shares. The final two sources of finance involve microeconomic action in the form of raising enterprise efficiency in order to reduce the cost of provision or, failing this, to charge higher prices.

While the Australian government has demonstrated considerable determination and ingenuity in turning around the stance of fiscal policy over the latter part of the 1980s, the way in which this has been done has been open to comment from a number of viewpoints. Perhaps the most important and vociferous of these comments has been the complaint that the fiscal contraction has been borne excessively by cuts to capital rather than to current programs. The result of this, it has been argued, is that the economy's infrastructure has suffered in the budgetary process, and this will adversely affect output growth, productivity and international competitiveness in the future.

Tables 4.7 and 4.8 provide a precise account of the government's record over the last decade with respect to its current and capital outlays. Figure 4.3 provides the background to these Tables by describing the structure of the Commonwealth Public Sector as the sum of the General Government Sector and the Public Trading Enterprise Sector. This is instructive in the present context because the latter sector accounts for approximately 80 per cent of total public gross capital expenditure. The sectors are divided into budget and non-budget sectors as indicated in the Figure. The Commonwealth Budget Sector includes departments and authorities whose transactions are recorded in the Commonwealth Public Account, (whether through the Consolidated Revenue Fund, the Trust Fund or the Loan Fund). The Commonwealth Non-Budget Sector consists of agencies which are budget-dependent but whose transactions are recorded outside the Public Account.

Table 4.7 provides the details of the Commonwealth Budget and Non-Budget Sector current and capital outlays over the last decade and Table 4.8 indicates how total outlays of these sectors are divided between current and capital expenditure programs. The important conclusion which emerges in the current context is that the increased tightness of the fiscal stance has been achieved largely by reductions in capital rather than current outlays. For example, within the Commonwealth Budget Sector, current outlays as a per centage of total outlays increased from 91.5 per cent in 1980/81 to 96.0 per cent in 1989/90, while capital outlays as a per centage of total outlays declined from 8.5 to 4.0 per cent in the same sector over the same time period. In fact, public investment expenditures in Australia have declined as a proportion of GDP since the mid–1960s with the exception of 1973/74.

This trend has been observed by, *inter alia*, Alesina, Gruen and Jones (1990), who note that the fiscal adjustment over the latter part of the 1980s was achieved by a combination of reduced outlays and higher revenues. The latter were achieved mainly from "fiscal drag" on income taxes which grew by 6.1 per cent on average from 1983/84 to 1988/89 while real household income grew by 3.1 per cent on average over the same period. In addition, a number of studies have sought to place this trend in historical and economic context and to analyse its implications for the provision of infrastructure and for the future performance of the Australian economy. In addition to the National Infrastructure Conferences over the 1980s, the important studies in this respect are Langmore (1987), EPAC (1988) and McDonell (1990).

The Langmore Report focused upon historically declining trends in the public provision of infrastructure relative to GDP, it analysed the political and institutional mechanisms through which public investment funds are allocated and it pointed to the costs involved in the provision of less than optimal levels of infrastructure.

Amongst its main findings and recommendations were that first, the budgetary process should distinguish between current and capital expenditure programs in arriving at the fiscal balance; second, the funding of government business enterprises (GBEs) should be excluded from the public sector borrowing requirement; third, more attention should be devoted to relevant research and development; and fourth, the asset management techniques and overall performance of GBEs should be improved by the implementation of more market-oriented pricing policies, by the elimination of cross subsidies and by more extensive use of cost-benefit analysis in assessing the economic worth of projects.

EPAC (1988) argued that declining public expenditure on the provision of infrastructure does not imply that its provision is less than optimal, and it also pointed out that there are costs associated with over-supply as well as with under-supply of infrastructure. It subsequently argued that the optimal supply of infrastructure provision can only be decided on an individual program basis. It also echoed the findings of the Langmore Report that more market-oriented pricing policies together with more extensive use of cost-benefit analysis would enhance the performance of GBEs. Finally, EPAC (1988) advocated a three-pronged strategy for addressing the optimal and efficient provision of infrastructure as first, continued public provision under less regulated conditions; second, commercialisation within public provision; and third, privatisation. Privatisation is an issue we cover elsewhere in this report (particularly Chapters 10 and 11).

McDonell (1990) provides a comprehensive review of both the history and current issues in the provision of infrastructure in Australia. Amongst his major findings are the existence of an emerging consensus that first, aggregate levels of public investment do not imply over- or under-supply of infrastructure, rather, optimality conditions must be decided on a sector, program and case by case basis; second, that the optimal and efficient provision of infrastructure should entail an increasing amount of commercialisation and the application of formal cost-benefit analysis; and third, that the existence of natural monopoly and public good features of many infrastructure provision sectors necessitates a continued role for the public sector in planning for and providing for Australian infrastructure.

4.6 Macroeconomic Policy and the Electricity Industry

The provision of electricity infrastructure in Australia has traditionally involved extensive input by the public sector. This is not surprising in light of the previous discussion insofar as both the production and transmission of electricity as well as its distribution involve obvious cases of market failure. Some of the important examples of this are provided in the next few paragraphs.

The electricity industry, (at least in production and transmission if not in distribution) operates under substantial scale economies which imply a degree of natural monopoly. In an economy of Australia's size, this implies that the necessary scope of investment cannot be guaranteed unless planned for and executed on a national as well as on a regional basis. In addition, the existence of business cycles together with poor intertemporal allocation of resources which characterise market economies makes it unlikely that optimal provision of electricity — where investment is characterised by long time horizons — will eventuate in the absence of public sector involvement.

The electricity industry also incorporates many externalities which may not be internalised in private sector decisions. These externalities are pervasive and span the concerns of efficiency in domestic production, international competitiveness, environmental quality and social justice issues. Howe (1990) canvasses some of these concerns. For example, the current initiatives for enhanced electrification of rail transportation networks will have many positive side-effects such as improved trade performance due to less local demand for crude oil, less road transport congestion and improved environmental conditions.

This situation generates the need for continued public involvement in the electricity industry, both in the planning of necessary capacity as well as in carrying out the required investment. Recent macroeconomic policy, however, by focusing on fiscal restraint, has resulted in declining infrastructure expenditures. Tables 4.9 and 4.10 document the importance of electricity generation in overall government outlays over the last two decades, and Figure 4.4 illustrates the importance of this in the govern-

ment's overall capital expenditure program.

Looking firstly at the Tables 4.9 and 4.10, the programs which have gained most over this time period are education, health and social security and welfare, although even these programs have been curtailed during the latter part of the 1980s as part of the government's tight fiscal policy stance. Expenditure on fuel and energy (which mainly reflects capital expenditure on electricity generation capacity, see Table 4.10), has remained fairly static during this time period when measured in averages over five year periods, except for the rapid expansion following the resources boom in the early 1980s. The annual data reveals that capital expenditure on electricity capacity generation has fallen from a peak of 2.3 per cent of GDP in 1982/83 to current levels of 0.8 per cent of GDP in 1988/89. In comparison to the totality of public investment programs which declined by an average annual rate of 1.3 per cent between 1983/84 and 1988/89, real expenditure on electricity has been the fastest declining program — at an annual average rate of 11.4 per cent.

Figure 4.4 reinforces the lumpiness of this investment relative to other public investment programs. It is well documented that the reason for this lumpiness is to be found in the heavy investment in electricity capacity generation which occurred in the early 1980s. From 1981/82 to 1982/83, capital expenditure on electricity grew by 48 per cent due to the construction of four power stations, (namely, Bayswater, Eraring, Loy Yang and Northern).

Although the period of investment in electricity in the early 1980s has often been labelled as "overinvestment" (see, eg., Budget Paper No 1, 1990–91, p. 6.13), and this has been used to explain the subsequent decline in investment in electricity generation, a couple of points are worth making. First, real public capital expenditure on electricity in 1988/89 was more than 20 per cent below its level in 1978/79 prior to the resources boom; and second, the government itself (see Budget Paper No 1, 1990–91, p.6.12) admits that overall expenditure on infrastructure does not provide a reliable guide as to its optimal provision.

The conclusion which emerges is that there exists a trade-off within macroeconomic policy between the desire for fiscal austerity and the need to ensure that the economy is supplied with optimal quantities of infrastructure necessary to ensure improved international trading performance over the long run. The electricity industry provides a case in point.

It is clear that overinvestment occurred in traditional area of electricity generation capacity in the early 1980s. In the context of the emerging demands on the electricity industry, it is not at all clear that the most recent declines in investment in the electricity industry have been warranted. This is because new investment in required on the demand-side; and, on the supply-side, future investment will be required to either refit or replace existing generating capacity, and that the establishment of a nationally integrated industry will require considerable investment in transmission assets.

It is interesting, too, that the types of investment required on the demand-side are more susceptible to overall democratic control.

4.7 Summary and Conclusions

This chapter commenced with an overview of developments which have occurred in the Australian economy over the past decade. Basically, strong growth in aggregate demand combined with poor export growth has culminated in declining net export performance and burgeoning foreign debt. A separate section pointed to problems which currently exist in incorporating resource and environmental effects into the standard presentation of national account statistics. The macroeconomic policy settings which have been put in place, viz, tight wages, monetary, and fiscal policies have been designed, along with microeconomic reform policies, to stabilise the debt problem and help to generate improved international trading performance.

It was pointed out that a trade-off exists within macroeconomic policy between the desire for fiscal austerity and the need to ensure that the economy is supplied with optimal quantities of infrastructure necessary to ensure improved international trading performance over the long run. The electricity industry provides a case in point. Although it can be argued that some overinvestment in electricity capacity generation may have occurred in the early 1980s, it is not at all clear that subsequent declines in investment in this sector have been warranted.

The monopolistic character of the electricity industry and its considerable externalities, and the need to make long run decisions in conditions of uncertainty, necessarily means government involvement.

As Howe (1990) has argued, what Australia requires is a coordinated policy on long-term infrastructure investment which will guide Australia into the next century. It is beyond our commission to outline what may be required other than in the electricity industry. We would, however, suggest that a national, public inquiry is required to ascertain the economic and social infrastructure needs in all sectors of the economy.

CHAPTER 5

THE ENVIRONMENTAL IMPERATIVES OF POWERING THE FUTURE

5.1 Introduction

Energy is not so much a single product as a mix of products and services, a mix upon which the welfare of individuals, the sustainable development of nations, and the life-supporting capabilities of the global ecosystem depend. In the past, this mix has been allowed to flow together haphazardly, the proportions dictated by short-term pressures on and short-term goals of governments, institutions and companies. Energy is too important for its development to continue in such a random manner. A safe, environmentally sound and economically viable energy pathway that will sustain human progress into the distant future is clearly imperative. It is also possible. But it will require new dimensions of political will and institutional co-operation to achieve it (World Commission on Environment and Development [WCED], 1987, p.176).

Until the 1970s, the environmental and socio-political costs of supplying energy used by the industrialised countries for heating, lighting, cooking and industrial processes were relegated to secondary status and considered as "local nuisances or temporary inconveniences". They have since become "pervasive and persistent liabilities". The combination of an over dependence upon Middle Eastern oil supplies, and the air and water pollution problems frequently associated with energy supply and use have been recognised as threats to human health, economic well-being and environmental stability (Holdren, 1990, pp.109–110).

One commentator has also noted:

> ...energy use has become a potentially destructive force, locally because emissions contaminate air, water and soil and globally because there is the possibility that energy use may enhance the greenhouse effect. We face a dilemma: properly used, energy technologies serve as instruments for realizing material well-being across the planet, but continuation of current trends could lead to a degraded environment, yielding a mean and uncertain existence (Davis, 1990, p.21).

The doubts and uncertainties that are currently expressed in the conservation/development debate of recent years concern the capacity of the environment to absorb the effluents and other impacts of the last two centuries of unprecedented economic development and demographic growth. In 1987 the WCED released *Our Common Future*, a report on the relationship between economic development and environmental conservation. With regard to population growth and resource use the report stated:

> Many present efforts to guard and maintain human progress, to meet human needs and to realise human ambitions, are simply unsustainable — in both rich and poor nations. They draw too heavily, too quickly, on overdrawn environmental resource accounts to be affordable far into the future without bankrupting those accounts (p.8).

The likely growth of energy consumption was the subject of a heated international debate during the 1970s, largely dominated by the oil, nuclear and coal lobbies, whose arguments for growth ignored whether energy being consumed was being used economically or, indeed, whether it was needed in the first place. Until the 1973 oil crisis, technological change had brought about a steady decline in the price of energy. Fossil fuels were accessible in one form or another in all regions of the world, and they were used with little concern about waste.

Since 1973 the OECD has documented reduced energy consumption accompanied by economic growth in its member nations, which confirms that there is no fixed nexus between economic growth and energy consumption.[1] Energy intensity is declining, in part due to the shift to service industries, the use of lighter materials and the incorporation of more efficient industrial processes and technologies.

There is, however, abundant evidence that industrial economies do not consume energy resources in an efficient or sustainable manner. Following the 1973 oil crisis there was extensive debate and discussion about energy use and the possibilities that renewable energy technologies and conservation strategies offered. A subsequent glut on world markets resulted in cuts in funding for research and development, and commercialisation. The debate became the province of technical specialists. However, concern about the greenhouse effect has heightened public awareness that global development has been proceeding along an unsustainable path and is once again focusing public attention and discussion on energy use (Greene, 1990, pp.1–5). And has elsewhere been noted:

> Concern over the environmental consequences of energy production and consumption has increased markedly in recent years. Governments at all levels both in Australia and overseas are assessing the extent to which policy actions may need to be taken in an attempt to reduce any damaging effects of these activities, particularly in response to concern over the greenhouse effect and acid rain (ABARE, 1989, pp.1–2).

5.2 The Australian Context: the Ideology of Electrification

In 1973 oil constituted nearly half of the world's annual energy forms (Holdren, 1990, p.109). Until the oil price rises in 1973 and 1979, when the real price of oil quadrupled, there had been an almost unshakeable belief that there was a positive correlation between energy consumption and economic growth. This belief was central to what we might call "the ideology of electrification". A decade ago, Saddler noted "the belief that electricity was the agent and harbinger of efficiency, modernity and the good life at home and the workplace alike" (Saddler, 1981, p.51). The influence of this view may indeed have waned considerably (due in no small part to success in connecting most Australian households and enterprises to the grid), but it remains entrenched within the culture of electricity authorities.

Until recently, electrification in Australia has been inextricably linked with developmentalism, a belief which has "always been much more potent at the State than at the federal level" (Saddler, 1981, p.4). This led to State energy policies which showed a marked preference for the expansion of supply to the neglect of any serious consideration of conservation methods. It was assumed that better living required more energy. It is the environmental consequences of coal-fired power stations that we consider first.

5.3 Traditional Environmental Issues Associated with the Construction and Operation of Coal-Fired Power Stations
Power stations
The electricity industry in Australia is a profligate user of non-renewable resources. This judgement can be made even if problems stemming from electricity being a major source of carbon dioxide (CO_2) emissions are not considered. There are traditional environmental issues associated with construction, operation and fuel supply to the additional power stations such as concern with waste discharges to the air, water and land. The experience of decommissioning has led to the inclusion of factors such as exposure to asbestos.

Issues such as land-use, resource-use, the economics of electricity generation and aesthetics have not been traditionally considered. However, in a number of recent disputes concerning power stations, such as Eraring in NSW and Mt Laseur in Western Australia, these issues have come to the fore. The experience with such disputes in Victoria has led to a more consultative approach in these matters, with the Brunswick-Richmond Power Lines dispute setting a bench-mark in the processes of community consultation.

However, even if environmental impact assessments (EIAs) take these factors into account, it is worth noting that, the Franklin River dispute notwithstanding, "no amount of EIA process public or parliamentary inquiry, and consultation will halt a controversial project that has the full support of an excessively pro-development government" (Rosenthal and Russ, 1988, p.277). At this stage, the Task Force Inquiry into the proposed Tully-Millstream hydro-electric scheme (a project which has echoes of the Franklin River dispute) has yet to make its recommendations:

> The controversial proposed Tully-Millstream dam will impact on a significantly large area within the Wet Tropics of Queensland World Heritage Area. This contains a diverse living record of the major stages of the earth's evolution, provides fundamental insights into ongoing evolutionary processes and patterns, contains areas of exceptional natural beauty, and is a habitat for rare and threatened species (Diesendorf and Sonneborn, 1991, p.5).

South Australia and Queensland differ from Victoria, NSW and Western Australia in that they have no State legislation to determine emission limits. Recent amendments to the Victorian Environmental Protection Act have placed far more stringent pollution emission controls upon coal-fired power stations and increased the annual operating licence fees from $16,000 to $304,000. Sulphur dioxide emissions are controlled through ground concentration limits. There are however no scheduled limits on the atmospheric ventilation of sulphur dioxide (SO_2), and carbon dioxide (CO_2) is not likely to be scheduled as a pollutant in the foreseeable future.[2]

Prior to 1988, there were no air regulations in the monitoring requirements for power stations in NSW. Ambient air is now monitored over a distance of up to 20 kilometres from the power station site, with the limits in accordance with the NSW Clean Air Act but using a higher de facto level taken from National Health and Medical Research Council ambient goals which are more stringent than US Environmental Protection Agency (EPA) limits. All power stations are required to submit a quarterly air and water monitoring report to the State Pollution Control Commission (SPCC). Water quality is controlled by the NSW Clean Waters Act which is currently under review by the SPCC. It is expected that the new criteria, adopted from US and Canadian

standards, will be considerably more stringent than the previous requirements. There will be more pressure for the facilities to control their discharge of trace elements into the waterways in order to comply with licensing conditions.[3]

Coal-fired power stations affect the ecosystem of waterways through the discharge of their used water. Hot waste water from the cooling of thermal power stations discharged into the waterways encourages the growth of algae. The use of cooling towers has reduced these discharges, but differences in temperature between the discharged water and water in the lake are still observable. Concentrated waste solids containing mineral salts affect the salinity of the surrounding area. For example, the environmental effects of waste water discharges from thermal power stations have given rise to concern around the Macquarie Lakes area of New South Wales and the Gippsland Lakes in Victoria.

> Given the federal and State governments' concern with soil and inland waterway quality, salt discharges into the Latrobe River and Lake Coleman have raised concern. SECV saline wastewater arises from the processes of hydraulically transporting the fly ash and boiler ash from Yallourn North, Hazelwood and Loy Yang power stations to ash ponds. The Victorian EPA has estimated that SECV discharges contribute over "50 per cent of the point sources of salt discharged to the Latrobe River and some 20 to 25 per cent of the total increase in salinity in the river" (Latrobe Valley Wastewater Review, 1990, pp.9–10, 75).

The Review found that:

> the power stations and their associated open cuts consume more water than is necessary and return a larger than necessary volume of degraded wastewater to the stream system of the Latrobe Valley.

One of the actions recommended by the Task Force included an "imaginative suggestion, which appealed to the Panel", of a resource charge as a means of promoting greater efficiency in SECV Production Centre water usage (Latrobe Valley Wastewater Review, 1990, p.74).

The Panel recommended that:

> [the] SECV develop a new wastewater management strategy involving a public consultation process by July 1991, for immediate

implementation. This strategy should aim to substantially improve the quality of any wastewater discharged and to modify the present system so that less wastewater needs to be discharged (Latrobe Valley Wastewater Review, 1990, p.75).

In addition the, Environmental Protection Agency was ordered to review the standards and objectives every five years on the basis of technological changes, community expectations and knowledge of environmental impacts (Latrobe Valley Wastewater Review, 1990, p.75).

Coal mining

The coal industry has a long record of environmental neglect, particularly in the areas of subsidence, dust, noise, mine site rehabilitation and the destruction of sensitive ecosystems which has only been reversed in the last decade. This was reinforced by "... a government attitude of development at all costs" (United Mineworkers' Federation of Australia [UMFA], January 1991, p.1):

> There have been considerable advances in the science and practice of subsidence and mine site rehabilitation. Stringent environmental impact assessment procedures and the recent federal government decision to make mine site rehabilitation expenditure a tax-deductible cost have helped bring about these much needed changes (UMFA, January 1991, p.1).

In order to meet environmental impact assessment requirements, coal mines cannot be operated without securing and continually complying with government regulations for controlling water pollution, land surface subsidence, mine site rehabilitation, air and noise pollution and the safe disposal of any coal tailings. Individual State legislation and regulations have a "no release" criteria on highly saline water and water carrying silt loads that exceed the requirements of their Clean Water Acts and noise safeguards are imposed on operating plant and blasting (Gilbert, 1990, pp.69–72). It would however appear that these criteria are not always as stringently adhered to as the industry would have us believe:

> Collieries have been known to release ash, salts and heavy metals into the waterways. For example in 1990, Huntley Colliery near

Wollongong was fined \$3,391 by the NSW State Pollution Control Commission for polluting streams near its coal washing plant. In Newcastle, NSW, environmental groups have expressed concern that monitoring of waterways is inadequate (Diesendorf and Sonneborn, 1991, p.4).

There is also little or no attention given to the question of the environmental effects of the volumes of water consumed by the industry in a country where, potentially, water is a scarce resource.

Acid rain is not as yet a problem in Australia due to the relatively low sulphur content of Australian coal and the continent's isolation from acidic pollutants produced by other countries. However, there are "localised sources of (mildly) acid rain in heavily industrialised areas" (Diesendorf & Sonneborn, 1991, p.4).

Land reclamation programs are generally designed to provide a "stable land form requiring no ongoing maintenance and ensuring no downstream water pollution through situation or salination at the end of the life of the mine" (Gilbert, 1990, p.73). The success of land reclamation programs is dependent upon whether the mine has been underground or open cut, as "... previously mined land over potential underground workings should not be progressively reclaimed". Instead, it should be considered as part of ongoing operations due to "safety and technical reasons". This requirement has in effect removed — or, as the industry would have it, "sterilised" — 55 per cent of recoverable coal reserves in NSW due to "... the spread of residential and industrial development, transport and communication corridors and National Parks" (Gilbert, 1990, pp.74–75).

Conflicts over access to resources have been a major feature of the conservation/development debate and the coal industry is clearly concerned about the constraints on mining in national parks:

> The nation cannot expect to maintain the environment at the expense of our curtailing mining and mineral processing (Gilbert, 1990, p.83).

However, it would seem that the excision of Energy Resources of Australia (ERA) Ranger uranium mine from Kakadu National Park has set a precedent on the purposes to which national parks can be put. The coal industry has claimed that underground mining beneath national parks "... is feasible particularly where mining facilities and infrastructure can be located outside park boundaries" (Gilbert, 1990, p.76). Any environmental or aesthetic concerns are summarily dismissed as the following quote shows:

> The overall effects would not be adverse other than a small amount of disturbance resulting from exploration and the construction and maintenance of ventilation and access shafts (Gilbert, 1990, p.76).

Whilst it may be possible to play down the effects of underground mining, surface mining is another matter, as ECNSW discovered when it gain approval for an open cut mine to serve Eraring (Rosenthal and Russ, 1988, p.282). The problem with work that is essentially aimed at "erosion protection, water management, stabilisation and aesthetic improvement", and which is usually directed towards "reinstating the agricultural productivity of the land", is that the habitats and ecosystems of national parks and wilderness areas do not have the same limited rehabilitation requirements as agricultural land (Gilbert, 1990, p.77). Diesendorf and Sonneborn make a strong point on this same issue:

> Flora and fauna depend upon the stability of their ecosystem for survival. Disruptions such as oil spills, mining, flooding and water pollution all change the balance and threaten the existence of plentiful and endangered species alike (Diesendorf and Sonneborn, 1991, p.5).

5.4 The International Perspective
Introduction
Australia spends about half the per capita average of IEA member countries on the research and development of renewable energy sources. There has also been an "extraordinary emphasis on nuclear energy, especially given that there are no serious plans to use nuclear power in Australia". Total government expenditure on nuclear energy related research is almost double the amount spent on all forms of renewable energy (Lowe, 1988, pp.606–607). Further, since 1978, federal funding of research and development and demonstration of renewable energy

has been reduced to one eighth of its original value (Diesendorf, 1990, p.4).

While there are historical factors which go some way to explaining this situation, a brief consideration of international energy initiatives yields some insights into the possibilities that, in Australia, are only just beginning to gain institutional acceptance as viable and feasible alternatives to fossil-fuel generation.

The United States
There is extensive documentation of the demand-side management practices and energy efficiency measures that have been taken up by utilities in the United States. For example, since 1977 California has pursued a policy of strict conservation standards for all sectors of the economy. This included mandatory building and appliance efficiency standards reinforced by massive utility conservation programs.[4]

Renewable technologies, with 16,000 wind generators feeding 1,400 MW into the grid, are used as grid energy sources. 184MW of solar thermal energy from parabolic trough solar concentrators manufactured by Luz International have been installed, with another 80–160 MW scheduled for 1993. Such use of alternative sources has been contrary to the forecasts of US energy planners in the early 1970s who were ignorant of the potential for conservation, and who based their projections upon supply expansion, and expected demand to continue to double every ten years (World Resources Institute, 1990, p.122).

Utilities in the United States have actively marketed energy efficiency technologies and services as an alternative to building more power stations. This has been driven by the fact that demand-side measures are often far cheaper than constructing new supply capacity, and do not carry the substantial economic risks involved in construction at times when demand trends are uncertain. In addition, there have been attempts to quantify demand-side externalities (the unpriced benefits derived from conservation) in the four states of the Pacific Northwest by including a 10 per cent cost advantage for conservation programs over traditional programs. The Wisconsin Public Service Commission (WPSC) has also examined ways to cost intangibles in supply and demand options, and has devised a ranking system called NEEDS to describe demand-side intangibles which cannot easily be expressed in dollars. NEEDS include positive environmental characteristics, resource conservation, flexibility and risk. The WPSC gives a credit to the NEEDS of between 10 and 25 per cent. Options are ranked twice by cost, with a 10 per cent credit, and then again with a 25 per cent credit, thereby providing decision makers with an understanding of the effect of the cost of intangibles on various options (Community Energy Network, 1990, p.3.2–3.3).

United Kingdom

Co-generation, also known as Combined Heat and Power (CHP) has met with considerable acceptance in Britain, particularly from British Gas, as have a number of energy efficiency measures, due in no small part to the rise in oil prices. Renewable Technologies have not received any such encouragement. The pro-nuclear lobby within the Central Electricity Generating Board (CEGB) and the United Kingdom Department of Energy (DEN) have effectively sabotaged any viable alternatives that could produce significant amounts of electricity cheaper than any of the British nuclear power plants. Despite considerable British expertise in building Californian wind farms, and opinion polls that favour wind power, the CEGB and DEN have managed to restrict the development of wind power to three small parks.

The public inquiry into the Hinkley Point nuclear power station and the recent House of Lords Committee of Inquiry into Renewable Energy Sources heard considerable evidence detailing the strength of the pro-nuclear lobby within DEN and the CEGB. Professor Stephen Salter of Edinburgh University is the inventor of a wave power device commonly known as 'Salter's Duck'. The history of the research and development if this device is a prime example of the dirty tricks that have been used by British energy authorities to discourage and discredit renewable energy research.[5] It also underlines the lack of government support and funding for this type of research, a familiar situation for Australian researchers who need funding to upgrade their prototype renewable energy applications to a stage where they are commercially viable. These researchers have to make do with what little funding is available — after the lion's share has been absorbed by coal technology.

In 1976, DEN considered wave power the most attractive renewable source, with wind power among the least viable. But by 1982 wave power research and development ceased, with a number of wave projects suffering in the process, among them 'Salter's Duck'. In simple terms, this device consisted of a canister which bobbed up and down on the waves like a floating duck. The resulting motion drives an electrical generator. The estimated development potential for electricity from the Duck was 7.5c/kWh, thus making it the first renewable generating source which could conceivably compete with nuclear power.

However, prior to the Duck's final year of development, a report from the DEN Energy Technology Support Unit (ETSU) persuaded the DEN Advisory Council that wind power had more immediate economic potential than wave power, and that the required $A7.5 million cut to the budget for renewable research would have to be met by closing down wave power research. At that time DEN had an annual nuclear research budget of A$500 million. Both wind and wave research could easily have been maintained.

In January 1983, not content with removing funding from the Salter's Duck project, ETSU proceeded to "massage the data" on costs of wave power by averaging out the best and worst estimates, arriving at a figure of 20c/kWh, which was henceforth quoted as the wave power *minimum* cost. This was followed by a change in the method used to calculate the capital cost, which added nearly A$7 million to the cost of each Duck, and pushed the unit cost up to 24.5c/kWh. The CEGB was then able to quote the 'new' costings at the 1987 Hinkley Inquiry in order to discredit alternatives to nuclear power. In his oral evidence to the Hinkley Inquiry Professor Salter commented that there was "abundant documentary evidence" that DEN and ETSU had indeed stooped to such processes (*The Ecologist*, Vol. 20, No.3, p.88).

Professor Salter spent much of 1983 disputing these figures, including a paper which asked 19 questions, all of which drew attention to some failure of the DEN consultants' reliability estimates. None of the questions were answered; any one of which would have made a responsible engineer or scientist realise something was wrong with the way wave research had been evaluated. He concluded his original memorandum to the House of Lords Committee thus:

> We must not waste another 15 years and dissipate the high motivation of another generation of young engineers. We must stop using grossly different assessments in a rat race between technologies at widely different stage of their development. We must find a way of reporting accurate results to decision makers with enough technical knowledge to spot data massage if it occurs. **I believe this will be possible only if the control of renewable energy projects is completely removed from nuclear influences** (Jeffery, 1990, p.90, emphasis added).

Denmark

In Denmark over the past 30 years there has been a major shift from dependence on imported oil to energy self sufficiency (Sorensen in ERDIC, 1990, p.8).

Between 1975 and 1990 Denmark invested A$4 billion into efficient uses of energy and wind power. Most investments were made in the building sector with economic advantages amounting to A$2.5 billion per decade — building energy requirements were first included in Danish building codes in 1967. There has been a high level of investment in energy efficiency in their domestic sector, including home insulation, lighting and appliances. Subsidies were phased out in the early 1980s, but the level of investment has not diminished, which suggests a high level of public awareness. Any new industry is planned in clusters so that waste heat can be used. Approximately 75 per cent of electricity is produced by combined heat and power plants with waste heat used for district heating.

Wind power was installed extensively and now provides 4 per cent of the country's electricity supply. The wind power industry now accounts for A$200 million in foreign currency from exports. Wind power was evaluated on the assumption that costs were the same as for fossil fuels, if the environmental costs of fossil fuels are taken into account. In addition, the economies of scale in power plants have changed so that smaller plants are no longer financially uncompetitive. It is also worth noting that Denmark, along with Austria, have banned nuclear energy.

As Sorensen notes, energy planning has been depoliticised to the point where policies on energy planning are recognised as working for the benefit of everyone:

> The result has been a broad based social and political consensus in energy planning. Changes of government are not associated with changes of direction. For example, a tax applied to primary energy sources has maintained the consumption price of energy at approximately constant levels since the early 1980s (after accounting for inflation). This has provided a stable economic environment for demand-side investment decisions. Further, the receipts from this tax have been invested in research and subsidies for renewables and end-use efficiency so that they remain competitive during periods of low primary energy prices (Sorensen in ERDIC, 1990, pp. 8–9).

The energy question in Denmark also opened up an area of social debate which changed the selection process used to evaluate projects. Now as many impacts as possible are evaluated so that the cost of investment is only one amongst global and social impacts, and health effects. The decision-making process has been devolved to individual communities who are able to choose which forms of energy they will use and how they will connect with the existing grid. Professor Sorensen notes that this is a very resilient system that allows for decentralised community based decision-making and provides an interesting contrast with a large, centralised political bloc such as ECNSW.

Sweden

In 1988 the Swedish Parliament approved a plan to freeze CO_2 emissions at their current levels and institute a tax on CO_2 emissions this year:

> There are only 8.5 million Swedes, and each is on average responsible for adding 2.2 metric tons of carbon to the atmosphere annually. There is not much they can do to offset the effect of 260 million US residents adding 5.5 tons per capita annually, or that of China's one billion adding 0.5 ton per capita. Nevertheless, a broad coalition in Parliament has determined that Sweden should provide an example of responsible behaviour in protecting the biosphere

(Burke, 1990, p.12).

The 1988 CO_2 freeze means that the loss cannot be supplemented with oil or coal generation, and a 1985 ban on development of Sweden's four major river systems that remain undammed removes the option of hydro.

Sweden has already benefited from conservation methods adopted after the oil price rises during the 1970s and plans to extend energy efficiency measures and technologies and introduce a major shift to biomass fuels. A study by the Swedish University of Agricultural Sciences has estimated the increase in biomass energy over the next ten years is equivalent to 20–35 TWh, or half the nuclear power currently generated. Wind power could also replace up to half the power currently generated by nuclear plants through the construction of 4,000 wind generators, a third based on the land and two-thirds in coastal waters. The Swedish government may soon introduce a subsidy for wind power which will make it a more attractive financial proposition (Burke, 1990, pp.2–7).

Nuclear power

To date, Australia's involvement in the nuclear fuel cycle has been as a source of uranium mining.[6] Abundant supplies of coal have rendered nuclear energy as neither feasible nor viable. However, advocates of nuclear energy have recently been using the greenhouse effect as justification for the installation of nuclear power plants in this country. The nuclear industry has claimed that new reactors in the 200 to 600 megawatt range are being developed which would be suitable for Australia's needs. New plant designs are in the pipeline with features such as modularity and passive safety systems. However, nuclear power's problems are not simply the result of a few engineering mistakes or mismanagement, and, as the Worldwatch Institute says, the entire concept of inherent safety may be an "engineering mirage", and further that:

> The problems stem from basic unresolved technological issues such as vulnerability to accidents and reliance on highly dangerous materials (Worldwatch Institute, 1990, p.24).

In their 1988 paper, *Greenhouse Warming: Comparative Analysis of Two Abatement Strategies*, Gregory Kats and Bill Keepin concluded that a significant number of nuclear plants would be required to replace fossil-fuel generators with nuclear generated power (Greene, 1990, p.6 Section 1) and would not work as a greenhouse abatement strategy, even if it were possible to co-ordinate on a global scale (in Falk and Brownlow, 1990, pp.127–130). A dollar invested in energy efficiency can displace seven times more carbon dioxide than a dollar invested in nuclear energy.

The figures used by Kats and Keepin are extremely generous to nuclear power in that they deliberately underestimate construction times and the cost of building and running nuclear plants. They ignore the problems and costs of nuclear waste storage and treatment, decommissioning costs, safety, environment and health effects, nuclear proliferation, and vulnerability to sabotage terrorism and acts of war. Nor do they take into account the energy required to build the plants.[7]

The American nuclear industry has received enormous government subsidies since the 1950s including: research and development; subsidies for uranium enrichment and waste storage; failure to include decommissioning costs; and federal tax subsidies which pay for almost a third of plant capital costs, compared with one sixth for fossil-fuelled plants. The Price-Anderson Act also limits the liabilities faced by builders and operators of nuclear power plants for any damages caused by their plants (Diesendorf, 1990, p.7).

Whilst fossil fuelled electricity in England and Wales is now privatised, the government did not proceed with the sale of the nuclear component of the industry (see Chapter 11). In 1990, Britain's House of Commons Energy Select Committee criticised the Department of Energy and came to a large number of unfavourable conclusions concerning the cost of nuclear electricity which included:

> Given the recent history of nuclear power it will never again be possible to take assurances as to the viability of any type of nuclear power on trust (cited in Diesendorf, 1990, p.3).

Globally, nuclear power has been in the doldrums for the past decade, there are currently 94 nuclear plants under construction, the smallest number in 15 years (Worldwatch Institute, 1990, p.23). In the United States, no new nuclear power stations have been ordered since 1978, and all orders from 1974 to 1978 have been cancelled. Construction costs are racing ahead of inflation as reactors take longer and longer to build and almost all new orders are in the Soviet Union and France where the market plays little or no role.[8]

With regard to nuclear waste, there is extensive documentation, particularly in the US, of the failure to safely store existing waste stockpiles, let alone develop a long-term solution for the disposal of nuclear waste. Citizen action groups and the "not in my back yard" (NIMBY) syndrome in the US have made it increasingly difficult for the US Department of Energy to maintain existing waste sites, and nearly impossible to select and locate future ones.

SYNROC, a special material, is frequently advocated as a long-term solution for the safe disposal of high-level nuclear wastes. However, glowing reports usually fail to mention that this method can only cope with a very narrow range of medium to high-level liquid wastes which require storage in politically and geologically stable countries. This of course rules out large areas of the world, with the exception of a few countries such as Australia.

In addition, Three Mile Island, the consequences of Chernobyl, and the notorious Sellafield reprocessing facility (which has made the Irish sea the most radioactive body of water in the world) and has an abnormally high incidence of leukaemia clusters in Sellafield workers' children, all contribute to the declining acceptance of nuclear power and the conclusion that it is not a valid option for slowing global warming.

5.5 The Electricity Industry and the Greenhouse Effect
Carbon dioxide emissions and fossil fuel combustion

It is not exactly certain in the scientific sense what this increased CO_2 production will mean for the environment, but there is no reason to be optimistic (Banks, 1985, p.168).

As a result of the greenhouse effect global warming is expected to lead to an average increase in the earth's surface temperature of between 1.5°C and 4.5°C, with a corresponding rise in sea levels of around 30 cm by the middle of the next century. In October 1990 the Australian federal government announced the adoption of the Toronto target of a 20 per cent reduction in carbon dioxide, nitrous oxide and

methane gases by 2005.

The greenhouse effect is the source of considerable debate, both within the scientific community and amongst policy makers. Many uncertainties attend the issues, some of which may take many decades to resolve. Nevertheless, it is now generally accepted that fossil fuel combustion contributes more atmospheric carbon dioxide than any other activity, including deforestation (Pearman, 1988, p.7):

> Carbon dioxide is on the increase in the atmosphere. The average measured concentration over 1988 was 351.2 parts per million (ppm), about 76ppm above the pre-industrial level. The exact contribution of the various mechanisms which may have led to this increase remains open to scientific debate. Nevertheless few would doubt that energy generation has played an important role (Falk and Brownlow, 1990, p.112).

The problem with a "wait and see" approach is that whilst information may expand, the effectiveness of any strategies may be reduced as damage becomes irreversible, dangerous trends become more entrenched, and technologies and institutions harder to steer and shape:

> It is likely to be easier to plan for a long-term shift in energy mix than to respond to regional climate variations if they occur. An adaptive strategy is open-ended; if atmospheric concentrations of greenhouse gases are not stabilised, then climate changes will be a continuing phenomenon requiring indefinite programs of adaptation (Senate Standing Committee on Industry, Science and Technology [SSCIST], 1991, p.5).

Professor John P. Holdren from the University of California, Berkeley, has proposed a two-pronged strategy consisting of "no regrets" and "insurance policy" elements to counter opposition that argues that there is insufficient data to warrant costly action:

> No-regrets actions are those that provide leverage against the dangers we fear but are beneficial even if the dangers do not fully materialise. In contrast, insurance-policy actions offer high potential leverage against uncertain dangers in exchange for only modest investment, although some of the investment may later turn out to have been unnecessary (Holdren, 1990, p.114).

Holdren further argues that there are two no-regrets programs that would internalise and reduce the environmental and socio-political costs of existing energy sources. The first is the abatement of emissions of sulphur, nitrogen oxides, and hydrocarbon and particles from fossil fuels using existing technologies, the costs being recovered by the reduction in damage to health, property and ecosystems. He further suggests that a carbon tax could develop and finance technologies for reducing world-wide fossil-fuel dependence. It remains true, however, that increasing the efficiency of energy use is undoubtedly the most effective way of all to abate environmental impacts:

> In the case of greenhouse much has already been written and said, including strategies and recommendations that would greatly reduce greenhouse emissions. The element that is missing is not information but action...Whilst community awareness and discussion are important the Committee's view is that it is now time for action. That action must be speedy and must be a practical solution in the short term. Setting up committees to further examine greenhouse issues or putting out press releases imploring the community to be more energy conscious does not constitute action that will result in sufficiently significant reductions of greenhouse gas emissions (SSCIST, 1991, p.7).

Implications for the Australian coal industry

> ...if the world introduces energy efficiency and no longer wishes to buy our coal or gas (imported fuels will be the first to go for these countries), then there is little we can do (Australian and New Zealand Solar Energy Society, 1990, p.10).

Coal is by far the most abundant and accessible fossil fuel source in Australia. Coal plant accounts for the bulk of the 35,000 megawatts of installed capacity in Australia (SSCIST, 1991, p.64). Until the greenhouse effect and carbon dioxide emissions became an issue, coal appeared to be a cheap and ideal fuel source for electricity generation.

When compared with the sulphur content of coals mined and used overseas, Australian black coal is considered "clean". However, coal combustion results in more carbon dioxide emission per unit of energy than any other fossil fuel. Black coal used in electricity generation typically releases approximately 25 per cent more carbon dioxide than oil and 50 per cent more than natural gas for the same amount of heat (Falk and Brownlow, 1990, p.118).

The problem is compounded by the relative inefficiency of conventional coal fired power stations where a maximum of 35 per cent of the energy in black coal can be converted into electrical energy. One Gigawatt hour of electricity from a black coal fired power station produces 940 tonnes of carbon dioxide. Modern brown coal fired stations such as Loy Yang have energy conversion efficiencies of 29 per cent and produce 1,110 tonnes of carbon dioxide per Gigawatt hour. The efficiency of thermal power stations is unlikely to ever exceed 50 per cent, despite current research by the CSIRO (SSCIST, 1991, p.55).

The SSCIST accepted that Australia's vast reserves of coal cannot be ignored as a source of energy in the short to medium term, as this is not an area where rapid change is possible, and economic considerations will be central to decisions made. However, if emission targets were to be met, the efficiency of coal based electricity generation must be improved and, as current coal stations reach the end of their life, they must be replaced with the best available technology. In the longer term, as alternative non-fossil fuel energy forms become available, "the requirement to utilise Australia's vast coal reserves will decrease" (SSCIST, 1991, p.65–66).

Carbon dioxide is not as strong a greenhouse gas as methane, nitrous oxide or CFCs but because it exists in such large amounts compared to those other gases its impact is more significant. The ability to effectively decrease methane and nitrous oxide emissions that stem from ruminant digestive tracts and agricultural practices is limited, whilst numerous options exist for the reduction in the use of fossil fuels and the phasing in of non-polluting renewable energy sources. Hence the overwhelming focus on carbon dioxide:

> The energy sector is responsible for significantly increasing the emission of carbon dioxide. In energy conversion, over 94 per cent of total estimated warming will be caused by carbon dioxide. Effective action to decrease

greenhouse warming must therefore focus on carbon dioxide (SSCIST, 1991, p.32).

Although Australia's global share of greenhouse gases is between 1 and 2 per cent, at 4 tonnes per person per annum, we are the fourth or fifth highest per capita producer of CO_2 emissions in the world (SSCIST, 1991, p.19). The energy sector also releases large amounts of other greenhouse gases including methane, from coal fields and natural gas pipeline leakages, and chlorofluorocarbons used in refrigeration and the manufacture of insulation materials.

Formulating an effective greenhouse policy is clearly politically difficult. In Australia it is compounded by the undue power of the coal mining lobby — Australia is the world's largest exporter of coal, and coal fired power stations account for a significant proportion of total energy consumption (ABARE, 1989, p.6). Energy supplies are subject to State control which further exacerbates policy formulation due to the vexed perennial question of State's rights and their ability to meet costs imposed by effective abatement strategies.

The resulting costs will vary from State to State, depending upon their ability to reduce greenhouse gas emissions and the resulting costs and the extent to which their regional economies depend upon coal mining and electricity generation. There is also little doubt that employees of both industries will suffer from the short-term costs and dislocations brought about by future fuel substitution measures.

The Australian Coal Association's (ACA) determination to shift the onus of greenhouse gas emissions onto the agricultural sector is hardly surprising given the industry's vested interest in the supply of local and export coal for electricity generation. Whilst lending their support to the concept of the efficient use of energy, their position paper on the greenhouse effect contains the following familiar elements: a reluctance to accept the gravity of the problem due to the element of uncertainty and lack of consensus amongst the scientific community; and the by now problematic view (at least for the developed world) that "Energy usage is linked directly to economic growth" (ACA, 1989, pp.6–8).

Ultimately the central problem is not so much the impact on the coal industry, but upon those who depend upon it (and its flow-ons) for their day-to-day survival. It could be argued that the coal industry has in previous years benefited by having the pollution which results from its product omitted from the economic calculations of those who buy it. The costs to future generations from carbon dioxide have been an externality, borne directly be no one, but indirectly by everyone (Falk and Brownlow, 1990, p.218).

The United Mineworkers' Federation of Australia (UMFA) estimates that if all coal-fired power stations were closed down by 2004–5 about half of the current workforce of 29–30,000 miners would be made redundant. The Australian Coal Association has used multiplier effects to estimate that "the black coal industry supports the livelihood of about half a million Australians" (UMFA, 1991, pp.18–19):

> It may be argued by some that new employment opportunities will open up in other industries; those that are less energy intensive or are concerned with environmental protection. Such industries will not develop spontaneously; if left to their own devices many Australian enterprises will choose to either import new technology or relocate to countries with less stringent environmental policies. Australian business management has an extremely poor record in developing new productive opportunities.
>
> Against the wider backdrop of Australia being a relatively remote, resource rich country with small domestic markets, the prospect of a shift away from resource and energy industries without concrete alternatives in place is alarming (UMFA, 1991, p.19).

In the absence of any clear policy directions or action it is apparent that "one of the least equitably distributed costs of a greenhouse emissions policy is likely to be its impact on employment" (Falk and Brownlow, 1990, p.220).

New methodologies for improvement

Techniques that are currently being developed which can increase the efficiency of coal generated electricity whilst decreasing emissions by 20–25 per cent. These include pressurised fluidised bed combustion, integrated gasification combined cycle, direct injection of pulverised ultraclean coal into gas turbines and solid oxide fuel cells.

Fluidised bed combustion boilers burn finely ground coal suspended on a strongly rising current of air. They allow for more efficient heat transfer to the boiler, and the coal is burnt at a lower temperature thereby reducing the production of nitrous oxide. The addition of materials to the bed, like crushed limestone, removes sulphur and other pollutants. Efficiency can be further improved by adding gas turbines to generate electricity from the exhaust gases. The Southern California Edison Company is operating a 100MW fluidised bed combustion station at its Cool Water site producing emissions that are equivalent to a comparable natural gas power plant (Falk and Brownlow, 1990, p.119). Fluidised bed combustion may also offer a solution for the costly problem of coal washery rejects.

Coal may also be converted to gas, cleaned of unwanted contaminants, and piped to the generating station. Both of these systems are not only cleaner than conventional coal-fired stations they are also economic as much smaller units. Thus it is possible to site them near end point usage which allows any waste heat to be used to warm water for domestic or industrial use.

The Brookhaven National Laboratory in Mississippi is investigating a process known as Hydrocarb which allows the hydrogen to be extracted from coal and burnt without producing any carbon dioxide. This is still at the experimental stage and is yet to be demonstrated as a feasible or economic process (Falk and Brownlow, 1990, p.118).

The problem inherent in all these developments is that they are extremely costly and the conversion processes themselves involve substantial amounts of energy to produce a non-polluting fuel source. If this is taken into account when they are compared with demand-side management and the incorporation of renewable technologies, which are after all occurring within the same time frame, it is difficult to justify the huge funding input they require.

New generating technologies which can supplement existing methods of electricity generation include solid oxide fuel cells (SOFCs), a relatively "clean" technology that has the potential to produce electricity from natural gas, hydrogen, alcohol and gasifies coal. The ceramic cell has no moving parts and operates like a battery continuously fed with reactants. The CSIRO is currently making breakthroughs in ceramic technology and SOFCs are considered by the Department of Primary Industry and Energy and the SSCIST as having "considerable promise". However, the raw materials used for the cells include rare earths, which naturally raise the questions of the environmental effects of mining, and the occupational and community health and safety aspects of radioactive materials. If the International Commission for Radiological Protection recommended a reduction in acceptable annual dose levels, rare earth processing may very well cease (*The Ecologist*, Vol. 20 No 3 pp.85–90).

Natural gas substitution

Natural gas has two immediate advantages over coal: less carbon is released for each unit of energy obtained and combined gas turbines are more efficient than coal-fired plant. However, the long economic life of coal-fired power stations precludes the "significant" replacement of coal plant by gas plant prior to 2010, although such substitution could cut CO_2 emissions by 15 per cent by 2010 if 50 per cent of power stations were gas fired.

Whilst it may be environmentally desirable to scrap existing plant and replace it with natural gas, it is neither economically or politically feasible. However, it is possible to ensure that "any decision to build new facilities should take account of possibly tougher emission restrictions next century than even gas fired power generation could meet" (SSCIST, 1991, p.61).

5.6 The Corporate Response — the Marks et al Report

Conzink Rio-tinto Australia Ltd (CRA) commissioned the Australian Graduate School of Management from the University of New South Wales and the Institute of Applied Economic and Social Research of the University of Melbourne to examine "the feasibility and implications of the adoption of the Toronto proposal for carbon dioxide emissions". The subsequent report, known as the Marks Report, "is generally accepted as predicting the most dramatic adverse economic impacts from the forced achievement of the Toronto target" (UMFA, 1991, pp.13–16).

The Marks Report forecasts energy price increases that give rise to a number of conclusions in terms of fuel prices, real wage levels and losses of GDP growth that are damaging to the economy and expensive for the community.

The report has been criticised by both the UMFA and the Australian Conservation Foundation (ACF). UMFA notes a "lack of realism in the study" (1991, p.16). The ACF also criticises the report's unrealistic assumptions which seem to be based "almost entirely on changes in a single variable: namely 40 per cent increases in the cost of electricity and 60 to 120 per cent increases in the costs of petroleum" (ACF, 1990, p.2). The report makes no mention of the potential in Australia for new and expanded industries in renewable energy or energy management services:

> The authors of the CRA report seem blissfully unaware that, in several northern European countries and North American countries and in Japan, the energy intensity (i.e. energy consumption per unit of GDP) has declined substantially over the past 15 years or so; there has even been a modest decline in Australia.

> It is ironic that the CRA report states that its baseline, business-as-usual scenario "implies a sombre future for Australia", yet still supports this black future which has presumably resulted from mistaken policies of the past, such as Australia placing excessive reliance upon "resource development" industries while its customers spread their purchasing wildly. The CRA report seems hindered by its pro-mining and mineral resource development ideology from serious consideration of an energy efficient, renewable energy scenario, where most of the technologies are manufactured in Australia (ACF, 1990, p.2).

The Marks Report would appear to have set the tone for the Australian corporate response to meeting the Toronto target, namely that the market rules and any form of government intervention aimed at environmental improvements is to be actively discouraged whilst maintaining that intervention will always result in additional costs to consumers. The counter view is that excess costs will be the result of inaction, and that a planned phased in changeover to clean energy sources may be the most cost-effective approach.

The exponents of the "business as usual scenario" ignore the possibility of international agreements designed to reduce the level of carbon dioxide emissions which would force a major revision of energy supply policy and practice. BHP Petroleum's Industry Commission submission shows an almost wilful neglect of any consideration of economically sustainable development (ESD) or environmental impacts. They do however note that amongst the list of conditions *not* required if they are to achieve their "view of the future" are the "imposition of government agendas on the industry, which often emphasise job creation and other 'social goals' over and above long term economic viability" (BHP Petroleum, 1990, p.7). Presumably the long term future of the planet is one of those "social goals".

The Australian Petroleum Exploration Association Limited maintain that "the market mechanism can be made to play an import [sic] role in controlling emissions of greenhouse gases" as this is likely "to be more efficient and less disruptive than direct regulations aimed at limiting some particular aspect of energy use" (Australian Petroleum Exploration Association Limited [APEA], 1990, p.10). The Report's policy recommendations included:

ii) Australia should not commit itself to artificial reductions in greenhouse gas emissions which mirror global targets. There are environmental benefits associated with burning Australian coal compared with Northern Hemisphere coals and burning Australian oil compared with Middle East oil.

iii) Domestic policy prescriptions should not involve significant interference with market forces. The greenhouse effect is a global issue. Consequently, activity directed at large scale reductions of greenhouse gas emissions can be commercially based on a global scale. **This may allow Australia to assume a greater economic role and increase greenhouse gas emissions relative to, say, Western Europe and North America, to the overall benefit of the global environment** (APEA, 1990, p.10, emphasis added).

If the abstruse logic of (iii) is anything to go by, it is clear that the Association is yet to comprehend fully the nature of the problem.

There is also considerable resistance to greenhouse abatement strategies from within the federal government. In September 1990, the federal Treasury was widely reported as using stalling tactics designed to undermine a submission by the Minister for the Environment for the immediate imposition of a target reduction of 20 per cent of greenhouse gas emissions by 2005. The Minister had based her submission on the Greene Report which argued that achieving the target is not only possible but easy and would bring economic benefits from investment in energy efficient measures.

The Treasury took the line that no conclusive reports on the value of the targets existed, and that more investigation was needed before any changes would be necessary to the "business as usual scenario". This view ran counter to the United Nation's Intergovernmental Panel on Climate Change and the conclusions of the CSIRO, but found favour with the ACA, the Mining Industry Council and the Departments of Transport, Primary Industry and Energy. The view is also shared by the Bush Administration which has so far vetoed any attempts to bring about a consensus amongst OECD countries with regard to collective strategies, actions and responsibilities to deal with possible catastrophic global climate change.

5.7. Survey of Demand-Side Management Strategies and Energy
Institutional barriers inherent in conventional forecasting methods

In Australia, the spread of technologies for energy efficiency and renewable energy is impeded by institutional barriers and a low level of research funding. A major contributing factor in this situation is a set of attitudes that are, arguably, part and parcel of the conventional wisdom. Engineering branches of electricity authorities have also been influenced by similar conventions. While this situation has begun to change, there has been a reluctance to consider the potential of, for example, renewable energy sources.

Reasoning is based upon the economies of scale that have been used to generate cheap electricity from fossil fuels. Thus, conventional energy planners proceed from the premise that it is impractical to build a 1000 megawatt solar thermal generating station, extensive wind farms, and install thousands of megawatts of wind machines. They are, however, beginning to learn the lessons from their colleagues elsewhere in the world who have adopted the approach of least cost planning. Nevertheless, their slowness in adopting this new perspective has contributed to an inability to conceive of future energy needs that can be met through energy efficiency and conservation methods combined with renewable energy technologies:

> If such a vision were to underlie planning decisions, then most of the non-technical barriers would dissolve or be legislated away. Such non-technical barriers include lack of a pollution and resource depletion tax on fossil fuels; poor assessment of wind energy by some electricity authorities; conservative opposition to non-conventional technologies; inappropriate grid extensions instead of installation of modular remote area power supply systems; unfavourable tax laws; and unfavourable financing arrangements for renewable energy systems, which tend to be capital intensive with low running costs (Blakers, Outhred and Diesendorf, 1988, p.16).

Energy intensive industries: the example of aluminium smelters

> The old reflexes of megaprojects and asset utilisation (whether brown coal in the ground or costly plants to burn it) die hard (Lovins, 1990, p.33).

Between 1979 and 1987 energy intensity declined in Australia as a result of major structural changes in fuel use technology instituted by industry. While this does not necessarily imply a reduction in the total energy used, the last three years have once again seen an increase in energy intensity as a result of lower real energy prices and a strong growth in the steel and aluminium industries which are themselves energy intensive (ABARE, 1989, p.5). Whilst some observers would disagree, Greene argues that although Australia's energy intensity has declined more slowly than most countries, the energy intensive industries mask the overall downward trend:

> When the energy used by those few very large facilities is removed, the decline in Australian energy intensity is quite clear (Greene,

1990, pp.2–7).

It is important, therefore, to consider the reasons that exist for Australia's attraction for aluminium producers.

Coal from mines owned by electricity authorities has conventionally been priced at "what it costs to dig up and transport", making no allowance for resource depletion or environmental cost (Saddler, 1981, p.137). One result has been to keep electricity prices low. This cheap electricity is a very attractive proposition indeed for the international aluminium cartel which requires vast amounts of electricity for smelting (some refer to aluminium as "solid electricity"). The States almost fell over one another in the rush to attract aluminium smelters, offering power at giveaway prices in "exchange for a relative handful of jobs (and a not inconsiderable amount of environmental pollution)" (Saddler, 1981, p.138).

By 1988, the situation had not changed dramatically. Rosenthal and Russ concluded that when all factors are taken into account, aluminium smelters pay less for their power than smaller industrial customers. They argue that if a subsidy is to be paid because of considerations such as the provision of employment then:

> ...it would be preferable that smelters take the standard industrial tariff for large customers and be given a direct hand-out from the State Treasury. Then at least governments would have to justify their decisions in the face of competing demands from smaller industries, welfare groups and other consumer groups. It may well turn out that the hand-outs cannot be justified (Rosenthal and Russ, 1988, p.186).

In their critique of the SECV/Department of Industry, Technology and Resources (DITR) Demand Management Development Project the Conservation Council of Victoria saw the link between utilities and aluminium smelters as integral to the pricing structures that underlie supply-side planning strategies and rationale:

> Low marginal costs and correspondingly low retail pricing encourages the use of electricity. This increases demand and perpetuates a 'build more' planning cycle. This vicious circle is exacerbated when the utility negotiates a cheap power deal with an aluminium smelter to justify the building of a power station (Conservation Council of Victoria, 1990, p.2).

In their submission to the Industry Commission, the Rainforest Conservation Society noted the pitfalls that have accompanied the active pursuit of this strategy by the QEC and the former Queensland government:

> In this study we have analysed the basis of the QEC forecast and we conclude that a significant proportion of the increased demand forecast by QEC is the result of existing policies and strategies that are specifically designed to increase electricity sales. **Of central importance is a policy of stimulating growth in sales of electricity that had its origins in the 1980s when abandoned aluminium smelter projects left Queensland with an oversupply of electricity and associated large debts** (Rainforest Conservation Society, 1990, p.1, emphasis added).[9]

There are sound practical reasons for locating aluminium smelters in this country. Simply, aluminium smelting adds value to a resource which Australia has in abundance. This increased value is extremely important in respect of export earnings, though it is recognised that even greater advantages would accrue from further, downstream processing. We need to recognise that in respect of the global environmental equation, this argument carries the underlying assumption that the use of fossil fuel to generate electricity for smelters in Australia is less globally damaging then the use of fossil fuels needed to transport bauxite to other smelters, and the use of any of the energy sources for those smelters.

The equation becomes more complex in terms of sustainable development: it needs at the very least to include the global environmental advantages which would flow from incentives for incorporating energy efficient plant. Subsidised tariffs to the aluminium industry can hardly be said to fall into that category.

On the other side, the equation needs to incorporate recycling, as recycling energy intensive products definitely has the potential to not only reduce greenhouse gas emissions, but also demand for primary aluminium production. For example, recycling aluminium cans uses approximately one twentieth of the energy required to produce a new can (SSCIST, 1991, p.116).

Demand-side management

Three recent reports (Greene, 1990; National Institute of Economic and Industrial Research [NIEIR], 1990; and Wilkenfeld, 1990) have challenged the underlying assumptions of energy planners in Australia, and proposed strategies that can meet the Toronto target of a 20 per cent reduction in greenhouse gas emissions by 2005. The basic underlying assumption of these reports is that rather than spending vast amounts of money developing ways to prevent CO_2 escaping into the atmosphere after fossil fuels have been burnt, or subjecting the fuel to costly and energy intensive technologies, it makes a lot more sense to reduce the amounts of fossil fuels that are consumed in the first place. This will involve modifying current patterns of energy use by making homes, offices, industries and transport more energy efficient.

Utilities also have to change their orientation from organisations whose business is to sell as many units of electricity as possible, into organisations which provide energy services. This creates a major need to review objectives, organisational structures and operating frameworks, and make finance available in ways that avoid the current discrimination of long term low interest loans in favour of new energy supply equipment. These are matters which we consider throughout this report, and particularly in Chapter 12.

The Greene Report states that every $5 spent on improving energy efficiency results in an average saving of over $15 that otherwise would have been spent on supplying energy. This is possible through examining the services and functions that energy is used for, and determining the most appropriate and economic way of providing the service. Identification and implementation of cost effective efficiency measures results in a much lower requirement for new generating sources. The lower requirement can be met by "small, flexible use of renewable energy". When the focus is on providing the services that consumers want, instead of determining which energy source can be used to meet demand, then "direct use of a renewable source, such as solar energy is a real option" (Greene, 1990, pp.7–8 Section 2).

Some of the most effective measures are:

- shifting from electricity to gas for heating and cooking;
- replacing electric hot water systems with solar hot water, which can be gas-boosted where necessary;
- use of compact fluorescent globes or reflectors for energy efficient lighting and electrical appliances, most notably refrigerators;
- retrofitting existing buildings so that they are well insulated and no longer function as "thermal sieves";
- co-generation of heat and electricity in industry, preferably by burning natural gas — this will require a pricing structure that incorporates a reasonable payback time;
- wider use of public transport, energy efficient motor vehicles and railways; and
- improvements to industrial motors used for fans, pumps, air compressors and conditioners, refrigerators etc. Motors consume nearly three quarters of all industrial electricity outside of the aluminium industry.

More than 70 per cent of the CO_2 produced by the electricity industry is associated with waste heat. Efficient energy use dictates that electricity is best used for applications for which other energy sources are inappropriate, such as lighting and powering appliances:

> The use of electricity for such purposes as space heating and the supply of domestic hot water is not only thermodynamically absurd, but also a very low priority if measured in terms of useful return per unit of CO_2 produced (Lowe, 1988, p.609).

To examine the possibilities for displacing fossil fuel use in Victoria, the NIEIR carried out a detailed study of the potential for more efficient and renewable energy use. NIEIR found that meeting the Toronto target for CO_2 emissions through expansion of energy efficient industries in Victoria could result in energy cost savings of $4.74 billion and the creation of 17,300 additional jobs (NIEIR, 1990).

The Wilkenfeld report calculated the emissions of CO_2 and methane for all forms of delivered energy on a state by state basis. Using measures which pay back in three years or less, the report found that energy consumption could be reduced by about 17 per cent, and CO_2 emissions by about 20 per cent (Diesendorf and Sonneborn, 1991, p.3).

The joint SECV/DITR demand management development project — A 'Claytons' energy strategy?

The SECV is the first Australian utility to make any serious attempt to implement demand-side management.[10] They have however been criticised for not "rigorously" considering demand-side options, and for "using demand management as a Trojan horse to push through their old plan of 'desired' load changes" (Community Energy Network, 1990, p.2.1).

Amory Lovins has also criticised the project's "excessively conservative" assumptions:

> Based on measured data and recent utility experience elsewhere, I cannot avoid the conclusion that the electrical savings available and worth buying are several fold larger and cheaper than the project has so far assessed, and can probably be captured more quickly and thoroughly than it has assumed...The Project's current assumption of a "moderate" level and pace of implementation...should be immediately revised to an aggressive level, with further upward revisions considered likely as experience to support them is rapidly developed (Lovins, 1990, p.2).

A key area of contention is that the SECV persists in offering off peak water and space heating. (Community Energy Network, 1990, p.19). It may be that a more rational policy would be to supplement the cost of installation of off-peak solar hot water supplementation. This would also have the advantage of providing a significant boost to demand for Australian manufactured solar hot water heaters.

Co-generation

Co-generation relies on production processes which produce, from the same fuel supply, both mechanical energy and heat used to generate electricity. As such, use can be made of the waste heat produced in electricity generation, making it a far more efficient means of supplying power with conversion efficiencies of up to 80 per cent in optimum conditions:

> The process was economic in the early part of this century, supplying a factory with its requirements for both steam and electricity. However, electricity was three to four times more expensive in real terms than it is today. The advent of cheap centrally generated

power saw the demise of co-generation as industries found it cheaper to generate their own steam and buy power from the grid. The additional costs of co-generation are the extra capital cost of the generating plant, additional staff for operation and some additional fuel — all factors which made co-generated power uncompetitive with the State utilities. (Rosenthal and Russ, 1988, pp.104–105).

Co-generation is an extremely attractive proposition as a CO_2 reduction strategy and an energy efficient measure. It also conserves water as water is not required to cool down the plant. There are however a number of barriers to be overcome. For example, co-generation is not a viable option for Australian power stations as they are located too far from major population centres. Their remote siting is due to a number of factors. These include: proximity to water supply; political considerations such as areas of high unemployment; and to some extent the NIMBY syndrome in that communities do not like living adjacent to power stations with their associated pollution.

There remains the possibility of small scale co-generation from industrial sources, but this will have to overcome the barriers described by Deni Greene in her report to the Victorian government.

She found that:

> in past years co-generation has been treated by the SEC and most authorities as a privilege to be discouraged where possible and tolerated where it could not be discouraged. To increase the use of co-generation, the benefits need to be recognised, rewarded and publicised (Rosenthal and Russ, 1988, p.104).

There are as yet only a few industries where co-generation can be profitably installed, as existing energy charges make the rate of return on capital investment unattractive to many industries who are looking for a payback time of one to two years. If utilities have excess generating capacity there is little incentive to seek extra sources of supply especially if this tends to be used for baseload purposes:

> While co-generation may be difficult to justify economically at present, it must be recognised that it has considerable value as a

carbon dioxide reduction strategy and may make a significant contribution to meeting demand in future years, particularly as older power stations are retired...The Committee recommends...that the energy utilities be required to assess the potential for co-generated power (as is being done in Victoria and New South Wales) and set targets concerning the minimum proportion of electricity to be obtained from co-generated sources within a five year period (SSCIST, 1991, pp.60–61).

The SECV has recently entered into a co-generation agreement with the Austin Hospital for the hospital to supply power to the grid during evening peak hours. The agreed buy-back price of 10c/kWh has made the pay-back time approximately three years, and may demonstrate that the gap between the Victorian government's rhetoric on co-generation and the commitment of its energy agencies is finally narrowing.

200MW of co-generated electricity will soon be produced in Victoria.

ECNSW has also started to look more favourably upon co-generation. The SSCIST noted that BHP informed them that buyback rates in NSW had recently changed from being "unattractive to attractive". The Greene report found that "there is up to 1800 megawatts of untapped potential in New South Wales alone, and nearly 1000 megawatts could be brought on line by 1996 if current economic and institutional barriers were removed". This is equivalent to half the generating capacity of Loy Yang A (SSCIST, 1991, pp.58–60).

If, during urban planning requirements and processes, potential co-generation needs were acknowledged it would be possible to site clusters of future industry, as is the case in Denmark.

5.8 Increasing Fuel Efficiency by Integrating Efficient Renewable Energy Sources into the Existing Grid

Three main possibilities currently exist for this, namely wind; parabolic trough solar collectors as manufactured by Luz International and currently installed in California; and mini hydro systems that are being trialled by the SECV in Victoria. However, consideration should be given to the rapidly developing solar thermal system from Sydney University, especially for industrial

process heat applications. The most technically and economically advanced form of renewable energy for grid connection is wind power, which is "already making valuable contributions to the grid in North America and Europe without additional storage" (Diesendorf,1990, p.5–6).

Renewables
Barriers to the acceptance of renewable energy

The Committee rejects the notion suggested by the Department of Primary Industries and Energy that technical limitations prevent Australia from embracing alternative technologies. Australia's role as a world leader in the design and manufacture of solar cells is evidence to the contrary. Rather the Committee is of the opinion that Australia currently has both the scientific expertise and the technology to develop renewable energy sources to the point where they can be manufactured locally and exported overseas (SSCIST, 1991, p.131).

The Australian Bureau of Agricultural and Resource Economics (ABARE) forecasts that the contribution of renewable sources of energy to total energy consumption is expected to remain small in the next ten years. Demand for solar energy will grow but its total contribution is "expected nevertheless to be very small". As far as ABARE is concerned, renewable projects have "generally failed to demonstrate the economic expansion of such uses on a significant scale given current energy prices and technologies...they are a both economically and technically viable alternative in some remote applications but...a major breakthrough in technology or a substantial change to the expected energy pricing structure would be required to increase the contribution of renewable sources of energy beyond that projected in this report" (ABARE, 1989, pp.24–25).

The ABARE assessment also bears a remarkable resemblance to the following statement by the Australian Coal Association:

While it is foreseeable that renewables and nuclear energy may play an expanding role their growth prospects would seem marginal. There is no major breakthrough such as solar on the horizon. Thus the major source of energy for the long-term future will most likely be fossil fuels and that assumption should underlie policy formation at this time (ACA, 1989, p.9).

Aside from the problems inherent in linking renewables with nuclear power, this assertion ignores the increasing use of wind generators in both the US and Europe, developments in photovoltaics at the University of New South Wales and the solar thermal energy project at Sydney University. Both these technologies had already demonstrated considerable promise with commercial applications. Whilst fossil fuels may remain the major source of energy in the short-term, it is clearly not certain that they will continue to do so in the medium to long-term due to a combination of increasing environmental constraints and advances in economically viable renewable energy technologies.

In Australia there is yet to be a comprehensive study of hidden energy subsidies, so the extent of depletion allowances, capital injections etc remain unknown. A recent study in the United States revealed that an annual subsidy of $44 billion largely went to the coal and nuclear industries, with a small percentage going to natural gas (cited in Mills, 1988, p.8).

In order to attain emission targets SSCIST has urged the federal government to accelerate the introduction of technologies that improve energy efficiency, given that efficiency improvements currently represent lower cost options than most renewable energy supply options. After 2005, the Committee determined that "renewable energy options are likely to become much more competitive with energy efficiency and non-renewable supply options" (SSCIST, 1991, p.125).

The Committee was also highly critical of the absence of any long term planning for new technology by either government or industry. The Committee noted that in Japan, Germany and the United States "governments support emerging technology by giving that technology large contracts." This helps build up large production volumes which allow the price reductions that are so necessary for solar thermal technology and photovoltaics:

When the production volume cannot get past a critical level in Australia, the technology ends up being bought by overseas interests (SSCIST, 1991, p.132).

Although ABARE at least acknowledge the role played by pricing structures in determining any increased contribution by renewable energy technologies, their forecast merely confirms Diesendorf's observation:

In Australian fossil energy circles, the conventional wisdom is that renewable electricity (apart from hydro-electricity) is only suitable as a remote area power source at present (Diesendorf, 1990, p.2).

Holdren (1990) argues that the acceleration of research and development of renewable energy technologies is "crucial to a sensible energy strategy". Some of the research will produce options that may never be exploited, but the funding required "to develop these alternatives is modest compared with the potential costs of having too few choices" (p.114).

Survey of renewable technologies currently available and under development
Solar

The granting of government contracts to develop these technologies would be extremely beneficial (SSCIST, 1991, p.134).

As mentioned in section 5.4, parabolic solar trough concentrators have been installed in California. The Australian National University has developed prototype paraboidal dishes which in theory are more thermally efficient than parabolic troughs, and the dishes could be produced more cheaply. Once this occurs, their potential contribution to grid electricity and remote area power supplies could far outweigh that of wind energy.

A solar steam generator that uses evacuated absorber tubes and low concentration seasonally adjusted parabolic mirrors is capable of generating thermal energy at up to 250°C. This system is "comparatively low-tech, having no moving parts in the collector except a mirror adjusted about once a month" (Mills, 1988, p.5). The collector is currently being demonstrated at Campbelltown District Hospital and is producing steam and hot water at a price which is competitive with electricity. Preliminary calculations suggest that once the system is mass produced "it is likely to become competitive with low-temperature heat from LPG and later, on a larger scale of production, with natural gas" (Diesendorf, 1990, p.5).

Solar thermal collectors have a "multi billion

dollar annual potential within Australia alone, and...sixty times that of Australia (in developing countries) by the turn of the century " (SSCIST, 1991, p.134).

Wind

Diesendorf explains that the main potential for wind power is on the coastlines of southern Australia. A small wind farm of six 60kW generators at Esperance in Western Australia is performing well, and a wind generator industry has recently been established in Perth. The potential for hundreds of megawatts of wind power generation exists in South Australia, Tasmania, Western Australia and possibly Victoria, without additional storage. He goes on to comment that:

> If mass-produced in Australia, wind generated electricity may be already economically competitive with new conventional electricity generation in States with high wind energy potential, such as South Australia and Tasmania. With growing interest in wind energy from India, China and the Pacific, it could become an export industry. Two States, Western Australia and Victoria have recently called for expressions of interest for megawatt-rated wind farms and this will clear the way for local mass production (1990, p.6).

Comparison of Costs of Renewable Energy Technologies and Fossil Fuel Generation.

> A power station built today, using gas or coal, that would have a forty year operating life could be rendered inoperative after less than half that period because it no longer met emission standards. **This would radically alter the economics of such plants and would make solar and other advanced technologies immediately competitive by comparison** (SSCIST, 1991, p.61, emphasis added).

According to the Australian Minerals and Energy Council, solar energy accounts for less than 1 per cent of Australian total energy consumption. Renewable energy sources are not seen as economically viable in relation to the relatively low prices currently charged for conventional energy sources which mitigate against the development of alternatives. This has been compounded by factors such as "the basic conservatism of industry, community resistance to

change, lack of public awareness of alternative technologies and the failure to give economic recognition to the environment" (SSCIST, 1991, p.123–24).

The method used to determine the costs of renewables has also acted as a barrier to their mainstream adoption. The Committee argued that capital costs associated with the implementation of solar technology can be comparable to conventional energy, provided they are financed in the same way:

> Utilities are able to spread their capital costs over 15–20 years and pass on a cost for the energy delivered to the consumer without the consumer having to pay a massive upfront charge. The installation of renewable energy could also be financed in this way, thereby making it comparably priced to the consumer (SSCIST, 1991, p.128).

This is the argument that has been advanced in order to make solar hot water systems competitive with gas and electric ones, and for a whole range of energy efficiency measures from the purchase of home insulation materials to complete retrofits for residential and commercial buildings.

The Committee also argued that whilst during their developmental stage the cost per unit of renewables is quite high, the price drops considerably once the volume of production increases. In the case of photovoltaics the price has dropped by 80 per cent in the past ten years:

> Improvements in photovoltaic cell design and production processes will ultimately decrease costs to a level where electricity produced would be cheaper than that produced by a coal plant (SSCIST, 1991, p.129).

In the course of its inquiries the Committee experienced "considerable difficulty" finding figures that could be used for comparative purposes, due to a lack of "consistency between the factors which are taken into account in calculating costs, and mention is rarely made of the social or environmental costs associated with a particular technology" (SSCIST, 1991, p.129).

Estimates of the environmental costs of coal, oil, natural gas, nuclear and wind power have been made by the Pace University in the United States:

> Making its assumptions explicit, the Pace University estimates range from 5.7c/kWh

for coal with 1.2 per cent sulphur down to 0–0.1c/kWh for wind. Scaling down to coal with 0.3 per cent sulphur yields an estimated environmental cost of about 3.5c/kWh. Although more work needs to be done in this area, it is likely that the external costs of using fossil fuels will become increasingly internalised in their prices (Diesendorf and Sonneborn, 1991, p.6).

5.9. Other Issues
Public health and safety impacts of fossils fuel generation
The most threatening aspect of fossil fuel generation is the prospect of global climate change. The well-being of the global population is dependent upon the environmental processes which govern climatic processes. The exact nature of these effects and the number of people that will be affected is a matter of speculation.

Air pollution from fossil fuels as a result of particulates formed from sulphur dioxide emissions is the dominant concern. Estimates differ wildly according to assumptions made about fuel composition, air pollution control technology, power plant siting in relation to population distribution, meteorological conditions that affect sulphate formation, and above all the relation between sulphate concentration and disease (Holdren, 1990, p.112). Nevertheless, recent documentation about public health problems in Eastern Europe that stem from environmental pollution associated with coal-fired power stations are a testimony to the extent of the problem.

Health and safety aspects of nuclear energy
The probabilities and consequences of large accidents at reactors and reprocessing plants during the transportation of radioactive wastes, and the health and safety of workers involved in the entire nuclear cycle, including uranium mining, are full of uncertainties. Documentation from Chernobyl reveals to some extent the effects of high doses of radiation, but it is too early to be able to appreciate the full impact upon the Soviet population, let alone Europe, since it is only in the next few decades that the full number of cancers and other effects can be quantified. Some predictions put the actual numbers of deaths at tens of thousands (Diesendorf, 1990, p.8).

The effects of exposure to low-dose radiation is a highly contentious topic. In 1959 the International Commission for Radiological Protection (ICRP), a body whose links with the International Atomic Energy Agency cast dubious light upon its claims of neutrality, recommended an exposure level of 5 rems per annum — equivalent to 50 milliseverts (mSv). The ICRP has long maintained that the health risks of radiation exposure below a certain level are minimal. This consideration has politicised scientific research in the field ever since. The ICRP still defends its current radiation standards despite increasing scientific disquiet and two recent reports that seriously question their validity.

The Gardner Report (in their opinion midyear 1990) found that the children of workers at the Sellafield reprocessing plant in Britain whose fathers received doses of 10 mSv in the six months prior to their conception faced a six to eight fold increased risk of developing leukaemia. The Biological Effects of Ionising Radiation (BEIR) Committee in the United States examined data from Hiroshima and Nagasaki and in their 1989 report observed that the number of tumours increased in direct proportion to the size of the dose of radiation, thereby indicating that there was no threshold below which the effects of radiation could be disregarded. The BEIR Committee recommended that the maximum annual exposure be reduced from 50 mSv to 15 mSv.

Dr Dennis Mathews, a chemist from Flinders University, who resigned from the South Australian Radiation Protection Authority in December 1989, maintains that the ICRP's slow and conservative actions have been to the benefit of the nuclear industry and the detriment of public health (interview with team member, 2SER-FM, 1990).

Electromagnetic fields
If a reassessment of what can be considered a safe level of exposure to ionising radiation poses an enormous threat to the nuclear power industry, the vexed topic of the possible increased cancer risks associated with electromagnetic fields from electricity transmission lines could involve fundamental changes in the way electrical energy is distributed and used in society. The outcomes of

future studies contain serious implications for any attempts to privatise the Australian electricity industry. For example, transmission line operators will have to bear the costs of any future changes to distribution, and, a further issue that will no doubt need to be contended with is that of litigation.

The United States

The New Yorker chronicled the history of the hazards of electro- magnetic fields (EMFs) in a 1989 three part series of articles "Annals of Radiation". The articles detail conflicts of interest amongst the scientific experts whose evidence has been used to challenge and disprove all studies that determined a relationship between EMFs and cancer. They also describe a coalition of powerful interest groups that includes the US Air Force, Navy, the utilities, the Electronic Industries Association and the National Association of Broadcasters that has worked long and hard to counter public fears of the health hazards of non-ionising radiation. Amongst their chief preoccupation has been concern over how to deal with litigation.

That strategy clearly has not worked as fears and uncertainties still surround the issue. Recently there have been two successful litigation cases. In September 1990, the Boeing Corporation paid US$500,000 in an out of court settlement to a former employee, Robert Strom, who claimed that he developed leukaemia from occupational exposures to electromagnetic pulse radiation (EMP). In addition, that agreement provided for a comprehensive medical program for approximately 700 Boeing employees who have worked with EMP since the 1960s.

Michael Withey who represented Strom claimed that the "landmark settlement confirms that electromagnetic radiation is hazardous to the public health and creates a mechanism for proving that fact in further cases". Unlike many previous EMF settlements, the Boeing agreement is a matter of public record (*Microwave News*, September/October 1990, pp.1, 11).

In June 1990, the US Environmental Protection Agency (EPA) released its long awaited draft report on EMF.[11] The report concluded that studies "show a consistent pattern of response that suggests, but does not prove a causal link" between EMR and human cancers. EMF must be

considered a "possible" human carcinogen. Due to the absence of "both a mechanism of interaction and an observed dose-response relationship" the draft report was published without the inclusion of a "B1" risk classification. This classification designates a substance as a "probable human carcinogen", based on "limited epidemiological evidence". Included in the B1 classification are formaldehyde and cadmium (*Microwave News*, May/June 1990, pp.1,9).

The question of how to deal with EMFs has been debated at the highest levels of the Bush administration and in Congress, and a major federal research program to resolve the uncertainties associated with EMF health risks is clearly needed. *Microwave News* noted that the following paragraph, which concluded the executive summary of the EPA report, was deleted following a White House briefing of EPA officials:

> Concerning exposure to fields associated with 60Hz electrical power distribution, the conclusion reached in this document is that such exposure is a 'probable' carcinogenic risk factor, corresponding to a 'B1' degree of evidence that it is a risk factor. This conclusion is based on 'limited' evidence of carcinogenicity [in] humans which is supported by laboratory research indicating that the carcinogenic response observed in humans has a biological basis, although the precise mechanisms [are] only vaguely understood (*Microwave News*, May/June 1990, p.1).

Australia

As yet, there have been no successful attempts at litigation on the matter in Australia, although the Richmond Brunswick Powerline decision to install underground powerlines can be seen as an acknowledgement of the possible public health risks. Utilities continue to assert that there are no health risks associated with EMFs. Public health policy in the area of environmental health has a range of conceptual tools to draw upon including: synergistic effects; threshold effects; interactive effects; and risk analysis, including risk loading and the cumulative effects of risk.

However, establishing and estimating possible links between environmental factors and public health are fraught with methodological difficulties. Unlike laboratory rats, it is not possible to isolate human beings from their environment and observe them in conditions that approximate living in a vacuum. This has tended to create a climate that favours conservatism on behalf of industry rather than public health. However, many observers would argue that if it has been observed that particular substances or conditions could be associated with adverse health effects, then it makes good sense to err on the side of conservatism in setting limits that may then help to ensure public health. In this respect, the recommendations of the Gibbs Inquiry (see below), are a sign of a change in attitude towards public health policy in Australia.

This issue has been attracting considerable attention following the publication of two new reports. The recent University of Melbourne meta-analysis of epidemiological studies for the Victorian Health Department coyly couched one of its conclusions in a double negative:

> We do not conclude that there are no cancer risks from electromagnetic fields in occupational settings. Rather, the present body of research is not adequate enough for a meta-analysis of occupational exposures to 50–60 Hz electromagnetic fields to be undertaken (Gordon, Motika, Nolan, 1990, Executive Summary p.7).

With regard to residential exposure the authors believed that:

> ...prima facie evidence that a residential exposure to powerline frequency magnetic fields of at least 3 mG is associated with an elevated risk of childhood cancer (Gordon, Motika, Nolan, 1990, Executive Summary p.6).

The Gibbs Inquiry found that the "fact the evidence on the question whether exposure creates a risk to health is so inconclusive suggests that if a risk exists it is a comparatively small one" (Gibbs, 1991, p.59).

The Inquiry determined that lack of sufficient scientific data raises a question of policy as to "what action should be taken to avert a possible risk to public health when it cannot be said either that it is probable that the risk exists or in what circumstances a risk, if one does exist, arises" (Gibbs, 1991, p.59). A policy of "prudent avoidance", is suggested by the Congress of the United States Office of Technology when it notes;

> By avoidance, we mean taking steps to keep people out of fields, both by re-routing facilities and redesigning electrical systems and appliances. By prudence, we mean undertaking only those avoidance activities which carry modest costs (Gibbs, 1991, p.59).

For the Gibbs Inquiry suggested possible prudent courses include attempting to route "new transmission lines so that they avoid people; widening transmission line rights-of-way; developing designs for distribution systems, including new grounding procedures, which minimise associated fields" (Gibbs, 1991, p.59).

The Inquiry dismissed a submission on behalf of the Electricity Supply Association of Australia which argued that prudent avoidance was an American concept which did not apply to Australia, and that until a risk was known to exist, prudence does not require steps to be taken:

> I cannot agree with these submissions. It seems to me that there is nothing peculiar to United States conditions in the suggestion that if something can be done without undue disadvantage to avoid a risk which may possibly arise, it would be prudent to take such action (Gibbs, 1991, p.59).

5.9 Conclusion

This chapter reveals the extent of the momentous changes likely to impact on the energy sector, as a result of the attention now being paid to environmental issues. Current debates in respect of environmental issues lead to a number of the proposals in Chapter 12. In summary the main points made in this chapter include:

- the ESI impacts significantly on the environment, including the land, water and air resources that surround it and with which it interacts and these should all be managed appropriately and openly;
- there is room for improvement in the monitoring of environmental impacts in the energy sector. This improvement is the responsibility of both the ESI authorities and regulatory agencies;
- there is room for significant improvement in the determination of appropriate environmental standards, and their enforcement;
- the ESI needs to make a substantial commitment to achieve an appropriate balance between supply and demand-side management;

- the renewable energy technologies capable of making a contribution to energy supply, including directly into the electricity grid, are now available and should be employed wherever possible;
- the economics of the nuclear power industry clearly indicates that the establishment of an Australian nuclear industry should not occur. This factor and the problems of waste, plant retirement and other factors show this is not a viable industry;
- the question of the greenhouse issue cannot be addressed with a laissez faire policy. The introduction of new technologies that produce lower levels of greenhouse gas emissions and improve ESI efficiency, or are renewable sources of energy must be a priority;
- public health issues such as those arising from air pollution, the nuclear industry and EMFs are likely to receive increasing attention. The health of those working in the industry and therefore those likely to be most effected by environmental threats are of particular concern;
- the most critical factor in the management of environmental issues and the future of the ESI is an appropriate set of representative institutions to control and regulate the industry in an open and responsive way; and
- it is clear that a vertically integrated industry would have more opportunity to deal with these issues because it could simultaneously introduce both demand- and supply-side measures designed to be more environmentally sensitive.

Tricks: How the Nuclear Lobby Stopped the Development of Wave Power in Britain", *The Ecologist*, May-June 1990 pp. 85–90.

6. While some consider weapons testing as part of the cycle, the implication is not considered in this report.

7. Kats and Keepin use two scenarios of high and medium energy growth whose building costs very respectively from $US8,390 to $US5,300 billion for the construction of one reactor every 1.6 to 2.5 days over the next 37 years. Both scenarios fail to prevent an increase in carbon monoxide emissions.

8. The huge capital costs make a mockery of the nuclear industry's claim that nuclear power is the energy solution for developing countries. The only way money could be made available is through foreign financing, thereby adding to their already crushing foreign debts. In this context it is worth noting that the French government's prevailing attitude that France must stay in the forefront of international atomic power has made Electricite de France one of the heaviest corporate debtors in the world (Banks, 1985, p.226).

9. Part of the reason for this, of course, is simple bad management.

10. SECWA is apparently giving demand management strategies high priority, due to Western Australia's perilous financial condition. However, repeated requests for details did not result in any documentation forthcoming.

11. US Environmental Protection Agency (June 1990), *An Evaluation of the Potential Carcinogenicity of Electromagnetic Fields (EMFs)*.

Notes

1. International Energy Agency (1984), *Energy Balances of OECD Countries, 1970/1982*, OECD, Paris; WCED (1987), *Our Common Future*, Oxford University Press, New York.

2. Telephone conversation with ESAA environmental officer, 12 March 1991.

3. Telephone conversation with Elcom Environmental Planning Section officer, 13 March 1991.

4. In the United States there are estimated to be 200,000 passive solar buildings and a further 1 million buildings with passive solar features.

5. The following account is taken from J. Jeffery "Dirty

CHAPTER 6

FORECASTING DEMAND

6.1 Introduction

As we have noted in previous chapters, the electricity supply industry is one of Australia's major industries. It is a significant energy user in its own right, a significant employer, and makes an important contribution to the nation's Gross Domestic Product (GDP). The capital intensity of the industry, together with its very rapid growth, has also resulted in it taking a strong presence in the capital markets.

One important characteristic which distinguishes electricity from other fuels is that it is effectively impossible to store it in large quantities. Consequently, the rate at which electricity is being used at any instant, by consumers connected to a grid, must be exactly equalled by the rate at which the power stations on the grid are supplying electricity. Fundamental to the industry, therefore, is the question of how best to match future supply and demand while avoiding either shortages or overinvestment in capacity. A further important factor is the need to provide sufficient flexibility in power station planning and construction programs to enable them to be adjusted to changing demand growth.

The various Australian State electricity authorities must have as their foremost objective the provision of an adequate and reliable supply of electricity to meet the current and future needs of their customers. Traditionally, this process has involved the provision of estimates of future requirements and a corresponding plant construction program to ensure that these requirements are met. More recently, however, this passive approach has been augmented by more active utility participation in "managing" demand (what we have previously referred to as demand-side management strategies) to improve the efficiency of the supply system, as well as a host of other objectives.

Forecasts of customer demands are essential for:

- estimation of generation and transmission requirements;
- preparation of plant retirement schedules;
- assessment of fuel requirements;
- assessment of capital requirements; and
- valuation of needs for demand-side management.

However, forecasting electricity requirements is likely to be a hazardous exercise, involving a projection of future trends in a large variety of interacting socio-economic variables. While planning in terms of a stable environment is a relatively straightforward matter, the past two decades have been characterized by energy "shocks" that have had drastic and long-term impacts on all energy related industries. Unforeseen events (such as the 1973 and 1979 oil price hikes, the 1986 oil price slump, and the 1990 Iraqi invasion of Kuwait) have the potential to undermine purely analytical methods of forecasting demand, with the possibility of severe financial implications for capital investment. This has been particularly the case in the electricity industry, where long lead times, high capital commitment, and community obligations combine to make strategic planning a difficult task in times of uncertainty.

In view of the great number of "surprises" which occurred in the 1970s and early 1980s, many utilities decided that it was useless to continue to use traditional analytical forecasting techniques in isolation, and that forecasting should become an integral part, and not the entire focus, of a broad-based strategic plan. Henceforth, the concept would be one of preparing for future uncertainties by considering a number of alternative scenarios and preparing response strategies for each. In the case of electricity utilities, the most conspicuous long-term practitioner of this approach would appear to be the Southern California Edison Company based in Los Angeles.

This chapter will provide a review of demand forecasting methodologies employed for the electricity and associated industries.

6.2 Forecasting Methodologies

A number of techniques can be used for forecasting electricity demand, each of which is described briefly below. It should be emphasized that these techniques are not mutually exclusive, and generally some combination of them will be employed.

Trend/time series analysis

Techniques based on trends simply attempt to project past demand experience into the future without regard to the variables which influenced that experience. Generally this is accomplished by projecting the (estimated) trend of a time series of demand data to derive estimates of future values of demand. More sophisticated procedures are associated with growth curves (e.g. logistic functions) and Box-Jenkins type techniques. All such techniques attempt to reproduce the underlying statistical relationship in the (sample) data and, if this can be done successfully, extrapolation can be undertaken for forecasting purposes. Since such methods assume unaltered growth patterns of the determinants of demand, they are generally considered appropriate for short term forecasting only. In addition, the lack of any causal relationships in time series analysis severely restricts their use for sensitivity analysis.

Econometric modelling

Econometric techniques are usually more sophisticated than the time series approach and should be capable of greater flexibility in forecasting exercises. However, depending upon the degree of disaggregation in the analysis, these techniques generally require substantially more data than time series applications, and consequently involve greater time and cost. Past electricity demand is first "explained" in terms of other variables, such as prices and consumer income, using (often relatively simple) statistical models. Such relationships are based upon causal relationships dictated by economic theory. Future energy demands are then related to the predicted growth of these "explanatory" variables. Econometric models vary from one equation, high aggregated, economic relationships, to multiple (simultaneous) equation systems involving a highly disaggregated blueprint of the theoretical relationships.

The advantages of econometric studies are that they can explicitly identify important demand determining variables. The disadvantages generally relate to data availability for large (i.e. highly disaggregated) models, and the seeming inability of economists to convince planners, and many others, that econometric models are simply approximations to reality and should be used as an aid (perhaps the major one) in forecasting but can certainly not provide definitive projections in their own right.

There are three major sources of error which arise from forecasting with econometric models associated with:

  i) functional form (i.e. the specification of the economic relationship);
 ii) estimation of the parameters of the relationship; and
iii) forecasting the explanatory variables.

In addition, errors are also likely to arise where the theoretical variable differs in definition from that upon which data are available, all of which should make planners wary of uncritical use of econometric forecasting techniques. Notwithstanding these drawbacks, econometric models are relatively flexible and provide a rigorous framework for policy evaluation.

Macroeconomic models

The demand for electricity is comprised of a large number of separate energy demand functions for various fuel types at the residential, commercial, and industrial levels. An analysis of the economy at this level of disaggregation requires macroeconomic models which are capable of estimating the individual impacts of a vast array of interacting technical, economic, social, and demographic variables on the final demand of electricity (in aggregate) from all sectors. Such models require substantial inputs of skilled labour, finance, and time, and relatively few have been produced in Australia to date. Perhaps the best known, commercially available,

macroeconomic models are ORANI, developed
by the Institute of Applied Economic and Social
Research, and the Institute Multipurpose Model
(IMP) developed by the National Institute of
Economic and Industry Research (NIEIR).

End-use models

In the end-use approach to modelling, electricity consumption is estimated for each major
process or application, such as space heating,
water heating, cooking, lighting, and so on. For
the residential sector, for example, electricity
consumption for household appliances is specified as a function of factors such as income levels,
household size, and climate. Total residential
consumption is obtained by multiplying average
appliance consumption by the forecast number
of appliances, which is in turn a function of
population, number of households, and assumed appliance penetration rates. The basis of
estimation of end-use consumption is generally
the application of econometric techniques to
data collected by means of survey.

The advantages and disadvantages of end-use
models are similar to those of econometric
models described above. The high level of
disaggregation permits great flexibility in modelling appliance-specific factors, but the
corresponding level of data requirements (in
addition to well-documented biases that can arise
in sample surveys) could act as a major disincentive for its application. Outhred (1989) lists
a number of other drawbacks associated with
ambiguities arising from the disaggregation
process and problems of interaction between
appliances. However, the data provided for end-
use analysis is particularly important when
planning demand-side management strategies.

Scenario analysis

Scenario analysis has gained popularity over recent years as an approach to accommodating
uncertainty in a planning context. Scenario
planning can be described as a process of simu-
lating possible future events in a specific context
with a view to formulating strategies. One of the
prime functions of scenario analysis is to permit
exploration of the uncertain future
unconstrained by past events and trends. Scenarios are not predictions or extrapolations,
essentially they are predictive judgements. The

use of scenario analysis has been hastened by the
fact that it is difficult to incorporate sudden
shocks and major shifts into econometric models
unless such events can be well defined and
quantified themselves. The problem is particularly acute when changes occur in qualitative
(e.g. Iraq's invasion of Kuwait), as opposed to
quantitative, variables.

Some of the key features of scenario analysis
are:

- it looks at many alternative futures, as opposed to one;
- it requires examination of underlying assumptions and permits planners to change
  their assumptions;
- it focuses on "what-if" questions;
- it encourages development of plans which
  are robust and resilient under alternative
  futures; and
- it emphasizes the significance of planning
  flexibility — development of built-in "on and
  off" ramps that allow quick responses to
  changing conditions.

Scenario analysis is, of course, only a tool. Its
usefulness depends on the creativity and imagi-
nation of those applying the technique and
interpreting its results. Furthermore, scenario
analysis is not an end in itself, but merely a means
of planning for uncertainty. Developing alternative futures does not solve any problems, but
it does identify potential weaknesses in a rigid
plan.

6.3 Combining Methodologies for Electricity Load Growth Forecasting

The starting point of load growth forecasting at
the State level is the design of basic economic
scenarios. This process essentially comprises
developing, on a judgemental basis, alternative
predictions in respect of certain exogenous
macro-economic variables such as world economic growth, terms of trade, foreign debt as a
percentage of GDP, inflation rate, population
growth, and the competitiveness of the States
relative to each other. These predictions can then
be used as input for a macroeconomic model
(such as IMP) in order to produce projections
of the determinants of electricity requirements
in various sectors of the State's economy.

The main determinants of electricity consumption include volume of output, turnover,

value added, weekly earnings of labour, employment, and electricity and gas prices in the respective industries. The projection from the macroeconomic model are then used as input for electricity demand models (econometric and end-use) in order to arrive at electricity consumption forecasts over the medium term (say, ten years). Finally, the load growth forecasts derived by using this methodology are adjusted for the impact of demand-side programs likely to be initiated by the electricity supply industry.

Where forecasts can go wrong

Economic forecasting is not a precise science. A multitude of complex socio-economic variables interact in a way which defies accurate modelling of all influences on the variable under consideration. Nevertheless, by constructing a (relatively) simple behavioural model it is possible to achieve a fundamental understanding of the factors that "drive" certain sectors of the economy.

A major problem faced by economic forecasters is that of projecting future levels of the explanatory variables in any behavioural relationship. Once this has been done, the future time path of the dependent variable(s) can be derived simply by substituting into the estimated relationship. Conventional wisdom suggests that such projections are relatively straightforward since the variables concerned, by definition, follow fairly well defined patterns over time. Changes when they occur tend to be slow and relatively minor in magnitude.

As we have noted, faith in such assumptions was badly misplaced in the case of energy forecasts for the 1970s. The 1960s had been a decade of rapid and relatively continuous growth in most developed nations of the world and, in the erroneous belief that such trends would continue unchecked through the 1970s, forecasts of energy requirements were made which simply extrapolated past rates of growth. The 1973 OPEC oil embargo and major oil price hikes led to a sudden drop in the rate of economic growth in the developed world with a resultant fall in energy requirements. Although most economies recovered within a couple of years, another oil price hike in 1979 had a similar, but longer lasting, impact. These unforeseen events shattered the ten year forecasts produced by US utilities as

illustrated in Figure 6.1 (see Appendix 2 at the end of the book) and led to a substantial overcapacity in the industry which lasted until the late 1980s. The errors were compounded by the growth of energy conservation measures and public education programs encouraging energy efficiency.

Forecasting electricity demand

Each electricity supply authority prepares its own forecasts using a variety of historical data and modelling techniques. Consequently, their results may not be strictly comparable, as their methodologies may assign different values and weighting to factors such as economic climate and outlook, changes in the price of competing energy sources, and in patterns of energy consumption, and recent demand trends. Demand forecasts based on a common methodology, by State, are prepared annually by the Australian Bureau of Agricultural and Resource Economics (ABARE).

In 1981, the Department of National Development and Energy (DNDE) published forecasts (based upon conditions prevailing during 1979–80) of energy demand and supply in Australia for the period to 1990. These forecasts were based on an assumed rate of growth in real GDP of 3.5 per cent per annum, although it was recognised that such growth would not be smooth and continuous over the decade. The demand for energy is particularly sensitive to changes in GDP, and the unforeseen recession of the early 1980s introduced a sizeable error into DNDE's projections.

Table 6.1 (see Appendix 2) gives the 1981 DNDE projections of total end-use demand for electricity in Australia to 1990, divided into public and private suppliers. The actual level of demand experienced over this period is also given.

In total, demand was expected to rise at an average annual rate of growth of 6.0 per cent, although when disaggregated by State this figure ranged from 9.8 per cent (Queensland) down to 2.2 per cent (South Australia). This forecast reflected the buoyant economic forecasts then being made in anticipation of the "resource boom" and projected construction of aluminium smelters in several States. Thus the rate of growth of electricity demand was anticipated to be relatively high (up to almost 9 per cent) over the first half of the decade, falling to under 5 per cent by the late 1980s.

A significant downturn in the economy occurred in 1982 at a time when (real) electricity prices were experiencing large increases. These factors coupled with the initiatives to encourage conservation of energy combined to depress demand in that year. Cancellation of a proposed aluminium smelter in NSW and the rapid disappearance of the resource boom further aggravated the situation.

Consequently, not only was the average annual rate of growth of electricity demand lower than projected, but the major growth period was the late, rather than the early, 1980s.

Overall, the forecast errors associated with the projections in Table 6.1 are relatively minor compared to those experienced with projections of demand for primary fuels during the 1980s, particularly for crude oil. The recent history of load growth forecasts in NSW is illustrated in Figure 6.2. The recession of the early 1980s can be seen to have caused a major hiccup in the forecasts, but a substantial revision placed them back within a reasonable range of accuracy post-1982.

A major source of both historical and projected energy consumption data is the biennial Fuel and Electricity Survey (FES) conducted by ABARE. This survey covers major consumers in the mining, manufacturing, communication, health, public administration, and electricity generation sectors. The FES provides forecasts by consumers of the amount of energy each expects to use. The forecasts are then compared with energy suppliers' forecasts and estimates of the amount of energy available. Econometric models are used in the derivation of consumption projections for those sectors not covered by the FES.

Over the period to the year 2000, the 1989–90 ABARE projections of energy consumption are based upon a moderate 3 per cent a year growth in real GDP. Further, world oil prices are assumed to rise over the projection period to an average US$18 a barrel (1988 dollars) in 2000 (in 1988 the world trade-weighted average oil price was US $13.83 a barrel). However, it was expected that considerable price volatility would be present in the oil market.

Prices of petroleum products in Australia are expected to rise in real terms in line with move-ments in world oil prices. Natural gas and electricity prices are projected to remain virtually unchanged in real terms, as most utilities have announced pricing policies which peg price rises at rates close to the rate of change of the consumer price index. Prices of the other main fuels (coal and wood) are projected to rise in real terms over the projection period.

Generation of electricity accounted for over 27 per cent of total energy consumption in Australia in 1988–89. A large majority of coal production and a substantial proportion of natural gas production are consumed in the generation of electricity. In turn, electricity provides the major source of energy for the residential and commercial sectors and significant shares of the energy consumed in the manufacturing, mining, agriculture and rail transport sectors.

Over the period to 1999–2000, growth in electricity consumption is projected to average 2.3 per cent a year — representing a significant slowing from rates of growth experienced over the past few decades. This slowing will be particularly pronounced in the manufacturing sector, where few large energy-intensive projects have reached the committed or final feasibility stage, and the residential sector, where the electricity market share is assumed to be virtually saturated. Private generation of electricity, which accounted for only 7.1 per cent of the total in 1988–89, is projected to increase slightly at an average rate of 1.1 per cent a year, while public generation is projected to increase at an average rate of 2.4 per cent a year. The pattern of electricity consumption by sector is illustrated in Figure 6.3.

The rapid expansion in electricity consumption which occurred in the manufacturing sector during the 1980s was largely a result of growth in the aluminium industry. While there appears to be scope for substantial further expansion in that industry during the 1990s (several projects have been subject to prefeasibility assessment) in the absence of firm industry plans or expectations of major changes in market conditions no provision has been made in these projections for any such expansion. Electricity consumption in the manufacturing sector is projected to increase at 1.6 per cent a year overall between 1988–89 and 1999–2000.

Consumption of electricity in the residential

sector is expected to increase at an average rate of 2.3 per cent a year over the projection period, down from an average 3.3 per cent a year over the preceding eleven years, although total residential energy consumption growth is projected to be higher than in the previous period. Throughout the 1970s and 1980s, natural gas rapidly gained residential energy market share due to its significant price advantages over other fuels. Natural gas and LPG also replaced town gas to a significant degree. Consumption of other residential fuels, including wood, petroleum products and briquettes, declined rapidly due to changing energy price relationships and consumer preferences. Along with natural gas, electricity also gained market share over the period at the expense of these other fuels.

Many of these substitution possibilities are now virtually exhausted. Electricity, natural gas and wood between them made up 93 per cent of total residential energy consumption in 1988–89, as compared to about 75 per cent at the time of the first oil price shock in 1973–74. Over the period to 1999–2000 petroleum products and wood are projected to continue to lose market share, mainly to natural gas, but at a slower rate than previously. The share of electricity is expected to remain at about 45 per cent of total residential energy consumption.

In order to meet the increased demand for electricity, significant new system and generation capacity expansion is expected to be required in all States (but not in NSW or the Northern Territory) over the projection period. The most significant of these expansions will be the interconnecting of the New South Wales, Victoria and South Australia's peak demands. This will result in significant energy savings in South Australia and will defer the need for additional capacity there until the mid 1990s at least. The Industries Assistance Commission has concluded that there are longer term opportunities for further interconnection between New south Wales, Victoria and South Australia, and eventually with Queensland and possibly Tasmania (IC, 1991). Such interconnections could mean substantial changes to the projected type and location of any new generating plant constructed over the projection period in these States.

In the absence of such interconnections, it is expected that base-load capacity for New South Wales and Queensland will continue to be fuelled by black coal, while in Victoria additional units are expected to be installed at Loy Yang using brown coal. Base load generation in Western Australia has over the last few years been increasingly fuelled by natural gas. A shortfall in consumption of North-West Shelf gas below contracted take-or-pay volumes led to the State Energy Commission of Western Australia reducing consumption of coal for electricity generation and burning increased quantities of gas for this purpose in order to boost overall gas consumption. This situation has eased in 1988–89 as consumption of gas for other uses has boosted overall consumption to above the minimum contract volumes. As a result, black coal use in electricity generation increased from 46.6 PJ in 1987–88 to 63.7 PJ in 1988–89, while that of natural gas fell from 52.1 PJ to 44.8 PJ. This trend toward greater use of coal is expected to continue over the projection period with natural gas expected to stay at around current levels. Tasmania's electricity needs are expected to be met by hydro-electric stations to the end of the century.

6.4 Australia's Energy Resources

Australia's identified resources of the major energy minerals and fuels are given in Table 6.2. Relative to current rates of production, as measured by the reserve-production ratio, Australia has a substantial endowment of coal, natural gas, and uranium, and significant, but more limited, resources of crude oil, condensate, and LPG. There are also extensive, currently subeconomic, resources of shale oil, and vast inferred coal and uranium resources which are potentially significant sources of energy for future development.

Australia also has substantial resources of some renewable energy resources, although the potential for expanding the contribution of traditional renewables is limited. With the exception of Tasmania, Australia is not well endowed with hydro-electric potential and most of the economically favourable sites have already been exploited. Potential for expansion of wood and bagasse use is also limited. Australia's overall geothermal and wave energy potential is moderate, resources in general being limited to remote locations. Australia does have significant wind resources along the south of the continent, good solar radiation, and theoretically very large amounts of tidal energy available. However, a major factor inhibiting the market penetration of many renewable sources of energy is that at current costs they are not economically competitive with conventional fuels.

The geographical location of Australia's energy resources is important in determining the pattern of production. Location has also played a significant role in determining the pattern of use, particularly for electricity generation. The vast majority of Australia's petroleum resources are located off Victoria and Western Australia, with crude oil concentrated in the Gippsland Basin off Victoria and natural gas and condensate concentrated in the Carnaervon and Browse Basins off Western Australia. The bulk of black coal is found in Queensland and New South Wales, and brown coal in Victoria. Uranium resources are more widely distributed, although no demonstrated economically recoverable deposits have yet been identified in New South Wales, Victoria or Tasmania.

6.5 The Australian Coal Industry

Australia possesses vast reserves of black coal relative to its domestic requirements, although by international standards its reserve base (amounting to 7 per cent of the world reserve base) is small compared to those of China (24 per cent), the USA (20 per cent), and the USSR (16 per cent). Nevertheless, Australia is currently the world's leading exporter of black coal and the industry is the country's major source of merchandise export revenue (accounting for about 15 per cent of the total — around $6 billion in 1989–90).

During 1989, Australia's 119 black coal mines produced 154.6 million tonnes of saleable black coal with NSW producing 73 million tonnes and Queensland 74 million tonnes. Of this total, 49.6 million tonnes was consumed domestically, mainly in NSW and Queensland, with electricity production accounting for the majority of coal use. All domestic production of brown coal is located in the Gippsland Basin in Victoria. The vast bulk of production is used in that state's electricity generating industry, and exports are negligible.

Over the decades of the 1970s and 1980s, domestic consumption of black coal rose from 27 Mt/y (million tonnes per year) to 45 Mt/y, with electricity generation accounting for almost the entire increase of 18 Mt/y. Metallurgical uses for coal increased gradually during the 1970s, but slumped during the recession of the early 1980s and has yet to regain its previous position. The disappearance of coal use in "railways and gasworks" has, in part, been offset by a corresponding increase in coal consumption for electricity generation following electrification of railways.

There is clearly little doubt that Australia has coal reserves adequate to meet greatly expanded levels of domestic and export demand until well into the next century. However, brown coal is likely to be an early victim of escalating levels of concern over the environmental consequences of using coal as a major source of energy, and in particular for electricity generation. As the century draws to a close, technological developments designed to deliver "clean" black coal are likely to be increasingly favoured at the expense of the brown variety.

Vertical integration of coal production with electricity generation is exemplified by the Electricity Commission of NSW (ECNSW) and its coal mining arms of Elcom and Newcom as well as contract mining operation with such companies as Costain. The eleven NSW mines owned by the ECNSW have a combined output of 10.7 Mt/y, with an additional 5.4 Mt/y provided from other mines through contractual agreements with private companies. Similarly, the Electricity Trust of South Australia has captive supplies of 2.5 Mt/y from Leigh Creek, and the State Electricity Commission of Victoria 42 Mt/y from three open-cut brown coal mines.

Coal-fired electricity generation currently accounts for about 97 per cent of total electricity generation in Queensland, 94 per cent in NSW, 87 per cent in Victoria, 62 per cent in Western Australia, and 40 per cent in South Australia. Gas-fired generation is particularly important in the Northern Territory (100 per cent) and Western Australia (31 per cent) whereas hydro power dominates (98 per cent) the Tasmanian generation industry.

Projections of electricity requirements through to the year 2005 were given in Figure 6.3 (by State). The corresponding black and brown coal requirements are 1330 PJ (about 57 Mt) and 478 PJ (about 49 Mt) respectively. These figures are 56 per cent and 9 per cent (respectively) higher than the corresponding figures for 1990. Thus while the expected increase in annual consumption of brown coal for electricity generation is almost negligible, black coal requirements are expected to rise by almost 3 per cent a year.

6.6 Energy Efficiency

From the outset it is important to distinguish between energy efficiency and energy conservation. Energy efficiency implies actions that will reduce energy consumption per unit of output without a corresponding increase in costs. There are ample opportunities to do both simultaneously by substituting an inefficient technology or appliance with a more efficient one. Little or no financial loss to consumers is associated with most energy efficiency improvements.

On the other hand, energy conservation has the connotation of increasing the consumer's costs as a direct result of conserving energy. The distinction is important because energy consumers are likely to be much more receptive to energy efficiency improvements than to conservation.

There are a number of reasons for the increased popularity of energy efficiency in recent years including the following:

- increased opposition to conventional supply-side options on environmental and risk aspects;
- increased concerns about environmental issues such as global warming, ozone depletion, acid rain, and hazardous waste associated with traditional supply-side resources;
- increased recognition of the cost-effectiveness of energy efficiency and demand-side options relative to their supply-side counterparts;
- increased awareness of the large potential scope and scale of available energy efficiency opportunities on the customer side;
- rapid pace of technological advancements in efficient electrical appliances, lighting, motors, heating, ventilation, and air conditioning equipment, and a variety of other applications; and
- increased interest on the part of regulators, policy makers, conservationists, and politi-

cians to promote energy efficiency and demand-side options.

However, the principle of diminishing marginal returns applies to efficiency as to anything else. Stated simply, it means that as one starts to implement energy improvements, initially very large gains can be had with very little effort and expenditure. But as the obvious and inexpensive options are exhausted, the subsequent options become progressively more expensive and difficult to capture. At some point, the marginal cost of additional energy efficiency improvements exceed the marginal benefits. It is not cost effective to pursue energy efficiency programs beyond this point.

Energy efficiency offers the greatest scope in the short/medium term for conserving fossil fuel, but at the same time it has a number of practical difficulties. Despite great technical and economic potential for improved efficiency, it is widely recognised that free market forces have not been effective in improving the energy efficiency of consumer durables. In the US, this has been recognised by the National Appliance Energy Conservation Act of 1987 which sets minimum energy performance standards for twelve such products.[1] The Act also established a timetable for periodic updates of the standards. While there are numerous examples of improved energy efficiency in the area of industrial production processes, even here the rate of change has been relatively slow. The major reasons for this apparent reluctance to adopt energy efficient technology are:

1. energy use may be peripheral in many purchasing decisions, particularly for applications where the energy operating cost of equipment is small relative to its capital cost (e.g. house purchase);
2. there is a lack of awareness of the part of potential beneficiaries, compounded by a shortage of specific and unbiased information;
3. the most cost-effective opportunities are limited because of the slow turnover in equipment, and especially in buildings;
4. studies of consumer behaviour on durable appliances suggest that consumers use fairly high discount rates when evaluating the financial benefits of energy efficient appliances over the, generally cheaper, less energy

efficient models. US studies have indicated that implicit discount rates of around 50–60 per cent are not uncommon. This contrasted with producer criteria of the order of 10 per cent return; and

5. benefits do not accrue to the person investing in the more efficient use of energy. The person owning a building or energy-consuming unit may not be the user, and consequently there is little incentive to invest in improvements in energy use.

A range of measures has been proposed for encouraging the adoption of greater energy efficiency. These include regulations to impose higher efficiency standards in building, and labelling to give greater information to purchasers which will enable them to weigh up potential future savings against any capital cost or other differences between the products on the market. Labelling of many appliances is now mandatory in NSW and Victoria, a move that has been credited with increasing consumer awareness of their ability to actually reduce the energy requirements for such products.

Incorporating improvements in energy and (for our purposes, electrical) efficiency into demand forecasts will clearly depend upon the rate at which consumers are encouraged (or forced) to adopt the improved technologies. This will depend on a large number of factors including cost of the appliance (and the cost of borrowing), the length of a typical product cycle (i.e. when does one scrap the existing product?), and the relative savings received from using the new technology. Electrical efficiency improvements may reduce electricity demand, but could also be expected to result in increased appliance penetration through improved cost effectiveness. An example of this is the use of microwave cooking which in terms of both energy usage and greenhouse impact is more efficient than either gas or electric stoves.

Quantifying the possible impacts of efficiency improvements on consumption is, therefore, a rather subjective exercise. The ECNSW (1990) in its forecasts to the year 2000 has estimated that, by that date, the overall impact on residential electricity consumption of efficiency improvements will be in the order of (a reduction of) 2.5 per cent. The figure is calculated after assigning improvement factors to a range of appliances,

e.g. 0.5 per cent efficiency improvement for off peak water heaters, 4 per cent for dishwashers and air-conditioners, 5 per cent for clothes dryers, and so on. The overall reduction is calculated using an end-use econometric model.

The overall picture is further clouded, however, by likely tends in substitution, depending on the aggressiveness of the marketing of gas domestic appliances.

In the industrial sector, improvements in electrical efficiency will result from the introduction of a number of improved technologies. Although these improvements in electrical efficiency would be expected to have a negative impact on electricity demand, if such improvements enhance the competitiveness of electricity relative to other fuel sources this substitution effect may offset the fall in demand. The anticipated improvements in electrical efficiency in the industrial sector to the year 2000 for NSW are given in Table 6.3, together with an estimate of the substitution effect.

In the commercial sector, ECNSW estimate that efficiency improvements, largely from improved lighting, air conditioning, and building design, will amount to 7 per cent in NSW by the year 2000. Again, however, there is the opportunity for substitution gains to offset this anticipated decline in electricity demand.

6.7 Utility Load Forecasts

Table 6.4 gives load forecasts by State, published by the Electricity Supply Association of Australia (1990) (ESAA). Assuming that the Snowy Mountains Hydo Electric Authority (SMHEA) continues to provide 4236 GWh to the system, by the year 2004–05 total energy consumption is estimated to be 217.8 thousand GWh. This aggregate figure is very close to the ABARE projection of 216.1 thousand GWh for the same year (228.5 thousand GWh if private generation is included), but at the individual state level there exist some marked discrepancies. In particular, the ESAA projection for Queensland is 12.3 per cent above that of ABARE, whilst the corresponding projection for NSW is 6.3 per cent below ABARE's estimate.

The forecasting methodology adopted by the ECNSW is illustrated in Figure 6.4. To varying degrees, a similar methodology is pursued by other state electric utilities. It is clear that the state utilities can engage in a much greater degree of analysis of end-use evaluation studies and regional demand patterns than the more aggregated approach of ABARE. In addition, the construction of alternative scenarios permits greater flexibility in strategic planning. As a consequence, the utilities tend to use ABARE's projections more as a cross-check than as a basic input into their deliberations. Indeed, an officer responsible for load forecasting in one state utility felt that "ABARE's forecasts of (the State's) electricity demand have proven to be too unreliable".

6.8 Conclusion

Projecting electricity demand through to the early years of the next century is fraught with difficulties. The industry has experienced a major shift of emphasis over the past decade, from a position of supply-side dominance to an increasing emphasis on demand-side management and the provision of electricity auditing services. This shift has been driven largely by concern over environmental issues and the high cost of over-investment in generating capacity during the 1970s and early 1980s. It must be assumed that environmental concerns will continue to drive energy conservation and efficiency efforts into the next century, but the scale and scope of future actions is difficult to evaluate in the present climate.

Forecasts of energy demand are an essential input to infrastructure and pricing decisions. It is therefore essential that forecasters remain as cognisant of developments within the energy sector and the electricity industry. These are features of the forecasting role that are given attention in Chapters 7 and 8.

Notes

1. Refrigerators and freezers, room air conditioners, central oil conditioners and heat pumps, water heaters, furnaces, dishwashers, clothes washers, clothes dryers, room heaters, kitchen ranges and ovens, pool heaters, and television sets.

CHAPTER 7

ENSURING APPROPRIATE LEVELS OF LONG TERM INVESTMENT

7.1 Introduction

Supply- and demand-side options

Electricity is an intermediate form in an energy conversion process linking a wide range of primary energy forms (e.g. coal, gas, hydro) to a wide range of end-use energy forms (heat, light, mechanical work, etc). Being such an essential commodity, it is reasonable that society should take an interest in ensuring appropriate levels of long-term investment in electricity infrastructure. Nor is it sensible to ignore the relationship between electricity and competing energy forms such as natural gas and renewables.

The electricity industry as a whole has many social impacts, both in terms of lifestyle and employment. These may be positive, such as the provision of employment, street lighting, refrigeration and reticulated water supplies, or negative such as atmospheric pollutants that are injurious to health.

For the purpose of considering investment, the industry should be considered in its totality, from primary energy sources to end-uses. For example, adequate investment in improved end-use efficiency is a direct alternative to investment in new generating capacity, because improvements in efficiency release existing generating capacity to supply other loads.

Improvements in end-use efficiency have the advantage of being, in general, environmentally benign whereas the use of some important primary energy forms such as coal has significant environmental impacts. As well as their other benefits, improvements in end-use efficiency and renewable energy forms also reduce exposure to uncertain fuel prices.

Improvements in the technologies for electricity generation, transmission, storage and use are providing new options for electricity infrastructure. Renewable energy forms, combined heat and power and improvements in end-use efficiency are all becoming important alternatives to the currently dominant technology of large central power stations burning fossil fuels.

Many new options can be located at points of end-use and owned and operated by consumers. These are referred to as demand-side options (DSOs). They form part of the electricity industry infrastructure, because although purchased by consumers they directly reduce the need for additional supply-side capacity. Consumer decisions to purchase DSOs are thus equivalent to supply-side decisions made by utilities to invest in new generating capacity.

We are entering a new era where supply authorities no longer have direct control over all decisions to invest in electricity infrastructure. Indeed there are many who believe that the supply authority's role in investment decisions about DSOs may be limited to the provision of information and possibly the provision of financial incentives; they could also encourage manufacturers to develop consumption equipment with appropriate characteristics.

Investment in DSOs also reduces the amount of electrical energy that must be transmitted across the transmission and distribution network. This reduces the need to invest in network augmentation, with consequent social and environmental benefits.

Investment coordination and timing under uncertainty

In common with other industries, uncertainty about the future affects many of the key parameters in electricity infrastructure planning. These include the capital and operating costs of the various expansion options and the future demand for electricity (see Chapter 6). Because of uncertainty over time, the case for modular, short-lead-time options at the expense of large, long-lead-time ones is strengthened (see also Chapter 5).

The question of investment timing is also important. Traditionally it has been felt that excess supply capacity is preferable to a shortage because interruptions to supply cause disruptions to consumers. However, it is now acknowledged that there are financial costs associated with excess supply capacity. On the other side, modern electricity pricing theory and communications technologies can be used with DSOs to alleviate greatly the disruptions caused by supply shortages. For example, uninterruptible power supplies and end-use storage can then be used to support the power system as well as an individual consumer. This would allow supply systems to be operated with reduced capacity reserve margins.

End-use efficiencies can also be altered to shift load, and there is clearly a role to be played by energy audits in this process (see Chapter 12).

Reducing the capacity reserve margin would allow infrastructure investment decisions to be deferred until closer to the time that the new infrastructure is actually required. This reduces financing costs and helps to avoid the selection of technologies that are no longer appropriate by the time they enter service. The deferral of investment decisions to the last possible moment would allow more time for innovation and would encourage the development of new electrical technologies that may have substantial potential for import replacement and export. For example, in New South Wales gas-fired cogeneration, solar water and space heating, gas water and space heating, gas or high efficiency electric cooking, increased insulation, improved air-conditioners and heat pumps, high efficiency lighting systems, high efficiency appliances and variable speed motor drives could now be considered in combination as a serious alternative to the Mt Piper Power Station. However the contract for Mt Piper was signed in 1982 (it will be nearly 15 years later before Mt Piper is expected to be required for service [ECNSW, 1989, p.55]).

A related problem is the coordination of the timing of the decisions taken by consumers and by the supply authority. Supply authorities have traditionally relied on demand forecasts to predict the aggregate outcome of the independent purchase and operation decisions being taken by consumers.

Short term demand forecasts are used to schedule the operation of power stations in merit-order to minimise the cost of meeting the forecast demand. Long term demand forecasts are used to select the type of new generating capacity that is most appropriate for the expected load characteristics and to determine the timing of investment decisions.

However consumers are not given the opportunity to assist in the cost-minimisation process by modifying their purchase and operation decisions when it is cost-effective for them to do so. For example, some consumers may have low priority loads that they would be happy to reduce temporarily if there was a generator failure when demand for electricity was high (perhaps on a very hot or cold day). Others might be prepared to operate stand-by sets. These activities could defer the need to invest in new capacity. A further option is to establish a market in "interruptability" i.e. large users might be prepared to suffer interruption in return for lower tariffs. Such arrangements are used internationally, and it is believed that ECNSW may be considering such options.

The problems of investment coordination and timing are becoming more difficult as the range of DSOs available to consumers increases. A further problem is the serious imbalance between the investment criteria used on the supply and demand-sides of the industry, with both publicly owned and regulated private supply utilities taking a more lenient attitude to rate of return on investment than consumers considering DSOs.[1] This discrepancy in investment criteria has been one factor leading to excessive investment in supply capacity compared with investment in DSOs (Outhred, 1989).

There are a number of questions that must be addressed in assessing long-term investment in electricity infrastructure:

- what level of capital funding is required;
- how should that funding be obtained;
- what is the significance of the timing of capital raising;
- when should new infrastructure be built and brought into service;
- how should funds be allocated between the competing supply and DSOs and how should the imbalance in investment criteria be

overcome;

- how can the investment decisions taken by independent parties be properly coordinated; and
- what obligations are associated with the ownership of electricity infrastructure (network, supply or demand-side)?

Perhaps the most critical issue is that uncertainty about the medium and long-term future precludes the possibility of a uniquely correct, objective decision making process for electricity infrastructure investment (Outhred, 1989).

Institutional arrangements for electricity planning

In traditional electricity supply planning, the suppliers — either publicly owned supply authorities or private utilities in conjunction with their regulators — were charged with the responsibility for electricity infrastructure planning. The approach taken was to forecast both the future demand for electricity and the future performance of existing supply capacity and then to build new supply capacity to keep the predicted reserve capacity margin close to an agreed target value. Consumers played a passive role in this planning process.

This approach worked satisfactorily in the 1950s and 1960s when growth in the demand for electricity was strong, environmental impacts were not seriously considered and there were still supply-side economies of scale to be captured. These conditions no longer apply and new approaches to electricity planning are being explored. Broadly speaking, the goals are to provide equality of treatment for the supply and demand side options in the industry; and to provide economic, social and environmental accountability.

Two competing philosophies are available to achieve these goals. Broadly, one could either adopt a coordinated approach, or assume that the best outcome will be achieved if decisions are left to participants in a competitive market environment.

An example of the former is the process of 'least-cost planning' implemented by public utility commissions in the United States (Kahn, 1988; Hirst et al, 1990). The objective of least-cost planning is to ensure that supply and DSOs are given equal consideration in the planning process. An example of the latter is the market

process being adopted in England and Wales, where it proposed to leave all investment decisions to individual participants; however, the assumption is that the market will guide them in the right direction (Dettmer and Littlechild, 1990). These examples are discussed more fully in Section 7.4 (the assumption of market wisdom is examined more fully in Chapters 9 and 10).

The following criteria may be useful in deciding the appropriate institutional arrangements for electricity planning:

- social, economic and environmental accountability (including regulation or other means to avoid excessive influence by large organisations or owners of key primary resources or items of infrastructure);
- consideration of the industry in its totality, from primary energy forms to end-uses (including equality of treatment for supply and DSOs and coordination of investment decisions);
- reasonable assurance that end-users will be serviced in the future;
- public participation (important because there are many value judgements to be made, such as valuing the impacts of environmental degradation on the welfare of future generations);
- support for innovation (if only to demonstrate that the status quo has not yet been superseded); and
- effective procedures for risk sharing and recovery from the mistakes that will inevitably occur because of future uncertainty.

7.2 Relevant Features of the Electricity Industry

The components of the electricity industry can be categorised in a number of ways, each of which provides a useful perspective on the industry.

Participant/network

The producers and consumers of electrical energy are the participants in the electricity industry whose interchange of energy provides the reason for the industry's existence. The function of transmission/distribution networks is to connect the participants so that the flow of energy from primary to end-use forms can occur. The physical laws that govern the flow of electrical energy mean that it is impossible to distinguish between units of electrical energy produced by different generators once they have been injected into the network.

Supply/demand

The supply-side of the electricity industry includes electricity generation and the transmission/distribution network, while the demand-side consists of the consumers' electrical equipment and wiring. The demand-side of the electricity industry is mainly unregulated, diversified and predominantly privately owned, while the supply-side is usually centralised and either regulated or publicly owned. This distinction is becoming more blurred as consumers become more heavily engaged in electricity generation (e.g. cogeneration). This is an important issue for investment decisions due to the (common) relationship between types of investment, their methods of financing and the costs associated with them (see above).

Transmission/distribution

There is no clear technical distinction between transmission and distribution networks; however transmission and distribution organisations should have distinct functional roles: transmission organisations can provide the link that allows electrical energy to flow from generators to consumers, while distribution organisations should provide customer services such as information and advice about competing energy options. There will, however, be points of overlap between the two functional organisations (see above).

Primary/intermediate/end-use energy forms

Electrical energy is a difficult-to-store intermediate energy form, the main merits of which are ease of transport and conversion to, or from, a wide range of primary and end-use energy forms. The shortage of cost-effective intermediate storage, the speed of electricity transmission, and the physical laws of network operation create unusually strong links between all participants in an electricity industry, whether they are producing electricity from primary energy forms or converting electricity into end-use forms.

Degree of dependence on the supply network

Consumers (and suppliers) of electrical energy who cannot change their physical location depend on the electrical network to which they are connected to provide adequate opportunities to buy (or sell) electrical energy. Their investment decisions are based on assumptions about the future ability of the network to satisfy their needs: a consumer, having established a track record of willingness to pay, might reasonably expect to be supplied in the future at a 'fair' price. A viable network is a necessary condition for such expectations to be met, and interconnection between networks will generally increase the chance of satisfaction. By contrast, consumers (and suppliers) of electrical energy using portable equipment will be less concerned about network viability. Those who consider the network to be too unreliable or too expensive to meet their requirements will invest in stand-by generators or fully independent supply systems.

Physical/intellectual assets

Intellectual assets are extremely important to the effective planning and operation of an industry as complex and capital-intensive as the electricity industry. Even more than most other segments of industry, attention must be paid to the maintenance and continuing development of the workforce skills of the electricity industry. In Chapter 12 we note that the expertise currently residing in the industry could be effectively utilised to implement the changes which will occur as a result of the challenges with which the industry is faced. If for no other reason, this factor illustrates the necessity for adequate trade union representation in all decision-making fora.

7.3 The Process of Investment in Electricity Infrastructure

The decision-making process

As previously discussed, electricity infrastructure includes both supply-side equipment and DSOs that release supply-side equipment for other uses. Decisions to invest in additional infrastructure are based on perceptions of the future supply-demand balance. Electricity infrastructure also includes the transmission/distribution network. Decisions to invest in additional network infrastructure depend on technical assessments of the future ability of the existing network to allow energy flow to occur in a reliable and efficient manner and to provide adequate quality of supply to consumers.

Conceptually, the dominant cash flow in an electricity industry is from consumers to network operators and then to producers of electrical energy and finally suppliers of primary energy forms (although this may not be clearly defined in a vertically integrated utility). Several decision processes can be identified in this conceptual model:

1. each consumer chooses to purchase either a time-stream of electricity consumption or some combination of reduced electricity consumption, improvements in end-use efficiency and conversion to competing energy forms;

2. network operators budget for network augmentation from their projected operating surpluses (income from electricity sales to consumers minus costs of electricity purchased from suppliers and costs associated with the establishment of the existing network);

3. producers of electrical energy budget for new generation assets from their projected operating surpluses (income from sales to the network minus costs of primary energy forms and costs associated with the establishment of existing generation capacity); and

4. suppliers of primary energy resources also budget for expansions of their activities from their projected operating surpluses.

A number of procedural issues arise at each decision point:

- Accountability/public participation: to what extent is the broader public interest involved in this particular decision, and how should it be represented?
- Comparison of options: is there a range of options to choose from, are they considered on an equal footing, and what is the basis for comparison?
- Coordination: how does this decision interact with those being taken elsewhere in the industry?
- Risk allocation: does the allocation of risk to the decision maker reflect the underlying uncertainty associated with each particular option? Are there reasonable expectations about the future that participants may be entitled to hold in making their investment decisions?

- Sources of finance: to what extent is this investment to be financed by debt and how does this affect the problems of investment coordination and risk allocation? Do limits on access to finance seriously restrict the options that a participant can consider? Does the form of financing allow for inter-generational equity?
- What protection is required against the failure of equipment to perform to specifications or the relocation of assets away from a network, both of which may restrict the ability of the industry to meet future demand?
- Investment criteria: are the investment criteria used by participants distorted by inappropriate risk allocation or inadequate access to finance?

Broadly speaking, we may separate infrastructure investment decisions into two categories — those that are 'small' and have little individual significance for the industry, and those that are 'large' and have important consequences for the industry. The former may be considered in aggregate and appropriate ground-rules developed. The latter will always require specific consideration to ensure that they are in the best interests of the community as a whole.

Consumer investment decisions

It is normally expected that consumers will eventually pay for all electricity infrastructure on both the supply and demand-sides of the industry. Thus consumers should participate in all the industry's investment decisions. They exercise this right directly through choosing to either purchase electricity or invest in DSOs; and indirectly through Parliamentary representation. Ultimately, (and the same is true for the vast bulk of public sector organisations) it is in that forum that decisions regarding the structure of the electricity supply industry, its pricing policies and the regulatory system are taken.

The choice by a consumer to either purchase electricity or invest in DSOs will usually fall into the 'small' category. The public interest is then served by making available all relevant information (including soundly based electricity prices and price forecasts to perform the investment coordination role), ensuring that there is an adequate range of options available and that these are presented on an equal footing. Appliance standards and related measures are important because most demand-side decision makers do not have the specialised knowledge required to make informed decisions about technical matters. Disadvantaged groups may require financial or other assistance to ensure that they are in a position to choose the most appropriate options. For example, rental housing must be subject to oversight in relation to its energy efficiency. Legitimate consumer expectations about long-term supply availability must be safeguarded.

Network investment decisions

Two types of network investment decision may be identified — those that are associated with the main network and those that are associated with a radial connection to a particular group of participants. All participants share responsibility for the former while the particular group of participants concerned share responsibility for the latter.

There is a strong community interest in maintaining the main network in a sound condition and in exploring interconnection between electricity networks. It may be difficult to allocate financial responsibility among individual participants for this task. For example, protection devices form one important category of network equipment. These devices serve no useful function during normal operation, but minimise supply interruptions and damage to electrical equipment when a fault occurs. The level of investment in protection devices should be based on an assessment of the aggregate needs of industry participants.

Generally speaking, the distribution sector may be best placed to represent the interests of small consumers attached to radial or near-radial parts of an electricity network, although it may be possible to separate responsibility for the wires from responsibility for other services. A radial link that connects a large generation project to the main network should be considered to be part of the generation project. Such a project should also contribute to any augmentation of the main network that is required to ensure the continued viability of the network when the project is brought into service.

Grid extensions in remote areas pose difficult problems. Connection costs can be very high and uncertain and independent supply systems offer a realistic alternative. The options should be presented to the participants involved in a way that does not distort the balance between them, and hidden subsidies have to be carefully examined. Thomas et al (1990) illustrates the pitfalls involved if this strategy is not adopted.

Generation investment decisions

Generation investment decisions are often large and have long lead times compared to DSOs. There is also a wide range of generation technologies to choose from, each with a different construction lead time, capital cost, operating cost and preferred type of operation. Generation technologies are often categorised as base, intermediate, peak or emergency duty, where base duty implies operation whenever the unit is available (e.g. brown coal units in the Latrobe Valley).

The lack of cost-effective storage for electricity favours a mix of generating technologies with different capabilities. The nature of the mix depends on characteristics of the demand for electricity, the available generating technologies and the available primary energy forms. There is a need for careful coordination between individual generation investment decisions and between investments in generation and investments in DSOs so that the generation mix remains in balance with the characteristics of the load.

The larger size and longer lead time of most generation projects compared with DSOs means that the former tend to carry greater investment risk than the latter. Generation projects also tend to carry greater environmental risks. These considerations, plus the nature of the cash flow in the industry (from consumers to producers) implies that consumers should be given the opportunity to consider investment in DSOs prior to commitments being made to large generation projects. This can best be done by minimising debt financing of generation projects and by providing consumers with forward projections of the electricity prices that would be required to finance future generation projects.

The effects of debt financing

Access to debt financing depends on the lender's perception of the borrower's ability to repay the loan (among other factors: see Chapter 12). There is a finance sector bias towards supply-side investment. The problem of supplier bias in debt financing has been exacerbated by the tariff policies and accounting practices used by Australian electricity supply authorities. Finance charges on loans taken out for long-lead time power station construction are capitalised until the station enters service. Interest and depreciation payments then appear in electricity prices, possibly causing them to rise. Price rises that occur when a unit enters service are too late from the perspective of investment coordination and may encourage consumers to invest in DSOs at the very time that there is spare supply capacity.

This will only be resolved by either weakening the borrowing power of electricity suppliers or assisting consumers to invest in DSOs. Disadvantaged consumers with limited ability to borrow should be given special consideration.

Nevertheless, the intergenerational equity issues associated with large, long-life capital works imply that any capital-intensive expansion of the electricity supply industry which does occur, could best be financed through borrowings.

7.4 Some Planning Approaches in Current Use

Recent developments in the US

The evolution of electricity planning in the US may be traced from traditional supply-side planning to 'least-cost' planning, in which equality of treatment for both supply and DSOs is stressed and public participation in the planning process is encouraged (Kaye and Outhred, 1990).

'Competitive resource procurement' is a feature of the US implementation of least-cost planning (Charles River Associates, 1990). The steps in this procedure are to, first, identify the need for new electricity infrastructure, and then undertake a bidding process in which a wide range of organisations bid to provide either new generating capability (which may be independently owned and operated) or DSOs. This is complemented by strong innovation in demand-side technologies and a system of steadily tightening appliance standards. Utilities in some US states are now permitted to earn profits on

expenditure they make on DSOs (Californian Collaborative Process, 1990).

At the same time, there has been a trend in the US towards deregulation in electricity generation, aided by deregulation in the natural gas industry and developments in renewable energy technologies, particularly wind, solar and municipal waste. The Public Utilities Regulation Act (PURPA) has played a significant role in this development.

Finally, many state regulatory commissions are beginning to incorporate environmental externalities into electric utility planning and regulation (Cohen et al, 1990).

While there has been considerable progress in the US in the treatment of DSOs, environmental externalities and public participation in electricity planning, a number of weaknesses remain.

Least-cost planning is a centralised procedure and the industry regulators risk becoming implicated in the outcome, thus losing their independence and distorting the allocation of investment risk. Electricity pricing is still determined on rate-base and allowed rate-of-return considerations, rather than on a sound basis where externalities are considered. This means that electricity prices are unlikely to convey the information on supply/demand balance that is critical to the coordination of investment decisions by independent participants (e.g. consumers). Questions of transmission access and transmission pricing remain unresolved. However the US now has well-established procedures for reform of the regulatory process that could allow these remaining problems to be resolved without sacrificing the strong and effective regulation that currently exists.

Privatisation of the British electricity industry[2]

The stated motivation of the British government for the privatisation of the electricity supply industry was to distance the industry from political interference, which was claimed to be hampering its ability to operate efficiently and to respond to the needs of its customers. It was claimed that a competitive environment could be created that would encourage economic efficiency and minimise the need for regulation.

Monopoly aspects of electricity supply (e.g. transmission) are regulated by a price-cap system

(CPI-x) and competition will be fostered in generation and supply in the belief that it will encourage economic efficiency. Competition in generation is to be achieved by a short-run marginal cost pricing (SRMC) based bidding procedure for the sale of energy to the transmission company, while competition in supply is expected to flow from the removal of franchise rights (see Chapter 8 for an explanation of pricing systems). Energy efficiency will not be specifically promoted but it is felt that the industry structure will favour it. There are no specific provisions to address planning and investment issues or to provide for social and environmental accountability.

The main drawback of the British approach is that it is biased towards financial accountability at the expense of social and environmental accountability. In addition, the implementation of the SRMC pricing arrangements has important weaknesses — in transmission pricing (the concept of the network as a common carrier has important technical complications that are not dealt with); in the handling of externalities, reliability and debt; and in the provision for confidential generator-consumer contracts that bypass the network-based trading arrangements.

These weaknesses mean that free and effective competition is unlikely to occur. In particular, the new structure may allow the existing generating companies (particularly the larger of the two — National Power) to have excessive market influence. Investment is to be left to market forces and the important relationship between the electricity and gas industries has yet to be addressed. The CPI-x price regulation applied to transmission and distribution will interfere with the investment coordination components of SRMC prices that fluctuate according to the evolving supply/demand balance.

The British government's insistence on a 'non-fossil fuel' levy to finance its nuclear power stations and its acceptance of vertically integrated supply industry structure for Scotland contradict its claim that political interference in the industry has been eliminated or at least substantially reduced. In addition, the broad powers of the government-appointed Director-General provide many opportunities for on-going political influence on the industry. The government will retain 'golden shares' in the privatised compa-nies, allowing it to become directly involved in management decisions as a last resort.

In summary, it appears likely that the British regulatory process will steadily become more complex in a similar manner to the evolution of the US regulatory process.

Restructuring of the New Zealand electricity industry

Restructuring of the New Zealand electricity industry has so far followed similar lines to the British model (Hewlett, 1990 provides a recent summary of the process. See also Chapter 11). However, important decisions are still to be implemented and the recent change of government has introduced some uncertainty into the final outcome. Decisions taken to date (some of which have yet to be implemented) include:

- corporatisation of the former Electricity Department to form Electricorp and its division into business units for generation, transmission, engineering services and marketing;
- implementation of a new bulk supply tariff with a SRMC pricing option;
- corporatisation of the former electric power boards into distribution entities and the abolition of franchise areas;
- the transfer of ownership of the grid company (Trans Power) to a club with equal shareholdings for the generation and distribution sides of the supply industry plus other participants; and
- information disclosure requirements for dominant firms in the new electricity supply industry structure.

As in Britain, the current preoccupation in New Zealand is with the establishment of the new trading arrangements and the transition from the previous industry structure. This means that other equally pressing issues are not receiving the attention they deserve. These include social and environmental accountability, investment coordination and equality of treatment for both primary and end-use energy forms. However the opportunity to learn from the British experience should give New Zealand the opportunity to incorporate improvements in their practical implementation of network-based trading arrangements.

One noticeable outcome of the corporatisation

process in both Britain and New Zealand has been a substantial reduction of the amount of information in the public domain. The key argument for this has been the increased need for confidentiality now that the supply organisations are operating on a commercial basis. By contrast, the open nature of the US regulatory process ensures that this problem does not arise to the same extent, despite the emphasis on private utilities in the US.

Current Australian practice

Frost (1990) summarises the size of the investment problem for the Australian electricity supply industry. He points out that apart from meeting increased demand for electricity, the existing generation, transmission and distribution infrastructure will require almost complete replacement by the year 2020 because it will have reached the end of its working life. This raises the possibility of a complete reconsideration of the industry, including choice of major primary energy forms, balance between supply and DSOs and organisational arrangements.

If this daunting task is to be tackled, Australia will have to come to terms with the need to broaden planning and investment arrangements from the traditional supply-based model of the electricity industry. Sound procedures must be developed for public participation and for consideration of DSOs.

New South Wales has instituted a strategic planning process (Electricity Commission of New South Wales, 1990), but it is still biassed towards supply-side options. Few details of the Commission's technical analyses reach the public domain to allow independent verification.

Other States have adopted *ad hoc* public inquiries in response to specific problems that have emerged. Victoria has developed the most effective procedures for public inquiries in the electricity industry, and has acknowledged the need to balance social, economic and environmental accountability in both the Brunswick-to-Richmond Powerline Inquiry (Powerline Review Panel, 1989) and the Inquiry into Electricity Supply and Demand Beyond the Mid 1990s (Natural Resources and Environment Committee, 1988).

Weaknesses of the current electricity planning arrangements in Australia include the following:

- reliance on *ad hoc* inquiries rather than an on-going process for public participation;
- imbalance between the treatment of supply and DSOs;
- failure to link electricity pricing to planning, including investment coordination and the incorporation of externalities into electricity pricing;
- failure to ensure equality of treatment between electricity, gas, efficiency and renewables at the point of end-use;
- failure to ensure equality of treatment of primary energy forms, particularly coal, gas and renewables;
- failure to balance the needs for social, economic and environmental accountability; and
- failure to address the need for federal as well as State government involvement in the above issues.

The moves towards national integration of the electricity industry could, at least, remove the motive for parochial decision-making, which has contributed to the existence of excess capacity.

7.5 Conclusion and Recommendations

There are sound reasons for public involvement in the electricity industry:

- the importance of electricity to modern society means that there is a strong public interest in achieving and maintaining an appropriate electricity industry infrastructure, including ongoing support for innovation;
- the social and environmental impacts of the industry are such that there are many externalities to be considered;
- the value judgements involved in assessing these external impacts and choosing between available options means that a high level of informed public participation is essential;
- major primary energy resources and electricity networks both have features that imply a strong public interest in decisions about their use; and
- the distributed nature of demand-side decision making implies the need for public support in the form of meaningful options, all relevant information and financial resources for disadvantaged groups.

There are also clear reasons why the present arrangements for public electricity supply are not working satisfactorily:
- planning is supply-centric and both demand-side and public participation is minimal;
- electricity pricing is based on outdated concepts and is not linked to electricity planning;
- supply authorities are able to transfer their investment risks to consumers without forgoing their decision-making power;
- externalities are not adequately considered in planning or pricing; and
- politicians and special interest groups have many opportunities to interfere in ways that may not be in the public interest.

Rather than using the failures of the present arrangements as dubious arguments to withdraw public involvement from the industry, it would be more sensible to adopt a strategy of reform. The following steps would eliminate many of the existing shortcomings:
- support for national integration;
- establishment of balanced approach to planning such that the distribution sector undertakes an enhanced customer service role, offering disinterested, end-use advise and a wide range of end-use options on an equal financial basis;
- appropriate reform of the primary energy resource sector to achieve equality of treatment of all primary energy forms and appropriate allocation of investment risks;
- appropriate reform of the natural gas industry to ensure equality of treatment for electricity and gas; and
- incorporation of externalities into the energy industry through processes of public participation, taxes on primary energy forms and the like.

Notes

1. Simply, interest rates for large investments are likely to be lower than interest rates on borrowings for consumer goods.

2. More details are given in Chapter 12.

CHAPTER 8

PRICING THEORY AND PRACTICE

8.1 Introduction

The role that the electricity industry plays in meeting our overall energy needs is the product of electricity's flexibility in use, its availability and its price to the consumer. The price at which electrical energy is traded, in turn, plays a key role in determining the structure and the operation of the electricity industry and the way in which that industry evolves. Pricing issues are also considered in Chapters 10 and 11. The main reasons for this are:

- price level and changes to price level affect consumer decisions on both operations and the purchase of new equipment. Consumers will usually compare a number of alternative plans and choose the cheapest. Thus price affects the allocation of resources between and amongst consumers and suppliers of electrical energy. Price acts as a decision co-ordinator;

- price thus influences the competition between end-use energy forms such as gas, electricity, renewable energy, end-use efficiency and conservation. For example, if the price of electricity is set too low, then cost effective energy efficiency opportunities can be lost; and

- price has a strong impact on the revenue for the supply-side, being used for operation and investment costs. In general there has been an attempt to cover present operations costs using present revenue. Investment costs have often been paid off as instalments on loans (see Chapter 7).

Thus price strongly affects the evolution of an electricity industry and price levels do not appear unbidden. Pricing policies and other organisational objectives are used to produce *tariffs*, which are statements of the charges which will be attached to the trading of various amounts of electrical energy. The process of establishing tariffs is referred to as *tariff setting* or *price setting* and the overview of their application is called regulation. Price setting and regulation have equity, social justice and socio-economic development dimensions. Price can be used to direct resources towards certain social groups. Examples include pensioner rebates, low-income assistance, rural cross-subsidies and industry development tariffs.

A key feature of modern electricity industries is the growing importance of *demand-side options* (DSOs). These are defined as whatever can be done on the demand-side to contribute to the economic efficiency of the system as a whole.

DSOs include:

- input substitution such as using gas or solar for hot water heating;
- third party (i.e. local or private) generation of electrical energy, including cogeneration;
- improved end-use efficiency;
- lifestyle changes which, for example, result in conservation;
- end-use storage; and
- utility initiated load shifting programs.

Many of these opportunities arise because of changing technologies and, in some instances, there will be DSOs with variable costs that are less than the variable costs of some supply-side sources of energy available at that time. Significant savings to the industry and to society can thus be achieved if the operation of those supply-side sources are replaced by cheaper DSOs. Further, because of their lower capital costs and shorter installation lead times, many DSOs offer substantially lower risks than large capital investments on the supply-side. In most cases, DSOs also have lower environmental impacts than supply-side options. In order to fully realise the benefits that DSOs offer to the electricity industry, it is necessary to coordinate operation and investment decisions of the supply and demand-sides.

An electricity industry should be viewed as one of many paths between a set of primary energy resources and end-use requirements (Kaye and Outhred, 1988). In this view, the industry is composed of a set of *participants*, some of whom are consumers of electrical energy, some suppliers and some who are both. Participants have a number of end-use requirements which can often be satisfied with a variety of mixes of energy forms. An electricity industry also requires transmission and distribution infrastructure to facilitate energy trading.

One large participant with particular characteristics is the utility which has traditionally been the dominant supplier of electrical energy. Utilities are either vertically integrated with generation, transmission and distribution functions owned and operated by the one company or else separated into distribution authorities and transmission and generation utilities. Utilities are now facing increasing competition from third party sources and some DSOs and the role of the traditional utility is changing. One important issue for society to resolve is how to best balance demand and supply-side options. The objective of this trade-off should be to develop an industry which achieves desirable outcomes in economic, social and environmental terms. Price and the methods used to establish it will be important in this regard.

In Section 8.2, the historical background to changes in the electricity industry is outlined, establishing the industry conditions under which price setting occurs. A detailed examination of the importance of price to both the supply and demand-sides of the industry is given in Section 8.3. The ways in which price affects both operation and investment activities are considered. Electricity industries also have a number of unique technical features which differentiate them from other industries. A consequence of these features is that many of the traditional microeconomic and price setting models are not valid. These features are described in Section 8.4.

A number of different principles have been applied to price setting in electricity industries in Australia and elsewhere. In Section 8.5 the most important of these are discussed in terms of their advantages and disadvantages within the Australian context. Price setting practices also vary between industries. A critical analysis of current Australian practices and a contrasting description of practices in the US are given in Section 8.6. These matters are also discussed in Chapter 10 where the accountability issue is considered. Finally, the interaction between price setting and privatisation is discussed in Section 8.7. Section 8.8 sets out our conclusions.

The reader should be aware that, in this chapter, the term "investment decision" is used to denote any decision to purchase an item of equipment which satisfies an end-use or which generates electrical energy (or both). In the case of domestic consumers, an "investment decision" is thus a decision to purchase a consumer durable, while for an electricity authority it is a decision to purchase either generating equipment, which converts primary energy to electrical energy, transmission equipment or demand-side infrastructure.

8.2 Historical Perspective

Over the last decade, electricity industries in most developed countries have experienced a significant and, at times, traumatic period of change.

The years from the mid 1940s until the early 1970s can be viewed as the "golden age" (Smith, 1989). During this time, electricity industries in most developed economies were characterised by the following:

- falling real unit costs of supply;
- growing demand; and
- a perception of future certainty: future conditions could safely be predicted by extrapolation from past history.

The economies of scale favoured large supply-side generation options and the industry faced limited competition from DSOs and other energy forms. Traditional economists maintain that the characteristics of the industry in this period met the criteria of a "natural monopoly".

Utilities were mostly concerned with the "technical issues" of design, construction and management of the generation, transmission and distribution systems. The most important goal seemed to be satisfying the load growth, with the major emphasis being placed on achieving or maintaining a high reliability of supply. Planning was a relatively straightforward matter.

Since demand for electrical energy over the planning period could be forecast with some accuracy, it was possible to calculate a schedule of new plant installation which minimised costs within constraints set by a predetermined quality of supply. Further, errors in timing were not critical because the rate of demand growth was large compared to unit sizes. For example, if the planned generating capacity turned out to be in excess by one 500 MW unit and if load were growing at 1,000 MW per annum, then a six month delay in installation would resolve the error. Setting the price for electricity was usually based on financial considerations such as balancing revenue. Falling real unit costs thus implied reductions in real prices.

Since the oil crisis in the early 1970s, the technological, economic and environmental conditions faced by the supply industries of North America, Europe and Australia (Murphy, 1987) have changed dramatically. In particular:

- load growth has been far below its forecast level;
- the economies of scale in conventional generation technology have been exhausted;
- the economics of co-generation and third party generation have improved significantly. In the US, this effect has been amplified by the PURPA regulations which resulted in very attractive buy-back prices for some co-generators and renewable energy sources (Berg, 1981);
- real supply-side costs have increased and, in particular, construction and capital costs for large base load units have escalated;
- concerns about the environmental impacts of the electricity industry have steadily increased. Particular issues have involved the greenhouse effect, acid rain and, most recently, the health effects of low frequency electromagnetic fields; and
- it has become impossible to make accurate predictions of future conditions affecting the planning process. Uncertainty has been increasing in regard to:
  a) security of future fuel supplies and costs;
  b) construction costs;
  c) demand (i.e. composition and quantity of end-uses);
  d) supply- and demand-side technologies; and

e) environmental factors.

As a result, supply authorities in many developed countries are suffering from an over-supply of base load generating capacity and financial difficulties such as large debts. Further, the competition from third party generators, DSOs and other energy sources is intensifying.

It is thus no longer correct to view all aspect of the electricity authorities as monopolies in all aspects of the industry. Rather they have become "dominant players" in that their historically acquired generating and transmission equipment places them in a pre-eminent position within the electricity industry. Around the world, even that position continues to be challenged.

Thus the electricity industry needs to develop a new perspective on its likely future role. In particular, the objectives should now be:

- optimal utilisation of existing supply-side and demand-side resources to delay further construction requirements;
- diversity and flexibility in planning to cope with a variety of possible future outcomes;
- seeking cost-effective supply options which have lower environmental impact than the traditional fossil fuel based supply-side options. These include renewable energy; and
- consideration of supply and demand-side options on an equal basis.

All these concerns must now be incorporated into decision-making to ensure an optimal social outcome.

8.3 The Importance of Price in the Electricity Industry

Introduction

Operating decisions are those choices a participant makes about how the equipment under its control is used. For a supply authority, the set of operating decisions made at any one time include:

- which generating units to bring "on-line";
- the level of output of each "on-line" unit; and
- the settings on the various pieces of transmission equipment.

For consumers, operating decisions include determining the level of end-use satisfaction and the way in which end-use equipment will be operated to achieve it.

The price at which a unit of electrical energy is traded has significant effects on the decision-making of both the supply and demand-sides of the industry. In particular, electricity prices strongly impact on the revenues of each participant. They thus strongly influence the operating and investment decisions of both suppliers and consumers.

Supply-side

The largest component of the income of most electricity utilities is derived from the sale of electrical energy. In many cases, all of the revenue is thus derived. Price is thus a key determinant of the revenue available to a utility to pay for its operating and investment costs. This is particularly true since electricity utilities have not had access to funds from Consolidated Revenue.

Using the revenue obtained from the sale of electrical energy, a utility must pay for all of its variable and fixed costs including:

- the fuel used in its thermal generators (e.g. coal, gas and oil);
- maintenance and repair of generation, transmission and distribution equipment;
- labour costs; and
- capital costs of purchase and construction of new plant (investment costs).

In many cases, a large component of a utility's costs involves supporting investment. Most commonly, new equipment is purchased using long-term borrowings. Income from the sale of electricity is then used to not only repay the principal but, in a period of historically high interest rates, large debt servicing costs.

In traditional supply-side strategies, two problems arise. The first has to do with uncertainty. The future demand for electricity is unknowable at the time that an investment is made and any forecast will contain errors (see Chapter 6). Hence, at the time of commitment to the investment, the utility will be uncertain of the need for the equipment.

The second problem arises from the dependence of demand for electrical energy on price. If the need to raise money to service a loan on new equipment causes an increase in price then this can cause a reduction in demand as consumers either switch to other end-use energy forms or reduce their end-use satisfaction. While some consumers are quite inelastic to price, many can exhibit large consumption responses to changing price levels. The result can be that the

original investment is no longer required. These issues are further investigated in Chapter 7.

Demand-side

The price of electricity and the quantity consumed determine the consumer's electricity bill, which is often a significant component of the total energy cost structure of an electric consumer. In a few cases this will, in fact, amount to a significant proportion of total costs. Thus price setting can play a key role in influencing a consumer's economic decision making.

An important example of this is where one end-use can be satisfied by a number of different energy forms. Water can be heated, for example, using electric resistive heating, electric heat pumps, gas and direct solar energy. The choice between these energy forms will be based on a comparison of the economics of the energy forms. Thus, the assessment of each energy form will be based on:

- the price of a unit of that energy form;
- the costs of end-use equipment using it;
- the reliability of its supply; and
- the amount of that energy form required to satisfy the end-use.

Consumers thus analyse and compare the costs and benefits of using each energy form. Two other end-use considerations which are affected by price are:

- the purchase of new equipment or modifying existing equipment to improve end-use efficiency (i.e. reducing the amount of energy form consumed without changing end-use satisfaction); and
- conservation which involves using less energy by reducing the satisfaction of the end-use.

Both these outcomes can be desirable in terms of reducing the environmental impacts of electricity generation and transmission. The price of each energy form has a key impact on the economics of both end-use efficiency and conservation and will thus need to contain the correct cost and environmental impact information to encourage participants to make appropriate decisions.

Operating decisions mostly react to the changing level of price. For example, time of use (TOU) tariffs usually involve a higher price for electrical energy during peak demand periods

(Tolley, 1987). Consumers with the ability to delay the satisfaction of an end-use until off-peak periods can reduce their electricity costs. Residential end-uses for which satisfaction can easily be delayed include water heating and clothes washing and drying. Broadly speaking, end-uses which can be delayed involve the use of storage to transfer operation between different time periods.

Investment decisions, on the other hand, react to longer term forecasts of future prices. In the absence of better information, participants often use past price movements as a guide. Such a strategy can be based on erroneous assumptions, resulting in unfounded confidence in the validity of the forecast. In any event, the wide range of uncertain factors that can affect future prices implies that any "single line" forecast for future prices will almost surely be incorrect. Probabilistic forecasts which take into account all possible outcomes and their likelihoods contain more appropriate information about forecast risk.

Third party generation has become increasingly important in electricity industries. This includes co-generators, renewable sources of energy and other privately owned generators. Electricity prices are very important to these participants in determining their operating and investment decisions. The economics of co-generation, for example, are often quite marginal and small differences in the income gained from the sale of electrical energy can determine the viability of the activity.

Tariff structures and prices

The tariff structure is the way in which electricity charges relate to consumption. That is also important in determining participant responses. The most common components of tariff structures are:

- energy only charges where a price is paid for each unit (kWh) of electrical energy. In some tariffs, this charge can vary with time, either in a pre-determined fashion — time of use prices (Tolley, 1987) — or in an unpredictable manner — dynamic prices (Tabors et al, 1989; Sanghvi, 1989);
- block tariffs, in which the price per unit of energy varies with the amount traded;
- maximum demand charges, which are proportional to the largest quarter or half hourly demand for electrical energy within the billing period; and
- standing charges (also called fixed charges), which do not vary with consumption levels.

Each of these has a different effect on consumer reaction to price.

For example, the use of maximum demand charges can have undesirable outcomes. Consumers faced with maximum demand charges can allocate significant resources into reducing their use of electrical energy at the times of their own maximum demands. In some cases, this involves using storage such as increasing the use of compressors on cool stores before and after the maximum demand periods. If a consumer's maximum demand periods do not correspond to times of system peak demand, then demand charges can result in that consumer increasing their demand during system peak times as a result of reducing its demand during system off-peak periods. From the industry's point of view, it is clearly irrational to have participants allocating resources to increase their demand during system peak times. Maximum demand charges, because they do not include information about the supply/demand balance, transmit the wrong information.

Standing charges, on the other hand, have no influence on participant decision making, other than reducing capital available for other activities. Since they are unavoidable, participants will not change their consumption or production patterns. The exception is where a consumer feels they can leave the industry and satisfy their own energy needs without grid connection. Standing charges are the most useful tariff component for collecting revenue without distorting participant decisions.

Dynamically varying energy charges can be used to reflect the supply/demand balance. At times when supply is constrained with respect to demand price is increased so that consumers can have an opportunity to respond to high prices by reducing their loads and hence their electricity bills. This would alleviate system stress conditions. Similarly, periods of higher prices would encourage the operation of those demand-side options, such as third party generation and co-generators, which can respond to occasional or regular periods of higher prices.

It is thus clear that price is a key determinant of the evolution of the electricity industry, particularly the balance between supply and demand-side options such as energy conservation and end-use efficiency. Price should contain the correct signals to consumers to enable appropriate participant choices.

8.4 Technical Features of Electricity Industries
Introduction
There are a number of features specific to an electricity supply industry which separate it from other industries. These arise from the technical nature of the industry.

Transmission and distribution
In electrical power systems, end-uses and generating equipment are connected by a set of electrical lines, transformers, switches and protection equipment. The transmission of power over long distances (for example, from the Latrobe Valley to Melbourne and from the Hunter Valley to Sydney) tends to be performed at higher voltages (e.g. 500,000 volts) in order to reduce the energy losses in transmission. However, this incurs higher capital costs per unit: length of line and the protection and switching equipment is more expensive. Further, high voltages are not suitable for most end-uses.

Electricity is thus retailed to most customers at lower voltages. Domestic consumers usually receive supply at 240 volts line neutral (i.e. 415 volts line to line) and some commercial and industrials receive supply at 11,000 volts (line to line). Between the highest voltage used in transmission and the final distribution voltage there are usually a number of levels. For example, in Victoria, electrical lines operate (line to line) at 500,000, 330,000, 275,000, 220,000, 66,000, 33,000, 22,000, 11,000, 6,600, 3,300, 2,200 and 415 volts (SECV, 1990, pp.124–5).

The equipment connecting end-users and generators of electrical energy is usually partitioned into distribution and transmission. Distribution can be thought of as retailing electrical energy while transmission is similar to wholesaling. The distinction however is blurred and no generally accepted technical definition of the boundary between transmission and distribution exists. However:
- the distribution system always contains the lowest voltages (415 and 11,000 volts) in the system and is usually characterised by a complex grid of lines. Direct connection to residential and smaller commercial customers is usually through the distribution system. Much of the distribution system can be radial in nature. That is, from each participant there is a single, unique path through the distribution system to some point in the transmission system; and
- transmission systems contain all the higher voltage equipment. In most cases, major generating stations are connected to the transmission system. Distribution systems usually receive power from one or more transmission systems. In many systems, a few of the largest consumers and third party generators connect directly to the transmission system.

The classification of mid-range voltage equipment (e.g. 33,000 volt) is often a matter determined by historical evolution or political fiat. In NSW, for example, ownership of the 132,000 volt lines have been transferred from ECNSW to the County Councils.

Accepting these definitional difficulties, distribution systems have two special characteristics within the electricity industry:
- opportunities for direct competition between two distributors are quite limited. While customers at the boundaries of the service areas might be able to exercise choice between two distributors, it is unlikely to be economic for two separate distribution companies to compete within the interior of one area. The cost of dual provision of distribution infrastructure would be too great. Further, while there have been some proposals for service competition based on a forced energy wheeling (i.e. each distribution authority is obliged to carry electrical energy through its lines for another company), establishing and regulating appropriate legislated wheeling tariffs at the distribution level could be quite complicated. Thus, small participants connected to a distribution system, and domestic customers in particular, are "captives" of the distribution franchise holders; and
- distributors are physically closest to the end-users of electrical energy. They are thus best

placed to understand customer needs and to respond to them. To some extent, distribution authorities have an advantage over other organisations in the provision of direct end-use services including information and advice on energy options.

The social role of the transmission system

Trading in electrical energy depends on the existence of a transmission system to interconnect the participants. Without such a system, the industry would cease to exist. Further, even with the transmission system, pair-wise trading between two participants is impossible. Quanta of electrical energy cannot be identified nor can a supplier of electricity specifically "target" its output to a particular consumer. Instead, it is more accurate to think of suppliers putting into a common pool from which consumers remove energy.

The expertise required to run a transmission system and the high capital costs associated with the construction of lines suggest that competing transmission systems in one area would be uneconomic. Thus the transmission grid needs to be thought of as a "social" system in that its specific role and economics imply that it is a community asset. It sits at the centre of the industry and it is appropriate that it remains in public ownership to ensure it achieves a socially optimal trading outcome.

"Quality of supply" issues

The laws of physics which govern the operation of an electric power system imply that individual participants cannot determine many features of their supply. These include such aspects as frequency, voltage fluctuations, voltage wave-form and reliability of supply. These are all quantities which result from the complexities of the interaction between the participants and the transmission system. They therefore cannot be specified as factors which differentiate the product in the way in which, for example, quality of wool can be used.

Storage

The electricity industry is marked by an absence of cost effective intermediate term storage for electrical energy *per se*. Thus, the rate at which energy flows into the grid must instantaneously match the rate at which energy leaves the grid. Traditionally, the instantaneous balance between supply and demand has been maintained using utility-owned load-following generators which alter their outputs according to the instantaneous needs.

Hydro-electric dams and pumped storage systems such as the Snowy Mountains Scheme store potential energy in the form of water held in dams. Water is then released through turbines to generate electrical energy. In pumped storage schemes, this process can be reversed so that electrical energy is taken from the system and used to pump water back into the storage for release and generation at later times.

Hydro and pumped storage schemes play a particularly important role in electricity industries. Their ability to withhold generation at one time instance in favour of increased output at another offers opportunities for inter-temporal transfers of energy. This can have the effect of smoothing out cyclical variations and random fluctuations in the (variable) cost of energy supply. Thus the amount of water in storage can be a strong predictor of likely future system conditions. Such effects have not been traditionally considered in economic models although some work has been reported recently (Kaye and Outhred, 1988).

A second feature of most storage schemes is their ability to respond rapidly to demands for sudden changes in output. This makes them better suited than most thermal generating units for emergency response to system contingencies such as the unexpected failure of a large generating unit or transmission line or an unexpected rapid increase in load. To achieve the rapid response required to realise the system support requires that control of the hydro or pumped storage scheme should be tightly coupled to the control centre of the electricity system.

The water in many hydro-electric schemes also has down-stream values, such as irrigation uses, flood and drought mitigation and environmental impacts. In the case of the Snowy Scheme, this imposes another set of costs and benefits on longer term operational strategies. The special features of hydro and pumped storage schemes include:

• operation of the storages can have a key effect on smoothing fluctuations in variable

system costs;
- the level of storage is an indicator of likely future system conditions;
- while hydro and pumped storage have excellent potential to supply system emergency support, tight control coupling is required to achieve it; and
- down-stream water values often impinge on the operation of schemes.

In consequence the responsible exploitation of the potential benefits of hydro and pumped storage schemes requires that :
- management of the schemes takes into account the social benefits of water, including down-stream water values. There is a need to balance benefits between different users and different times;
- the system control centre has short term access to the scheme for emergency responses; and
- the public has access to information about the state of the storages so that all participants can make sensible forecasting decisions.

This can be achieved using either public ownership of the scheme with improved management structures and clarified responsibilities and objectives or significant regulation of a privately owned scheme. "Light handed" regulation would be insufficient to achieve the above objectives. Thus significant and intrusive regulation would be required for a privately owned scheme of significant storage and generating capacities. This would probably be expensive and ineffective.

Market power of large participants
Economies of scale on both the supply and demand-sides of the industry have resulted in a diverse mix of sizes of participants. Most industries have a small number of large generators and consumers, and a much larger number of smaller participants. Opportunities for industry manipulation and the formation of cartels clearly exist. Large privately owned generating units would be seeking profit opportunities from the system with little or no regard for social goals. Large scale private ownership of the larger supply units could thus lead to price fixing arrangements. To avoid this, significant and expensive regulation would be required. The issue

of investment in large private generators is addressed in Chapters 11 and 12 and proposals in Western Australia and Victoria are discussed.

Conclusion
The special technical and organisational features of electricity industries outlined in this section indicate that the normal economic concepts of the "market" do not apply. In particular:
- large scale private ownership of large generating units would require heavy handed price regulation; and
- the price setting principles of the "free market" based on the dynamics of supply and demand would not work.

It is thus necessary to establish price setting procedures and authorities which take account of the economic and social goals of government, authorities and the community.

8.5 Price Setting Principles
Introduction
The principles that have been or could be applied to price setting in Australia are discussed in this section. Chapter 10 provides further the detail of pricing practices and techniques; how they have been used in practice in Australia and elsewhere; and how pricing questions bear on the question of accountability.

Pricing principles encompass a variety of objectives. Some of these are:
- supply-side cost recovery;
- rate of return (ROR) on investment,
- price capping (e.g. "CPI-x");
- welfare maximisation; and
- social and community objectives.

Each of these is described in the next section. It is clear, however, that these principles often translate into conflicting practical objectives for price setting. Thus actual price setting is usually based on a series of compromises. In the following section, the practical issues of price setting are discussed.

Cost recovery
This pricing principle suggests that the price of electricity is adjusted so that the total costs of the utility are recovered. The objective is to maintain the financial viability of the utility without allowing surpluses to accumulate. Thus price is set so that the projected revenue collected by the utility covers:

- operating costs such as payments for fuel, maintenance and labour;
- fixed costs such as administrative charges; and
- capital costs such as debt servicing payments.

Prices are fixed periodically and adjustments are usually required to correct for any errors in previous projections of either the utility's costs or the demand for electrical energy.

While maintaining the solvency of a utility is a laudable objective, cost recovery pricing has a number of disadvantages. These include the following:

- it is difficult to meaningfully define the actual costs. For example, a utility such as ECNSW might experience difficulties in placing a commercial value on coal purchased from its own collieries;
- prices which are set to recover supply-side costs do not contain useful information on the supply/demand balance. Because cost recovery is concerned merely with supply-side costs, this method, by definition, ignores the longer term effects that price can have on demand, for example, a utility that has just invested heavily in new generating plant. Its debt servicing payments will increase so that the price will also increase to cover them. However, an increase in price can suppress demand for electrical energy as end-users employ other options such as improved efficiency or fuel substitution. Thus the price increases required to cover costs can suppress load and result in underutilised assets. The problem is an absence of appropriate system cost information in the pricing signal;
- cost recovery prices imply that any cost incurred by the utility can be recovered from consumers. There is thus no financial incentive for the utility to contain costs. Further, the principle ignores the ability of end-users to be satisfied by other energy forms; and
- under cost recovery pricing, the financial risk of an investment not being required is borne entirely by the demand-side. Uncertainty is an inherent feature of electricity industries. If it is not reflected in the price of electricity then it is possible that there will be uneven or unfair risk sharing.

Note that cost recovery does not in principle imply any allocation of the costs between different consumers, nor does it suggest any way of setting buy back rates for third party generators.

Rate of return

Rate of return pricing involves adjusting the price of electrical energy so that the utility earns a surplus which is a fixed percentage of the value of its assets. A value for the assets of the utility is established and prices for electricity are set which enable the utility to earn a rate of return on those assets. Clearly this involves recovering costs, as in the above description of cost recovery pricing as well as earning a surplus.

This approach is utilised extensively in the US for the price regulation of investor-owned utilities (IOU) (Kahn, 1988, pp.12–13). The value of an IOU's assets is known as its "rate base". The main price regulators in the US, the Public Utility Commissions[1] (PUC), thus determine what investments can be included in the calculation of the rate base. The main regulatory objective is to avoid "gold plating" by the utility. Gold plating refers to the practice of inflating the rate base by installing plant that is unnecessary from the industry's point of view. The price regulator thus becomes involved in approving utility investment decisions.

In some instances, investments have been excluded from the rate base or their entry has been provisional on meeting certain performance standards (e.g. capacity factor). The rate of return has been adjusted to maintain return on bonds to attract capital into industry. This has resulted in some cases of "rate shock" where the addition of an expensive investment item to the rate base has caused sudden increases in prices. Some operating costs for IOU's are also recovered in the tariffs as "pass-through costs".

Rates of return are also in force in Victoria and South Australia where the utilities are required to earn a 4 per cent real rate of return on assets at replacement value.

Rate of return pricing suffers from all the disadvantages of cost recovery pricing outlined above. In addition, there are a number of other problems, some of which are as follows:

- determining the value of the rate base can involve arbitrary decisions. Accounting standards vary between public authorities and the accounting techniques used will have a significant impact on the actual price. For example, particular difficulties have been experienced in defining sunk costs. These can be defined as either historical costs adjusted for depreciation and inflation or the replacement costs of the same equipment. Both approaches are problematic. The present value of historical costs depends on the choice of parameters such as depreciation rates. The use of present day replacement costs suggests that the utility would want to replace equipment with the same or equivalent equipment. This might not be sensible. This topic is further discussed in Chapter 10;

- rate of return pricing supplies a financial incentive to the utility to over-invest since it is guaranteed to earn a surplus on any investment. Regulation has been required to avoid this gold plating problem (Kahn, 1988, p.14);
- rate of return pricing for a publicly owned utility raises the question as to which body should receive the surplus. If the government takes the surplus in the form of dividend payments which enter the Consolidated Revenue account and utilises those funds outside the industry, then this could be viewed as a tax on the electricity industry. A commonly used justification for this action would be that the government is the owner of the public enterprise. A countervailing argument is that the government only holds the enterprise in trust for its real owners, the Australian people and the consumers of electrical energy; and
- in a privately owned utility, the return on the investment could be paid to shareholders implying that surpluses from the sale of electrical energy can leave the electricity industry.

Price capping (e.g. "CPI-x")

Price capping involves holding down the real rate of increase of prices for electrical energy. In the "CPI-x" form, prices for electrical energy are adjusted so that the average price increases at a rate which is less than the Consumer Price Index (CPI) by a fixed amount "x". In most applications x is a couple of per cent. Other adjustments can be made for operating costs which are often dealt

with as pass through costs. That is, any unexpected increase in, for example, primary energy costs are passed directly onto the consumers as price rises.

The philosophical justification of price capping is that it encourages utilities to control their costs. For example, it financially penalises utilities which gold plate their investments. Price capping is used in the recently restructured electricity industry in Britain. It is also used in New South Wales to regulate gas prices. In all States there have been political directives to the electricity utilities to hold average price increases below CPI.

Price capping is politically popular in the short term because it gives the appearance to electricity consumers that the utility is being well managed. However, using capping as a price setting mechanism takes no account of supply-side costs nor of the possibilities for demand-side alternatives to supply-side decisions on operation and investment. Thus, the outcome for the utility will be either:

- when the need for new capacity is great there will be revenue starvation, in which case the utility will need to either borrow to cover costs or reduce the quality and standard of services. Examples include reduction in the level of maintenance, reduced quality of supply and delayed investment in new equipment; or
- when there is spare capacity there will be unnecessary and unjustifiable accumulation of supply-side surpluses.

In either case, the outcome is inappropriate because price does not react to the supply/demand balance or the costs of supply. Additional problems which arise with price capping include the arbitrary nature of the selection of the parameters such as:

- the calculation of "x";
- the choice of base case (first year) prices; and
- the set of costs which are allowed to flow through to consumers.

Price capping, cost recovery and rate of return cannot, on their own, provide the means by which to utilise the demand and supply-side mechanisms to resolve problems which might exist in the electricity industry. There needs to be a means of doing so. One such method which has been utilised elsewhere is described in the next section.

Industry short run marginal cost pricing (SRMC)

The most sophisticated of the pricing principles in current use is that price should reflect the marginal industry cost of supplying an additional unit of energy. Thus electricity price should track the supply/demand balance and supply a feedback signal to participants. When supply is constrained with respect to demand, the industry cost of supplying an additional increment would be high and a price based on marginal cost would indicate to consumers that any further consumption would incur a high industry cost.

The reader should note that this is not the same concept used in neoclassical theory of the firm (Varian, 1978, pp.34–46). The SRMC referred to in modern electricity pricing theory relates to marginal *industry* costs, whereas the SRMC of an individual firm relates only to the cost structure of that firm. For this reason the mechanism has also been called socially optimal pricing.

The objective of this approach is optimal allocation of activities between and amongst participants. *Socially optimal decisions* by participants are defined to be those which maximise global welfare. *Global welfare* is defined as the sum of the benefits of all participants. Socially optimal decisions are thus those which minimise costs to the industry as a whole with each end-user and each generator being treated equally. To incorporate environmental concerns, the SMRC must be accompanied by a tax or system of charges that reflect the environmental costs of the form of generation selected to produce the electricity so that prices reflect total costs including externalities. The tax or charge could reflect the costs of CO_2 or other polluting emissions. Other measures would also need to be developed to deal with the distributional consequences of this type of pricing system as we outline below.

In principle, it can be shown that if price is set equal to SRMC, then each participant makes optimal decisions when they attempt to maximise their own benefits (Caramanis et al, 1982, Kaye and Outhred, 1988). SRMC is a number (in units of ¢/kWh) defined as the minimum social cost of supplying one additional unit of energy. SRMC pricing is the tariff where the trading price — buying and selling — of all units of electrical energy is set equal to SRMC.

Because SRMC reflects the supply/demand balance, its future values cannot be predicted exactly. SRMC pricing thus takes on the attributes of spot pricing, where uncertainty in future prices reflects uncertainty in the future condition of the industry. It thus facilitates appropriate risk sharing between supply and demand-sides of the industry.

It has been argued that the dynamic interaction of supply and demand would result in prices which naturally trend towards SRMC. Such arguments are usually based on very simple models of consumer and supplier reactions to prices and of market interactions. The special nature of electricity industry as discussed in Section 8.4 would imply that these simplified models are not valid for the electricity industry and that regulatory interference and the cooperation of participants would be required to achieve SRMC pricing.

In theory, calculation of the value of SRMC requires knowledge of the cost structures of each participant (producers and consumers) and the current states of their equipment. This is, of course, impossible and it is also unnecessary in practice. In situations where supply is not constrained with respect to demand, the cheapest next increment of energy will come from a supply-side option. Thus, in these situations, the value of SRMC will be determined by the variable cost (i.e. variable operations and maintenance costs) of the marginal generating unit (i.e. the most expensive unit presently on line, which, in principle, will almost always be the only unit not fully loaded).

On the other hand, when supply is constrained with respect to demand and all available supply-side generating units are fully loaded, SRMC will be determined by the variable costs of demand-side options such as curtailing end-uses or switching to other, more expensive, energy forms. In these situations the exact value of SRMC will be more difficult to approximate but experience with demand response to price will be of assistance in setting a price that balances demand to the available supply.

A useful feature of SRMC pricing which follows from the above discussion is that if each generating unit is operated under SRMC pricing such that it generates only when it is economic to do so (i.e. only when SRMC is above its variable cost), then supply-side units will be dispatched according to their *merit order (economic dispatch)*. Merit order loading is the technique commonly used in centrally dispatched utilities to minimise costs. Units are ranked in increasing order of variable cost and load is met with the cheapest available units, thus minimising supply-side variable costs (Wood and Wollenberg, 1984, pp.23-58).

The concepts behind SRMC based pricing of electrical energy are relatively new. However, they have been applied in many parts of the world including New Zealand, France, and in some experiments in the US. Most Swedish tariffs are now based on SRMC pricing. A number of tariff based demand management schemes are also being developed. One, which is oriented towards dual fuel boilers, offers cheap electrical energy for a minimum of 3,000 hours per year, at times determined by the utility (Outhred, 1987).

Electricity pricing has in some cases been based on the concept of long run marginal costs (LRMC). In these tariffs, the capital costs of system expansion are allocated to different periods of the day (week or season). However, due to imprecision in the concept of LRMC, and difficulties which arise from uncertainties in future system capital needs, a number of definitions have been used in different countries. It was believed for some time that at "equilibrium" LRMC and SRMC pricing would be equivalent, however this has been shown to be untrue (Andersson and Bohman, 1985). Significant losses in global welfare can result from LRMC based price setting.

Electricite de France (EDF) base their tariffs and load management initiatives on LRMC (Lescoeur and Galland, 1987). The French generation mix of nuclear, oil and increasingly scarce hydro leads to a 20 to 1 range in marginal energy costs. One optional tariff offers low prices for most of the year in return for 22 eighteen hour days of higher prices. These are specified at short notice by EDF and correspond to days of supply constraint.

In the US, there has been a growing move towards "real time" (i.e. spot) pricing. State regulators in New York, Wisconsin and California have shown particular interest. The Pacific Gas and Electric (PG&E) company in Northern California has been developing, since 1985, a pricing experiment (Heffner and Ahlstrand, 1987). The prices for one day are fixed at 3pm the previous day and communicated electronically to the participating consumers. The hourly tariff is a mixture of, *inter alia*, estimated marginal cost and revenue recovery terms. However, the price does reflect evolving system costs. There are a number of other tariff experiments under way in the US, including one at Southern California Edison.

While SRMC pricing has a number of advantages and is consequently gaining popularity in various countries, there are a number of difficulties that a full implementation of SRMC pricing would encounter. These include the following:

- exact calculation of the value of SRMC would require complete knowledge of the cost structures of all participants . However, as discussed above there are good approximations available which require only information which could reasonably be expected to be available to the system control centre. Unlike rate of return pricing, the calculation of SRMC does not involve capital and investment costs. SRMC is only a function of the variable operating costs of each participant in the industry;

- regulation would be required to ensure that price remains equal to SRMC. While it has been argued that price regulation is required with any regime, SRMC regulation is somewhat more data intensive such that complete system conditions for each pricing period are required to verify SRMC pricing was used. On the other hand, SRMC regulations can be specified in terms of principles and procedures rather than outcomes; and

- in common with all pricing regimes, SRMC pricing raises a number of social justice issues. By treating all end-users equally, SRMC pricing will result in periods of high price which could prove to be difficult for low income consumers unless they were protected by other mechanisms. However, low income households which could reduce their consumption of electrical energy during occasional periods of high prices would potentially see a reduction in their overall electricity bills. This might involve, for example, shifting some end-use satisfaction until times of lower prices.

One of the advantages of SRMC based pricing is that it provides a rational framework for the inclusion of environmental and social impacts of the electricity industry by the use of taxes. For example, concerns about the greenhouse effect associated with the carbon dioxide (CO_2) emissions from the combustion of fossil fuels could be addressed by a "carbon tax". Under this scheme, the relevant government(s) would impose a tax on each form of fossil fuel (natural gas, brown coal and black coal) at the mine. The tax levied on each unit of fossil fuel would be proportional to its carbon content.

Thus, for "carbon-dirty" sources of energy, where the production of a unit of electrical energy involves a large emission of CO_2, a carbon tax would increase the variable cost of operation, while carbon clean sources such as renewables would be unaffected. This implies that, under SRMC pricing, the operation of carbon dirty sources would be curtailed in favour of carbon clean sources. For example, when a carbon-dirty source was marginal, the SRMC would be increased by the coal tax, thus encouraging carbon-clean sources such as increased end-use efficiency. Further, the operating surpluses accumulated by carbon-dirty sources would be reduced.

The revenue collected from the carbon tax should be spent on the development of carbon-clean sources, in order to encourage longer term reductions in price without incurring environmental damage. However, even if the tax revenues are removed from the industry then the carbon tax will still have the beneficial effect of reducing CO_2 emissions in the short term and encouraging investment in carbon-clean sources in the longer term.

One of the argued benefits of privatisation is that assets will be better managed because of the introduction of market forces. However, if price is set so as to reflect the marginal costs and externalities, then profit maximisation would imply socially optimal behaviour. Thus, at least in principle, publicly owned utilities can achieve operational efficiency by being assigned simple operational profit maximising objectives. Thus privatisation is, in this sense, unnecessary.

Further, maintaining the price at SRMC in an industry dominated by a small number of pri-vately owned generators would require significant regulation. Clearly a publicly owned utility would be more amenable to such regulation if properly controlled.

Social and community price rationales

A number of problems associated with the use of prices to effect social and community objectives have been identified. These mostly relate to the provision of deliberate cross-subsidies to certain groups. Some of these problems are as follows:

- it is not always clear that members of the targeted group receives the greatest benefit from a cross subsidy. Distortions in price will often deliver the largest cross subsidies to those who consume the most — often not the targeted group. Care should therefore be taken in the design of these measures;
- because the quantity of money being transferred through cross subsidies is the product of the distortion in price and the quantity involved, it is difficult to control the size of the cross subsidy; and
- it is not clear whether electricity pricing is the least social-cost vehicle for delivering benefits. For example, it might be more efficient in some cases to pay direct subsidies to targeted groups than to offer reductions in electricity prices. Those groups could then use the additional funds in a fashion that is more suited to their own needs.

An interesting alternative to using price to achieve social objectives is suggested by the arrangements for subsidies paid to remote consumers in New South Wales (Department of Minerals and Energy, NSW, 1990). For these consumers, the costs of grid connection are often prohibitively high due to the long distances of line and the small number of consumers involved. Stand-alone remote area power supply (RAPS) systems, which consists of a selection from diesel sets, batteries, wind generators and solar cells are often viable and cheaper alternatives. It is important that tariffs for grid supplied electricity reflect the true costs of supply, including grid connection costs, so that grid connection and stand-alone alternatives are treated equally. Price-based subsidies could distort these decisions.

Under the New South Wales scheme (Department of Minerals and Energy, NSW, 1990), eligible consumers could receive a subsidy for either grid connection or for a stand-alone RAPS. In the former case, consumers received a direct contribution to the costs of grid connection. If they opted for a stand-alone RAPS system, the subsidy was paid in two parts: as an annual subsidy on the operating cost of the system and as a capital contribution to the purchase cost of the system.

8.6 Price Setting Practice

The final price reaching the participant is not only the product of the *principles* which were used to establish it. Of equal importance is the *process* used to establish price, which includes:

- the relationship between the price setting agency and the rest of the industry;
- the guidelines under which that agency operates;
- the degree of openness and public accountability; and
- the degree of public involvement in the decision making of that agency.

Unfortunately, existing price setting practices within the Australian electricity industries are marked by *ad hoc* decision making leading to unsatisfactory outcomes. In many cases there have been no consistent guidelines for price setting. Prices are often held artificially low as a result of political pressure to suit short-term partisan political requirements. Prices have mostly been established by *ad hoc* committees or by the utilities themselves and there has been no attempt to establish arrangements for industry regulation by disinterested parties. The outcomes of this process have been that:

- the real opportunity costs of primary energy are often ignored;
- the effects of prices on end-use alternatives such as renewables and end-use efficiency have not been properly taken into account;
- secret deals have been done with special interest groups leaving the industry open to charges of "sweet-heart" deals;
- rate of return and cost recovery pricing principles are in widespread use with their associated accounting problems; and
- external effects such as employment, socioeconomic and environmental impacts of the electricity industry are usually not properly

accounted for.

It is interesting to contrast this situation with price setting practices within the US. While it would be foolish to view American practices as a paradigm which should be slavishly followed, there are many features which are worthy of study. The most important of these is that the price for electrical energy charged by each generating and transmission monopoly is set by an independent body, the PUC. Because many utilities in the US are privately owned the PUCs have to shadow manage these utilities with a regulatory organisations that are nearly as big as those they regulate . With a publicly owned system like Australia's this necessity would be reduced, but only if the range of institutional reforms outlined in this report are implemented to ensure there is an accumulation of independent expertise on pricing and industry issues, outside of the utilities.

Since prices for most or all generating and transmission monopolies utilities in the US are set as a rate of return on assets as described above, there arises the problem of determining which investments should be included in the rate base. This is recognised as a difficult question with significant social consequences and therefore all PUC determinations are held in public, with serious public involvement in the process. For example, financial assistance for case preparation is often made available to regular participants such as consumer rights groups, environmental groups and the representatives of large consumers.

Many benefits of public involvement in decision-making have been recognised. In the context of PUC price determinations in the US. Some of these are:

- improved technical outcomes resulting from better demand-side information and a wider ideas base;
- improved public acceptance of the outcome
- improved relationships with consumers and public interest groups;
- improved information exchange between the traditional supply-side decision makers consumers and the public process participants;
- increased participant skills and sophistication;
- opportunities for union involvement; and

- societal improvements including broader social consensus.

There are also a number of costs associated with public participation. These mostly result from the expenditure of additional time and personnel resources and a slower price setting process. The benefits of a greater level of participation in decision-making offset these disadvantages as they would if the industry in Australia was opened up to closer scrutiny and a higher level of trade union and community participation.

8.7 Price Setting and Privatisation

As discussed in Section 8.4, electricity industries exhibit a number of specific features which suggest that "free market" price setting would not lead to efficient outcomes. These include the fact that there are few technical criteria when setting a boundary between transmission and distribution. Further, breaking up systems will incur an efficiency cost and create problems of coordination. In addition, it is inappropriate to have a major participant in the industry, such as the utility, setting prices such that their own self-interest could prejudice social goals. Thus an independent authority with price setting powers is required .

One of the key arguments advanced by supporters of privatisation in the electricity industry is that the introduction of private ownership will improve the management of resources. However, it has been suggested in Section 8.5 that optimal utilisation of resources from an industry perspective can be achieved using appropriate pricing signals. Optimal operation of the supply and demand-side can be achieved by the correct combination of management objectives and pricing signals.

Further, privatisation can make price setting more difficult. The specific technical nature of the industry implies that immediate cooperation is required to maintain system integrity. Public ownership of the supply-side makes this easier to achieve and also reduces the cost of regulation of price.

8.8 Conclusion

In this chapter, it has been argued that price is a key determinant of the evolution of the electricity industry, particularly with respect to the balance between supply and demand-side options. From an environmental perspective, two very important demand-side options are energy conservation and end-use efficiency.

In order for participants to make appropriate choices, the price level should contain the correct economic and environmental signals. The encouragement of environmentally benign cost effective alternatives is particularly important.

A number of significant problems were identified with current price setting practices in Australia. Chief amongst these are the absence of generally applicable guidelines, and the low level of trade union and community involvement. Good quality price setting outcomes can only be expected to flow from consistent pricing rules administered openly and with public participation and accountability .

A key conclusion is that if price is set appropriately, effective utilisation of assets will occur. This does not depend in any way on privatisation. In particular, if price is set so as to include all avoided costs, then profit maximisation implies socially optimal behaviour. However, the particular nature of the electricity industry implies that significant regulation is required, and the need for regulation is likely to be much greater if the industry is privatised.

Notes

1. A generic term used in this chapter referring to the state body which regulates investor owned utilities. Actual names vary from State to State and include Public Utility Commission, Public Service Commission and Department of Public Utilities.

CHAPTER 9

POWERING THE PUBLIC SECTOR: THE INSTITUTIONS

9.1 Introduction

The recent history of public administration in Australia is characterised by the re-emergence of the demand that public bodies involved with the delivery of goods and services be managed more effectively. The common policy implication of this demand emerges in recommendations that the structure and operations of public authorities either emulate the structure and operations of private sector companies, or that they be privatised. Both these policy prescriptions are now fundamentally changing the electricity industry, and for that reason it is important that these demands be examined so as to assess their relevance and usefulness.

In this chapter we place the institutional arrangements for statutory authorities in their historical and parliamentary context. We show that the claims made for the "reforms" which are being made to statutory authorities are shown to be unrealistic, in both economic efficiency and accountability terms. In Chapter 10, we go on to examine how these reforms have been put into practice. We also raise some important issues concerning privatisation.

9.2 Why Examine Statutory Authorities in General

Throughout Australia, electricity generation, transmission and distribution are the responsibility of statutory authorities.[1] Statutory authorities are peculiar organisations so it is worthwhile considering the origins of statutory authorities *in general* in Westminster-style Parliamentary democracies. Only by doing this can general principles relating to the management and accountability of these public sector bodies be developed. These general principles apply to the electricity authorities as much as to any other statutory authority.

The statutory authorities with which we are particularly concerned manage public sector assets i.e. assets owned, finally, by the citizens of the Commonwealth, State or Territory (Burt, 1989; Commonwealth Parliamentary Accounts Committee, 1989, p.102), or perform other functions of government (e.g. regulation, marketing, etc). The expansion in the number of administrative law bodies (for example, the Administrative Appeals Tribunal) has resulted in some statutory authorities having an adjudicating function.

While some commentators have drawn a distinction between the statutory trading *corporation*, and other statutory authorities, this distinction is rejected in this chapter for the following institutional reasons. First, the overwhelming majority of statutory authorities are required to report to Parliament, as specified in Annual Report Acts and similar legislation. Though the specific details of the structure and content of this report may vary, it nevertheless remains the means by which legislatures are acquainted with the activities of the authority.

Second, with very few exceptions, statutory authorities' financial dealings are controlled by the terms of Acts, sometimes known as Public Finance and Audit Acts (though other titles are also employed) and their audits are usually carried out by the relevant Auditor-General or that officer's agent. Recently, there have been moves away from this requirement, though considerable opposition has been voiced by Public Accounts Committees in various States, the Commonwealth and elsewhere in the Asia/Pacific region.

But what is meant by the term statutory authority? Put simply, a statutory authority is a public sector organisation established by a specific Act of Parliament. On this definition, central banking, State Government insurance activities, some parts of the transport sector, and telecommunications, among many others, are all operated by statutory authorities. A department, on the other hand, does not require legislation to be created or destroyed. Nevertheless, it should be emphasised that even this definition has some deficiencies due to the confusion that has resulted from centuries of development in the Westminster system (see Wettenhall, 1986, for an indication of the definitional difficulties).[2]

In respect of the position of the statutory authority in a Westminster-style Parliamentary system, Lewis makes the following statement:

> The existence of statutory authorities such as the Reserve Bank presents the student of the Australian Constitution with something of a paradox. Statutory authorities are commonly formed out of a belief that certain objectives of government are better pursued free from direct political interference and accordingly are usually invested with a greater or lesser degree of autonomy.
>
> And yet the Australian Constitution is said to be one in which the conventions of responsible government form an integral part (notwithstanding the fact that the Constitution itself contains no express reference to them).
>
> Within the Westminster model, the term 'responsible government' has always assumed that the accountability of government is achieved through ministers to the representatives of the people in Parliament. The model is deceptively simple.
>
> Plainly the exercise of government functions by statutory authorities tests the internal consistency of such a model.

As Archer observes:

> The theory of responsible government was never an accurate explanation of British political life. It was an idealised picture of British politics which was passed into the twentieth century as constitutional mythology (Lewis, 1987, pp.348–349)

Lewis goes on to conclude that the development of the public statutory corporation in particular "... is further evidence of a functional breakdown in the Westminster model" (Lewis, 1987, p.350).[3]

History of statutory authorities

It will probably come as a surprise to many that the statutory authority has an older history than the ministerial department; and that the recent move towards the establishment of statutory authorities rather than departments was pioneered in Australia in the second half of the nineteenth century. As Wettenhall points out "... Australia innovated dramatically in the 1880s when it transformed the management of its state railway enterprises" (Wettenhall, 1990, p.14; Wettenhall, 1985).

Earlier this century, Beatrice and Sidney Webb documented the emergence of statutory authorities in England, and the principles that governed this development are illustrative of many of the principles on which we still rely.[4] They sum up the twin development of statutory authorities, and the development of government departments in the following words:

> Prior to 1689, indeed, the innovations of Parliament in Local Government had been few and far between, and more by way of prescribing new functions than in materially altering either the constitution of Manor or Parish, Borough or County, or their ancient authority. But at the close of the seventeenth and throughout the eighteenth century we find, as we have described, ever-increasing crowds of innovating statutes. As the century wore to its close, Act after Act, of a character at once unusual, imposed general rules and wide-reaching prohibitions upon all the Parishes in respect of their relief of the poor, upon all the Turnpike Trusts in their maintenance of the roads, upon all the courts of Quarter Sessions in their upkeep of the bridges and their management of the Houses of Correction and County Gaols.
>
> But it was in the nineteenth century, and particularly in its second, third and fourth decades, that this tendency for Parliament to prescribe, by statute, general rules in supersession of Local Custom and the Common Law for all the Local Authorities from one end of England to the other, became a regular habit.
>
> The gradual development of general statute law, introducing a measure of uniformity in the several branches of Local Government, was accompanied by a still more gradual and

tentative development of the authority of the
National Executive, with regard to one
function after another, taking eventually the
form of the establishment of specialised
Government Departments of supervision
and control (Webb, 1922, pp.458–459).[5]
Australian statutory trading authorities' structures and responsibilities can be traced back to
the Australian railway corporations (Goldring
and Wettenhall, 1980, p. 136), and the importance of the statutory authority in the history of
the Australian public sector can be seen in the
following:
  Today we are inclined to think of the ministerial department as the orthodox form of
  central administration, yet the 'mushroom
  growth' of the modern public enterprise
  boards and commissions (the statutory authorities, public corporations, or semi-gov-
  ernment bodies) has accounted for about
  three-quarters of all employees of Australian
  State governments (Wettenhall, 1963,
  pp.255–256).
Yet, despite the broad range of functions performed by statutory authorities "there appears
to be no consistent rationale applied in deciding
to place a particular function in the hands of a
statutory authority over other organs of public
administration" (Lewis, 1987, p.351).
  Such lack of consistency can be seen in the case
of government transport responsibilities in New
South Wales in the inter-war years, and summarised by Wettenhall in relation to transport:
  (Premier Lang had established an integrated
  Ministry of Transport. In 1932)…when
  Lang's short-lived integrated Ministry of
  Transport was broken up. Bruxner's Transport (Division of Functions) Act
  re-established the separate transport authorities — Railways, Road Transport and
  Tramways, Main Roads — but retained a
  coordinating public service secretariat to aid
  the minister in exercising his supervisory
  duties over them. The legislation retained
  the term 'Ministry of Transport' to denote
  the whole composite organisation — minister, secretariat, and autonomous operating
  authorities. But the colloquial language of
  public administration soon came to apply the
  term in a more restrictive context i.e. to denote only the ministerial secretariat [staffed

from] within the public service.
  More recently, this practice has extended to
Victoria (e.g. in Transport and in Fuel and
Power) (Wettenhall, 1986, p.13).
  This experience of statutory authorities coming and going, change in names (of the
organisations and their officers), and changes in
responsibilities and ministries is common to the
history of every Australian State and the Commonwealth.
  It should not be considered that the fact that
elected representatives may sit on the board of a
statutory authority differentiates it from the
more usual statutory authorities which have appointed officials. The County Councils in New
South Wales are statutory authorities responsible
for electricity distribution and other activities
(such as abattoirs) which have elected
alderpeople on their boards.
  We would also include as another type of
statutory authority the "company established by
legislation" such as the British East India Company and the Australian Gas Light Company.
These companies were established by legislation,
but their capital was provided by private investors.
Because they were established by legislation, the
government retained certain rights over them,
though this was often vigorously opposed (see,
for instance, Sutherland, 1952). The most recent
case of an Australian government exercising
control over a company established by legislation
occurred as recently as the 1980s in the case of
the Australian Gas Light Company in New South
Wales. In that case, the majority shareholder was
precluded from exercising the voting rights that
such a shareholding would normally have given
him. The government argued that it was inappropriate that any single shareholder should be
granted power over such a basic energy industry.
  The dissolution of these quasi-private companies resulted in one or other form of public
sector institution, illustrating again the arbitrary
nature of the nomenclature and organisational
form of many statutory authorities. Governments
could establish, from such a company, a public
sector owned company, a statutory authority, a
government department or a new set of responsibilities for an existing public sector body.
For example, a completely new responsibility
devolved to one of the British Secretaries of State
in 1858 when the British East India Company was

dissolved (Maitland, 1968, p.411).

Conversely, the transfer of ownership from the private sector to the public sector can result in one or other form of public ownership: the South Australian Electric Company was converted to the Electricity Trust of South Australia; the Balmain Power Company was made part of the Electricity Commission of New South Wales; and Qantas is a 100 per cent government owned company.

Statutory authorities can also be converted to government departments (for example, the New South Wales Water Resources Commission was converted to the Department of Water Resources); and departments can be converted to statutory authorities (for example, the Australian Trade Commission was formed out of a number of Divisions of the Department of Trade).

9.3 Managerial Autonomy

Lewis' understanding of the reasons for the creation of statutory authorities is benign. They are, he says, "... created out of a recognition that the restrictions imposed by the normal departmental structure make it unsuitable for some government functions" (Lewis, 1987, p.351). Similarly, and more specifically, Kewley included the following reasons:

- the technical legal advantages of an entity empowered and capable of suing and being sued, of having perpetual succession and owning and controlling property;
- freedom from party politics;
- the ability to place experts and professionals on the boards, rather than reliance on public servants; and
- the use of commercial accounting practices (Kewley, 1957, p.4).

Despite these stated advantages of the statutory authority form over the departmental form, it is interesting to observe that:

> While appreciating the technical legal convenience of the statutory corporation, trade union and labour leaders developed a suspicion of the theory of collectivist activities beyond 'political' interference... Hence consistent advocacy of the statutory corporation has tended to become an aspect of conservative parties in Australia (Sawer (1954) quoted in Kewley, 1957, p.7).

It would appear that it is the emulation of the private sector forms that appeals to conservatives. We should also recognise that the marketing authorities which were formed to provide income support and market stabilisation for agricultural and pastoral producers were also statutory authorities. There is clearly a degree of self-interest in some of the (traditional) conservative advocacy for statutory authorities in Australia.

Notwithstanding this traditional reluctance on the part of labour/Labor to embrace the creation of statutory authorities, the Chifley Government made considerable use of them, and the Whitlam Labor Government of 1972–75 dramatically altered the landscape of the Australian public sector. For instance, Telecom and Australia Post were created out of the single Postmaster General's Department (PMG); and Medibank was a strictly "Whitlamesque" body.

Where the actual (as opposed to stated) reason for the creation of a statutory authority is often little more than to place the government at arm's length from painful decisions, the traditional labour/Labor concerns are seen to be both understandable and defensible. The so-called independence of the Reserve Bank, the State Electricity Commission of Victoria (Watson, 1990), and the State Insurance Corporation of Western Australia (Evatt, 1989) are cases in point.

It is this realisation that has led to calls for accountability on the part of statutory authority managers, or as Goldring and Wettenhall put it:

> ...because statutory authorities are essentially public, there is a demand that they should be accountable and responsible to the public, or to its representatives in Parliament, for their activities. There is also a recognition that the policies and activities of most statutory authorities are, in a real sense, political (Goldring and Wettenhall, 1980, p.136).

So while governments claim that statutory authorities are created in order to reduce their own involvement in the activities of these authorities, demands for accountability, combined with a realisation that governments can create or destroy statutory authorities at will, have necessarily meant that governments determine the degree to which the operations of a statutory authority will in fact be autonomous.

But, as we show later, this involvement by government should not be considered as unarguably indefensible. Bodies such as the Industries Commission (and its predecessor, the Industries Assistance Commission) fail to realise the nexus between citizens' ownership and their right to expect their elected representatives to safeguard both the assets and the services delivered by authorities.

In fact, statutory authority managers in many aspects of their operation still remain largely controlled by the Parliamentary system, and hence by the exercise of political power by governments and, in some cases, minorities or independents in Upper Houses.[6] The following is a short list of government decisions which illustrates this point:

- the transfer of the 132kV lines from the Electricity Commission of New South Wales to the County Councils;
- the sale of Electricity Commission coal mines in New South Wales;
- the application of the Public Finance and Audit Act to the financial undertakings of statutory authorities and departments alike;
- the responsibility of the authority managements to appear in front of Parliamentary Accounts Committee; and
- most significantly, the Loan Council disciplines on the borrowings of many statutory authorities.[7]

Based on the failure to understand citizens' legitimate expectation that their representatives will oversight the management of public sector bodies, there have recently been renewed calls for managerial autonomy in the public sector:

> A new slogan gained currency in 1988 (in New South Wales) as the old one was discredited. It began as 'managerial authority' in official reports, but was translated to 'downstream autonomy' by middle managers who read some of the more trendy business journals. It was meant to reflect Greiner's philosophy of letting managers at all levels get on with the job, with minimum interference from above (or 'upstream'). The Premier began by abolishing the Public Service Board and giving department heads the power to create or abolish jobs, and to recruit their own staff (Moore, 1990, p.21).

These calls have their origins in various conservative economic analyses, to which we return

in Chapter 10, and which are also discussed in Chapter 11.

And with this trend towards managerial autonomy has come the re-emergence of the demand for statutory authorities to be managed by professional business-oriented personnel, and for the public sector as a whole to be managed cost-effectively. The implications of these developments are dealt with in the following sections.[8]

The implications of managerial autonomy

In a 1990 article Yeatman detailed the differences between two models of public sector management:

> It is important to appreciate that the cost-effective achievement of outcomes is logically distinct from the generic features of management for results. An emphasis on outcomes or results can encourage consultation with citizen users of public services to determine what results and outcomes they want.
>
> Cost-effective achievement of outcomes is an economistic orientation to outcomes guided by the interest of the executive levels of government in the rationing of scarce public resources at a time when those levels of government have accepted the radical liberal agendas of small government, economic rationalism and deregulation. It is an orientation to outcomes which de-authorises the participation of citizens as individual and community users in the planning and evaluation of services. Such participation is not cost effective.
>
> In the ethos of cost-effective management for results, management prerogatives are fully reinstated within public bureaucracies to enable executive rationing of public resources with minimum input from lower and middle ranks of public servants as well as of citizens (Yeatman, 1990b, p.16).

In an interesting re-emergence of traditional conservative values, one of the characteristics of the trend towards cost-effective management is that managers are placed in statutory authorities in order to run them as businesses and their service role is devalued.

Or, as Yeatman has expressed it:

> ... public servants who are committed to the contemporary public service value of in-

volving citizens in the planning of services discover they cannot deliver on this value at the present time (Yeatman, 1990b, p.20).

One of the characteristics of this trend is that accountability is reinterpreted to mean, predominantly, accountability for financial management, not accountability for the quality or extent of service provision. This re-emphasis occurs despite the establishment of performance criteria which purport to ensure that the authorities meet the stated social/equity goals of the government:

> Performance control is designed to meet taxpayers' expectations of value for money — in its directing of resources to objectives, in its spotlighting and trimming of slack in the governmental production process, in its enhancing of managerial flexibility to deploy resources efficiently, and in its clarification of public sector functions. To the extent that the only relevant inputs are economic ones, it can promote public sector efficiency, effectiveness and quality.

> But to the extent that the manager also requires political consent to do his/her job... then performance control fails to acknowledge and provide guidance for a large portion of the public sector production process. It is true that it acknowledges the nature of government outputs, but it does not recognise the nature and role of a significant stream of public sector inputs or conversion processes.

> This is like trying to drive a coach pulled by a pair of horses but only focusing attention (such as carrots and sticks) on one of the horses (the economic resource), while ignoring the other horse (the political resource) (Alford, 1989).

While it is, of course, necessary to have confidence in the financial operations of statutory authorities, there must also be a recognition of the *legitimacy* of other goals, a legitimacy which many overlook. The Industry Commission, for example, has stated:

> ... utilities' objectives should relate solely to commercial performance. Each utility should be required to supply electricity or gas... in the most economically efficient manner. This would overcome difficulties caused by current requirements to under-

take non-commercial functions. A simply stated commercial objective would also avoid problems in accountability and performance monitoring which can result from multiple and ill-defined objectives (Industry Commission, 1991, Vol. 1, p.4)

Suggesting, as the Industry Commission does, that non-commercial objectives can be met through the setting of Community Service Obligations, glosses over the difficulties inherent in the application of this concept (see Chapter 10).

9.4 Recent Trends

The term "interference" is now used perjoratively to describe the involvement by governments, such as we have listed above, in the operations of statutory authorities. However, despite historical precedents to the current demands for less political "interference", there is now a radically different solution posited.

That solution is summarised in the term "corporatisation". There is a great deal of confusion about the precise definition of corporatisation and, incidentally, privatisation. The terms are generally used as part of "political" debate (either by politicians or other professionals seeking to market consultancy services) and as such they are often used emotively or persuasively. For example, a paper published by the Australian Society of Accountants (1989) noted:

> ...the terms "privatisation" and "corporatisation" carry with them implicit views about the deficiencies of public sector performance (p.1).[9]

To the anonymous author of the Australian Society's discussion paper, "corporatisation" meant "to re-organize a government enterprise so that as far as possible it emulates private sector behaviour" (p.1). To those who recall the recent history of companies such as Ariadne, Bond, Bell, Budget, Duke, Elders, Entity, Girvan, General Investments, Hookers, Quadrax, Qintex, Rothwells, Spedley, Tricontinental and Westmex, that statement seems, at best, somewhat imprecise. Some aspects of private-sector behaviour might well be left unemulated.

In current usage, the term "corporatisation" seems to assume differing meanings in different contexts:

- the restructuring of a public-sector body so

as to change the way ministerial responsibility is exercised;

- changes in the legal form with which certain public sector activities are undertaken — so as to free those organisations from certain of the restrictions imposed elsewhere within the public service;
- the restructuring of some statutory authorities as "companies" in terms of the Companies Act or State Companies Codes, or (after 1991) the Commonwealth Corporations Law — or (in the case of NSW) in terms of the 1989 State Owned Corporations Act;
- the specification by governments (either through statutory amendments, or by formal directives) that the overriding objective of a government-owned enterprise is to make a profit, or to "maximise" the net worth of the enterprise; or
- some combination of the above features.

The foregoing comments may indicate that the term "corporatisation" evokes a conceptual quagmire. Plainly these usages overlap — so that "corporatisation" does always involve major differences from existing arrangements. For example, statutory authorities are already "corporations" or "bodies corporate", being established by statute and having certain formally-stated objectives. As noted above, statutory authorities share many of the features of companies formed by a process of registration under companies or corporations legislation: they have the capacity to enter into contracts in their own name, they may sue or be sued, and they have an unlimited life. Legislation creating statutory authorities may require adherence to reporting procedures which are similar to those adopted by ordinary companies; some statutory authorities may be required to be profit-seeking.

To some "corporatisation" may be seen as substituting traditional notions that a minister is "responsible" for the conduct of statutory authorities, with a new view: that the conduct of a statutory authority is the responsibility of the statutory authority's board, while the minister's role is simply to appoint or remove members of that board. Again, governments do not need to "restructure" enterprises in the form of incorporated companies in order to claim that a minister is insulated from responsibility for the conduct of a statutory authority.

In any event, disclaimers of ministerial responsibility, and claims that the boards of corporatised entities bears full responsibility for the conduct of those enterprises, are of doubtful effectiveness. Plainly if they were effective, the community (and governments themselves) would be prepared to accept those claims. Recent experience suggests otherwise; for example, after the disastrous losses of the Victorian Economic Development Corporation, the State Bank of Victoria, and the bank's subsidiary Tricontinental, the Victorian government's response was to secure the resignation of directors and to reshuffle ministerial portfolios.

"Corporatisation" may involve a change in the *status* of a body — from "statutory authority" to a company which is formed in terms of the Companies Act or Codes (or, more recently, the commonwealth Corporations Law). Such companies may have far broader powers than a statutory authority: for example, modern companies are virtually unconstrained by statements of objectives. Whereas government departments must operate within the limits of the resources appropriated to them by parliament, a government-owned company may be free of any such legal constraints.

Indeed, a company which is effectively owned by a department will have greater legal powers than its parent. That means, for example, that a company would have the power to make loans to its directors or employees, to acquire major assets from friends or relatives of management without resort to tender processes, or to acquire houses, cars and aeroplanes for the use of executives. In the absence of any formal legal code of conduct for government-owned companies, the only restraints on such potentially opportunistic behaviour will come from agreements negotiated privately between ministers, departments and the boards of these government-owned companies.

The main significance of the use of incorporated companies to conduct government activities may be that corporatisation (in this sense) liberalises the rules which affect the conduct of public-sector managers. Corporatisation may remove restrictions on the level of salaries and other emoluments payable to senior managers, or establish a second set of salary scales and employment conditions, in parallel with those being applied elsewhere in the public service. Managers may be permitted to engage independent legal advice, rather than use the services of the attorney-general's department. For some enterprises, the removal of red tape may enable them to maintain greater operational flexibility.

On the other hand, as noted by the Senate Standing Committee on Finance and Public Administration (1989, ch. 4) it would be possible to reduce or modify operational controls on existing government organisations, without restructuring them as companies.

There is clearly a continuum of meanings to the term corporatisation. At one end are those changes which have previously been described as commercialisation at the other are the extreme versions such as the restructuring of statutory authorities operating under the accountability provisions of the companies code or its equivalent (Thynne, 1990).

Illustrative of this latter form of corporatisation is the situation in the New where the government has used the State Owned Corporations Act, and related Acts to achieve corporatisation of particular authorities.[10] This orientation by the New South Wales government was reiterated in its submission to the current Industry Commission's Inquiry into Energy Generation and Distribution:

> It is believed that the greatest efficiency improvements in the generation, transmission and distribution of electricity and gas will be gained by the introduction of reforms which would lead towards free market arrangements.
>
> In respect of the electricity industry, the New South Wales government is moving towards the introduction of free market arrangements through a phased approach to industry reform. The decision has been made to corporatise the Electricity Commission of New South Wales by the end of this financial year... (New South Wales Government, 1990, pp.ES3–4)

The New South Wales government has summarised the expected advantages of corporatisation in the following way:

> Corporatisation, as espoused in New South Wales, focuses on making Government Trading Enterprises operate on a commercial basis.
>
> • Business decisions, including investment decisions, cost reduction efforts and pricing, can be made without undue influence from special interest groups.
>
> • Management compensation structures can be developed to focus attention on the controllable factors that influence organisational performance.
>
> • Trading among corporatised entities can be on a much freer basis than among government instrumentalities.

In the specific case of the Electricity Supply Industry (ESI), corporatisation has the potential to obtain some important benefits:

> • Corporatised State entities, freed of political influence and intervention, may be able to develop a joint planning mechanism to develop an co-ordinated system on a multi-state basis
>
> • Under corporatisation, there will be a strong motivation to select the best new source of generation, regardless of supplier, based on rate of return targets and more flexible commercial arrangements.
>
> Corporatisation would permit joint ventures with outside suppliers, which are specifically prohibited as a government instrumentality (New South Wales Government, 1990, Vol. 1 pp.19–20).[11]

In respect of the point made regarding the ability to enter into joint ventures, the New South Wales government has clearly "forgotten" that the Commonwealth's Superannuation Fund Investment Trust and the Australian Industry Development Corporation (a McMahon-McEwen creation) entered into joint ventures.[12]

The State Electricity Commission of Victoria has also made the following statement regarding the advantages of corporatisation:

> The corporatisation model is favoured as the next step because it makes management more responsible for achieving clear goals and objectives by operating in a well defined business environment (SECV, 1990, p.9).

It is possible that the Victorian government does, in fact, mean commercialisation: the New South Wales government is not alone in advocating ill-defined and misunderstood "reforms".

The Industry Commission is as strongly committed to the concept of competitive pressure and private sector operations as a means of ensuring that the most efficient outcomes are achieved as the NSW government. This shared perspective is particularly obvious in the Commission's view that:

> ... administrative changes can be viewed largely as an attempt to replicate the pressures to minimise costs experienced by enterprises operating within a competitive market (Industry Commission, 1990, p.10).

In summary, we have noted that statutory authorities exist within the political realm; and we have also referred to the traditional concerns of the labour movement with attempts to remove such decision-making from the political arena. The recent experience of the operations of statutory authorities which have been "freed" from direct political control (in Victoria, New South Wales, Western Australia and South Australia) indicates that this so-called "freedom" operates against the best interests of citizens and governments. It is to this matter of accountability that we now turn.

9.5 Implications of Corporatisation for Accountability

The issue of accountability for statutory authorities has been exercising the minds of public sector analysts for a considerable time (Wettenhall, 1985), and in variety of nations (Rosas, 1988, p.35). Recently, Ian Thynne from the Institute of Southeast Asian Studies in Singapore noted:

> The issue of the appropriate balance between autonomy and control is fundamental to the structure and operation of public enterprises in most countries of the world. On the one hand, for instance, their relationship with members of the community is the discharge of their commercial responsibilities is usually expected to be that of "producer" and consumer" or "producer and client", rather than that which is more readily associated with the notions of "provider and recipient" or, very generally, "governor and governed" and "state and subject"; while, on the other hand they do, after all, exist within, rather than beyond, a governmental system and therefore are rightly subject to some form of political control as a means, among other things, of ensuring

their accountability to the public at large (Thynne, 1990, p.5).

If government business enterprises are to be given the objective of earning a "profit" or a "target rate of return", then social or community objectives may be disregarded or devalued.[13] One such argument was recently outlined by the Industry Commission (1991):

> Even after corporatisation, public enterprises would remain untouched by a number of market disciplines which automatically apply to incorporated private enterprises:
> - the ability of private shareholders to trade in the equity capital of the enterprise;
> - the requirement to compete for debt capital on commercial terms;
> - the exposure of investment and/or borrowing programs to continual monitoring by the capital and share markets;
> - the sanctions of takeover or merger for inferior performance arising from, say, the under-utilisation of capital; and
> - the risk of insolvency (Industry Commission, 1991, pp. 129–20).

Yet traditional claims about the "discipline" of the market on private-sector enterprises are not based on realistic assumptions. First, only some private-sector enterprises have their securities publicly traded. Second, of those entities whose securities are publicly traded, many are "controlled" through the shareholdings of the entrepreneurs who formed those companies or had them floated on the stock exchange — so that owner-managers may not be subject to the threat of dismissal or takeover. Third, and more importantly, traditional arguments about the effectiveness of market discipline generally assume that the information being provided to securities markets is extensive, and of high quality.

In practice:
- managers may engage in "creative accounting" to create an illusion of profitability and financial strength. Consider, for example, the way Bond Corporation and Ariadne reported profits on the sale of assets in transactions which were only "contingent" since the purchaser was entitled to exercise "put" options;
- investment and borrowing activities are not effectively monitored by the stock market,

since listed entities do not provide continuous disclosures about their borrowing and investment activities. Consider, for example, the fact that loans of around $875 million made by Weeks Petroleum to Bell Resources, and loans of around $1.2 billion from Bell Resources to Bond Corporation, were not disclosed to shareholders at the time they were made, and were only revealed much later with the publication of annual financial reports. Consider also, the failure of the accounts of Trustees Executors and Agency Co Ltd, Pyramid Building Society or Estate Mortgage to reveal that a substantial proportion of their "mortgage loans" related to unfinished, speculative property developments; and

• investment and borrowing activities are not always effectively monitored by lenders, who may be impeded by (for example) the widespread use of "trusts" and other off-balance sheet borrowing arrangements.

Nor have corporate business practices been consistent with so-called "market discipline":

• the incidence of takeovers is closely correlated with changes in the stock-market index, with more takeovers occurring during bull than during bear markets. Under these circumstances, entrepreneurs may be able to acquire enterprises at prices which are inflated, relative to prospective earnings. Consider, for example, the outcome of recent takeovers in the radio and television industry. Under these circumstances, bidders have been able to acquire businesses at excessive prices through "paper" share issues or through borrowings which they were unable to service;

• while insolvent trading may expose directors to prosecution if they continue to trade when a company is unable to pay its debts as and when they fall due, the evidence suggests that this "discipline" is often ineffective, since many companies continue to fail without being able to pay creditors even 50 cents in the dollar — yet the directors of those companies have not been prosecuted for insolvent trading; and

• the "insolvent trading" provisions of companies legislation have been of such doubtful effectiveness that the Australian Law Reform Commission has recommended that they be entirely restructured. Even so, one commentator has suggested that the proposed reforms perpetuate both procedural and substantive obstacles to creditors seeking to invoke those provisions to place a company in liquidation, and are flawed since directors of insolvent companies can continue to incur liabilities to creditors other than trade creditors "with impunity" (Herzberg, 1991, pp.3–4).

Claims about the efficacy of "market discipline" often imply that there are no equivalent disciplines operating in the public sector. Yet the mechanisms for external review of management practices are stronger in the public sector than in the private sector.

For example, unlike their counterparts in the private sector, public sector auditors may report publicly about weaknesses in internal controls. Most Auditors-General now adopt the practice of reviewing aspects of managerial performance in selected auditees, and reporting their findings publicly. In recent years the activities of Public Accounts Committees have provided another avenue for external review of managerial performance, and often undertake reviews of management practices within individual departments, or of particular activities within a cross-section of government organisations.

In addition to these arrangements for external audit and review, most governments engage internal management review teams (located in central agencies, such as a Department of Treasury, Department of Finance or a Premiers' Department). Those teams review the operations of units or programmes which are thought to be not operating efficiently or effectively. Further, individual governments have adopted policies regarding the engagement of internal auditors; even Queensland, which has been tardy in this regard, is now addressing the need for greater commitment to the use of internal auditors (Electoral and Administrative Review Commission, 1990). Moreover, arrangements for permanent internal audit within government organisations may be established under the oversight of a central agency (see, e.g. Victorian Department of Management and Budget, 1987; NSW Treasury, 1990a), and be subject to periodical review by a Public Accounts Committee (see, e.g. JCPA, 1989) or an auditor-general (see, for example, Australian National Audit Office, 1990).

One suspects that the authors of documents promoting the merits of exposing public-sector organisations to "the discipline of the market" have neither looked critically at the operations of business in the private sector, nor have much awareness of the range and scope of arrangements now adopted to ensure the accountability of public sector managers Indeed, many of these arrangements have been established or upgraded within the past decade. Unfortunately, the reports of auditors-general and public accounts committees attract less media attention and analysis than they deserve — and this contributes to a lack of awareness of the nature of the arrangements established to make public sector managers accountable in a number of ways to a range of parties.

That is not to suggest that accountability arrangements within the public sector are universally effective. Some of the most vocal advocates of strengthened accountability relationships may be found within Public Accounts Committees; yet if promoted to ministerial office, they develop new perspectives. Governments may seek to restrict opportunities for politically-damaging revelations by limiting the funding of office of auditors-general, or of parliamentary committees.

However it is important to note that there are significant differences between the accountability arrangements adopted for departments, statutory authorities, and government-owned companies or joint ventures. *Indeed, the wider use of the corporate form as a vehicle for conducting the business of government can be expected to weaken arrangements for accountability within the public sector.*

There may be those who read these remarks with some scepticism, in the light of the financial disasters which have recently engulfed some major government-owned organisations: the Victorian Economic Development Corporation, the State Bank of Victoria and its subsidiary Tricontinental, and West Australia's State Government Insurance Corporation. Hence the point should be made at the outset that those organisations were operating outside (or on the fringes of) the network of accountability arrangements adopted for most public sector organisations. They were operating under independent "boards", and their affairs were subject to a limited form of audit by private-sector auditors, rather than the wider scope of auditing conducted by the auditor-general. Those bodies had, in several senses of the term, been "corporatised".

At root, the trend towards corporatisation (particularly of the most extreme form) is based on the confusion which exists between *financial accountability*, such as is provided (however inadequately) through the relevant sections of the companies code (or their equivalent), and the necessary *political and social accountability* expected of authorities in a Westminster-style parliamentary democracy. Put simply, decisions regarding the proper legal or constitutional form for public authorities should a take account of their special situation arising from their public ownership.

As the Western Australian Burt Commission expressed it:

> The Commission is of the opinion that there is a fundamental difference between the ideas of accountability and of public scrutiny when applied to the investment activities of individuals, partnerships and companies incorporated under the Companies Code on the one hand, and the investment activities of government agencies on the other (Burt Commission, 1989, p.15).

In this respect, it is instructive to consider the findings, in 1989, of the Senate Standing Committee on Finance and Public Administration (SSCFGPA) which had conducted a study of companies in the federal sphere . The Committee's references include "... the continuing oversight of the establishment, operation, administration and accountability of bodies established pursuant to Commonwealth Statute...". This includes the non-departmental area of public administration (Coates, 1990, p.7).

The Committee found the following:

- that many departments did not understand that companies in which they had an interest were subject to Parliamentary scrutiny. The Committee therefore recommended that a register of all companies in which the Commonwealth has an interest should be established;
- that the procedures covering the involve-

ment of the Commonwealth in companies was confused, and that the requirement for Government Business Enterprises (GBEs) to table information relating to the establishment of subsidiaries be tabled in Parliament was never practiced! (Coates, 1990, p.9);

- that "... ministers, acting through their departments, can apparently form, participate in and even dispose of companies in the ordinary exercise of the executive powers. They need not inform Parliament nor table annual reports (Coates, 1990, p.9);
- "... that, as is already a requirement for public and private sector companies, all statutory authorities should present consolidated annual accounts incorporating all subsidiary companies" (Coates, 1990, p.10); and
- "... all government companies should be required to conform to the reporting requirements of statutory authorities as well as meeting those of the Companies Code for listed public companies, and all such reports should be required to be tabled in Parliament. We do not believe that this would place an unduly heavy burden on government companies. **But, even if it did, the principle of responsibility to Parliament demands it be done**" (Coates, 1990, p.10; emphasis added).

Coates' personal conclusion was that he:

...could see no advantage in the use of the company form over statutory authority structure and considered that its use is likely to complicate, and probably reduce, accountability in practice. Reputable observers, including significant sections of the accounting profession, share this concern. No substantial official justification has been offered for the trend towards incorporation... (Coates, 1990, p.9).

These are significant findings, and all governments (State and Federal) and public sector managers should be aware of them as the demands for "reform" via incorporation of public sector institutions gathers pace.

Put another way, decisions made which are targeted to improve an authority's business orientation or management structure must take into account the particular characteristics of statutory authorities, embodying as they do the community's ownership of considerable assets.

9.6 An International Perspective

The trends we see in the development of strategies such as corporatisation are premised on attempts to minimise "interference" by governments and replace political accountability with a limited managerial accountability (in the sense that it is solely concerned with financial results). These trends are not isolated to Australia: similar developments are evident in many of the advanced parliamentary democracies. In fact, such developments are common enough for theories to have been developed concerning the political consequences of such actions. One such theorist is Claus Offe, and it is instructive to consider his conclusions regarding the sorts of changes which have been occurring in the developed world.

Offe suggests that laws — made in the political sphere — which retain their applicability because of their interpretation in the administrative sphere are inadequate as a guide to the political legitimacy of administrative action (Offe, 1985). It is as if administrative action legitimises itself because it is administrative action. The law in this situation can have only limited power over the administrator. This can create as many problems in the *explicitly* political arena (the legislature, government, executive and ministry) as well as the *implicitly* political arena (the administration). To see how this problem could arise, consider the following hypothetical example.

A government decides that each major government authority is to be responsible for its own purchasing, and that each of the purchasing sections thus established is required to ensure that the lowest prices and highest quality goods and services are procured. At the same time, the government decides (administratively) that its purchasing agents are also to purchase, wherever possible and under certain conditions, goods and services produced in the domestic economy. It is clear that in some cases these goals will conflict.

The day-to-day resolution of any conflict rests with the administrators as those responsible for the application of policy, but the ultimate responsibility lies with the government for the formulation of policy. However, it becomes possible for both groups to evade responsibility for any unpopular decision by reference to the power of the other! The apparent self-interest of both the administrators and the government lies in maintaining a "polite silence" about the problems which the application of these two policies may create. Accountability is compromised in the interests of goal-oriented decision making and the abrogation of ultimate responsibility by the explicitly political arena.

More generally, Offe goes on to summarise his thesis in the following terms:

> On the first level, the administrative process is tied to legal rules as its standard of "correctness"; all that administrators are supposed to do is act in conformity with politically pre-established formal-legal rules. This model of action may be rational in the Weberian sense, but it is hardly rational in the functional sense, according to which the administration must respond to concrete needs and requirements of the larger society (and not just to the will of its political "master"). On the *second* level, therefore, the test of *functional effectiveness* underlies administrative action. The direction of the conversion process is reversed, and the problem of the administration henceforth becomes that of choosing and extracting *adequate* legal, organisational, and personnel resources and action premises. The dividing line between "administration" and "politics" disintegrates, since parliamentary bodies as well as the political heads of ministries have themselves become dependent on the administration and respond to its needs rather than guiding, directing and controlling it. By partly reversing the authoritative relationship between "politics" and "administration", however, the administration also subverts its authority relation with social actions and clients; this relation is often transformed from a relationship of "vertical" authority into one of bargaining and cooperation. Thus, a further, *third* standard of administrative action emerges: the generation of consensus, support and cooperative relations between the administration and its specific clientele
>
> These levels do not follow one another in a historical sequence, although it may be plausible to speak of a shift of emphasis towards the second and third levels (Offe, 1985, pp.315–316).

Various Public Accounts Committee Reports testify to the existence of public policy problems which result when the first two developments summarised by Offe have not yet been overtaken by direct community involvement in decision-making. In October 1989, for instance, the New South Wales Public Accounts Committee reported in the following terms:

> Reforms begun under the New South Wales Labor Government and accelerated under the present Liberal Government have shifted public sector management away from a focus on inputs and processes, towards an interest in outputs, efficiency and effectiveness. Responsibility for the management of individual enterprises is being devolved; "let the managers manage" is the catch-cry. Increasing emphasis is being placed on commercial management principles.
>
> The greater emphasis on commercially-oriented management has already led statutory bodies to form a number of subsidiary companies and to have greater involvement in trusts, partnerships and joint ventures. **These developments raise questions about the adequacy of existing arrangements for accountability to government** (NSW PAC, 1989, p.6; emphasis added).

It is interesting to note, again, that the sorts of "reforms" we are seeing in Australian public administration are by no means isolated to this country.

Rather than slavishly follow ideologically determined agendas, therefore, it would be more advantageous to examine the overseas experience for its applicability. Of course, this is not the first time that such a conclusion has been drawn, but it is, nevertheless, important to restate that Australia is in the fortunate position of being able to examine the impact of changes before they are introduced. That this happens so rarely bears out our earlier comment regarding "fashion" in public administration.

9.7 Conclusion

In this chapter we have briefly outlined the reasons for the development of statutory authorities and, at the same time, the development of the departmental form in public administration. We have noted that debates concerning the degree of autonomy and accountability are not new.

Corporatisation has been shown as fundamentally flawed in both conception and application, and we have noted that it could be seen as a logical precursor to privatisation.

We have also noted the reality of ultimate political control over the formation, structure and operations of all public sector institutions, whether departments, authorities or companies. The objective of providing ultimate autonomy for public sector management will always be confronted by this political reality.[14] The economic conservatives argue that such a situation is inimical to "efficiency". However, they ignore the larger roles of public sector bodies in a parliamentary democracy.

We have also dealt with the role that government "interference" has played in ensuring an electricity supply to the bulk of Australian citizens, a role which they needed to undertake because of the intransigence of previous public and private sector managers.

The findings lead, inexorably, to the conclusion that neither corporatisation nor privatisation are strategies for solving those problems which may exist in the public sector. The contents of the following chapter (where we examine the practical application of such policies, and also examine some of the issues associated with privatisation) serve to bolster this conclusion.

Rather, genuine accountability should be introduced to the management of citizens' assets through more effective representative and participatory structures.

Notes

1. In common with other areas of political life, there is a fashion in nomenclature for public bodies. Statutory authority is a general term used throughout this document to describe the legislative basis of Public Trading Enterprises (PTEs), Government Business Enterprises (GBEs) and corporatised authorities.

2. In fact, the introduction to Wettenhall's book is titled "So You Think You Know What Government Departments Are?". The New South Public Works Department is a statutory authority.

3. See also Harden, 1988 where some problems associated with the role and accountability of statutory authorities is discussed in the British situation. Interestingly for our dis-

cussion of the secrecy of some Inquiries mentioned later Harden states: "At worst, therefore, the existence and workings of certain forms of indirect public administration in Britain can amount to a state secret".

4. Primarily in relation to municipal authorities (see bibliography). A perusal of this work has done much to elucidate some of the ideas in this section.

5. The Webbs also inform the reader that the statutory authority and the department were developed to protect the government from the financial excesses, and the citizen from the human depredations of contractors, including in the area of prison control.

6. The Democrats in the New South Wales Legislative Council (the Upper House) have successfully forced the Greiner Government to ensure that employee representation is provided on the Boards of corporatised authorities. The terms and conditions of employment which applied in an earlier incarnation can also be continued in the new form (e.g. maternity leave in the Australian Defence Industries Companies).

7. Economic rationalists would not describe privatisation as interference in the operation of statutory authorities.

8. Further, it should be acknowledged that even if privatisation occurs, the existence of "golden shares", with a consequent potential Ministerial involvement, (where the government recognises a continuing need for ultimate political control to protect consumers) does not mean that any problems associated with Ministerial "interference" are resolved.

9. Mark the assumption that there are "deficiencies of public sector performance" — a proposition assumed without analysis or evidence.

10. Both Victoria and Queensland have announced moves in that direction, though it is unclear what these governments precisely mean by the term.

11. An even more disturbing rationale for corporatisation has appeared in New South Wales which compares corporatisation with *perestroika* and *glasnost*. This analysis is simplistic in the extreme: the differences between centrally-planned economies and mixed economies cannot be glossed over so easily. In any event, *perestroika* has a primarily progressive political role.

12. We are grateful to Roger Wettenhall for pointing this out to us. The New South Wales government also seems to have forgotten the joint ventures associated with the Harbour Tunnel and Darling Harbour.

13. From there, it is a small step to argue that statutory au-

thorities might just as well be in private as in public ownership.

14. This situation has recently been seen in the formation
of the Aboriginal and Torres Strait Islanders Commission
(ATSIC). ATSIC was formed out the Department of Aboriginal Affairs (a department) and the Aboriginal
Development Corporation (a statutory authority). It has
also been structured to ensure the election of its office
holders. In theory, the Minister has limited powers, but the
political sensitivities of the portfolio require the Minister to
intervene in virtually all important decisions.

CHAPTER 10

THE IMPLICATIONS OF RECENT REFORMS

10.1 Introduction

In Chapter 9 we outlined some of the theoretical and practical deficiencies associated with strategies designed to make the public sector operate similarly to the private sector.

The objectives of this chapter are to review the effect that "corporatisation" or "privatisation" may have on the accountability arrangements, accounting practices and overall pricing practices adopted by organisations engaged in the generation and distribution of electricity. Many of the comments offered here are based on comparisons of institutional arrangements variously adopted to regulate the conduct of statutory authorities[1] (including government business enterprises, government-owned companies, and companies operating in the private sector). Some comments are necessarily speculative, based as they are on observations of past commercial conduct, and on the recent practices of enterprises which might be viewed as wholly or partially "corporatised".

We have chosen to examine this aspect of public sector reform due to the stress that is placed by the "reformers" on the financial performance of authorities, and their simplistic adherence to the view that the private sector "does it better" in all cases. As we will show, nothing could be further from the truth.

10.2 The Role of Accounting

Many may regard "accounting" as a neutral form of record-keeping. Yet the choice of accounting techniques and methods can create illusions.

Recent Australian experience underlines how financial reporting by companies in the private sector can provide a misleading impression of profitability and prosperity — an impression later corrected by reports of losses running into hundreds of millions of dollars. Accordingly,

when arguments that public sector organisations should adopt private-sector approaches to accounting and financial reporting are encountered, a modicum of scepticism is warranted.

Recent changes in the accounting methods being adopted by some government departments, and by statutory authorities, have profoundly affected the financial information about those organisations which is being presented to parliaments and the public. Those changes may be a precursor of more substantial changes in the way the financial standing and profitability of electricity authorities is prepared, as those organisations are progressively "corporatised".

Governments have the power to determine what accounting policies are adopted by statutory authorities (whether "corporatised" or not). At the same time, governments may also use accounting numbers to justify their policies, or to support claims about their managerial efficiency. Governments are, in effect, both players, and score-keepers.

In such a situation, particular attention must be paid to the role of the auditor. Indeed, claims about the "benefits" of corporatisation have been accompanied, at times, by claims that there are advantages in allowing the managers of statutory authorities to "slip the yoke of the auditor-general" and select their own auditor from the private sector. Those claims have largely been discredited, largely through the efforts of Public Accounts Committees in the Commonwealth and several States. But suggestions that there are advantages in employing auditors who are more "commercial" may continue to be aired.

"Privatisation" — the whole or partial sale of those enterprises to private interests — may lead to further changes. A privatised electricity generating body is likely (some might argue, inevitably) to be subject to some form of price-regulation, since governments have been unwilling to allow suppliers of essential services in markets where competition is a problematic occurrence (such as monopolies and duopolies) to operate totally free of all controls. In effect, then, privatisation may lead to the substitution of one form of government involvement (the conduct of trading and investment activities) with another form of government involvement (price regulation). Or, as it has sometimes been expressed, the replacement of "regulation by ownership" with "regulation by legislation".

The adoption of a scheme of price regulation will in itself create incentives for managers to select operating and accounting policies which are "optimal" in the context of the regulatory controls being applied.

"Corporatisation" and the specification of performance objectives in terms of profitability is frequently associated with the proposal that governments should formally purchase certain services, in order to meet "community service obligations". The argument is often advanced that this approach will remove hidden subsidies, while giving managers unambiguous targets and performance measures. Yet the introduction of a system of payments for "community service obligations" will establish another set of incentives for managers and governments to calculate the "cost" of those services in particular ways.

10.3 The Terminology — and the Rhetoric

Before analysing changes in regimes for accountability under corporatisation, it might be noted that *privatisation* would probably involve use of the corporate form — though not necessarily so. It is possible to operate commercial activities using vehicles such as "trading trusts" (which are subject to even lesser reporting requirements than companies. See also Chapter 5, Evatt, 1989 for a list of some forms of privatisation). Private-sector purchasers may elect to acquire the assets of a previously government-owned enterprise by using more than one company or unincorporated association — thus compounding the difficulties faced by outside parties (including agencies involved in price regulation) who seek to assess the profitability of those activities. The task of monitoring the finan-

cial performance of statutory authorities after privatisation may be formidably difficult, if not impossible.

10.4 General Public Sector Accounting and "Privatisation"

The limitations of contemporary public-sector accounting practices may have contributed to the "push" towards the sale or partial sale of public-sector assets and activities to the private sector.

Presently government departments and the "public accounts" are presented on a cash basis. If revenues exceed payments, governments record a *surplus*. If payments exceed revenues, governments record a *deficit*. These terms have become potent political symbols. Governments may express their aims as being to produce a "surplus"; oppositions may attack the government for the failure to meet their targets.

Despite the emphasis on surpluses or deficits, accounting data about the activities of government departments or programmes may provide a thoroughly distorted impression of a government's financial performance. Preparation of the public accounts on a cash basis enables the proceeds of asset sales to be recorded as receipts (which many commentators interpret as equivalent to "revenues"). In contrast, if a private-sector company using accrual accounting were to sell one of its subsidiaries, then the transaction would be treated as the substitution of one asset (an investment) for another asset (cash); the difference between sale price and book value would give rise to reports of a profit or loss.

If the ordinary woman or man in the street were to sell her or his house and car, s/he would be appalled if the net proceeds were to be regarded as part of his/her "income". Yet that is the impression conveyed by the form of accounting presently adopted by governments.

Hence, privatisation can produce a short-term cosmetic effect on the public accounts. While the proceeds may be applied to reduce debt — and hence, debt servicing commitments — over the long term the States or the Commonwealth will lose revenues from the profits of the businesses which have been sold. There will also be a second-order effect: the Commonwealth may lose tax revenues, since a statutory authority in private hands is likely to pay less tax than a statutory authority owned by the commonwealth and paying tax on its income. This will arise because the purchasers of a business are able to revalue the assets and liabilities of an acquired business. In the simplest case, the revaluation leads to higher tax deductions for "depreciation", and thus reduces taxable income, which in turn reduces the stream of future tax payments made to the Commonwealth.

In addition, the States have tended to levy charges on their statutory authorities equivalent to the tax that would be paid to the Commonwealth if they were in private hands. This loss of revenue could contribute to further financial difficulties of the States.

There are grounds for supposing that some government agencies have not always paid close attention to these factors (particularly the loss to revenue from taxation) when selling-off assets or businesses: indeed, in some asset sale proposals, commonwealth tender documents have virtually invited potential bidders to consider what arrangements were the most "tax effective" for them.

Correspondingly, there are grounds for supposing that, for a government as vendor, some privatisation proposals are commercially unsound, since the present value of projected cash inflows from continued ownership may exceed the projected cash inflows associated with the sale (having regard to sale proceeds, interest savings on retired debt, and the taxes imposed on revenues of businesses under new ownership).

However, the short-term political objective of wanting to boost the level of "receipts" in the cash-based public accounts seems to overcome most such concerns. It is not possible for outsiders to review the merits of most privatisation transactions since the particulars are kept secret in the name of "commercial confidentiality". Paradoxically, there is less concern about commercial confidentiality in the private sector. The corporations law requires the approval of shareholders before major assets or undertakings can be sold; similarly the listing rules of the Australian Stock Exchange require shareholder approval before assets constituting more than 10 per cent of shareholders' funds can be sold to certain parties (such as directors or former directors). In either case, shareholders of public companies (and the community) are provided with full particulars of the transactions before

they are consummated — the kind of information which governments keep secret. This is one of the few areas where accountability in the private sector is actually stronger than in the public sector!

10.5 Current Accountability Arrangements for Electricity Generation Agencies

Government-owned electricity generation bodies have been formed as "statutory authorities" in terms of specific legislation, which in turn establishes the major accountability arrangements for those bodies. While a detailed review of the particulars of relevant State or Commonwealth legislation is beyond the scope of this chapter, there are some common features.

Accounting

Most Australian electricity generating bodies use a form of "accrual accounting". That means they provide financial statements setting out their "financial position", and their profit or loss. These financial statements look beyond receipts and payments, and have regard to the effect of transactions which involve borrowing and lending activities, and to reductions in the value of assets over time. Similar forms of accrual accounting are adopted by companies in the private-sector — however, there are wide differences in the way in which accrual accounting can be applied, so that there is great flexibility in the way that authorities may calculate their profit or loss (see also Evatt, 1989, pp.73–74).

A notable exception has been the style of accounting adopted in Queensland.

The accounts of the Queensland Electricity Commission (QEC) have been maintained on a "cash" basis. The QEC's reports have taken the form of a "Statement of Receipts and Disbursements" for "operating funds", "capital works funds", "special funds" and "trust funds" (with separate reports on an accrual basis for appliance trading activities).

While the QEC has also furnished a "statement of assets" and a "statement of liabilities", those documents record "assets" at cost, and make no allowance for depreciation or adjustments reflecting differences between book and market values. Similarly no adjustments are made to reflect any differences between the face value and the current value of liabilities (especially loans undertaken in foreign currencies). The 1989–1990 Annual Report records that the Commission has appointed the Queensland Treasury Corporation to manage its risks arising from foreign currency exposures. At 30 June, 1990 offshore borrowings totalled A$1.166 billion though that figure reflects historical data rather than the market value of those commitments (which was not disclosed). Also undisclosed was the extent of any "unfunded liabilities" arising from the QEC's sponsorship of defined benefit superannuation schemes. (A difficulty faced when examining Queensland public-sector financial statements is that the state's Treasury describes its superannuation schemes as "fully funded" but uses that term in an unconventional way).

However, it is anticipated that the QEC will soon adopt some form of "accrual accounting", in common with the accounting practices adopted in other States (see Queensland Treasury, 1990).

Statutory authorities in Australian jurisdictions are required to follow guidelines set down by central agencies concerning the content of their annual reports. These guidelines often require the presentation of some details of categories of costs and sources of revenues; in contrast, neither companies legislation nor Australian Accounting Standards require the preparation of a detailed profit and loss statement.

In recent years, central agencies have been formulating accounting rules which are in some respects more comprehensive than those contained in accounting standards produced by the profession:

- the Commonwealth Department of Finance has produced guidelines for the financial statements of statutory authorities which incorporate rules regarding bad-debt write-offs, ceiling values for non-current assets (matters addressed in companies legislation but not in Australian Accounting Standards); prescribe the general basis of valuing and presenting liabilities; and in particular, have recently prescribed new disclosures concerning superannuation commitments (a subject not addressed by accounting standards);
- the NSW Treasury pioneered Australian requirements for disclosure of unfunded su-

perannuation liabilities as notes in the balance sheets of statutory authorities; subsequently those liabilities were to be brought to account on the face of the balance sheet. With the decision by the NSW government to introduce accrual accounting in annual reports issued by departments, this practice will be progressively extended. The Commonwealth guidelines for statutory authorities have been amended to require disclosures similar to those adopted in NSW from 1991. Equivalent reporting rules have not as yet been prescribed for corporations in the private sector (see Evatt, 1989 for a discussion of the applicability of accrual accounting to government departments); and

- NSW Treasury has prepared a set of accounting guidelines for recognising and reporting assets within the "budget sector" (i.e. those agencies which are principally reliant on budgetary allocations rather than revenues from trading activities). Noting that a major issue in applying accrual accounting "is the basis of the values to be assigned to physical non-current assets such as schools, police stations, Opera House, and monuments" the code outlines valuation methods which are also expected to be "useful" in other authorities (NSW Treasury, 1989).

However, given that public sector organisations are employing "accrual accounting", the procedures following in preparing the financial statements of statutory authorities may have regard to "Australian Accounting Standards" – rules which have been developed by the Australian accounting profession. The antecedents of these rules lie in efforts by the profession to interpret the reporting requirements of companies legislation. Some features are:

- the range of topics covered by Australian Accounting Standards is far less than those covered in standards produced by similar bodies in other countries. While the number of standards which have been issued is not an exact measure of the coverage of standards, it is indicative. From its establishment in 1974 to December 1990 the Australian accounting profession issued 25 accounting standards. The US's Financial Accounting Standards Board issued more than 100 standards between July 1973 and July 1990;

these were in addition to extensive rules previously issued by the FASB's predecessor body, the Accounting Principles Board; moreover an "Emerging Issues Task Force" has produced a series of detailed interpretations of existing rules, and examines around 40 topics per annum; and

- the drafting of individual rules often leaves room for a range of interpretations: rather than prescribe rules to be followed, the standards have referred to "usual" practice, or have permitted a wide range of alternative treatments, or indicated that rules are only to be applied if their effect is "material" — though without setting out concrete tests of "materiality". The issue from 1984 of legally-backed "approved accounting standards" by the Accounting Standards Review Board incorporated some tightening of the drafting style, though subsequently the drafting was again relaxed, principally by the frequent incorporation of statements that individual rules need not be applied to items which are not "material" — a concept commonly interpreted as involving items which affect items which constitute more than 10 per cent of aggregate assets, liabilities, revenues or expenses.

In the early 1980s the profession established a Public Sector Accounting Standards Board. In 1984 the Board issued a statement indicating that certain accounting standards presently on issue should be applied to public sector business undertakings. The profession's standard setting organisation, the Australian Accounting Research Foundation (AARF) has pursued a policy of issuing "common standards" for both the public and private sector. By 1990 the Public Sector Accounting Standards Board had issued nine standards jointly with the private-sector standard setting body.

Pronouncements by the accounting profession have no direct authority on State or Commonwealth governments. However, the two major professional bodies have issued statements on ethics which impose a professional obligation on members to adhere to Australian Accounting Standards, and suggest that non-compliance will lead to exposure to possible disciplinary action. In practice, disciplinary action over non-compliance with accounting standards has been minimal, or non-existent.

Several State Auditors-General have been enthusiastic supporters of the application of Australian Accounting Standards to the public sector, and several have been active on committees of the Australian Society of Certified Public Accountants, or the Australian Accounting Research Foundation.

In that way, the profession's standards have come to influence the accounting practices adopted by statutory authorities, including electricity generating authorities. On the other hand, it must be recognised that in practice, the authorities have in some respects provided more information than that required by the profession's standards (particularly with regard to the disclosure of individual items of revenue and expense).

It must also be recognised that Australian Accounting Standards have major gaps. Arguably the major "gaps" in the standards are the absence of any requirements:

a) concerning the basis used to revalue assets. In Australian accounting practice, companies frequently revalue assets upwards, but the profession has yet to introduce rules restricting the basis of those asset valuations, or formally requiring disclosure of the assumptions and methods used to arrive at the new figures. While companies legislation has required companies to provide full explanations in situations where non-current assets are recorded at figures in excess of the amount which it would have been reasonable to pay to acquire them at year end [subsection 269(7)(c) of the Companies Act and Codes; subsection 294(4) of the Corporations Law], that provision has never been enforced by the regulatory authorities;

b) concerning the basis used to identify and value "liabilities" — whether at face value, or at "present values"; and

c) requiring the presentation of "cash flow statements" in parallel with accounting reports prepared on an accrual basis. Publication of cash flow statements (now required disclosures in the US and New Zealand, as well as South Africa) would indicate the capacity of an enterprise to service its debt, while material divergences between the trend of cash and accrual-based accounting reports provide warning signs as to the possible use of "creative accounting" techniques to either inflate or deflate reported profits.

Some of these deficiencies have been addressed in a partial way by regulatory authorities. For example, the now-defunct National Companies and Securities Commission (NCSC)[2] urged companies to disclose the methodology and assumptions used to arrive at asset revaluations (NCSC Policy Release 135, 1988). Recently the Australian Stock Exchange proposed the introduction of requirements for cash flow reports, and has urged listed companies to produce those statements on a voluntary basis (Australian Stock Exchange, 1990).

But it is inescapable that the limited scope and loose drafting of Australian Accounting Standards prescribing the contents of "accrual accounting" reports leaves plenty of latitude for private and public sector entities alike to choose accounting techniques which enable them to shape accounting representations of an entity's profitability and financial position. Some speculations about the way those discretions may be exercised by electricity generation authorities — and the significance of those choices on reported indicators of profitability and financial position — are discussed later in this chapter.

In this setting, and in the absence of an widely agreed framework for the valuation of assets or liabilities, the rules issued by the NSW Treasury on the valuation of physical assets are likely to influence practices adopted elsewhere in Australia when "corporatised" public sector organisations adopt accrual accounting. We discuss those matters in the following paragraphs.

Government-owned companies would be subject to the reporting rules established in companies legislation. Much depends on whether they are formed as public companies, or as exempt proprietary companies. An exempt proprietary company need not place any financial information on the public record, provided it appoints an auditor. Without express agreement to the contrary, government-owned companies need not table their reports in Parliament, but only distribute them to the nominal "shareholders" (which may be ministers or public servants as nominees). Plainly these arrangements weaken traditional arrangements for the public disclosure of information concerning the use and application of taxpayers' funds; while there may be some situations in which use of private-sector corporate forms may be warranted, those situations are few in number.

In this context, a development worth noting has been the introduction in 1989 by NSW's Greiner Government of a State Owned Corporations Act — a move which the Premier explained as being designed to ensure that state-owned companies "will become accountable under the ordinary laws of commerce". The statute required government-owned companies to be accountable to Parliament in terms of several steps. They were to table a statement of "corporate intent" setting out their corporate objectives, and a statement of their main undertakings, the nature and scope of their activities, statements of accounting policies, and performance targets. Later they were to file six-monthly reports, which detailed actual performance against targets for the half-year.[3]

Unfortunately, the NSW legislation is somewhat flawed: for example, it requires state-owned corporations to prepare financial statements which conform with the requirements of the Companies (NSW) Code, but does not specify exactly which sets of financial reporting requirements were applicable: whether those prescribed for exempt proprietary companies, or for listed public companies.

Auditing

In general, the financial statements of statutory authorities are required to be audited by the public sector auditor, the (Commonwealth or State) Auditor-General. There have been exceptions: for example, the Commonwealth permitted certain marketing authorities to engage their own auditors. The quality of the audit conducted by a private audit firm for the Australian Wheat Board was later the subject of adverse comment in a report to Parliament from the Auditor-General. It is understood that the Commonwealth has subsequently agreed that the Auditor-General be reinstated as auditor of these bodies, with the right to engage private-sector auditors under contract.

The powers and duties of auditors-general vary in some minor respects, but in general terms they are wider than those adopted by private-sector auditors engaged to audit companies.

Furthermore, public-sector auditors often disclose more in their published audit reports than their private-sector counterparts. Private-sector auditors are required to provide a report expressing an opinion on the financial information contained in the statutory financial statements; they are also obliged to report if there have been certain breaches of companies legislation. They do not see their brief as encompassing reports on the adequacy of the financial controls adopted by managers, or on whether there have been breakdowns in those controls. Nor do private-sector auditors see their brief as being to disclose that a company has been engaged in illegal activities. The accounting profession has prepared standard-form audit reports (see Statement of Accounting Practice AUP 3), and it is rare for an auditor to stray too far from the stereotyped wording contained in these documents.

At times, public sector auditors have been quite outspoken about breakdowns in internal financial controls and "compliance" issues (though it

appears that standards of public disclosure may be greater for, say, a government department than for a statutory authority engaged in commercial activities). Public sector auditors also may have an implicit or explicit brief to undertake "performance audits" i.e. audits concerned with assessing the economy, efficiency or effectiveness with which government activities or programmes have been pursued. At times the rights of auditors-general to undertake this work has been contested; however several States have made explicit that public sector auditors have a mandate to undertake "performance" audits.

Accordingly, the engagement of private-sector auditors by "corporatised" entities may bring a change in the regime of accountability provided by the audit function. This arises because private-sector auditors following the accounting profession's Statements of Auditing Standards and Statements of Auditing Practice generally limit their activities to expressing an opinion on financial statements, except when expressly required to address other issues. A summary of the different arrangements for financial reporting is set out in Table 10.1.

Table 10.1
Accounting and Audit Rules Applied to Statutory Authorities and Companies

	Statutory authorities	Companies
Financial reports	As specified; usually accrual accounting	Balance sheet, profit and loss statement (which necessitates use of accrual accounting)
Distribution	Parliament; some libraries; some on request for certain exempt	Shareholders; also placed on public record (except proprietary companies); may not be tabled in Parliament
Accounting methods	Usually unspecified; usually Aust Accounting Stds	Approved accounting standards; rules specified in Schedule 5 of the Corporations Law
Auditor	Auditor-General	Auditor-General or agent; or private sector auditor
Audit reporting	Audit of: * financial statements *compliance issues *performance (elective)	Audit of financial mandate statements (only)

While the engagement of private audit firms may be regarded as somewhat attractive by public sector managers, it may reduce the accountability of public enterprises to Parliament and the community, since it may reduce the range of issues which are addressed in an audit and which are reported publicly by the auditor: there will be less emphasis on "compliance" issues, and the exclusion of the Auditor-General may avoid the possibility of an activity being subject to a performance audit by an independent party not subject to direction from the executive.

The implications of the use of companies, joint ventures and trusts on financial reporting and accountability have been (or are being) considered in Commonwealth, State and Territory Parliaments.

It appears that most governments have formed exempt proprietary companies and have taken advantage of the "privacy" concessions available to those entities. Such practices have been criticised in various ways by a variety of Parliamentary committees (see e.g. Senate Standing Committee on Finance and Public Administration, 1989; NSW Public Accounts Committee, 1989).

In 1989 the commonwealth Joint Committee of Public Accounts issued a landmark Report 296, *The Auditor-General: Ally of the Parliament and the People* which recommended *inter alia* that the Auditor-General be reinstated as auditor of commonwealth marketing authorities, but be permitted to "contract out" certain audits. The effect would be to ensure that audits of such bodies would continue to emphasise "compliance" issues, and could also encompass "performance auditing".

Subsequently, the NSW Public Accounts Committee has made similar recommendations (see NSW Public Accounts Committee, 1989); the role of the Auditor-General has been reviewed by Parliamentary committees in Queensland (Electoral and Administrative Review Commission, 1990); by a policy advisory committee to the Auditor-General of Western Australia (1990); and is being considered by the Public Accounts Committee in the Northern Territory. The reports so far published have indicated strong support for the retention of the auditor-general as the "lead" auditor for all government-owned enterprises (including

companies), with power to contract out. There has also been some concern about the adequacy of existing auditing standards for application to the public sector (see e.g. NSW Public Accounts Committee, 1989, pp. 85, 125–7).

Mention has already been made of the NSW State Owned Corporations Act of 1989. If governments are to use the vehicle of a company or trust, there is some merit in making the accountability arrangements to be applied to those entities quite explicit. This statute (while flawed in other respects) formally states that the Auditor-General is to be responsible for the audit of state-owned corporations.

Overall, then, it appears that the argument for the retention of the Auditor-General as the auditor of government owned companies has been largely won throughout Australia; correspondingly, a consensus has emerged that there may be merit in engaging private sector audit firms to perform work under contract for the Auditor-General — a compromise which may lead to higher standards of audit work from both sides.

10.6 Incentives Facing Governments and Managers which may Affect the Choice of Accounting Techniques by a Statutory Authority or "Corporatised" Entity

Why would governments want to influence the reported profits and financial position of a statutory authority? Why would managers wish to influence the accounting numbers? Would their various interests coincide, or conflict?

There are no simple answers to those questions. The incentives faced by governments are likely to be contingent upon a range of factors, which vary in significance from time to time. For governments, the two most important factors concern political aims and the need to raise funds through taxes and charges, without losing too many votes. As for managers, they may variously wish to inflate or depress asset values. Much would depend on the processes used to allocate resources to those enterprises, and whether managers' employment and remuneration arrangements are linked with the financial outcomes of their work.

A starting point is to consider the nexus between the financial performance of statutory authorities, and the pricing practices of those bodies.

Accounting reports may depict the results of a statutory authority's activities in providing and selling services; correspondingly, managers may attempt to influence the content of accounting reports so as to legitimise their pricing practices.

Prior to the debate and discussion about the supposed merits of corporatisation, it appears that statutory authorities tended to set prices at a level such that the enterprises neither recorded high levels of profits nor high levels of losses. Some public sector managers suggest that their target was to "break-even" over the long-term. High levels of losses or profits were a source of political embarrassment.

In the mid 1980s, in an effort to understand the basis upon which one state statutory authority had determined the scale of its provisions for employee superannuation — a practice which had apparently led to a material understatement of the authority's liabilities — one of us arranged an interview with a senior member of the accounting staff. The staff member explained: "The minister has told us he doesn't want any price increases before the next election. So we are keeping the provisions down so we don't have to show a loss".

But if a "break-even" outcome could not be secured from *trading*, then it could be secured from *accounting*, or by designing financial transactions so that a loss-making enterprise was not responsible for all of its "costs".

The NSW State Rail Authority recorded a modest surplus of $78,000 in 1986–87. But that was after a host of subsidies and after some large expenses (such as lease charges for rolling stock) had been met out of consolidated revenue. These were disclosed in notes to the SRA's accounts which thus suggested an excess of expenses over earnings of $868 million. However the NSW Auditor-General reported that these figures did not include interest charges on $1.5 billion capital debt that was met from the consolidated fund. Nor did they include increases in the SRA's liability for superannuation commitments, amounting to $56.9 million in the 1986–87 year.

Further, the SRA had only charged losses on foreign currency borrowings of some $6 million against the year's results, while some $155 million losses were recorded as an "asset". The Auditor-General observed that it "would not be

unreasonable" to assess the 1986–87 losses of the SRA at around $1.25 billion (see Walker, October 1987, p.92).

The political interest in "corporatisation" has seen a changed emphasis: instead of quiet attempts to secure a "break-even" result, the argument is shifted towards showing a profit. In the quest for greater productivity and efficiency, a key element has been the establishment of target rates of return for statutory authorities. But there has not been any great uniformity of approach:

- Victoria established rate of return targets in terms of the "current values" of the net assets being utilised in particular enterprises. In 1986 the Department of Management and Budget explained that the policy was designed to achieve a 4 per cent rate of return in "real" terms by cost reductions without "real" increases in charges (i.e. price increases at a rate higher than inflation);

  Victorian statutory authorities (including the State Electricity Commission of Victoria) report their "rate of return" performance in their annual reports;

- the Commonwealth uses rate of return targets — but does not establish across-the-board target rates of return, and does not report the results publicly. The calculation of rate of return data does not utilise published accounting figures, but is based on adjusted data (see Department of Treasury, 1990). Representatives of the commonwealth Department of Finance have advised that target rates of return are generally "negotiated" between a minister and a statutory authority within his portfolio; and

- the NSW State Owned Corporations Act 1989 indicated that corporatised entities were to have key financial targets, expressed in terms of a "rate of return" — but did not indicate how such indicators would be calculated. However the accounting guidelines being developed by the NSW Treasury involve the valuation of physical assets in terms of a form of "current replacement values" — so that reported profit and balance sheet figures may be used as the numerator and denominator in rate of return calculations.

The establishment of rate of return targets will affects the behaviour of public-sector managers.

"Corporatisation" may also involve those managers being engaged in terms of short-term performance-related contracts – so that salaries and tenure are conditional upon meeting target rates of return.

Overall, managerial incentives are likely to be contingent upon the nature of employment contracts, the "actual" profitability of a statutory authority in a given year, and the difference between those levels of profitability and any pre-set targets. For example, managers may be tempted to "manage" reported earnings and asset values in order to meet their targets; if those targets were met rather easily in a given year, it may be possible to reduce reported profit through "deferring" some income or recognising high levels of expenses (through depreciation charges or provisions for bad debts) thus establishing a cushion to assist in meeting targets in future years.

On the other hand, governments may face different sets of incentives. Most political parties make claims about their effectiveness as economic managers, and the way governments calculate and report accounting numbers can play a significant part in promoting those claims.

When statutory authorities have been making significant losses, an incoming government may wish to turn that around. When statutory authorities are making significant profits, and are a major source of cash flows to support other, electorally significant projects, then the government of the day may wish to continue that arrangement while understating the level of its profit in order to avoid criticisms of excessive pricing.

No doubt governments of all persuasions are reluctant to raise charges. But circumstances may sometimes dictate otherwise. Some States may have inherited commitments to construct capital works, or may have themselves initiated new infrastructure developments. In those situations, governments may seek to increase revenues in one area in order to fund other projects: increases in the price of (say) electricity, or road taxes, may be used to improve water quality, or sewerage treatment facilities.

Overall, the incentives likely to be faced by governments and public-sector managers, and some of their implications, can be outlined in summary form in the following five propositions:

1. Newly-elected governments face incentives to write-down assets or report previously undisclosed liabilities — and explain that any accounting losses were attributable to poor management by their predecessors;

2. Long-serving governments face incentives to suggest that their financial administration has contributed to the attainment of a strong financial position;

3. Governments wishing to increase charges face incentives to minimise the scale of profits and the rate of return being reported by statutory authorities. Hence they may seek to write-up assets, recognise additional liabilities, increase reported expenses or reduce reported revenues;

4. Managers of government agencies which are not predominantly trading enterprises face incentives to portray their area of administration as demanding and important. Hence they might wish to write-up assets so as to support claims for higher budgetary allocations; and

5. Managers of statutory authorities provided with rate of return targets face incentives to make those targets more readily attainable. Hence they might endeavour to record poor results just prior to the introduction of targets; they may endeavour to maintain the value of assets at low values, or to recognise liabilities which previously were off-balance sheet — both having the effect of reducing the denominator in the rate of return calculation; or by deferring revenues or increasing reported expenses in years in which the targets have been achieved with ease.

10.7 Accounting Choices in the Public Sector — in Practice.

The foregoing list of the incentives facing managers and governments is readily supportable by reference to recent events in the public sector.

The first two observations — concerning the wish of governments to blame their predecessors for losses or liabilities, and to claim responsibility for a strengthened financial position — are reflected in recent experience in NSW:

• on attaining office, the Greiner Government appointed a NSW Commission of Audit which reported that "state borrowings had increased to $24.7bn in 1987, compared to disclosed borrowings just five years ago of $11.7bn. In addition, the State has liabilities of some $14.5bn for which provision has not been made" ("Curran Commission", 1988, p. v). The annual operating deficit was $1.2bn, "of which an increasing proportion comprises debt servicing costs and losses incurred by the major State transport undertakings". In fact, many of the matters raised in the Curran Commission report had been disclosed to Parliament by the NSW Auditor-General and been highlighted in media reports (see, e.g. "Reading between the railway's lines, *Australian Business* 21 October, 1987; see also "NSW Sorts Out its Debt", *Australian Business*, 4 May, 1988, pp.80–83; a brief analysis of the Curran Commission's efforts was made in Evatt, 1989); and

• three years later the Greiner Government issued a summary of its budget documents claiming that it was "A Triple-A State", and quoting the Premier as stating that NSW "leads the nation as a model of good government, financial responsibility and managerial competence" (*A Triple-A State*, 1990, publisher undisclosed).

No doubt many governments from either side of politics make similar claims. However a feature of recent political rhetoric has been an emphasis on the notion that hidden subsidies should be exposed, that pricing should be based on the precept of "user pays", and that charges should "accurately reflect costs".

There are also signs that managers of organisations which may be privatised are taking steps to "defer" revenues so as to make it easier to meet rate of return targets:

• the 1990 annual accounts of the State Electricity Commission of Victoria (SECV) were qualified by the Auditor-General over the treatment of gains made on the early extinguishment of debt. The SECV had not brought all those gains to account as revenues, as recommended by an Accounting Guidance Release issued by the Australian Accounting Research Foundation; rather it had resolved to bring those gains to account in instalments over the remaining years of the term of the now-retired debt. The effect was to understate profits for the year ended

30 June, 1990 by $39.1 million; similar treatments had been adopted in previous years, so that a total of $76.8 million had been deferred to be recognised as revenues in later years.

There is also an abundance of evidence that government bodies which are facing corporatisation (and the imposition of rate of return targets) have revalued assets so as to change the basis upon which "costs" are recorded and calculated. This phenomenon was particularly evident in NSW during the 1989 and 1990 financial years (at a time when NSW was yet to introduce rate of return targets).

As already acknowledged, NSW was the first government in Australia to apply what might be termed "full accrual accounting" to all statutory authorities; other States, and the Commonwealth, have made similar claims, which can not be taken too seriously in view of their failure to disclose and record their emerging liability for superannuation commitments. Moreover, NSW was the first Australian government to make a commitment to implement "accrual accounting" in the preparation of annual reports by government *departments*. It also pioneered the preparation of a form of "consolidated statement" encompassing the financial statements of statutory authorities and departments.

Accordingly, the accounting practices adopted in NSW deserve close attention for they illustrate the manner in which government bodies in other jurisdictions may present financial information in the future if they are "corporatised", and also adopt "accrual accounting" methods, similar to those used in the private sector.

The guidelines produced by the NSW Treasury for the valuation of physical assets suggests that, as a general principle, "assets should be brought to account at their current cost valuation measured by the lowest cost at which the service potential or future economic benefits of the asset could currently be obtained in the formal course of business" (NSW Treasury, 1989, p.9). The accounting practices adopted by some NSW authorities during 1989 and 1990 before these guidelines were codified (see Treasury 1990) have involved the upward revaluation of physical assets to "current cost valuations".

The scale of some of these upward revaluations has been extraordinary, both in percentage terms, and relative to the scale of balance sheet revisions which have previously been undertaken in the private sector:

- ECNSW's 1989 annual report disclosed that it had undertaken substantial revaluations of property, plant and equipment. Book values had increased from $4,503.6 million in 1988 to $5,600.2 million in 1989. The book values of hydro-electric equipment at Brown Mountain, Burrinjuck, Hume, Keepit, Shoalhaven and Warragamba dams — some of which date back to 1938 — had been revalued upwards from $41 million to $134 million i.e. by 287 per cent; and the NSW Auditor-General noted that the revaluations had contributed $101.99 million in extra depreciation charges in the 1988–89 financial year.

The major write-ups by ECNSW in 1989 were followed by further revaluations the following year: during 1989–90 ECNSW revalued its 132 kV transmission lines, underground feeders, substations and transformers of 132 kV and above, from historical cost to depreciated replacement value. That increased book values by $904.4 million[4].

But even larger write-ups were recorded in 1990 by NSW's Water Board. The Water Board wrote-up certain of its infrastructure assets by more than $2.5 billion — arguably the largest balance sheet revision ever undertaken in a single year by an Australian business. The write-ups involved pipes and tunnels which were said to have been only 18.5 per cent of the Board's infrastructure assets (presumably the calculation was based on prior book values); in those terms, 81.5 per cent of the Board's infrastructure assets await revaluation. The write-ups were said to have increased depreciation charges during the year by $35 million over what would have been charged had valuations based on historical cost been retained for the full year.

Even though these revaluations were possibly an Australian record, they were of a small scale compared with the valuation placed on infrastructure assets by the State's Roads and Transport Authority when it prepared its first set of financial statements on an accrual accounting basis.

The 1990 annual accounts of the NSW Roads and Transit Authority (RTA) incorporated for the first time the value of certain infrastructure assets: Roads $17,778.3 million, Bridges $3,813.7 million, Traffic Signal Control Network $5.7 million and Land Under Roads and Within Road Reserves $20,922.2 million. The basis of valuation was "written down replacement valuation where each road is assigned a value which equates with what it would cost to replace that road to its current condition, without improving the road". Land Under Roads was valued "according to the average rateable value per hectare of urban and rural areas" (RTA Annual Report 1989–90).

The RTA's upward revaluations totalling around $43 billion might be seen as entirely consistent with the hypothesis outlined above: that managers face incentives "to portray their area of administration as demanding and important". It might also be regarded as a precursor to future arguments about the "need" to lift government charges (such as motor vehicle registration fees, road taxes) in order to meet the "true" or "full cost" of services. The RTA did not record depreciation of "infrastructure assets" as an expense in its 1989–90 accounts but revealed that it was reviewing the issue and that "current indications favour the adoption of the remaining life method". If that method is adopted, the RTA's assets (other than land) will be depreciated over the estimated remaining useful life — thus increasing the "costs" reported in the Authority's financial statements.

The NSW Auditor-General Ken Robson did not make any direct comments about the RTA's accounting practices in his 1990 report, but did devote some attention to the revaluations by the Water Board, and other agencies, and the effect of those revaluations on reported "costs":

> It is the flow-on effect of additional depreciation charges following asset revaluation which is my major concern. This effect is displayed by increased costs and depressed operating results in the Income and Expenditure Statements.
>
> My concerns in this area are that costs will be overstated, that increased prices will be more easily justified and that depreciation charges will in time exceed original cost.

One of the rationales for the commercialisation and corporatisation of statutory authorities is the suggestion that government charges should cover costs, and also provide a return on capital invested. Yet the "costs" being recorded by government bodies in NSW are of a very different order from the "costs" which are brought to account in conventional accounting.

There may be good arguments favouring the pricing of services at a level which permits a trading organisation to generate cash flows sufficient to finance the replacement of capital equipment. But decisions about pricing can be undertaken without making accounting reports a vehicle for persuasive stories about the "full costs" of providing services with existing equipment.

The accounting practices being seen in NSW reflect confusion or disagreement about whether the accounting of statutory authorities is intended to provide a formulation of "current costs" to aid (or legitimise) pricing decisions, or whether statutory authorities' accounting should set forth the resources which are available for adaptive behaviour. If one adopts the latter view, then it does not make sense to record roads at replacement values, and then to add the selling price of the land under the roads — since that land cannot be sold while it is committed for use for transportation. Indeed, it seems that the NSW Treasury make have taken the same view: in consolidated statements prepared for the 1989–90 year, the value of land under roads was deducted from the RTA's values as a "consolidation adjustment".

Of course, one should not suggest that the choice of accounting methods is the sole way of weaving financial illusions about the profitability of statutory authorities: one should not overlook the way that transactions with central agencies can influence reported profit and financial position; nor should one overlook the way that a "restructuring" can completely change an enterprise's financial position.

As noted above, for many years the NSW State Rail Authority systematically understated the extent of its operating losses, after the NSW Treasury assumed responsibility for commitments to pay employees' retirement benefits, and for the leasing of rolling stock. The SRA had also, in substance, incurred substantial losses on foreign currency borrowings undertaken on its behalf, after adverse shifts in exchange rates. However those losses were not recorded in the

SRA's books because the loans had been taken out on its behalf by another statutory authority (which, incidentally, did not record a loss either because responsibility for meeting the higher payout figures rested with the SRA).

The scale of the losses being incurred by the SRA were subject to adverse comment in the report of the Greiner Government's Curran Commission, which contrasted the figures being reported in annual accounts and the actual level of losses, when adjustments were made by transactions entered into by central agencies.

Ironically, in 1990 the Greiner Government has set about to achieve a similar result, but using different methods. The 1990 Report of the NSW Auditor-General reveals that the "financial framework" of the SRA had been "restructured":

> An agreement was entered into whereby outstanding loan liabilities amounting to $2,511.2 m were assumed by the NSW Treasury from 1 July, 1989. In addition, from the same date all future payments required under the Authority's finance leases amounting to $400.6 m were also assumed by the NSW Treasury. In consideration for the assumption of this debt the Authority has agreed to assign to the NSW Treasury future net proceeds from the disposal of surplus land and the disposal will be by way of sale (Vol. 2, p.240).

The NSW Grain Handling Authority was officially "corporatised" on 1 October, 1989 and its role in administering the State's bulk grain handling network transferred to the NSW Grain Corporation Ltd ("GrainCorp"). GrainCorp was a company established under the Companies Code rather than the State Owned Corporations Act — possibly a sign that it is slated for sale. The financial restructuring involved writing-down assets from $348 million to $62 million, writing off $185 million debt, and converting $58.5 million debt into "equity". The revaluations were based not on the resale value of assets, but on the present value of expected future earnings from use of the company's facilities.

These financial and accounting changes were said to enable GrainCorp to compete on a "level playing field" (NSW Auditor-General's Report, 1990, Vol. 1).

The point might be made that the "corporatisation" of government bodies will not

Table 10.2
MODELS OF PRICE REGULATION

Method	Explanation	Agency which adopted similar procedures	Comment
I. Per centage limitations on price increases	Firms permitted to increase prices by specified (or calculable) percentage	U.S. Price Commission 'Phase I' Aug-Nov, 1971; 'Phase III' June 1973.	Short-term 'price freeze.
		U.S. Council on Wage & Price Stability (June 1979–1982)	Described as a 'price deceleration' standard. Permitted prices to increase by rate of increase during base year (1975–77) less 1.15%.
II. 'Pass through' cost increases	Firms permitted to increase revenues so as to recover the dollar amount of cost increase.	U.S. Price Commission Nov. 1972–Nov. 1971–Jan. 1973 ('Phase II')	(NB limited to of specified costs; could be adjusted for productivity gains while avoidable costs, or costs arising from 'inefficiencies', could be disregarded).
III Maintenance of gross profit margins	Firms permitted to increase revenues so as to recover the dollar amount of costs increases plus a margin (at some rate as was obtained in earlier periods)	U.K. Price Commission 1973	Permitted margin — normally that in best two years of the five year period to April 1973 (period later revised).
		U.S. Council on Wage & Price Stability (June 1979 1982)	A *net* profit margin relevant for wholesalers and distributors together with a 'dollar profit limitation,. as an exception to the price deceleration standard (Method I).
IV Return on investment	Firms permitted to charge prices which would enable them to secure a 'fair' rate. of return on investment (*or* a rate of return 'sufficient to attract new funds *or* a rate	U.K. National Board for Prices and Incomes 1967–71 U.K. Price Commission 1974.	Target rate of return for nationalised industries
			Permitted surplus

of return 'sufficient to support new investment proposals')	U.S. Interstate Commerce Commission	2% on turnover of 10% on assets (Stage 4 code)	
V Price caps	Price increases constrained by a per centage – (CPI–x)	U.K. Oftel (1984)	Together with periodic reviews of adequacy of returns.

prevent accounting reports on statutory authorities being used to convey illusions of profitability and financial strength. Rather, the game of accounting will be played within new parameters.

Overall, an immediate effect of corporatisation on public sector accounting practices is likely to be the widespread use of asset revaluations. For successful statutory authorities, asset write-ups will produce higher levels of reported expenses — and which in turn may support plausible stories about the need for statutory authorities to levy higher charges. For loss-making statutory authorities, judicious write-offs may enable them to start reporting profits in later years — a technique which may be used to prepare an enterprise for privatisation, or to ensure that politicians can point to improvements in profitability under their astute financial management.

10.8 Pricing Practices under "Privatisation"

It can be reasonably assumed that many targets of corporatisation are being prepared for privatisation. It can then be expected that governments will be compelled to introduce some form of controls over the pricing practices of any privately-owned business enterprises which are engaged in the generation and distribution of electricity. One can speculate about the form of price regulation likely to be introduced in the 1990s, and how privatised firms will respond to those controls (see also Chapter 8).

Historically, various approaches to price regulation have been used, in different circumstances. Price regulations were widely adopted during war-time conditions. During the 1960s and 1970s high levels of inflation led several governments to introduce price controls aimed at moderating changes in the general level of prices. Note that both war-time price controls,

and the anti-inflationary price controls, were political devices designed to limit the scale of price increases in the short-term.

Several countries have also maintained some form of surveillance or control over the pricing practices of privately-owned public utilities (operating in the energy, transport or communications industries). Presumably the aim of these forms of regulation has been to ensure that utilities do not adopt pricing practices which exploit their monopolistic position and so disadvantage consumers. Correspondingly, regulatory agencies have tried to maintain incentives for companies to improve their efficiency and the quality of service to consumers.

Table 10.2 describes some models of price regulation which have been adopted in Australia, the UK and the USA.

Method one (percentage limits on price increases)

This method has generally been used as a short-term exercise. This technique was adopted by the US Nixon administration in 1971 to freeze prices and hence reduce expectations about inflation. It was intended to be applied economy-wide, not to specific industries. While simple to administer, it could have serious disfunctional consequences if applied over the long-term, or to specific industries. For example,

- it takes no account of the level of inflation within the economy during the base year, and subsequently. The method leads to regular fixed-percentage price increases which could be either "too high" or "too low". This could permit the regulated industry to reap high levels of profits (regardless of its efficiency) or it could erode the profitability of regulated firms, and destroy any incentives for firms to undertake new investment;

- it sets levels of prices regardless of the impact of changing costs of inputs;
- it sets levels of prices regardless of whether the regulated firms are enjoying economies of scale through increases in volumes of production, or whether they are suffering through a contraction of volumes in times of economic recession; and
- it contains no incentives for firms to introduce new products or to vary product mix in response to changing patterns of demand.

Method two ("pass through of cost increases") and method three (maintenance of gross profit margins")

The methods have also been used to permit firms in regulated industries to secure short-term rate increases. Both methods were used by the US Price Commission (which had earlier applied method one) — apparently in response to some of the disfunctional consequences flowing from the application of a "percentage increase in prices" approach to a range of industries which were facing different types of problems.

Likewise, both method two and method three ("maintenance of gross profit margins") were used by Australia's Price Justification Tribunal (PJT) in the course of periodic reviews of particular industries. At times the PJT permitted firms to "pass through" cost increases; at other times it permitted them to vary the level of margins (and occasionally considered those margins in the context of profitability).

Method two ("pass through of cost increases") might seem simple to administer — but in practice its application can be fraught with complexity. When used in the short term, regulated firms can apply to translate increases in (say) wages and supply-costs into a schedule of increased prices. Some of the difficulties encountered in application are as follows:

- decisions must be made about whether the "pass through" technique is to be applied using historical cost data or "annualised" cost data (represented current levels of expenditure). In either case, without some additional adjustments the regulated industry will "lose" every time there is a lag between increases in the cost of inputs and permitted increases in the price of outputs;
- decisions must be made about the treatment of changes in costs of imports which are as-

sociated with changes in the value of the Australian dollar (exchange rate changes);
- decisions must be made about whether the method looks only at direct costs of input, or whether it should have regard to changing overhead costs, or changing costs of securing finance;
- the method ignores the impact of economies of scale arising from variability in output;
- assuming stable volumes, the method effectively pegs the quantum of gross profits to the level prevailing in the base year. With inflation, this quantum of gross profits is eroded in real terms. Hence the method can discourage new investment. This is perhaps the most significant problem associated with the method; and
- choices which have to be made in handling reductions in costs which arise from technological change. Are these to be shared between producer and consumer?

One response to these difficulties is illustrated by the PJT's approach to regulation of the petroleum industry. In 1979 the PJT permitted firms to "pass through" both actual costs and some imputed costs — apparently in order to give the industry some increases in gross profits. The imputed costs considered by the PJT were hypothetical financing costs associated with greater investment in inventories after the price of crude oil increased. The amount of these imputed costs was calculated by applying the marginal weighted average cost of capital of a representative firm to "standard" volumes of inventory.

If reductions in costs are to be translated into lower prices, then firms have no incentive to increase their efficiency. Correspondingly, if there is no penalty imposed on firms which incur increased costs through inefficiencies, there is no incentive to them to seek to improve management and work practices or to undertake new investment, or apply techniques, aimed at enhancing efficiency and improving the quality of service to customers.

If a regulatory authority were to attempt to permit firms to retain the benefits of efficiency gains in the "pass through" or cost recovery model, then to be consistent it should not permit any initial short-term cost increases associated with the installation of new equipment to be "recovered" through increased prices. Hence it would face the problem of identifying those costs associated with new investment.

Yet another difficulty relates to the extent to which depreciation charges are to be regarded as costs which can "pass through" into increased prices. Judgments must be made about what is an appropriate depreciation "base" (whether represented by historical cost figures or current replacement prices). Judgments must also be made about how to apportion the costs associated with increased investment if that investment increases capacity at a time when production or distribution volumes are less than capacity.

Regulatory agencies face the problem of a lack of expert technical knowledge of the industry they are regulating. Hence, they either become dependent upon the information provided to them ("captured"), or they find it necessary to embark on long and extensive inquiries into the circumstances of the industry under review — thus adding to industry costs, consuming management time and possibly contributing to inefficiencies. Both these characteristics have been said to apply to the privately owned US electricity supply industry.

It has been claimed that, at times, this form of price control is used by industry to secure government legitimation of increases in prices (which otherwise might not have been undertaken).

Method four ("rate of return" regulation)

This method has generally been adopted in some form or other where price controls are applied to public utilities and other firms which enjoy a monopolistic position. It has also been used in conjunction with methods one and two when regulated firms complain about the impact of those methods upon profitability (see, e.g. the first and fourth BHP cases before Australia's PJT).

Two key issues in the application of the "rate of return" approach are:
a) setting target rates of return; and
b) calculating actual rates of return (for the purpose of reviewing past experience).

A US "solution" to these matters has been to constrain regulated public utilities to use historical cost data, where "cost" in this context generally refers to the cost of an asset when first

applied to service. Criticisms of US rate of return regulation have pointed to the incentives it creates for firms to over-invest in plant and equipment, since a return on that investment is virtually underwritten by the regulatory agency.

It would seem highly unlikely that rate of return regulation would be adopted, on its own, in any arrangement for the regulation of electricity prices in Australia. If it were to be adopted, one would expect that the price-regulating authority would be confronted with claims that the appropriate way of valuing assets in this context was some variant of "current replacement value" — probably the method of valuation (written down replacement value) being adopted by several NSW statutory authorities. That would compel the regulatory agency to address such issues as:

* why is it appropriate to use the values ascribed to generating equipment and transmission lines based on the continued use of coal as a primary source of energy — when any replacement might well involve the use of natural gas, and the location of generating equipment closer to metropolitan centres?
* why should a rate of return be calculated on the aggregate value of all generating equipment when there is excess capacity in the industry?
* given the long lead-times to re-equip electricity generating plants, are "current replacement values" estimates of replacement (or reproduction) values if the new equipment had been ordered some years ago, or are they estimates of what would be paid if new equipment was ordered now?

We must admit that there are no easy answers to those questions. But they are serious questions nevertheless, and there is little evidence to suggest that they are being addressed.

Method five ("price cap regulation")

This is a form of price regulation finding favour among regulated industries: it permits firms to raise prices at the level of inflation (as indicated by the consumer price index - CPI), or some other indicator (such as the "retail price index") - less a margin, the "x" factor. Hence the formulation,

$$CPI - x$$

The role of the regulatory agency is to determine the level of "x".

The major advantage claimed for this method is that it establishes incentives for firms to seek efficiency gains, since it will be entitled to retain the rewards of such savings. From the regulator's point of view, it narrows the area of judgment to a single factor: the level of the x factor. Determination of the level of x involves the regulator to consider a host of factors, and then make a single overall calculation which balances all variables. The reasoning behind that interpretation is virtually beyond enquiry, or challenge.

Price-cap regulation has been adopted in the UK in the regulation of the gas and telecommunications industries; it has also recently been adopted in NSW to regulate the activities of gas distribution. This method would seem to be the favoured candidate for price regulation of "privatised" electricity generation authorities — certainly among the business community. From the perspective of government, price cap regulation also has some advantages. Use of the CPI - x model does not require regulatory agencies to justify their decisions in terms of a mechanistic formula. As such, it can minimise political exposure: governments can point to the fact that decisions have been made by experts who have exercised expert judgment.

10.8 Possible Impact of Price-cap Regulation on "Privatised" Electricity Generation Authorities

Under "price-cap" systems of price regulation, the process of permitting price increases which are linked with the level of inflation, but which do not constrain the extent to which an industry can retain additional profits arising from lowering its costs, the regulatory body aims at fixing a level of "x" so as to create incentives for the regulated firm to pursue efficiency.

A privatised electricity authority would be expected to argue that the "x" factor should be very small, since the smaller that factor, the greater their expected profitability. The argument might be framed in terms of the need for the firm to retain the capacity to acquire new equipment and take advantage of new technologies — steps advocated in the name of enhancing productivity in the future so that consumers can enjoy reduced prices in future.

In this context, use of price-cap regulation would create incentives for regulated firms to understate their current profitability.

One way in which regulated firms could understate their profits might be to establish a complex corporate structure in which different elements receive management fees, provide loans, or provide goods or services which are used in the production of the regulated commodity or service. The use of transfer prices may enable "profits" to be withdrawn from the regulated firm, in the guise of expenses.

In some industries — such as telecommunications — technological change is so swift and (in some respects) uncertain that the regulatory body faces a daunting task in ensuring that the industry obtains adequate returns for replacement and upgrading of equipment. Other industries (such as those engaged in gas distribution) are employing relatively stable technologies, so that assessments of claims about the need for incentives for the acquisition of new technologies would not be as significant.

Two major implications of the use of price-cap regulation can be identified.

The first concerns the capital structure of the regulated firm. Price-cap regulation may be administered with regard to the rate of return being enjoyed on the assets employed in an industry, but it does not seek to restrict the returns available to the providers of equity capital. Electricity utilities whose pricing policies are supported by government regulation in any form are likely to be perceived as being of relatively low risk, so that they may be able to obtain loan funds at relatively cheap rates. The private owners of an electricity utility may be attracted by the idea of establishing a highly-geared capital structure which enables shareholders to increase their returns on funds employed — provided the cash flows generated from their business operations is sufficient to service debt.

Hence, the introduction of price-cap legislation could create incentives for privatised electricity authorities to establish highly-geared capital structures (relative to the gearing levels in comparable manufacturing organisations).

A second likely outcome of the application of price-cap regulation is that it would create incentives for a privatised industry to expand sales of electricity.

The price-cap model does not incorporate any mechanism to adjust returns enjoyed by an industry in times of changing volumes. One might suppose that regulated firms will produce arguments about the need to reduce the "x" factor when times are bad, and why it should not be increased when times are good. But overall, the model implies that a regulated industry is entitled to retain all additional profits derived from marketing efforts to increase sales.

Since the electricity industry includes several State systems which are presently operating at below technical capacity, price-cap regulation is likely to establish clear incentives for privatised firms to encourage increased sales. No doubt some would argue that such an outcome would be less than optimal, given concern about such factors as the depletion of finite reserves of fossil fuels, and the impact of continued use of fossil fuels on the environment.

10.9 Community Service Obligations

The 1989 NSW State Owned Corporations Act introduced to Australia the notion that statutory authorities would be directed to earn a profit, while government would make direct payments to those enterprises to meet the cost of meeting "community service obligations" (CSOs).

Subsequently the idea of making payments for CSOs has obtained wider currency, with the Industry Commission recently recommending the adoption of that scheme by both gas and electricity utilities. The Commission was critical of what it regarded as "unclear objectives":

> Loosely specified and sometimes conflicting goals can result in efficiency being compromised and/or managers implementing policies which are inconsistent with government's intended policy direction. Poorly stated objectives may also provide management with an excuse for unsatisfactory performance (IC, 1991).

This led the Commission to recommend that electricity and gas utilities should be given straightforward profit seeking objectives:

> In the Commission's view, the problems caused by multiple, unclear and sometimes conflicting objectives could be largely avoided if, consistent with the objectives of private enterprises, public utilities' objectives relate solely to commercial performance (IC, 1991).

Such arguments do not stand up very well to analysis.

Table 10.3

Major CSOs fulfilled by public utilities

	Type of utility	
CSO	Electricity	Gas
Uniform pricing within customer class	All	TPA, GFCV, SECWA
Concessions to domestic users	All	GFCV
Pensioner rebates[a] Sagasco	All	GFCV,
Low income household concessions	All	GFCV
Subsidies to large users	NSW ESI, ETSA, QEC, SECWA	—
Emergency payments	NSW ESI, ETSA	Sagasco
Remote area connection subsidy	NSW ESI, QEC, HECT, SECWA	—
Remote area supply	NSW, ESI, ETSA HECT, PAWA	GFCV (tempered LPG) SECWA, HECT, PAWA

[a] A private utility — AGL — is also required to offer pensioner rebates

Source: Extract — Industry Commission Report. Based on information supplied by participants

For example, the premise that private enterprises are solely concerned with "commercial performance" sits a little uneasily with expectations that private sector organisations will also be "good citizens". Indeed, private-sector businesses are expected to have regard to the environment, to pursue employment programmes which are not discriminatory, to provide opportunities for staff education and training — and generally to temper their pursuit of profits with regard to their social responsibilities. In short, private sector organisations themselves face multiple objectives — and many corporations actually use their "contributions" to the community as a marketing tool. Cigarette and alcohol marketing strategies are a case in point.

The argument also presupposes that there is no ambiguity about what constitutes a CSO. But do such obligations arise from the provision of a particular type of service; from providing a service to consumers in particular localities; or from the maintenance of common charges — so that consumers in the more remote areas can be seen as enjoying the benefit of concessional pricing? These are just some of questions that should be considered.

Table 10.3 comes from the Industry Commission's 1990 report, and illustrates the way that the concept of a "community service obligation" can be interpreted.

Most of the items in the table concern tariff scales. It will be noted that "low" pricing to domestic consumers, or concessions to pensioners, are regarded by the Industry Commission as CSOs. The reasoning is that establishment of common charges for all classes of customer could be regarded as an "obligation" (or concession) to the smaller customers.

The term "community service obligation" is so value-laden and imprecise that it invites all kinds of interpretations. For example, contrary to the assertions of the Industry Commission, the provision of services to bulk users at cheaper rates than domestic users could be described as a CSO (reasoning: the supplier has a monopoly on distribution, and within certain price ranges, demand is inelastic, so that bulk users might be prepared to pay higher rates). Or one could identify as a CSO the supply of electricity at cheap rates for the purpose of street lighting, and the illumination of parks, museums and monuments. Much depends on how CSOs are defined — and detailed definitions are hard to find.

Indeed, the Curran Commission referred to CSOs in a wider sense — suggesting for example that loss-making rail passenger services were provided out of obligations to the community. That in turn suggests that the criteria used by the Commission to identify CSOs was that they were any activity which was making a "loss" rather than a "profit". In that case, an accountant would immediately wonder: how does one identify whether certain services — part of such an integrated activity as the distribution of electricity — could be regarded as making a profit or a loss?

The techniques of cost accounting enable one to calculate the performance of a section of a business, by making certain assumptions about what kinds of costs and revenues can be traced to that activity, and how certain common costs can be calculated.

In broad terms, choices have to be made about whether the cost of meeting certain CSOs is to be calculated in terms of purely "marginal" costs and revenues, or in terms of a method which allocates common costs and overheads. The apparent precision of the calculations can be misleading. Widely different estimates can be obtained, on different assumptions.

It has been reported that Telecom and the Bureau of Transport and Communications Economics produced widely different estimates of the cost of meeting community service obligations through the provision of rural services: Telecom estimated the figure at $800 million per annum, the Bureau at only $200 million per annum. The Bureau was said to have calculated "avoidable costs" — the savings which could be made if the service was not provided. Telecom was said to have included a share of overheads, on the ground that such expenses were part of the true commercial cost of providing the service (see *Sydney Morning Herald*, 16 September, 1989 p.39; Guthrie, 1989).

Students of accounting are familiar with examples of how abandoning a loss-making division can actually make a firm worse off: the loss-maker may have been contributing to the recovery of common costs. That insight suggests that public sector managers, and their governments, may both face incentives to identify certain services as CSOs. If a statutory authority is not securing high levels of profit, payment for CSOs can be a way of providing subsidies — perhaps enabling the statutory authorities to be seen as financially successful. Instead of having their statutory authorities report losses, a political "negative", governments can be seen as taking the positive step of continuing much needed services through subsidies.

The subsidies would in that case be "open" rather than hidden. But governments may also face incentives to avoid revealing some subsidies — for example, the provision of loss-making services to key electorates. The solution lies in so defining the ambit of CSOs that they are not seen as pork-barrelling activities.

Still, claims that "corporatisation" and abandoning of "hidden subsidies" in favour of open payments for CSOs will lead to "improved accountability", must be treated with scepticism.

It seems significant that proponents of these policies have avoided discussing whether the basis of identifying and calculating the cost of CSOs should be subject to guidelines, and whether the basis used in particular circumstances should be disclosed in reports of government and the recipient. But without disclosure, the introduction of policies of paying corporatised or privatised firms for the delivery of CSOs will give rise to doubts and concerns about whether those transactions are just another form of hidden subsidies or ways of disguising the differential impact of policies on different sections of the community.

10.10 Summary and Conclusion

Accounting and auditing practices in the public sector have been undergoing considerable change in the past decade. Public sector auditors and parliamentary committees have been active in promoting debate about the desirability of strengthening accountability arrangements, in order that the financial performance of the public sector is more open to review by parliament and the community.

Proposals for the "corporatisation" of public sector bodies have, and will, lead to further changes in the arrangements for financial reporting and audit of government-owned bodies. The enthusiasm of public-sector managers to be allowed to operate through the vehicle of a private sector corporate form, or in terms of rules which emulate private-sector arrangements, may be symptomatic of a desire to avoid both public-service red-tape and the demands placed on them to be accountable for their use of public monies. The fact remains that corporatisation involves a change in the regime of accountability faced by public sector bodies — a change marked by the reduction or elimination of the safeguards established through financial disclosure and wide-ranging audit. In many respect, corporatisation may mean that the financial affairs of government bodies is less open to scrutiny that before.

Claims that corporatised bodies will be subject to the discipline of the market can be seen as questionable rhetoric. Market disciplines have been unsuccessful in the private sector; they appear less effective than the disciplines established in the public sector through the complex web of accountability relationships involving managers, central agencies, public sector auditors, parliamentary committees, parliament and the community.

If public utilities supplying electricity services were to "privatised", one might expect that information about the activities of those bodies — which enjoy benefits of a monopolistic position in their markets — will be even less accessible than at present. This seems especially likely if governments introduce price regulation, since private sector firms will face incentives to present their financial affairs in the optimal light, relative to the regime of price regulation being implemented.

The argument progresses that, whatever the ownership of bodies engaged in electricity generation and distribution, the restructuring of those bodies as predominantly profit-seeking entities will lead to enhanced accountability through the establishment of clear goals and clear-cut measures of performance. Again, such arguments do not stand up to close analysis. If the provision of electricity services is to be subject to price controls, and if governments are to pay for CSOs, those steps simply shift the arena in which illusions about the financial performance of statutory authorities can be created.

The foregoing indicates that there needs to be greater recognition of the principles of public sector performance and accountability by those who are, for a time, responsible for decisions which affect every citizen. There is very little evidence to suggest that this recognition will be forthcoming without significant pressure being applied at the workplace and by the community in general.

The following chapter examines the arguments advanced to justify privatisation in the electricity supply industry and, in particular, arguments based on the concept of efficiency.

Notes

1. We would reiterate, however, that the definitional problems we noted in Chapter 9 must be borne in mind when considering the issues raised in this chapter. Not all statutory authorities are required to meet the conditions which are discussed in this chapter.

2. A statutory authority.

3. It might be noted that some NSW public servants restrict use of the term "corporatisation" to organisations listed as state-owned corporations in terms of this legislation.

4. In this respect, it is noteworthy that these assets were then "sold" to the County Councils (the distribution authorities).

CHAPTER 11

EFFICIENCY AND PRIVATISATION

11.1 Introduction

As we outline in Chapter 12 the focus of debate about microeconomic reform has been on government business enterprises' (GBEs)[1] efficiency or capital needs (see Chapter 4) rather than on private sector undertakings. This concern with GBEs' efficiency, or lack of it, has resulted in the development of a variety of tools to measure that efficiency.

When inefficiency has been detected, rather than address its causes if these are known, or find out what they are, some agencies and groups have suggested privatisation and the establishment of a competitive market discipline as a "cure-all". Chapter 10 showed that this is a misplaced faith. There is, in fact, little evidence that competitive forces can be brought to bear, let alone solve the problem.

This chapter addresses similar issues, but begins with problems of measuring organisational efficiency and effectiveness from an economic perspective, the primary medium of the debate so far. We then go on to show, from a theoretical and empirical viewpoint, how the measures of efficiency used by organisations like the Industry Commission (IC) are deficient and provide no basis for the claim that privatisation is the answer to any problem revealed.

The view that there is gross inefficiency in the electricity industry and that the only solution is privatisation has been put forward by a number of business, political and institutional groups. In particular the IC has taken this view in its 1991 Draft Report on Energy Generation and Distribution. The title suggests that a wide ranging study of energy institutions and policy was carried out, but the Report is, in fact, limited in its scope to the gas and electricity industries' productive efficiency and the IC's suggested solution — exposure to "market discipline", or (better yet)

privatisation. That Report is examined in this chapter to assess the basis for charges of electricity industry inefficiency. On the basis of this assessment we go on to suggest why the IC's claims are, at a minimum, grossly extravagant and, probably, wrong. We then look at possible reasons why the Report's view that privatisation is the only answer is misplaced due to deficiencies in their analytical tools.

Finally we look at the corporatisation and privatisation experience in the United Kingdom and New Zealand, both OECD economies which are performing poorly at present. Both nations are considered by conservatives to provide a model for privatisation as the solution to the electricity industry's problems.

11.2 Measuring Efficiency in Enterprises and Industry.

Measuring the productive efficiency of any business has necessarily been a question of developing a range of input, output and outcome measures, as well as identifying links between these measured characteristics. The reason is that, in the real world, no one measure provides an accurate or appropriate measure of efficiency, productivity, or effectiveness. This is particularly so for GBEs because they operate in a regulatory environment that is often a product of their monopolistic character; the externalities they generate; and their diverse objectives. Despite the fact that, for such enterprises, diverse efficiency measures are essential to accurately monitor performance, there has been a tendency for many economists to advocate, and focus on, a single general measure of a GBE's productive efficiency and use this as an exemplar to characterise the industry as a whole. Some economists believe they have found the appropriate measure through the construction of measures of total factor productivity (TFP) and a few have developed it as the major indicator of factor efficiency (see, for example, BIE, 1991). The IC's Draft Report referred to above placed a great deal of reliance on TFP.

This section examines the measure's appropriateness and accuracy. We examine whether any limitations on data or conditionality in the theory are observable; whether they are made explicit; and whether they limit the Report's application. The case is extremely important because the major thrust of the IC report is that the industry is generally inefficient as measured by TFP, and that, therefore, privatisation is the only solution to the problems of the industry. This line of reasoning seems to be logically impeccable to the economists of the IC and, of course, to those private firms wishing to secure parts of the industry, hopefully at a discount because it is "run down" and "inefficient".

It should be remembered, of course, that the discussion here does not suggest that the question of productive and allocative efficiency or its measurement is not important or not examined in the IC Report but, rather, that *the key* measure of efficiency employed is the TFP measure. Some partial productivity measures are also used (and are also flawed) and some provide some support to the TFP argument, but it can be claimed that the IC's TFP analysis distorts the assessment and directs the debate away from the development of other productivity measures which could provide a more accurate view of what the dimensions (and causes) are of inefficiency in the ESI. Instead of taking the time and trouble of developing a *full range* of partial productivity measures that show the source of the problems in the industry and suggest the solutions to them, the limited and no more than indicative TFP measure used by the IC allows an ideological solution, privatisation, to be advocated rather than a list of practical recommendations to address the industry's problems.

Most economists in their analysis of an enterprises' efficiency, use a variety of partial measures. These measures might include the capital/output ratio, output per employee (labour productivity), cost per unit of output and a range of financial indicators (such as profit to equity, and equity to debt ratios). None of these measures, of themselves, provides a single accurate gauge of efficiency of an enterprise let alone an industry, although they can provide a rough guide. The reason for this is the different internal and external environments of each enterprise that arise, for example, from the variations in the age structure of fixed plant (or plants) and types of fuels and technologies used; or the impact of geography; and the different regulatory environments. This suggests that aggregative enterprise measures of efficiency as single measures are suspect and tell little about a diverse individual enterprise's efficiency. It also suggests that there a range of causes, quite separate from ownership, which contribute to inefficiencies.

This has not deterred or moderated the IC's analysis. The IC has made aggregation and generalisation a "high art" through its dependence on TFP to give a guide to the efficiency of the electricity industry in Australia.

Using this analysis, the IC can then justify its claim that the gains from an improvement in TFP in all States to the level of that of the most efficient State are between, at a minimum, $850 million (from efficient use of resources); and $1.4 billion (achievement of best world practice). The total benefits to the national economy estimated by the IC of the industry being optimally efficient might be an increase of $2.7 billion in national output (measured as GDP).[2] While savings are available to be made, this section now will suggest that savings on the scale estimated by the IC, are unlikely; and that even if they were available, the years it will take to earn them could range to that time in which Keynes said "we are all dead".

11.3 The Theory and Practice of Measuring Total Factor Productivity

Economists have correctly pointed out the limitations of single (partial) factor productivity measures like output per unit of labour input (Deakin and Seward, 1969, p.17). For many, the solution to this problem is the construction of a measure of output per unit of total factor input as a ratio, where the latter is an index of fixed proportions of capital and labour determined by their contribution to final output (TFP).

To the extent that the proportions of the values of output, and fixed proportions of capital and labour (the production functions) are changed according to estimations of changes in relative factor prices at different points in time it may provide a comparative static approach to measuring efficiency changes over time. We can express this as:

$$o_e = \Delta_{f(l,\,k,\,t)}$$

Where o_e = net value added
f = the functional relationship of the sum of the inputs
l = a productive unit of capital
k = a productive unit of labour
t = fixed technical conditions of production
As a ratio of output to the sum of inputs to produce the output — at a point in time with perfect information — TFP provides one possible empirical measure of efficiency. In order to provide a measure of changing efficiency this measure must be repeated at two points in time and a difference calculated to provide a measure of efficiency differences. Under these conditions a range of measurement and index number problems emerge which can undermine the concept to make it little more than the provision of a rough indicator or at worst an exercise in crude empiricism. The reasons for this include:

1. the measurement problems are associated with the difficulty of differentiating the factors and in fixing accurately the relationship between capital, labour, technology and output at a point in time, let alone over time. As Green commented in a recent paper that canvassed the subject of TFP, the idea that the measures of capital, labour and technological inputs can be easily separated was suggested as "absurd" by Nelson as far back as 1973 and yet this is vital for the measurement of TFP (Green, 1991, p.26). These problems were also identified in the "capital controversies" of the 1970s (see Harcourt, 1972);

2. the aggregation of measures of levels of technology and the difference between them in different enterprises and industries are particularly problematical; and

3. difficulties with the theory behind the TFP measure itself because of the limited range of factors with which it deals (l, k, t) that mean that where productivity gains are recorded they may be due to factors that are

not included, like institutional change. Other limitations are the functional relationships within the index itself that can only work if the factors are measurable and their quantities can change by small quantities. Further, all prices must be known and any regional or other differences in these must be adjusted for, as these differences can have significant effects on results. Knowledge is considered to be perfect and the TFP measure includes all the other conditions that apply to a neoclassical production function based model.

It is no surprise given the foregoing difficulties in the theory and the measurement of TFP, that it can often be called an "index of ignorance".

11.4 The Industry Commission's View

The basis for the IC's TFP measure and the efficiency gains it says can be achieved rests on a long chain of reasoning that begins, correctly, with dismissal of the use of a comparison of prices in selected countries to roughly measure efficiency (IC Draft, 1990, p.20; ESAA Submission, 1990, p.6). The IC rejects this measure for the quite legitimate reason that the obvious advantage of some countries (Canada in hydro or flare gas in the Gulf for example) makes comparison difficult and in any case comparisons should be only made with Australia's competitors. The IC should have also noted that there is no sound common pricing model used and this is also a problem. For comparison, the IC suggests Australia's competitors are third world countries like Brazil. It should be pointed out however, many of these also have natural advantages like the cheap hydro power, and of course Australia does have first world trade competitors like Canada and the United States in the OECD and it compares favourably with these countries as a group in general efficiency terms. Instead of turning to a range of partial indicators first, the IC in its analysis of the ESI, turns to measures of TFP and uses the work of Lawrence, Swan and Zeitsch (here notated LSZ) that compares the TFP of the five mainland utilities in 1990 (Lawrence, Swan and Zeitsch, 1990).

The LSZ system uses the technological efficiency calculations for the ESI worked out in the Industries Assistance Commission Report on Government (Non Tax) Charges of 1989 (IAC,

1989) as the basis for its analysis. It recognises that separating the sources of productivity differences (from geography or management) is difficult, (although the challenge of the aggregation of diverse outputs and inputs as single measures are not) despite the fact the use of these measures over time for comparisons is recognised as possibly inappropriate (Lawrence, Swan and Zeitsch, 1990, pp. 1–2).

The factor inputs into the LSZ System are labour, fuel, capital services and other inputs. It should be noted that the total money and quantity value of all the factors inputs in each state utility must be known and the list of components in each factor category must be the same. The analysis must only compare like with like, and provision must be made for differences (such as some utilities having a higher level of integration in some States than in others). Taking one factor, it can be assessed whether the IC estimates overall are reliable. In this study we have taken labour. In the IC's analysis, labour inputs include all operating and maintenance personnel, but do not include contract workers as this data does not exist. This exclusion was interpreted by the IC Draft Report as a sign of productivity gain (IC Draft, 1990, p.28) but this cannot be correct as this labour is still an input into the industry and must be included. The value and number of the labour force in each State directly employed by the authorities is known, and although it is not clear in this paper, some contract labour may have been included in the model to try and make the data of all the authorities comparable, but the report suggest this was not so with Queensland. This means the total value of labour input was not calculated appropriately. The problem is multiplied because the quantity and type of contract labour in each authority, in each State, is quite different depending on the technology the authorities use, skilled labour availability inside and outside authorities and so on. If this is the case, and it is almost certain it is, and contract services are lumped in with "other inputs" the data to produce a comprehensive labour input index for each State authority has not been constructed. The results reflect this – the State where contracting out is probably highest, Queensland, is shown to be most efficient in the LSZ results, with the highest TFP growth rates (See Lawrence, Swan and Zeitsch, 1990, pp. 4 &

7). These results are replicated in the IC Draft Report and are wrong for the same reasons.

The source of TFP differences is, to some extent, is to be found in factor differences and LSZ realise State differences must be transformed in partial productivity measures of inputs to outputs (Lawrence, Swan and Zeitsch, 1990, p.8) to be properly explained. The partial measures reflect, in terms of labour inputs at least, the source of Queensland's top TFP performance in the study of the five authorities examined (see also IC, 1991, p.28). The rest of the partial productivity measure differences used by the IC indicate (as a result, for example, of Victoria's investment in its capital intensive brown coal system compared to the other utilities) the source of capital use efficiency difference. This analysis is not going to show in detail why the capital input measures in the IC's TFP calculations are likely to be flawed, as some often suggested deficiencies are outlined in the ESAA and SECV responses to the ICs Draft Report (SECV, 1991, March, pp.18–19; ESAA, 1991, March, pp.13–14). The deficiencies suggested by the SECV are concerned with "poor and out of date data... data quality... current values of assets must be considered suspect... and failure to make allowance for technological change ... (and) the authors fail to find evidence of scale economies" (SECV, 1991 March, p.18). The ESAA response suggests similar deficiencies (ESAA, 1991, March, p.13). These criticisms suggest the measurement of efficiency by the IC is seriously deficient and the TFP approach must be abandoned. This is unlikely to occur in the IC's Final Report because it is on the basis of this general measure of inefficiency, that the call by the IC for corporatisation and privatisation is based. In contrast, the partial productivity measures begin to show why better investment and technology choices must be made in future years, but they also fail to provide a guide as to why the private sector would do this better than the public sector. It must be said, although we do not have the opportunity to expand on it here, that a lot more work is required on developing the partial measures as well.

Savings can be shown to be possible from a comparison of costs between each State following the LSZ system to suggest that $851 million can be saved by moving all authorities to Queensland's estimated TFP productivity level. The IC suggests even greater gains when a comparison is made with best international practice (see above). These claims are based in the IC Draft Report on international comparisons from the estimates of a private consulting firm done for an electricity authority and submitted as evidence to the Inquiry. The basis for these estimates is not available and must be treated with scepticism.

A further reason why the estimated savings calculated by the IC will not be realised is because the real economic system, unlike the IC's analysis, is not in theoretical static equilibrium but in real dynamic disequilibrium. The savings outlined by LSZ and the IC in reality, can only be achieved over an extended time period. Over time, when changes in relative prices of inputs and types of technologies employed change they alter the efficiencies of authorities differently. In other words there is no basis for saying whether they may or may not be realised, or when.

However, let's for exposition sake play the LSZ and IC game. If we assume 20 per cent of the total Australian savings calculated by the LSZ/IC system could be made in Year 1 of reform programs this will equal about $170 million or 1.9 per cent of the total revenue of the authorities. This compares with the TFP compound growth rates actually achieved as reported by the IC (IC, 1990, p.7) for NSW of 3.53 per cent for 1982/83 to 1988/89 and 6.19 per cent for Victoria, although South Australia's TFP growth was negative (and its causes were not explained in the IC's paper). It could be realistically said then, that these sorts of additional efficiency gains would not be beyond the existing five authorities analysed who have already made significant efficiency gains in the last five years when measured in terms of supply-side efficiency rather than end-use efficiency. This should be particularly so, if the management of the authorities and their political authorities were made more responsible for the performance, investment and other decisions they make. This means corporatisation, privatisation or the break up of authorities is unnecessary and may in fact be disruptive, as goals other than efficiency are pursued in the carve up. In any case, the private sector is not above making poor investment decisions and escaping the "discipline" of the market as recent events outlined in Chapter 10 show. In fact, it can be argued that in a real world

of high levels of uncertainty in the energy sector as a whole, large, integrated, publicly owned electricity enterprises employing large capitals and diverse technologies are essential to spread the risks of operating in such an environment.

11.5 Doing More with Less with ORANI

As we have shown, the basis for the efficiency gains claimed as possible in the IC report are the estimations based on a highly questionable theory and poor data. This is not seen by the IC as a deterrent from further claims of possible benefits from efficiency gains. These possible gains are estimated by taking the gains the IC calculated and previously outlined and input them into the ORANI macroeconomic model to suggest a rise national rise in GDP of $2.7 billion, and an extra 9,400 jobs generated. It is not proposed here to detail the reasoning employed to get the "headline getter" produced, except to make a few summary points.

The IC itself in its Draft Report, admits inadequacies and inconsistencies in its data and accepts its methodology is speculative (IC, 1990, pp.34, 35 etc.). This does not deter it from making further claims of efficiency gains built on the data produced in its models and confidential data supplied to it of further capital and other factor input savings projections in future years produced by the Queensland Electricity Commission (IC, 1990, January, p.35). An approach that surely cannot be taken seriously, and makes a mockery of a supposedly public inquiry, that should generate informed discussion, but reduces the process to an opaque manipulation of secret data by economic technocrats whose theory and empirical methodologies are highly suspect.

This approach is adopted despite the fact that the IC in its Report does include a wider range of productivity measures covering factors like reserve plant margins (RPMs) and pricing decisions that indicate poor management capital investment decisions and technological choices in the past with considerable room for efficiency gains. At the core of the problem is the industry's history in the 1970s, under the leadership of the federal Fraser Government that over-estimated the industrial capacity needed to provide electricity for the aluminium plants and other energy intensive industries that were to lead the "minerals boom". Plants were built in the 1970s (and they take a long time to bring on stream and last on average, for over 30 years) that created excess capacity and the inefficiency and waste of the 1980s. Reserve capacity still exists in New South Wales while energy deficits are emerging elsewhere. A partial solution to this problem is the future development of the National Grid to use it and not destroy this capacity or sell some of it off.

The inadequate labour measures (in contrast to the capital measures which themselves are deficient) are emphasised in the IC Draft Report and are used in such a way as to suggest an almost pathological desire to indicate labour inefficiency through over manning, despite the acknowledged fall in the labour force over the last five years (IC, 1990, January, p.28) and the recognised substitution of authority employees for contractors, which may not indicate any efficiency gain or loss to the industry as a whole. It should be remembered that cuts in the labour force may not mean cuts in labour costs over time as managers and directors may increase their salaries and fees to offset gains from this source. Labour force reductions may also mean demand-side activity cuts to staff working on energy end-use efficiency (which bring a wide range of benefits: see Chapters 5 and 12) as these are relatively easy to make .

The question of what is wrong with the claims of GDP and job gains resulting from feeding ORANI, a static linear econometric model of the Australian economy, is that all gains are recorded as being made at once. This is unrealistic as gains will accrue, if at all, at a lower accumulative level, as we have suggested, over time. The markets clearing assumption in the ORANI model means that jobs and GDP will be generated but this may not be the case (see Chapman, 1990, pp.10–17). To the extent that efficiency gains are translated into higher employment and output, it will also reduce electricity prices (see IC, 1990, January, p.41) and increase electricity usage. The consequences in terms of the social cost of the externalities like environmental damage from higher electricity use may be considerable and erode the economic gains ORANI calculates (Chapman, 1990, p.13).

Emphasising the hidden cost of externalities is not in the purview of the IC however, who

suggest (IC, 1990, January, p.43) selling of excess capacity to force prices down and electricity consumption up; the capacity to be sold at "bargain basement" prices. A privatisation objective that is a recurring theme in the work of Professor Swan as well (see Swan, 1989, p.57) whose work has been heavily drawn on by the IC and other institutions, like CRA involved in the energy area (see Dixon, et al, 1989). The sale of the ESI would be a cost to the community equal to the undervaluation of the assets necessary to sell them. England and Wales' experience indicates public asset value losses will be large as we indicate later in this chapter.

In Australia, privatisation would not, of course, reduce the ESI's monopoly character or bring down prices in the longer run, as privately owned power stations would demand and probably get base load supply privileges and require heavy regulation, and leave the residual public sector still a high cost industry. These are the microeconomic consequences of the suggested process of privatisation before the macroeconomic and monetary policy consequences in terms of greater debt, possible contributions to the balance of payments imbalance are dealt with and these may not be to Australia's benefit. The IC Draft Report itself does not deal with these questions in any detail at all and this is yet another major weakness in it.

If we take the foregoing to account, the IC's claims made on the basis of its ORANI projections (IC, 1990, p.47) that national output will increase by $2.7 billion annually in 1989/90 values; that 9,400 jobs will be created; that annual disposable income per household will rise $330 and income taxes will fall by 0.7 per cent as a result of its proposed reforms could seem to be a gross misrepresentation of the facts, based as they are on long questionable chains of reasoning with results that will, at best, take a long time to be realised. If we are prepared to accept worthwhile savings are to be made, and we do, the "cargo cult" of ORANI generated gains, delivered via TFP improvements are distractions from the real world of practical programs for improving productivity. As Green has commented in another context which is applicable here "*a priori* economic reasoning, plus measures to force a complex bundle of technologies, organisation, institutions both functional and instrumental to conform to its simple price nexus is disastrous" (Green, 1990, p.53 his emphasis). This is shown graphically in the IC's Draft Report.

Under-developed and flawed productivity measures like TFP gain prominence through their use by the IC, yet organisations like EPAC (1990b, p.90) have warned these are suspect and, as we have pointed out here, when these are coupled with market models like ORANI they assume the efficiency gains will automatically be turned into jobs and money incomes. These issues were also of concern to Associate Commissioner Webb, the industry's representative on the IC Inquiry who said at a seminar at the University of New South Wales in 1990 that he was concerned about the use of the TFP methodology as well as other matters. This concern did not seem to change the ICs view, or his ideas were ignored, and the latter is more likely, as the 1991 Draft Report of the IC is merely an expanded and updated version of its 1989 report on Government (Non-Tax) Charges which it said in 1991 was deficient (IC, 1991). The illusion of gross inefficiency in the ESI that is created by the IC, can only be seen as ideological in nature to provide the basis for policy proposals like privatisation. This report considers this view is not justified due to the conditions which operate in the monopolistic markets in which the industry works, and avoids the organisational and political reforms that will make them operate better in the long run. This is despite a range of ideas for improving efficiency being put forward by EPAC (see EPAC, 1988, EPAC, 1990a) or others with both supply and demand suggestions for change (see for example Hilmer, 1990). The work to improve long term efficiency is already under way as the IC report shows (IC, 1990, pp.26–31) and this should be increased rather than dismantling the system and putting back necessary change on both the supply and demand side of the industry.

11.6 The Pressure for Radical Change: Privatisation

Conservatives argue that any problems arising from inefficiency are best resolved by privatisation and the creation of a "competitive" environment. Usually the two solutions are conflated, though the IC (for instance) in its 1991 Draft Report on the industry does assume that privatisation alone confers certain efficiency advantages — a claim we have already shown is not well supported but which we now examine again to see where this idea comes from in economics and what it means.

The Commission has listed the disciplines which it thinks that authorities are not subject and to which they would become subject after privatisation (we have listed these in Chapter 10). The IC recognises that these disciplines "may operate imperfectly", but the Commission retains the belief that imposition of these disciplines would enhance the efficient operation of the electricity authorities (IC, 1991, Part 1). In this respect, we suggest, for example, that it is necessary to recognise that only some private sector enterprises have their securities publicly traded, and even where they are traded "discipline" is often weakened (or made non-existent). Further, the development of private company holdings in listed companies (for instance) has burgeoned in Australia; and the rapid growth of institutional shareholdings, especially superannuation funds, often means that shareholdings are retained on the basis of *security* of return rather than *rate* of return. This serves to weaken market "discipline".

Traditional arguments about the discipline of the market assume an extensive quantity of high quality information being released to the market. In practice, managers may and, as recent events have shown, often do manipulate information released, while investment and borrowing activities are not effectively monitored by the stock market since listed entities do not provide continuous disclosures about their borrowing and investment activities.

In respect of raising debt capital on commercial terms, it must be pointed out that borrowing by all enterprises including State enterprises is influenced by a number of factors that serve to regulate their borrowing. The level of interest rates, for example, include components for the actual cost of funds, the credit risk, the tradeability of the issued paper and the inflationary expectations.

The rates of interest charged to government bodies do vary on the basis of these commercially determined components of the rates. For example, the "tradeability" of paper issued by a large State is greater than the tradeability of paper issued by small States. Further, rates do not only vary between States, but between authorities in one State. It was precisely this variability which led to the creation of centralised borrowing agencies such as the Treasury Corporation (T-Corp.) in New South Wales and similar borrowing authorities in other States (Evatt, 1989, p.148). However, when comparing public and private borrowing there is also a fundamental difference in the maturity structures of corporate debt and government debt which makes direct comparisons difficult.

11. 7 Views on Competition

There is a tendency among many advocates of competition to do so without any analysis of how it is to be achieved. For example, the New South Wales Government's Submission to the IC lists the following advantages of competition in the ESI:

> It is believed that the free market approach has the potential to offer advantages over more traditional co-ordinated planning models in three main areas:
> • more appropriate capital investment decisions
> • more pressure to reduce operating costs
> • more economically based pricing arrangements (New South Wales Government, 1990, Vol.1, pp.11–12).[3]

The State Electricity Commission of Victoria has also adopted this view of the benefits of competition:

> SECV's experience suggests that internal administrative changes must be reinforced by external market forces if substantial improvements are going to be made and sustained (SECV, 1990, p.1).

But this still does not tell us how a free market (i.e. competition) is supposed to deliver these goals. To reach an understanding of how competition is automatically supposed to enhance the operations of an enterprise, it is necessary to consider the central role which competition plays in the (dominant) neoclassical economic paradigm; to investigate why it has that role; and to critically examine the implications for policy development and implementation of the policies.[4]

Competition in the neoclassical paradigm

The source of the belief in the efficacy of competition as a solution for every economic problem is contained in the dominant paradigm in economics. That paradigm is neoclassical theory and its attendant derivative applications, one of which was the TFP measure which we have already discussed. The core of the theory maintains that the factors determining supply and demand and the mechanisms that clear markets in the short run are competitively driven, and it is this core belief and its myriad permutations that is the focus in the teaching and practice of many economists. The centrality of competition has been noted by Demsetz:

> Competition occupies so important a position in economics that it is difficult to imagine economics as a social discipline without it (Demsetz, 1982, p.1).

Some commentators, indeed, argue that competition is a cornerstone of society:

> Western society is organised on the assumption that firms freely compete for markets for goods and services, for access to factors of production and for ownership of other less efficient firms. In this competitive game, there are high rewards for successful players and a promise of ever rising standards of living for all spectators (Burke et al, 1988, p.ix).

We can describe this attitude towards competition as an *artide of faith*, or *dogma*.[5] The claim made by the neoclassicists can be considered grandiose, ignoring as it does the institutions, structures or the historical context that play such an important role in understanding the real economy and how it works. Nevertheless, the sorts of views advanced by Demsetz are also evident in the policy prescriptions developed by the IC (and its predecessor, the Industries Assistance Commission — the IAC) in virtually all their Reports. For example:

> Chapters 5 and 6 explained how the Hearing Services Program and the Free Limbs Scheme have led to productive inefficiency and less competition in both the private and public markets. Demand for free services has exceeded supply for some years. However, even though there have been long waiting lists, competition from the private sector has remained restricted. Where goods are pro-

vided free and competition is restricted, prices do not operate as a market signal to either producers or consumers. The result is that the options available to people with disabilities are reduced (IC, 1990b, p.152).

What is not said here, is that the distributional consequences of the IC's proposal are that the poor (while they may not queue) are likely to be unable to afford the limbs etc, and will thus be unable to continue to make a worthwhile contribution to the community, to the community's cost. The conservatives' views are not shared by all economists for, as Groenewegen, notes:

> The economic theory of the efficiency consequences of competitive market adjustment is filled with traps for young players (including young Turks). The pure concept of economic efficiency is linked to both the market condition of perfect competition and equilibrium states. Equilibrium states are a tool of analysis essential to much economic theory and useful to focus attention on some propositions which otherwise are not logically attainable. However, the limitations inherent in such propositions need to be fully understood. Prefect competition is likewise an artificial construct which by its very, definitional, nature, can never exist because this contravenes the physical laws of time and space (Groenewegen, 1990, p.10).

Neoclassical economists claim to have inherited their view of the effectiveness of competition from the classical foundations of the discipline (Demsetz, 1982, p.1; Clower, 1988, p.95). However, this neat view of the continuity of economics over a period in excess of two centuries is not borne out by a closer examination of the matter. As Clifton comments:

> *Perfect* competition is a particular theory of competition that arose only at the origin of neoclassical value theory in the late 19th century. The concept of competition used by the classical economists and Marx did not require atomism of independent agents — the essential "perfection" of perfect competition. With the development of neoclassical price theory perfect competition was modified to imperfect competition, in order to add realism to the analysis. Although imperfect competition was viewed at the time as being a significant improvement in the neo-

classical theory, it did not really stand apart from perfect competition, which was seen as an ideal or "benchmark", from which the capitalist reality deviated to a greater or lesser degree as history unfolded.

Another remnant of imperfect competition remains, however: the vision of capitalist development implicit in the evolution of neoclassical theory from perfect to imperfect competition. It is only under conditions of perfect competition that competition freely reigns in the neoclassical system (Clifton, 1988, pp.137–138).

Clifton goes on to argue that it is the modern corporation that can achieve the competitive advantages which follow from capital mobility, rather than the small atomised firm. This is because the corporation is more flexible, and hence is able to more quickly and effectively shift capital between alternative uses. It is necessary to fully understand the implications of this analysis for neoclassically based policy initiatives in the public sector. It is interesting to note, too, that such optimally efficient outcomes are achieved from this view-point as from "bureaucratic" decision-making, not the operation of an unfettered market.[6]

The neoclassicists argue that competitive behaviour which occurs in the realm of distribution (via the price mechanism) provides the signals whereby atomistic firms will shift capital to alternative uses (Clifton, 1977, p.146). It should be noted that this idea can only have validity where capital is mobile and this is only usually true where capitals are small and the business is serving consumer goods or service markets where entry and exit is comparatively easy. Clifton goes on to elucidate the two fallacies on which the neoclassical view is predicated:

> The first is the fallacy that the conditions of free capital mobility are established in the context of exchange, as of course they can be for merchant capital. The second is the mistaken notion that durable capital goods are equivalent to financial capital and can therefore be transferred from sector to sector, establishing competition (Clifton, 1977, p.146).

On the other hand, the large corporate enterprise can more closely approximate the condition of capital mobility:

The fixed capital of the firm has become increasingly mobile as the firm has grown, by industrial and geographical diversification, out of its original sphere of production. Such a firm may be called a "unit of general production", because it organises production across a wider spectrum of the full range of production possibilities than the single product firm itself to achieve a more efficient allocation of its capital between several activities and regions, in accordance with changing market conditions (Clifton, 1977, p.147).

If the neoclassical view of the social advantages resulting from capital flows from less efficient to more efficient uses is correct, then it would appear that, rather than breaking up the various electricity authorities, there is no reason to fragment the industry, and it would, in fact, be more efficient to extend their range of activities in ways that we propose in Chapter 12.[7] It also has important implications for the implementation of national integration.

11.8 Exceptions within Neoclassical Economics

In neoclassical economics, the achievement of Pareto optimality (i.e. the position where the existing resources of the economy cannot be re-allocated without making somebody worse off and the ultimate goal of competitive pressure) depends on the following conditions being met:

> ... profit maximisation on the part of producers, prices equal to costs (marginal or minimum average) and consumer freedom (sovereignty) to maximise want satisfaction (utility) (Groenewegen, 1988, p.9).

Further, we should add these conditions must apply in all sectors of the economy at the same time, which means that there is no room for a government role in this economy if an optimal outcome is to occur. These conditions cannot be met (only second best at best) but has not hindered the economic theologians from continuing to advocate the extension of competition to public sector bodies: they discuss "approximations" to the competitive ideal (see Groenewegen, 1990, pp.11–12). Nevertheless, most neoclassicist do admit to limitations of the application of competition: natural monopolies, the existence of Community Service Obligations (CSOs), externalities and public goods.

A natural monopoly is one where technical conditions and market size are such that it would be impossible or undesirable to have more than one incumbent firm. Monopolies are characteristic of the capitalist economy, as Kalecki notes:

> A world in which the degree of natural monopoly determines the distribution of national income is a world far removed from the pattern of free competition. Monopoly appears to be deeply rooted in the capitalist system: free competition may be useful as an assumption, may be useful in the first stage of certain investigations, but as a description of the normal state of the capitalist economy it is mainly a myth (Kalecki, quoted in Kriesler, 1988, p.16)

In recognition of the adverse effects (for example, high price and low quality) which could result from the unfettered operation of a private monopoly in such a market, Australian governments have tended to "grant" the monopoly to the public sector, subject as it is to political and social control.

The existence of natural monopolies, and the limitation this poses to the introduction of competition has led to the development of the concept of "contestability" by the conservatives. In its crudest form this suggests that the removal of legal barriers to entry can have the same impact as the existence of competition. This is because, it is argued, the threat of competition acts as a disincentive to the existing monopoly suppliers to extract monopoly profits. If they did, new entrants could enter and soak up part of this profit and, over time, establish themselves as long-term viable competitors at any price level. There are weaknesses to such an argument.

For example, even when the legal barriers to entry are removed, monopoly profits can continue to be extracted. The logical explanation for the failure of any such strategy is that the costs of entry are still prohibitively high. As Fine has noted:

> In general, contestability has received quite a cool reception on the ground that its prerequisite, the absence of sunk cost (and hence costless exit and the impossibility of effective 'incumbents') is far from realistic (Fine, 1990, p.129).

On a theoretical level, Groenewegen has been even more scathing:

Although still prominent in the textbook world, where fairy tales tend to linger on in economics, the notion of contestability has theoretically lost its sheen in the policy world designed to ensure practical extensions of competition (Groenewegen, 1990, p.12).

Realistically, therefore, regulation of existing public monopolies will remain a more successful way of ensuring that price levels and service quality are maintained.

Traditionally, progressives have argued that, *though monopoly profits might continue to be generated,* they can be distributed to the community in the form of free-to-user services, subsidy-to-user services and income transfers. However, a more realistic analysis is required. This re-analysis needs to begin with a realisation that a price charged by a public sector monopoly which contributes to monopoly profits has, in effect, two components. First, there is, as conventionally understood, a charge. Second, because the monopoly supplier is free to charge a price containing a constant element of over-charging, its incidence is similar to that of a consumption tax. In this situation an observation made in 1989 regarding the equity implications is pertinent:

> It seems clear from the available evidence on tax incidence and the final beneficiaries of subsidies that the distributional impact of free-to user and subsidy-to-user services is by no means invariably to the benefit of "widows and orphans", to use the old cliche, that is to say, there are extensive benefits to people who fall outside the objectives of a policy designed to benefit working people and the poor (Evatt, 1989, p.189).

Admitting, then, that the equity implications of a publicly-owned monopoly earning monopoly profits (even where they fund income transfers or subsidisation) is problematic, there may indeed remain the need for a regulatory body to be created. Such a regulatory body could be similar to that proposed for New South Wales in 1986 (McDonell, 1986).

11.9 The Electricity Industry and Natural Monopoly

In respect of the electricity industry and the natural monopoly argument, neoclassicists usually break the industry down into its constituent parts: generation, bulk transmission and distri- bution to final consumers, though in some States this distinction is not apparent in the institutional arrangements (New South Wales Government, 1990, p.18).

These economists admit that electricity transmission falls into the recognised category of "natural monopoly". Rarely do they acknowledge, however, that the point at which transmission becomes distribution is not clear (see Chapters 7 and 8). For instance, the New South Wales transmission system in 1989 consisted of 734km of 500kV transmission circuits, 4826 km of 330 kV circuits, 681 km of 220 kV circuits and 8666km of 132kV transmission circuits (Elcom, 1989, p.15). However, in 1990 the New South Wales government transferred ownership of the 132kv lines from the Electricity Commission to the County Councils, so they are now counted as part of the distribution system.

The transmission system in Victoria includes high voltage lines and equipment from 66kV to 500kV, and also includes some 22kV of subtransmission ties (SECV, 1990, p.46). Moreover, there remain strong technical arguments for also considering distribution as a natural monopoly. This has been tacitly accepted by the SECV:

> There is no clear evidence that either corporate separation or privatisation results in a more efficient distribution system (SECV, 1990, p.11).

We are left with the conclusion therefore, that electricity transmission and distribution should be retained as publicly owned monopolies. There are also strong *technical* arguments for considering electricity distribution as a natural monopoly. Plants cannot directly compete because each has specific technical and capital-cost characteristics.[8]

In this situation, those who maintain that changes are required in the institutional arrangements of the transmission and distribution sectors of the electricity industry in order to achieve efficiency gains are left with two alternatives. First, retention of public ownership with significant internal reform to the agency, or tight regulation of a private monopoly. There are certain efficiency losses associated with the second alternative, clearly seen in the United States where a virtual shadow management operates, duplicating the functions of the utilities' own bureaucracies (Evatt, 1989, p.203; SECV, 1990, p.10). This shadow management exists in the attempt to ensure that the operations and decision-making of the utilities are transparent and, thus, that the utilities are accountable. It could hardly be asserted that efficiency advantages accrue from this situation.

It is often argued that electricity generation falls into a separate category:

> To ensure that a competitive force is maintained some private generation should be encouraged as soon as is practicable (SECV, 1990, p.13);

and, from Wicks:

> ... efforts to maximise efficiency in other areas of power generation, transmission and use become very important.

> Key areas where the scope for such an increase in economic efficiency exist [include] — increased competition, particularly through greater private sector participation (Wicks, 1990, p.3).

These statements are made on the assumption that greater competitive pressure will enhance efficiency. Such statements validate Groenewegen's statements above that the theoretical benefits of competition have achieved almost mythical proportions. Moreover, the emergence of lower-level technologies in electricity generation do not inexorably lead to the conclusion that more competition will result, or is desirable.

In fact, the Swedish situation illustrates quite the converse. At the World Conference on Electricity held in London in late 1989, Mans Lonnroth delivered the final paper. In that paper he stated:

> Public ownership may not have been terribly important in the past. Now, with technology being steadily more diverse, public ownership becomes important (Lonnroth, 1989).

The reason for a necessary expansion of the public sector resulting from these new technologies is that access to them will need to be guaranteed by the state. The market dominance of the existing technologies which, over many years have been refined and perfected (as well as the upstream industries' comfort with those technologies) could make the application of alternative technologies difficult. As we have previously noted, expansion into these tech-

nologies (even utilising a realistic version of neo-classical theory) could enable the existing authorities to achieve the competitive advantages which Clifton has noted occurred in the corporate sector. Given the social and political control exercised over the operations of public bodies, it would be preferable to maintain it.

11.10 Competition and Policy Development

It is also necessary to be aware of just how influential the mythology of competition is in the area of practical policy development. The example in Western Australia of the work of the Review Committee on Power Options for Western Australia is a case in point.

In May 1990 the Committee's Report outlined the options available for Private Generation Solely for Supply to SECWA – privatisation. It is the second of these options (Build, Own and Operate: BOO) with which we are primarily concerned. The Report notes:

> The BOO approach is an application of the concept of contracting out, which is always an option for the supply of services in any enterprise (WA Review Committee, 1990, p.63).

The Report also argues that:

> ... without the acceptance of private ownership, co-generation and renewable energy would have very limited market prospects (WA Review Committee, 1990, p.64).

In respect of the "Power Options" conclusion regarding private ownership, and co-generation, we believe that the Committee has incorrectly linked these two developments. Co-generation occurs where an enterprise either generates electricity directly, or produces the energy necessary to generate electricity. Electricity entering the grid from these sources is a by-product of enterprises' primary activities. Correctly analysed in this way, co-generation provides no basis for the extension of private ownership of large-scale generating plant.

In a paper delivered by the Chairman of the Review Committee at the 19th Conference of Economists, Dr. F.J. Harman identified the following limitations on the Review Committee's Inquiry which indicated that, to a significant degree, its outcome was predetermined:

1. the State Energy Commission of Western Australia had called for expressions of in-

terest in various forms of private sector participation *before* the Review Committee was established (p.1);

2. the Review Committee was not given the resources at the time to make its own analysis of private sector involvement in a power station (p.3);

3. the Committee could only consider broad estimates of costs as well as general principles (p.4);

4. the Committee "... chose to follow the terms of reference closely and to exclude from consideration a range of other policy criteria including employment and regional impacts from fuel extraction and power station construction and operation" (p.4); and

5. "... (the) narrow focus on lowest cost also meant that renewable energy sources did not get the support of the Committee on the grounds that while competitive in the non-interconnected system for remote area application, in the interconnected system renewable energy could not offer the lowest cost supply. That decision was made without the benefit of an analysis of external costs associated with the range of generation technologies available over the full cycle of the operation from fuel extraction to plant de-commissioning" (Harman, 1990, pp.4–5).

These limitations must be borne in mind when considering the Review Committee's conclusions on privatisation, especially those concerning private sector involvement and environmental issues. The use of the dogma of competition is even more observable in the IC Draft Report (IC, 1990c, pp.91–123), though here the Commission tacitly accepts that transmission is a natural monopoly.[9]

11.11 Conclusion

In this Chapter we have concentrated on a critique, both theoretical and practical, of the arguments for greater competition. We have noted that the economic arguments concerning competition are based on the elevation of a simplistic world view to the status of dogma. We have shown that in the area of policy development, conclusions regarding the advantages of competition are developed from an *a priori* position on the application of competitive

pressures, an *a priori* position which has little relevance to the situation in the ESI. We have concentrated on this aspect of the privatisation argument because it forms the backbone of the position that organisations like the IC have adopted

It is also worth noting that privatisation does not always result in competition.

What is required in the electricity industry is not so much competition between disaggregated authorities: there is no rational economic basis for this. What is required is better control of these enterprises and better production, distribution and end-use information as the basis for making better decisions about them. The hard work of developing appropriate performance indicators and doing the coordination to make them common across all authorities as far as possible has yet to be done.

11.12 International Comparisons

A major source of inspiration for bodies like the IC in Australia has been the experience overseas, especially that of the United Kingdom and New Zealand. We have suggested elsewhere in this report in respect to the National Grid the experience of countries other than these might be more relevant. In this section which deals with privatisation the situation in England and Wales and New Zealand are examined as these are the most often quoted in this debate.

England and Wales

We have noted that the State Electricity Commission of Victoria has been less than overwhelmingly positive in its assessment of the situation in England and Wales following privatisation of the electricity industry in parts of the United Kingdom's industry.[10] In this section we will point out why this is the case. We will also use it to illustrate some of the points we have made regarding the implications of implementing the sorts of policies the IC (and others) would like to see applied to Australia.

It is worth noting first the nature of the industry prior to privatisation.

Before the privatisation of the electricity industry in England and Wales, the bulk of the industry was owned and controlled by the public sector. In many respects, it had a structure similar to that of New South Wales. The Central

Electricity Generating Board (CEGB) was responsible for the generation and transmission (through the National Grid) of bulk electricity. The twelve Area Supply Boards received this electricity at "bulk supply points" and delivered it to customers through their own distribution networks. The Area Supply Boards also sold electrical appliances in retail outlets and ran electrical contracting businesses.

The passing of the 1989 Electricity Act means that British Coal (and the nuclear generators) will remain the only parts of the energy sector publicly owned. British National Oil Corporation, British Gas and British Petroleum had already been privatised. The industry has now been broken into four separate components:

Generation: the production of electricity;

Transmission: the transfer of electricity across England and Wales;

Distribution: the delivery of electricity over local networks; and

Supply: the acquisition of electricity and its re-sale to customers.
Supply is different from distribution in the following way: distribution carries power from the national grid to individual customers. Supply involves the purchase of bulk electricity from generators and its resale to customers.

The details of the structural changes are as follows.

Generation

Two privatised generators now operate: National Power PLC and Power Gen. The nuclear generators are now operated by a publicly owned company, Nuclear Electric. The pumped storage stations at Ffestinog and Dinorwig are owned by the transmission company.

Transmission

The National Grid Company is owned by the twelve privatised Regional Electricity Companies, which also have responsibility for interconnection with Scotland and France. It will also run ancillary services businesses.

Distribution

The government has recognised that the distribution system, like the transmission system, falls into the economic category of natural monopoly. Thus, while the distribution authorities have been privatised, they retain, as a group, their monopoly status for a time. They are obligated to offer terms to meet all reasonable demands for electricity from customers in their authorised areas. In the longer term, customers will be able to purchase electricity from any distribution company, generator or authorised supplier. They were floated on the stock exchange in late 1990. They are known as Regional Electricity Companies.

Supply

The distribution companies also operate the supply business. Other companies can undertake supply activity, becoming electricity brokers. Supply is divided into two groups of customers: those whose maximum demand is 10MW or less and are therefore entitled by law to receive their supplies from the local distribution company at a published tariff; and those whose demand is greater that 10MW who have to contract individually with their distribution company.

There are two features of the previous electricity industry which are (necessarily) incorporated into the privatised and competitive structure of the new industry. First, the load at a particular time determines the generation level required at that time. Second, the physical impossibility of determining the particular source of any generation and the load or customer to which it is applied. The first characteristic requires the retention of a central coordination/ scheduling despatch facility, and the second requires the effective combination of all generating output. The concept of a *Pooling Arrangement* is the result.

Thus, there should be a single market price for wholesale electricity at any time. The rules set down to govern the scheduling and despatch, planning, connection, operating and data registration procedures form a Grid Code.

The Pooling and Settlement System

The pooling and settlement system operated by the National Grid coordinates the supply of electricity to users and acts as a clearing house for paying the suppliers and collecting from the buyers. Membership of the System is a requirement for generators, distributors, suppliers and those trading over the interconnectors. Others who have an agreement with either their distributor, supplier or who are connected directly to the National Grid Company. There is a membership fee, and the members are responsible for ensuring that all relevant information is fed into the System.

In simple terms the pool works in the following way. By 1000 hours each day all generators must supply the National Grid a schedule of bid (or offer) prices for each generating unit for each half hour of the following day. The offer price are those that at which the operator is willing to operate, at different levels of output, each separate available generating unit for each half hour of the following day. Each offer price includes a start up price, a fixed price and up to three "incremental prices" per unit of electricity produced. Other information relating to plant availability must also be supplied. By 1500 hours on the same day, the National Grid Company will provide a schedule based, in the main, on merit order despatch which details the times and levels of generation required and any special operating requirements (MOA, 1991, p.11). Conceptually, this operates as a "spot market" with a market clearing price:

NGC will rank each generating unit in order of increasing offer prices. The ranking of stations in this way is called the "Merit Order". NGC will also examine its demand forecast for the next day, and large users' forecasts of their own demand, and calculate the operating regime for all the generating units that will meet expected demand over the next day at lowest cost. The calculations will take into account, amongst other things:

> *transmission constraints:* some combinations of operating regimes of the generating units would overload the transmission system and so will be avoided;
>
> *plant characteristics:* the dynamics of plant, for example some power stations take many hours to start and are labelled "inflexible". NGC must be informed of such constraints; and
>
> *system stability:* in order to maintain a stable system, it is necessary to have sufficient plant available as "reserve" and necessary

for some generating units to produce "reactive" power and provide other ancillary services (James Capel, 1990, p.22).

The NGC will, later on the same day as bids are made, publish a schedule advising when the generators' output is required and other operating requirements.

Price

The procedure by which price is set is extraordinarily complex, and we do not need to fully outline the procedure here.[11] In simple terms, the price normally paid will be the offer price of the highest price station operating at that time. Sometimes constraints within the transmission system can cause plant to be "constrained on or off" and other prices may apply. The price to be paid will compensate for the losses which result. This is known as the "system marginal price" (SMP) (MOA, 1991, p.11; James Capel, 1990, pp. 23–25).

As the transmission system is being retained as a natural monopoly, it will undergo a form of price control, similar to the CPI-x formulae used by various Australian governments to limit price increases of statutory authorities (including electricity authorities). One of the new features of the industry is the requirement to publish prices paid for electricity. The purchase price is not finalised until twenty-eight days after the sale occurred in order to allow for transmission costs to be met.

The industry is also regulated. There are three bodies primarily responsible for implementation of that regulatory regime operating under the authority of the Secretary of State for Energy. They are the Director General of Electricity Supply (DGES); the Monopolies and Mergers Commissions; and the Director General of Fair Trading. The DGES heads the office of Electricity Regulation (OFFER). The DGES also chairs a National Consumers' Committee. There are also consumer committees in each Regional Electricity Company's area.

The DGES is responsible for reviewing the terms of licenses for the system participants, and will undertake price reviews. S/he will also set the amounts to which consumers are entitled resulting from disconnection caused by breakdown or other causes. The Regional Electricity Companies are required to provide advice on the efficient use of electricity, and the DGES oversees this role to ensure that it occurs without diminution of the competitive environment. Disputes between members of the poling and settlement system are mediated and arbitrated by the DGES. Finally:

> The DGES has a responsibility to ensure that the industry makes satisfactory arrangements for the health and safety of the workforce and that the public is not at risk from the industry's activities. In addition, he has to exercise his functions in a manner which he considers is best calculated to secure that all reasonable demands for electricity are met (James Capel, 1990, p.37).

We have already noted the requirement that the Regional Electricity Companies provide advice regarding energy efficiency. The other (supposedly) environmental responsibility which the industry must exercise is known as the "Fossil Fuel Levy". However, this operates as little more than a direct subsidy to the expensive British nuclear fuel industry. The Regional Electricity Companies are required to purchase a specified amount of their supplies from Nuclear Electric through the Non-Fossil Purchasing Agency. The levy is designed to spread the additional costs over the whole industry. It appears that the incidence of this levy will be similar to that of an indirect tax (James Capel, 1990, pp. 28–29).

The results so far

Looking at the system in operation it is difficult to be certain of exactly how it is working as it has been in place for only a short time (MOA, 1991, p.13), and the fact that the regulator has only made one decision so far. This decision will be examined below. Nevertheless, there are certain features of the privatisation of the industry that can be questioned, both in terms of their implications for the responsibility of governments to exercise adequate stewardship of the citizens' resources; on the economic efficiency issue; and on environmental grounds.

On the first of these issues, it has been reported that the total revenue earned from the sale of the industry was £15 billion. The value of the assets, however, has been estimated as £39 billion (MOA, 1991, p.13). This raises serious questions regarding the actual motivation of the government in privatising the industry. It was also reported that the arrangements for sale of equity were specially designed to "gild the lily" for small purchasers:

> The incentives to small shareholders have been made particularly generous to try to avoid a flop. For those buying up to 1,500 shares there are discounts available on their electricity bills or the possibility of receiving bonus shares. For a minimum investment in 100 shares, investors will get a voucher worth £18.00 as a discount on their electricity bills. The main attraction of this privatisation is, however, the arrangements to pay in instalments. If the shares are priced at, for example £2.50 then investors will have to pay £1 on application, 75p in October 1991 and then 75p in September 1992. Not only is there plenty of time to pay but shareholders will actually be able to get their discount voucher and receive a first dividend payment then sell their shares before paying the second instalment (Labour Research, 1990, p.4).

The losses to the community are self evident and this is important if we consider that the responsibility of governments in respect of the assets it manages is to "... maximise social returns to social capital, of which, in a representative democracy, government is the mere custodian on behalf of the people" (Evatt, 1989, p.179). That any government is willing to alienate public assets in a fashion as cavalier as the British government is a matter of concern to all citizens in a Westminster-style democracy. It is illustrative, yet again, of a fundamental conceptual inadequacy whereby government custody and government ownership are confused. The sale of the assets of the people at bargain prices is the unseen part of the price of what may or may not be cheaper electricity far into the future in Britain.

In respect of economic efficiency, we have already noted the theoretical and practical limitations of policies which are designed to introduce competition to an industry. We must also ask whether the efficiency losses which are observable in the United States due to a large regulatory bureaucracy which "shadows" the operation of the private participants will not be duplicated in the United Kingdom.

Referring specifically to the British example,

the situation which now exists in respect of the costly and dangerous nuclear industry must also be questioned. The fact that the nuclear industry is to continue to receive subsidisation runs counter to the whole philosophy of the privatisation agenda. There is clear evidence that this resulted from a pre-conceived commitment to nuclear power on the part of the former British Prime Minister (*Economist*, 28 January, 1989, p.54).

In respect of the environmental issues which have been ignored in the British example, the point was made in the *Economist* as long ago as 1988 when it noted:

> Energy efficiency is cheap, too. The capital needed for each extra kilowatt of nuclear capacity is around £1,300. This is 6–12 times the cost of saving that same kilowatt. Energy-saving investments typically pay for themselves within four years at most, within four months if you are lucky.
>
> The government itself proclaims that £8 billion of the nation's £38 billion energy bill could be saved through greater efficiency. But it is not keen on subsidising users into doing what self-interest should make them do anyway. It is now "targeting" its fuel-saving promotional efforts — i.e., cutting them back (10 December 1988, p.70).

In respect of the regulator, the first decision on a dispute was handed down 27 September 1990. This dispute centred around the rights of a large purchaser to force a Regional Electricity Company to bear significant liability for the costs associated with connection to a generator through the transmission system. The regulator ruled that the Regional Electricity Company must bear a significant proportion of the costs of such connection. This decision has provided an impetus for the generating companies to aggressively market direct sale of electricity to large industrial users (Power in Europe, 1990, pp.8–9).

While seemingly a major victory for the policy of competition, the decision has potential serious implications. The upkeep of a transmission system is not a minor cost. For 1990, maintenance and other operating charges accounted for £164.7 million of National Grid's total Operating Costs of £792 million (i.e. 20.8 per cent) (National Grid, 1990, p.43). If large industrial

customers do not have to pay for upkeep of the system, or the Regional Electricity Companies are forced to pay a significant proportion of the costs of changed arrangements resulting from the use of the transmission system linking a private generator to a user, the result may be large increases in prices to the remaining users of the transmission system (i.e. smaller customers who cannot be linked directly to generators).

New Zealand

Australia and New Zealand have a long history of progressive public sector reform, but the changes which have taken place in New Zealand over recent years have somewhat reversed this progressive trend. "Reforms" to the New Zealand electricity industry have included commercialisation and corporatisation. It is instructive to consider the impact these "reforms" have had on the New Zealand industry and New Zealand society.

Prior to 1987, the New Zealand electricity industry was divided between generation/transmission and distribution. The generation/transmission aspects of the industry were undertaken by the New Zealand Electricity Department (NZED) and the distribution role was the responsibility of electric power boards or municipal electricity departments of territorial local authorities (supply authorities). While some reforms occurred from as early as 1967, the most significant changes have occurred since 1987 (see also Devine, 1990).

In 1987, Electricorp was established as a state owned enterprise. Electricorp had responsibility for generation/transmission, and was divided into four "business divisions". The supply authorities were also made more commercial: from February 1987, the supply authorities were able to adopt corporate structures including the appointment of directors rather than having them elected; in April 1987 they became liable to pay tax on any surplus after paying for bulk supply and other expenses (Rivers, 1990, pp. 10–13; Deane, 1990, pp.2–4).

However, the 1987 developments were more far reaching than we have outlined above. As Deane (1990) explains:

> At the same time, the government also moved to deregulate electricity generation. Immediately, a number of substantial pro-

posals were developed for competitive generation, in order to take advantage of a perceived gap between the wholesale electricity prices which had been set by the government, and the price which could be charged by a new entrant using the latest available technology. These proposals, which amounted to a total capacity of some 1400MW, involved a variety of players including CRA, as well as several of the larger New Zealand electricity supply authorities.

For the first time, then, there was a real prospect of competition in electricity generation in New Zealand. This was in addition to the competition which already occurred in the non-transport energy market between electricity and alternative energy sources, notably gas and coal. In this market, electricity had been steadily losing ground to competing energy sources for the previous eight years (pp. 2–3).

Similar changes are occurring in the distribution sector of the industry.

The similarities between the situation in New Zealand and New South Wales, and between New Zealand and England and Wales, are a recurring feature of the reforms which have occurred in New Zealand. That point will, necessarily, be reiterated throughout this section.

In February 1988, an Electricity Task Force was established to undertake a review of the industry. There were two reasons for establishing the Task Force: first, to ensure that the electricity industry "played its part" in achieving national economic vitality; and second, because the electricity industry, as one the largest public sector enterprises, was a possible target for privatisation. The Task Force's initial work was "… based on the presumption that all or most of the industry will be privatised" (Consultative Document Prepared by the Electricity Task Force, February 1989, in Rivers, 1990, p.13). The Task Force used many of the economic tools with which we have become familiar and on which we have commented elsewhere in this Chapter:

> … markets that are relatively more contestable or more competitive should be more efficient and prices will be lower. Market structures which provide for lower cost combinations of resources will be more efficient (Task Force, 1989, p.5).

The government's press statement announc-

ing the Task Force's findings also contained another familiar refrain: transmission in a natural monopoly (Caygill et al, 1989, p.2).

Given these views and tools of analysis, it is not surprising that the Task Force recommended the following:

> Generation: against the immediate divestment of generation assets, but that further work should be undertaken on forming competing companies;
> Transmission: that the National Grid (called TransPower despite its continued integration into Electricorp) should become a separate corporate identity, and that it should be owned by a "club" of distributors, but that the government retaining a "golden share"; and Distribution: that the supply authorities be incorporated as companies and then privatised via a stock market float. Vertical integration could be achieved subject to rules set by the Commerce Act. The geographic monopoly position of the resultant companies would be removed (Task Force, 1989, p.7).

The Task Force had obviously identified the situation in England and Wales as being worthy of emulation, which is surprising given the caution with which these changes have been viewed in Australia — even the IC has not been unequivocal in its assessment of the changes.

By April 1990, the following changes had been made to the industry. The electricity generators were required to release information to make monitoring easier; the government agreed that the Electricorp and the distribution companies would have equal shares with the possibility that a third party could also obtain shares; and the government agreed that the electricity supply authorities would be converted to companies. In this respect, it is worth noting that three New Zealand unions contributed to the government deciding not to privatise these authorities (Goodall, 1991).

What effect have these changes had?

The following assessment of the changes which have occurred fall under two headings: the isolation of transmission and industrial relations. Deane (1990) summarised the situation in the following words:

> The government-owned Electricity Corpo-

ration is the dominant generator, but faces potential competition from other generators as well as actual competition from alternative energy sources. The bulk transmission sector, as a "natural monopoly" is being separated out and is essentially to be owned by a combination of users. The retail sector is to remain in public ownership at this stage, but is to be commercialised and deregulated... (p.7).

Transmission

We have repeatedly noted that, in the Australian context, the distinction between transmission and distribution is difficult to make. In New Zealand's case, the break up of generation and transmission is likely to have a number of deleterious effects. These effects result from the more complex coordination which would be required within the industry.

The Electricity Corporation itself has objected to the break up on these grounds, as did the unions (Rivers, 1990, p.24). More recently Deane (1990), who is Electricorp's Chief Executive and commends the "efficiency" gains which have been made as a result of the structural changes which had already occurred, stated:

> In some ways it is a matter of regret that transmission is to be further separated from the Corporation, since this will inevitable result in significant additional costs, particularly from the reduced or at least more complicated information flows an coordination between generation and transmission decision-making, as well as from the duplication of company infrastructure which will inevitably be required (p.5).

The New Zealand Ministry of Commerce also rejected that a "club" of owners was the optimal way to parcel out the ownership of the "natural monopoly". It pointed out that the club would be made up of organisations which would have divergent interests, and that this could hinder the decision-making process (Ministry of Commerce in Rivers, 1990, p.25).

It also needs to be recalled that a government owned "golden share" was recommended by the Task Force. As we have noted elsewhere, the key question is: why. After repeated comments and analysis based on the purported superiority of market solutions, the more efficient methods of

the private sector and the need for governments to refrain from "interference", it seems that neither the British nor the New Zealand government is willing to allow the private sector to take full control of the industry. It seems however given the history of private sector involvement in the electricity industry in Australia, and the consequent need for the public sector to take strong action to ensure a safe and reliable industry, governments should be aware of the sorts of costs with which they risk burdening electricity consumers if the sorts of "reforms" undertaken in New Zealand are duplicated in Australia.

Industrial relations

In order to accurately assess the impact of what is (in Australian parlance) corporatisation of state owned corporations, it is important to understand the means by which this corporatisation has occurred.

Corporatisation in New Zealand is carried out under the auspices of the State-Owned Enterprises (SOE) Act 1986.[12] This Act states clearly that the principal objective of an SOE is to be as profitable and efficient as comparable businesses that are not owned by the Crown. They are obliged to be good employers and to exhibit a degree of social responsibility.

Walsh (1990) has noted the following tendency in the corporatised SOEs:

> Organisational restructuring and the swift restoration of profitability became the principal objectives of SOE management. Industrial relations and personnel policies were shaped to fit new organisational structures and modes of operation (p.4).

One of the features of corporatisation, both in Australia and in New Zealand, has been the idea that decentralised decision-making is more effective than centralised decision-making. In industrial relations terms such decentralisation can have negative effects. This has two causes.

First, both management and the unions have been "brought up" in a centralised system and find it difficult to make the transition to more line management autonomy. Second, and more significantly in the long term, the idea of managerial prerogative has been introduced to the public sector. This has occurred as a result of what senior public sector managers see as the more attractive features of the private sector, and the recruitment of private sector managers directly into the SOEs. This has resulted in a sustained attack on public sector working conditions:

> Existing statutory provisions with regard to merit appointments, appeals, promotions, transfers, classification, grading and termination were eliminated and replaced by provisions giving management vastly increased discretion. The statutory requirement to be a good employer did not prevent this (Walsh, 1990, p.10).

It is clear that the New Zealand government has failed to understand the positive results which can be achieved from realistic reform of industrial relations procedures and values. The degree of industrial conflict has been reduced in the electricity industry, but it is likely that this has more to do with the prevailing economic conditions in New Zealand, and the threat of unemployment than with an "appreciation" by the labour force of the "need" for the "reforms" on which there has been little or no consultation. It is to the issue of employment that we now turn.

Deane (1990) has made two comments which have a clear relationship to any dispassionate observer of the New Zealand situation:

> Throughout the organisation, it was apparent from the outset that economies needed to be made in terms of staff numbers. These have now been reduced by more than one third since corporatisation, without the need for forced redundancies.
>
> ... each business unit now negotiates its own voluntary agreement with union representatives drawn from its employees, and the agreements are beginning to reflect the commercial and operational needs of each business. These changes have not been achieved without cost, and industrial action was taken on one or two occasions early in the process. Since then, the industrial climate has been much more settled, and should continue to improve (pp. 5–7).

This is precisely the same attitude taken by various Australian governments, and can only be described as short-sighted. While it may be true that there was a degree of over-staffing in the New Zealand electricity industry there has been no realisation that the skills and experience of the workforce are a valuable resource that could be tapped by the industry in meeting the challenges faced by the industry over the next decades (see, for instance, Devine, 1990, pp.12–14). This is a major theme of this report and is addressed in Chapter 12 and in the interest of the community — which is the ultimate owner of all public sector assets — it would be better to take a longer term, consultative approach to change.

11.13 Conclusion

This chapter has examined three major areas of concern in the assessment and management of the ESI. These were the critical question of efficiency in the industry; the purported advantages of privatisation and competition; and the recent experiences of change in Britain and New Zealand.

It has been concluded that key policy making bodies like the IC have compiled suspect efficiency measures and that, therefore, new measures which provide a sound basis for measuring comparative industry and enterprise efficiency are essential. We have also shown that the IC's privatisation proposals are likely to retard further positive reform of the industry. It has also been shown that the reforms presently under way need supplementation to ensure that sources of profligacy can be reduced as far as possible.

This chapter shows that privatisation proposals are based on economic theories of the benefits of competition that show little appreciation of the dynamics of real world, large organisations operating in industries that are characterised by a high level of natural monopoly. Moreover, for an industry that requires both administrative reform and enhanced employee, customer and community participation, little positive guidance can be provided from the experience so far in either Britain or New Zealand.

The specific conclusions made in this chapter include:

- recognition that the TFP measures utilised by the IC are flawed in their construction and at best provide a rudimentary guide to static efficiency. To measure efficiency appropriately requires the development of a wider range of partial production, distribution and end-use measures over time that are accepted across the whole industry. This will also provide the capacity to do appropriate comparative analyses;

- in respect to the measuring the effect of changes in the industry on the economy as a whole more appropriate models than ORANI should be developed, and employed, to show the cost effects of the full range of externalities of the industry on all sectors of the economy and society. Chapter 4 has dealt with the necessary changes to the national accounts;
- recognition that the process of change in the industry has generated significant efficiency gains but this has been at the cost of significant human resources, whose skills and capacities have been lost to the industry and reduced its capacity of the industry to develop the demand side of the energy industry;
- recognition that the evidence linking inefficiency to the need for privatisation does not exist and for this reason should be resisted. The consequences of privatisation will likely be to create new inflexibility in the industry and reduce its capacity to contribute to Australia's energy management objectives;
- rejection of further corporatisation of the industry because, as this and privatisation progresses, new bureaucracies will need to be created to shadow manage utilities. This would be accelerated by industry disaggregation;
- resistance to the break up of utilities because of the reason mentioned above and because the internal efficiencies that are generated in properly managed integrated organisations will be lost;
- a suggestion that the management of utilities be made more transparent and participatory as a means of making them more effective rather than attempting to make them more susceptible to "market disciplines" (which Chapter 10 and this chapter show, produce only illusory benefits, and are unlikely to provide more in the ESI). Rather, better management review and accountability procedures should be applied across the whole industry;
- accepting that the experience of Britain and New Zealand shows that privatisation can only be done at the expense of a massive loss in the value of public assets; of creating an overly complex system with its attendant ef-

ficiency losses and the likely future creation of a massive regulatory structure dedicated to shadow managing the system as is already foreshadowed by the experience in the United States; and
- encouraging the development of representative institutions to research, produce information and coordinate the reform in the industry. This new organisation would replace the ESAA and provide a forum for the development of reform programs, advise governments on proposals, assist in the development of the national grid and sponsor specific and general research on the industry.

Notes

1. It should be recalled that GBEs are a subset of statutory authorities.

2. Using a static ORANI model, that itself incorporates some restrictive assumptions.

3. However, in a classic case of "hedging one's bets", the Submission also notes "Much of the appeal of the free market is (at this point) theoretical, since the best example of such a model, the UK, has only been operating for a short time and it may well prove necessary to reintroduce elements of coordinated planning arrangements to improve system reliability" (Vol.1, p.11).

4. "In many respects, competition has been elevated in the minds of the majority of economists as the great panacea for the nation's, if not the world's, economic problems" (Groenewegen, 1990, p.9).

5. "In English the word (dogma) can be used for any fixed and firmly held belief on any subject, but it usually suggests that the belief is a condition, or at least a sign, of belonging to either a secular (or more frequently) a religious group. The word can also imply that the belief rests on a special — often divine — authority; that any member of the group who attenuates or changes that belief is thereby a "heretic"; and that heresy is a moral, and perhaps also a legal, offence that merits the strongest condemnation (and perhaps also punishment" (Paul Edwards, [ed.] 1967, *The Encyclopedia of Philosophy*, Vol. 2, The MacMillan Company and The Free Press, New York, p.140).

6. See also Fitzgerald, 1990.

7. It is also a feature of classical economics that the movement of capital from less efficient uses to more efficient does create technical efficiencies.

8. However, the Industry Commission does not hold this view (Industry Commission, 1990c, Vol. 2., p.96).

9. "... the transmission grid (the natural monopoly)" (p. 100).

10. In Scotland the electricity supply industry is being privatised while continuing to be vertically integrated: two such integrated companies are being formed. That situation will only be referred to here to the extent that it impacts on the situation in England and Wales.

11. For those interested in the procedure, the James Capel document has a very good explanation of all details.

12. cf. New South Wales State Owned Corporations Act.

CHAPTER 12

POWERING THE VISION: ECONOMIC POLICY, AWARD RESTRUCTURING AND AN INDUSTRY STRATEGY

12.1 Introduction

Throughout this report, we have referred to deficiencies in the current arrangements of the Australian electricity supply industry and the challenges with which the trade union movement is faced in that industry. In this chapter we will outline the research team's proposals for significant reform, a reform strategy that draws together our conclusions regarding the industrial, environmental and public sector challenges with which Australia is now faced.

We begin with a discussion of the concept of microeconomic reform, looking in particular at the federal government and trade union positions. It is within this context that we examine the proposal for national integration of electricity industry. We conclude that national integration should be supported.

We then consider the employment situation in the industry, and suggest ways in which employment generating initiatives can be introduced which would have significant direct and downstream advantages. There is also a brief discussion of other components of an industry strategy which would have to be incorporated.

A discussion of the current industrial relations environment appears in the Appendix.

Finally, we put forward a proposal for an electricity industry strategy which would provide the opportunity for unions in the industry and the community, to have a voice in the management of that industry.

We do not maintain that these proposals will be easy to implement, nor are they likely to be adopted without significant opposition from those who have a vested interest in either maintaining the industry in its current form or "reforming" it along British or New Zealand lines. Or from those who have a strict and uncompromising ideological agenda of their own.

Nevertheless, the industry strategy we are proposing offers the most positive and realistic proposals for a process of necessary change.

Briefly, and before examining particular aspects of our proposals, we need to note again that the industry is currently organised on a State-by-State basis. The problems that such lack of uniformity can create are well known. However, the problems created by an industry (such as electricity) with a State orientation do not apply to that industry alone. They are also felt in industries which have strong links to that industry. In the case of the electricity industry, for instance, these negative effects are felt by suppliers of plant and equipment.

Even the negotiation of the National Preference Agreement between the States and the Commonwealth in 1986 did not resolve this problem, as there was no concerted, commensurate effort made by the State authorities to standardise. Thus, suppliers continued to be faced with limited orders when an integrated industry would have generated orders of a magnitude which would have yielded the efficiencies and productivity improvements obtainable from common standards. In some respects, this alone provides sufficient reason for the development of a national industry strategy.

12.2 The Rationale for our Proposal

Introduction

Considerable publicity has been given to the concept of microeconomic reform in recent years.[1] The achievement of such reforms has been tied to Australia's international competitiveness, improved quality of work (and outputs) and more efficient techniques. Such linkages have been made by governments of all persuasions, trade unions and (some) employers.

However, it is not at all clear that these groups

are advocating the same types of reform. It is worthwhile, therefore to begin this section with an outline of the various meanings of microeconomic reform in order to establish a clear picture of the priority of trade unions and how these priorities are consistent with the overall aims of improving Australia's competitiveness.

First, however, it is necessary to dispel a myth perpetrated by some employer groups which has significant implications. That myth can be summed up in the following words:

> Microeconomic reform covers a wide range of policies and programs designed to make public sector activities and markets more efficient. Its main focus is to create opportunities for growth and to remove impediments preventing resources from being employed most productively or limiting the flexibility of workers and enterprises. Many of these impediments result from government regulations and so require actions by governments. Others can be addressed directly by business and unions (Brennan, 1990, p.35).

The myth which this statement embodies is that microeconomic reform is concerned with the public sector. In this respect, it is worth recalling statements made in 1988 by the Economic Policy and Advisory Council (EPAC) which reported the Organisation for Economic Cooperation and Development's (OECD) view:

> Microeconomic policies can do much to raise employment and living standards. By calling forth more effectively the private initiative of firms and workers, and by improving the efficiency with which governments carry out their responsibilities, microeconomic reforms can reduce obstacles to the redirection of labour and capital towards greater production (EPAC, 1988, p.13).

By attempting to equate microeconomic reform with the role of government and the public sector, the private sector has sought to avoid any close scrutiny of its own role in microeconomic reform. This belies the fact that the private sector accounts for over three-quarters of total employment and 70 per cent of Australia's Gross Domestic Product (GDP).

To achieve its full and proper potential, microeconomic reform must apply to the private as well as the public sectors. For a considerable period of time this realisation has been shared not only by government but also by Australian trade unionists and some employers, particularly in the manufacturing sector.

In respect of the government's role EPAC also noted:

> Many of the key decisions relating to capital formation, technical efficiency and dynamic efficiency are in the hands of business and organised labour. The role of government lies essentially in providing an appropriate macroeconomic environment, implementing adjustment in the public sector, removing impediments to adjustment in the private sector and providing positive facilitation and support for development in the private sector (EPAC, 1988, p.17).

Put simply, the government's major role should be seen as a facilitator to microeconomic reform in the private sector, and to encourage reform in the public sector. This can only occur in the context of positive industry strategies which promote skills development, management efficiency, marketing, and product development, design and quality. It is our contention, based on the history and most recent experience of the electricity industry, that the orientation of these strategies need to emanate from a "bottom up" consultative processes, in which unions, governments and employers are involved.

Moreover, a leading private sector representative has stated that the private sector has a key role to play in aiding Australia's competitive position *by instituting reforms to its own operations.* Brian Loton, President of the Business Council of Australia and Chief Executive Officer and Managing Director of BHP, has been reported in the following terms:

> Half of the prize that is promised by reform to the year 2000 is in the business community's hands — we have to get on with the job ourselves.

> Many Australian businesses "lack a long term view", rank poorly in research and development and suffer from weak managerial skills, poor employee relations and weak incentives to perform.

> And exhibit a tendency to "over rely on the federal government to provide solutions".

Much of this is within the influence of management. Industrial relations, workplace reform, human resource development, investment and technology decisions are all the responsibility of management.... business can make a big difference regardless of what government or others can do. (A statement made at the Business Council of Australia forum "Developing Australia's National Competitiveness in *Australian Financial Review,* 26 February 1991, p.7).

It is clear that in a mixed economy such as Australia's, with both the private and public sectors playing a role in economic activity, it is essential that unions and employers in both sectors are intimately involved in the changes which are required if the nation's economic performance is to be enhanced, and if equity concerns are to be addressed.

The trade union perspective

A large part of the current microeconomic reform agenda (of which proposals for statutory authorities form a part) has been set by the trade unions. Much of this agenda has been embodied in the campaigns by the trade unions to achieve award restructuring. Such a strategy is closely tied to the Unions' analysis of the economic situation in Australia. For instance, in 1987 the ACTU stated:

> The economic circumstances have demanded that Unions in pursuit of more jobs, greater job security and the capacity to increase living standards are more closely involved in the processes of production and not simply in the distribution of the receipts of production. This changed emphasis has meant that unions must be interested and involved at the company and industry level about training, investment, production methods, and industry policy (ACTU, 1987, p.5).

Such statements — made both before and since 1987 — signal an important change in the orientation of the trade union movement. Though the trade unions did not relinquish their right to be involved in distributional issues (ACTU, 1987, pp.7–8), there has been a recognition that the process of wealth creation also requires the involvement of trade unionists if real and positive change is to be effected. This was

clearly articulated in 1987 with the release of *Australia Reconstructed,* though many would consider the earlier negotiation of the ACTU/ALP Prices and Incomes Accord in 1982 to be equally or more significant.[2]

Regardless of the precise date at which this change in orientation was institutionalised, it remains true that the labour movement adopted a radically different view of its role in the 1980s. This change in orientation was reflected in the importance (almost centrality) which was given to industry policy in that period. Arising out of that work and its reflection in the Accord Mark 1, the range of tripartite institutions which were established following the election of the Labor government in 1983 bears testimony to the matters which both the ALP and the unions realised had to be addressed if Australian industry was to effect a change in orientation:

- the Economic Planning and Advisory Council (EPAC);
- the Australian Manufacturing Council (AMC), and its associated industry councils;
- the Advisory Council on Prices and Incomes (ACPI); and
- the restructuring of the Trade Development Council (TDC) in the Department of Trade to make it genuinely tripartite and to undertake international research missions as well as the traditional marketing exercises.

It was out of a tripartite mission undertaken through the auspices of the TDC in 1986 that the pathbreaking *Australia Reconstructed* was prepared.

The initial Accord also embodied the concept of reductions in real wages in order to create the conditions whereby investment could recover. This was balanced by a commitment made by the ALP that real wages would be maintained "over time". Arising from the eight years of experience with the Accord, there have been increasing concern that the anticipated increase in investment did not result.

Being aware of these problems, in 1990 the ACTU Executive adopted a comprehensive industry and trade development strategy proposed by its Industry Development Committee. Martin Ferguson, President of the ACTU, made the following statement when releasing that policy:

> The federal government has a fundamental responsibility to provide the nation with a

vision for the future of industry development that industry and workers can relate to. That vision must project a future for this country. The 1990s is a decade where Australia must become a significant exporter of higher value added manufactures and services, as well as a leader in managing industry development and the environment in downstream processing. Such a vision gives credibility to Australia's claim to be able to resolve its external account problems without adopting a low growth, low living standards approach (ACTU, 1990, p.1).

The policy package prepared by the ACTU reflects the change in orientation that we have outlined. That package includes the introduction of a selective depreciation allowance, particularly for large capital intensive downstream processing projects; strategies to reform the rail industry to improve competitiveness; and a program for further reductions in tariffs. The power industry was also mentioned.

It is with awareness of the need for positive intervention in the economy, industry and (ultimately) the enterprise that our proposal for a national electricity strategy has been developed. Unlike the simplistic and flawed proposals advanced conservatives (see Chapter 11) what we will put forward for consideration takes cognisance of the complex economic and other challenges with which the industry is faced. It is necessary, however, to recall that part of the reform strategy advanced by the trade union movement includes award restructuring, and we briefly consider its meaning and implications in the next section.

Award restructuring

The ACTU has described award restructuring in the following terms:

Award restructuring is really a simple name for a very complex and wide ranging agenda of reform. Generally speaking there are certain common elements to the way award restructuring will operate in all industries. These include:
- a new classification structure based on nationally recognised contemporary standards for skills and training;
- the creation of career paths for all employees;

- the development of a new national training system which encourages increased skill formation and training;
- increased training opportunities for employees in all occupations;
- increased labour flexibility at the enterprise level and modernisation of awards so they are easy to read and capable of adapting to change through consultation and agreement.

However, the principles of award restructuring are the same in all industries, the environment of each industry is different as are the circumstances at the plant level (ACTU, 1990, p.120).

The ACTU has also emphasised the need for workers and their union representatives to be involved in the management decision making process:

This is absolutely fundamental if award restructuring is to make a real contribution to transforming the plants and bringing them into the twenty first century (p.121).

The industry strategy we advance has the following features which reflect the principles and aims of the award restructuring agenda. First, it is national in scope. We have repeatedly referred to the problems created by a fragmented, State-based industry, and we advocate that any program of reform must therefore have a national perspective.

Second, we emphasise that the human resources contained in the industry provide the opportunity for positive and far-reaching reforms. In order that the workers in the industry can contribute to the achievement of this type of reform they must have access to necessary and appropriate industry training, and confidence in their continued employment in the industry.

Third, we advocate that the workers' representative bodies — the unions — have representation at every level of decision-making. The necessary concomitant of this representation would be access to the information on which decision-making depends.[3]

The microeconomic reform environment

To a significant degree, the immediate environment in which such reforms can take place is conditioned by the policy decisions of the federal government. This is as true for State-based industries as it is for those which have a national base. While this has always been the case, the Premiers' Conference decisions of October 1990 (see below) make it even more important that we fully understand the federal government's microeconomic reform agenda.

We will briefly outline the various positions which have been adopted by a succession of federal Labor governments since 1983.

The history of the Labor governments' microeconomic reform initiatives are considerable. They include:

- deregulation of the finance sector, floating the Australian dollar and abolition of foreign exchange controls which created the conditions for a significantly increased volume and velocity of capital transfers;
- the abolition of the two airline agreement;
- opening up Telecom to competition;
- the extension of superannuation; and
- the extension of Australia-New Zealand Closer Economic Relations (CER).[4]

More recently, on 12 March 1991, the government released an Industry Policy Statement. The central feature of the Statement was the decision to drastically cut tariffs. By 1996 general tariff rates will be reduced from 10 and 15 per cent to 5 per cent; tariff rates on motor vehicles will be cut from 35 per cent to 15 per cent by 2000; and tariff reductions in the Textiles Clothing and Footwear industry will be reduced to maximum 25 per cent by 2000. At the same time the government announced a $90 million program to assist workers displaced as a result of the cuts in protection. In order to encourage a greater export orientation, the government announced a number of initiatives, in the form of enhancing existing programs and new schemes. The total cost of these initiatives was estimated to be $250 million. Anti-dumping procedures were streamlined, and the government reiterated its commitment to pursuing reductions in protection internationally.

The government also announced a number of taxation concessions. These included the broadening of exemptions from the Wholesale Sales Tax for goods used by manufacturers, miners and primary producers to pre-production activities, production related activities, post production activities and training of staff to perform eligible activities; a statutory definition

has been provided for the "effective life" eligible for depreciation allowances. $25 million was allocated to a program aimed at raising the efficiency of Australian enterprises to world levels. $1.45 million was allocated to assist the trade unions achieve amalgamation. This suggests that the government still has considerable resources which could be allocated to considered industry strategies such as is outlined below.

The ACTU's response to the Statement included the following:

> The changes to wholesale tax and depreciation will provide a substantial cost reduction for business and are welcomed by the ACTU. In addition the extension of the 125 per cent tax concession for research and development will continue to provide an important stimulus to the development of higher value added goods and services in this country. Taken together these taxation initiatives will assist Australia develop a more internationally competitive tradeable goods sector (ACTU, 1991, p.1).

The Prime Minister also announced the following:

> ... the government has decided to provide resource security for major new wood-processing projects. Resource security will involve undertakings, backed by legislation, guaranteeing an agreed volume of timber supply from an identified catchment area.

While assessing a statement of this complexity is difficult we can make the following suggestions.

There is the question of the wisdom of instituting a program of reductions in protection during a domestic economic recession and while our major trading partners are not committed to reducing their own levels of protection. A number of unions have already expressed reservations regarding this approach.

Second, it is important to place the government's decision on tariffs in the context of the detail of the ACTU proposals for tariff cuts. The government's timetable for tariff reduction is well in advance of that proposed by the ACTU. The ACTU position on the rate at which tariff reductions should occur is unequivocal:

> The ACTU reiterates its position that it will oppose tariff reductions unless they are part of a total package including positive industry assistance initiatives and structural adjust-

ment assistance. They should be part of what is undertaken by other countries as well (ACTU, 1990, p.127).

It is worth recalling the Prime Minister's actual words:

> With these tariff cuts, we demonstrate once again our commitment to liberalising international trade. The government has been fortified in this approach by a number of recent reports, not least Dr Ross Garnaut's Report *Australia and the Northeast Asian Ascendancy.*

However, the ACTU has extensively criticised the Garnaut Report. It is not necessary to restate these criticisms here. The ACTU's final assessment was:

> The trade union movement has serious doubts about the conclusions of the IAC/Garnaut analysis, and these doubts are reinforced by the recent study published by the Australian Manufacturing Council (ACTU, 1990, p.20).

Third, the ACTU position is that "the proposed Development Fund must be put in place to address the development requirements of medium size companies" (ACTU, 1991, p.3). There is little or no recognition of this in the Policy Statement.

Finally, in respect of the role of the public sector, the Statement contains little beyond a restatement of the goals of the series of Special Premiers' Conferences which commenced in October 1990. We have previously noted the importance of this initiative. However, we could have expected a greater commitment to the role of the public sector given the recognition of the central and vital role which the public sector plays in the Australian economy.

While the government's position as reflected in the Statement incorporated some features of the ACTU position, it was deficient in a number of areas. It is particularly significant that the Premiers' Conference decision suggests that the federal government will play an increasingly important role in the electricity supply industry. This was not reflected in the statement.

There is another, general, matter which needs to be discussed at this point. The current arrangements governing the provision of economic advice to the federal government contain two contradictory elements. First, the government has centralised its economic advice

in the federal Treasury, and it is now the Treasurer who is responsible for the Industry Commission. As we have shown in Chapter 11, the Industry Commission in unable to move beyond the provision of advice based on narrow, inadequate, ideologically-based theories which are then applied inappropriately (TFP is an example).

On the other hand, it has also recognised the need for structural change, and has encouraged the provision of alternative advice from participants in the industries it has targeted for reform. It is in recognition of this second trend that the unions have commissioned this report.

This then is the environment in which we are advancing our agenda for reform of the industry.

12.3 A National Electricity Industry Reform Strategy
Introduction

As we outlined in Chapter 9, the state has been required to "interfere" in the operations of markets to ensure both economic growth and socially equitable outcomes. Until recently, we would have mainly conceived such intervention in terms of tariffs, anti-dumping provisions and other protectionist measures.

Since 1983, governments have turned their focus from protectionist measures to development measures. Rather than protecting industry from competition in the international arena, governments are now considering ways to assist industry to compete in the international market. Such assistance has taken the form of an "industry policy", which seeks to co-ordinate inputs, infrastructure and market access while regularising industrial relations activities, rationalising legislative and institutional frameworks and establishing monitoring procedures.

It is also significant that the trade union movement has recognised that protective measures, such as tariffs, have provided a smokescreen behind which management became lethargic, lacking an "export mentality" and virtually ignorant of the importance of marketing strategies. In addition, there was a recognition that the object of post-war economic policy — to establish a manufacturing sector which could meet Australian demand in virtually every sector — was essentially self-defeating. In the simplest terms, the Australian market is too small to allow for this sort of luxury. That does not mean, however, that the trade union movement subscribes to the sterile and misconstrued notion of the "level playing field" and/or the "invisible hand".

In respect of the precise meaning of the term "industry policy", one commentator has noted:

Industry policy is simply a name for the set of actions — public and private — which nations can take in order to try and redefine their relationship with world markets on terms more favourable to them than those which they would have obtained by doing nothing... .is not about industry assistance ... [but] about acquiring information about markets ... and then using the resources of both the public and private sectors to exploit those opportunities (Stewart, 1990, p.11).

The benefits of industry policy do not accrue only to the target industry. In the process of establishing more favourable terms in international markets other, community-wide benefits are gained. Industry policy assists governments to regulate the relationship between industry and the wider society through the introduction of legislative and regulatory frameworks such as those pertaining to trade practices and consumer and environmental protection. Industrial relations activities can be regulated and some co-ordination between the various sectors of industries encouraged. Such activities assist governments in their economic planning by linking industrial measures with broader economic policies, such as reducing reliance on imports.

Why a strategy for electricity industry?

It is worth recapitulating some of the most salient features of the energy sector in Australia to again stress how important change can be in that sector to the Australian economy as a whole.

Energy is a key input to every stage of the production and distribution process. In 1989, the electricity and gas supply industries together accounted for 2.6 per cent of Australia's gross domestic product, employed 90,000 persons and supplied over 35 per cent of Australia's final energy requirements. Within this sector, the electricity supply industry forms one of Australia's largest industries. In 1986–87, value added was in the order of $5.9 billion. This was over

double that of other large Australian manufacturing industries, such as clothing and footwear, the motor vehicle and the basic iron and steel industries (IC Vol. 3, 1991, p.24).

This is not to suggest that size of an industry (or the fact that industries of comparable size are subject to an industry plan), is justification for the development and introduction of an industry plan in the electricity industry. It does, however, suggest that recognition of the importance of energy — and the need for structural reform in the industries which make up that sector — has been late in coming.

Put simply, there needs to be the development of an industry policy for the electricity industry. Energy is a major input to other industries, it straddles the boundaries between the private and public sectors, it is subject to a multitude of State government regulations and policies, it has a mixed industrial relations history and it provokes major concerns about its impact on the environment. The ESI exists as a major component of the Australian economy in its own right, a major employer, as a purchaser, as a catalyst for the introduction of new technologies and as a major producer of energy used by "downstream" industries. The performance of the electricity industry has been accused of limiting expansion in other industries (AMC, 1990, p.118).

There are many problems associated with having a multitude of authorities governing a major input to industry, particularly one in which a central government wishes to implement its own industry and economic policies:

With different policy makers and agencies responsible for each, policies tend to be discrete rather than integrated ... with rival bureaucracies, indirect policy tools and competing problems and solutions, the economic policy process becomes a fight about priorities (Davis, 1988, p.158).

As we have outlined in Chapters 5 and 8, the electricity industry currently faces a number of serious challenges. Some of these challenges include privatisation, commercialisation and contracting-out of functions and services — trends which increasingly are becoming the norm for government business enterprises. The sheer scale and costs associated with increasing energy output by conventional means are increasingly difficult to meet, and this increases the pressures to contract-out some functions. In a current example in Queensland, the entire operation of providing electricity to remote aboriginal communities, from construction of power generation equipment to wiring houses, has gone to tender (ATSIC, 1991).

A major impact of these changes in the electricity industry are reductions in employment, with the consequent loss of an essential and potentially vital skill base. Given the role that unions have played in other industries, and the role they could play in the electricity industry, it is imperative that they are involved in any articulation of the future image and arrangements in the industry. Also, the success of award restructuring and the productivity improvements which flow from it will depend on the adequate training and resources being provided to the workforce.

The electricity industry needs coordination and guidance. To ensure the success of economic and industry policy objectives, the government needs an energy sector and, within this, an electricity industry, that is efficient and well planned . The electricity industry needs a coherent image of future arrangements to enable it to develop and implement reform programs. These aims and objectives can be achieved through the formulation and implementation of an industry policy.

We begin by examining proposals for national integration.

National integration

While the research for this project was underway a number of other inquiries and research projects were also being conducted. These inquiries and projects included:[5]

- the Industry Commission Inquiry into electricity and gas;
- the Commission for the Future Inquiry into sustainable development;
- the Electricity Working Group established by the Premiers' Conference in October 1990; and
- the Inquiry into the Snowy Scheme conducted by the New South Wales, Victorian, South Australian and federal governments.

That all these inquiries were being conducted at the same time (sometimes with the same personnel) is indicative of two salient features, one relating to the electricity supply industry and the other to the nature of the Australian federation.

Clearly, the industry has a continuing importance in Australia's economic, social and political life. The short sections on the origins of the industry that occur elsewhere in this report illustrate that the importance of the industry has been recognised since its creation; and that a federal structure such as Australia's makes national coordination difficult.[6] We have only to witness how long it has taken for genuine attempts at integration of the railway industry or co-operation in credit and libel law to be aware of this fact.

In addition, two of the inquiries exhibited a feature which has also been characteristic of the industry. This feature raises serious questions relating to the mechanics of decision-making in an industry which so clearly has a great impact on the lives of the vast bulk of the population. It is to this feature — *secrecy* — that we now turn.[7]

In 1978 Muirden wrote:

In his history of Victoria's State Electricity Commission, *Brown Power,* Cecil Edwards observes that public electricity corporations throughout the world seem in general to be allowed greater independence than some other corporations because (1) they usually pay their way, and (2) electricity is an esoteric matter in which the layman admits himself lost (Muirden, 1978, p.13).

While there is no doubt that the technical aspects of electricity generation and transmission/distribution are complex, it requires the drawing of a long bow to move from this realisation to a position of support for decisions to be made by a group of self-replicating "experts" with no input from either the workforce or the consumers. This point has been realised by a number of commentators, including those appointed by governments to make recommendations on the structure of the industry:

1. Public access to information on electricity generation planning should be considerably enhanced.[8]

2. ... the problems which now confront the energy agencies and industries extend beyond ECNSW and involve the development of ... more adaptive relationships in the workplace; and the articulation of public processes which will allow the community

and its political, legal and administrative systems to interact with ECNSW in defining and resolving important, emerging questions of choice (McDonell, 1986, p.10).

Notwithstanding this advice, both the Electricity Working Group established by the Premiers' Conference in October 1990 and the Inquiry into the Snowy Scheme were (in March 1991) being conducted in virtual secrecy. There were no terms of reference issued for either Inquiry, nor were there calls for submissions. The findings of the Premiers' Conference Working Group will presumably enter the public arena prior to the 1991 Special Premiers' Conference, but the work of the Inquiry has been conducted in isolation from consumers and workers. The fact that it was only as a result of a "leak" that consumers became aware of all the matters which the October 1990 Premiers' Conference was to deal with is indicative of the degree of secrecy which surrounds such decision-making.[9]

The issue

The Special Premiers' Conference Communique of 31 October 1990 contained the following:

> Electricity generation, transmission and distribution
>
> Leaders agreed that there may be additional benefits from an extension of, and/or organisational changes to, the interstate electricity network covering NSW, Victoria, Queensland, South Australia, Tasmania and the ACT. Consequently, they further agreed that a working group be set up to:
>
> a. assess whether extensions to the interstate network are economically justified;
>
> b. if so, assess the organisational options for achieving this, including a jointly owned interstate transmission system, a pool arrangement, and other ways of improving the management of current interstate arrangements; and
>
> c. report to the next Special Premiers' Conference.
>
> The working group will include representation from relevant electricity authorities and policy agencies from the respective governments including the Commonwealth, and seek contributions from interested parties, including major users in the private sector. There is an appreciation of the need for action

among the *Powering the Future* team.

Nevertheless, we need to be aware of concern (expressed most strongly in South Australia) that the demand for national integration may be based more on NSW's over-supply than any real environmental or efficiency needs. This concern is not allayed by the following observation in the New South Wales Labor Party's Policy on Energy Conservation:

> Sharing power has obvious benefits for all States on the eastern seaboard. New South Wales currently has excess capacity ....

We make it clear at the outset that the project team had a broader perspective, recognising that national integration will provide benefits for all.

There is already interconnection between NSW, Victoria and South Australia. The interconnection between NSW and Victoria occurs through the Snowy Mountains Scheme and at several other points. Its capacity is five per cent of the load of either system on an annual basis. Victoria and South Australia are linked through one line. The capacity of this link is such that Victoria could supply a maximum of about twenty per cent of South Australia's load. In absolute terms, these interconnections are not "strong" (Hocking, 1991).

Hocking goes on to provide the reasons for this situation:

> ... (1) State rivalry and (2) technical reasons: Category one is familiar with each of the State electricity systems developing independently and the States competing against each other for energy intensive industries (particularly aluminium smelting). Technical reasons refer to the physical characteristics of the systems with the large load centres (Melbourne, Sydney, Brisbane) separated by considerable distances. It such circumstances it makes good sense to locate production plant as close as possible to end users. The actual site of plants is a compromise between these criteria and that of the cheapest available fuel source. In the case of coal it is generally a requirement to build the power station at the mine or open cut as transport cost can be prohibitive. Transmission losses generally mean that it is not economic to transfer large blocks of electricity more than six hundred kilometres. Direct Current (DC) transmission can reduce losses

(Hocking, 1991; see also Saddler, 1981, pp. 111–117; and Wicks 1990, p.9).

There is also a broader issue that requires consideration. That is, the form of national integration *must* take into account the increasing importance of Government Trading Enterprises (including electricity authorities) to the States' revenues: the surpluses of GTEs contributed around 7.1 per cent of total States' revenues in 1979/80; 7.4 per cent in 1985/86; and 10 per cent in 1986/87 (Evatt, 1989). That is, the States are increasingly reliant on the revenues earned by their statutory authorities, and would need to be *fully* compensated for any revenue losses suffered through national integration (see also Chapter 10).

Related developments are:
- the different institutional arrangements for generation, transmission and distribution in each State. The break-up of the authorities into separate generation, transmission and distribution entities (which has been suggested by the Industry Commission) would make the privatisation of generation and distribution much simpler (the experience of England and Wales illustrates this aspect of an industry break-up); and
- the increasing importance of co-generation, and the apparent failure of authorities to adequately define such arrangements. The Industry Commission has already suggested that the existence of co-generation provides a rationale for continuing privatisation (see also our comments in Chapter 11 regarding the Harman Committee Report).

Suggestions for consideration
There are five available models for integration which we examined:

1. System-independent integration
This would be similar to the present arrangements where each authority owns, operates and maintains its own transmission system. Each State and the Commonwealth could develop its own policies on the ownership and competitive environment for its authorities.

Each authority would remain accountable for reliable and efficient supply to customers within its own State boundaries. Coordination would occur through consultation between the various

State and Commonwealth authorities, and such consultation would have the goal of optimal utilisation of national fuel resources.

The existing regulatory environment would be maintained. Principles would need to be developed to guarantee "open" access to the national grid.

2. National protocol
A national protocol would formalise State and Commonwealth cooperation regarding planning, development and operation of a national transmission system. It would monitor and report to each State and Commonwealth government, and each of the State and Commonwealth — based utilities would be required to commit resources to the operation of the Council. Each State would retain ownership of its authorities.

A protocol for the operation of each of the State authorities within a nationally integrated industry would be established by the Council (for example, it could establish agreements regarding Unit commitment).

3. Representative secretariat
While each State and the Commonwealth would retain ownership of its authorities, a full-time secretariat would be established to undertake the functions of the Board, and it would have access to the State and Commonwealth information bases. Union, business and other community representation would be institutionalised.

The States and the Commonwealth would formally accede to the Board and its operations including its protocols.

Capacity expansion would be nationally coordinated.

4. System reservoir
The reservoir would coordinate the operation of State-based generation units. Its management would be on the basis of appointment by each State and the Commonwealth (i.e. a new statutory authority would be established).

The State and Commonwealth would be the owners of the national portions of the transmission system.

5. Transmission corporation
This model would operate in a similar fashion to the National Grid in England and Wales. It would

be similar to the system reservoir, except that management would be appointed on commercial grounds. Ownership of the assets would be vested in the Corporation.

Given the nature of the Australian electricity supply system, national integration will need to solve a number of problems.

First, in the absence of complete integration and standardisation of the existing resources and operational standards, difficulties are likely to arise. Technically, (as we have noted above) each State has different divisions between transmission and distribution. A national system based on (4) or (5) would need to overcome this problem.

Second, (4) and (5) are predicated on institutionalising the distinction between transmission and distribution. There are, as discussed above, dangers in taking this step. Further, the break up of the industry in this way makes it easier for those governments which have an "ownership" model of public sector stewardship to actually divest themselves of public sector assets. We must also recognise that option (1) does not appear to have operated optimally to date, and that some new model is required. The choice therefore is between options (2) and (3).

Our preference

The Scandinavian (Nordic) nations have a system which exhibits the features of options 2 and 3 above. The following summarises the major features of the system.

The system is governed by mutually agreed recommendations and principles and is directly managed by the national operations managements, alleviating any need for a superior body. It was established in 1963.

The basics of the system are set out in Table 12.1.

These interconnections have sufficient capacity for the Nordic systems to be regarded as a single power system which can utilise the combined production resources (Nordel, 1989, pp. 16 and 21). The system interconnects nations which have diverse sources of energy: Norway is entirely hydro based; Denmark is entirely fossil fuel based; Finland and Sweden have a mix of hydro, nuclear and fossil fuel generation.

The system is predominantly built around transmission voltages of 300 and 400 kV. A combination of AC and DC interconnection is used, the latter being used to reduce system losses. Nordel has described the interconnected system in the following way:

> In a perspective which ignores national and ownership boundaries, the Nordel system constitutes a combined hydro and thermal capacity which supplies a geographically unevenly distributed load. The hydro power sources are located largely in the system's north-western region and the thermal power in its south-eastern region. The transmission capacity between these regions is very strong (Nordel, 1989, p.17).

Nordel itself is an advisory and recommend-

Table 12.1
The Capacity of the Nordel system

(from) Finland (to) Norway	one 50MW (interconnection)		
Finland-Sweden	one 500MW;	one 700MW	
Sweden-Finland	one 900MW;	one 500MW	
Sweden-Denmark	one 1000MW;	one 600MW	
Sweden-Norway	one 1600MW;	one 500MW;	one 250MW
Denmark-Sweden	one 600MW;	one 1000MW	
Denmark-Norway	one 500MW		
Norway-Finland	one 50MW		
Norway-Sweden	one 1300MW;	one 500MW;	one 250MW
Norway-Denmark	one 500MW[10]		

Source: Nordel, 1989, pp.16 & 21

ing body made up of four representatives each from the participating countries. Its aim is to further international cooperation on production, distribution and utilisation of electric power. Nordel does not make any decisions regarding extensions to the system etc, merely issuing recommendations which constitute the guidelines for cooperation. It has no budget or personnel.

A large proportion of its work is carried out by three committees: the Operations Committee, the Planning Committee and the Production Committee. These committees are made up of experts from each of the Nordic countries.

The individual Nordic nations retain control of their own systems:

> The individual national operations managements are responsible for the operations management of the interconnected Nordel system. They are thus responsible for the operation of their own systems and for power exchanges with neighbouring systems, by bilateral agreements with the respective operation managements (Nordel, 1989, p.18).

The Swedish system (VATTENFALL) has a coordinating responsibility for frequency control and demands on operating reserves.

As will be noted, the Nordel example is relevant to Australia because the individual member nations have strongly integrated internal transmission systems with lower capacity interconnections between them. There are, however, a number of features of the system which would need to be altered before the Nordel system could be endorsed without qualifications. First, there would need to be a significant alteration to the current management style of each of the State authorities. The current methods of operation are inadequate for the current situation and should not be duplicated in the national sphere.

Second, there would be the need to ensure that adequate union representation was obtained on any bodies established to coordinate the integrated industry.

Third, there would need to be procedures put in place to ensure that the best working conditions applying in each of the State's transmission are applied generally across all interconnected States.

Fourth, to ensure that the system achieves its potential there would need to be agreement that

the considerable capital required to develop the system is made available from the public sector in order to limit the likely disadvantages which would result from privatisation.

A Nordel-type system would not require those authorities which are currently vertically integrated to be broken up. Generally an amended Nordel-type model meets most of the criteria for an interconnected Australian system.

The institutional mechanisms set up under our National Electricity Industry Committee proposal would have an oversight function of the direction and framework of national integration. Given the change in orientation which is occurring in the industry, it would also be worthwhile for such institutional mechanisms to be permanent bodies able to recommend industry strategies with a variety of time horizons. It would need a strong research base.

We move now to consider the potential that exists for significant restructuring of the electricity industry.

12.4 Employment in the Industry
Employment profile of various electricity authorities

The current employment profile of the electricity industry is largely unknown. Recent indiscriminate staffing cuts through processes of attrition or across-the-board staff cuts have left electricity authorities with only a broad picture of the staff they currently employ. This is an information gap that should be filled. The decisions to cut staff numbers have also combined with broadbanding of skill levels during the award restructuring process, so that data on the actual skill types used or possessed by workers in the electricity industry are not easily accessible.

Other information crucial for analyses of employment profiles which is not available includes the age, gender and location (rural or urban) of staff who are likely to face retrenchment. This information would assist analyses of the type of work which can be done, the likely success of retraining initiatives and the extent of retraining required. Location is important to determine what sort of business enterprise may succeed. For example, retrofitting may be more cost effective in urban than rural areas, while tourism initiatives may have more opportunity for success in rural locations.

Table 12.2

Persons employed in the Electricity Industry 1985–1989

Year	NSW	Vic	Qld	SA	WA	Tas	ACT	NT	SMHEA	Total
1985	28779	20693	12357	4971	5814	5247	875	925	730	80391
1986	28759	19989	11440	5111	5901	5123	929	878	774	78904
1987	28491	19793	10356	5323	5709	4757	886	797	809	76921
1988	27787	19421	9164	5386	5795	4153	830	721	903	74160
1989	24324	19224	8758	5376	5559	4030	803	760	746	71147
Percent decrease	15.5	7.1	29.1	-8.1	4.4	23.2	8.2	17.8	-2.9	11.5

Source: ESAA Annual Report 1988–89

Some minimal employment profile information is provided in the annual reports of the electricity authorities, but not in a useful matrix form. Consequently we can know how many women work for the State Electricity Commission of Victoria, and how many of them work in the design and construction group, but not how many women work in the design and construction group located in the Latrobe Valley.

It is known that there has been a steady decline in the numbers employed in the electricity industry. Table 12.2 shows a decline in numbers across Australia of 11.5 per cent between 1985 and 1989. The largest decline in employee figures occurred in Queensland, a 29.1 per cent decrease, followed by Tasmania with a 23.2 per cent decrease. Two authorities showed an increase in employee figures in this period; Snowy Mountains with a negative decrease of -2.9 per cent, and South Australia with a figure of -8.1 per cent. These data are important inputs to the type of (the inadequate) efficiency/productivity analyses discussed in Chapter 11.

Age
Age profiles have been obtained from the State Electricity Commission of Victoria (SECV) and the Electricity Trust of South Australia (ETSA). The SECV data is for 30 June 1990 and the ETSA data is for 21 January 1991. The data shows similar age profiles, with each having a relatively young labour force of more than 60 per cent of employees under 40 years old (see Tables 12.3 and 12.4).

Table 12.3

Age Profile of SECV Employees (as at 30 June 1990)

Age	Number
15–19	670
20–24	2184
25–29	2911
30–34	2753
35–39	2592
40–44	2384
45–49	1824
50–54	1445
55–59	822
60–64	377

Source: State Electricity Commission of Victoria Annual Report 1989 – 1990

Table 12.5
Full-time SECV Employees by Organisational Unit
(as at June 1990)

Organisational Unit	Males	Females	Total
Management, inc support	8	6	14
System Control	77	6	83
Corporate Services	108	57	165
Strategic Planning	10	1	11
Corporate Relations	4	2	6
Technology & Innovation	0		1
Human Resources	22	10	3
Finance & Admin:			
Corporate Transport	14	4	18
Treasury	29	13	42
Human Resources	5	2	7
Superannuation	20	13	42
Corporate Contracts	3	1	4
Accounting	97	54	151
Materials	50	22	72
Production Group:			
Strategic Support	158	78	236
Morwell	2890	115	3005
Yallourn	1718	54	1772
Loy Yang	1423	68	1491
Production Services	1857	120	1977
Design and Construction:			
Geotechnical & Design	55	2	57
Value & Quality	15	1	16
Construction	151	5	156
Consulting Services	11	1	12
Mine Technology	144	19	163
Power Technology	145	8	153
Loy Yang Project	94	14	108
Architectural	44	3	47
Research & Development	107	10	117
Business Perf & Supply	27	3	30
Environmental Mgt	9	1	10
Power Grid Support:			
Central	270	10	280
Northern	248	7	255
Eastern	195	10	205
Western	256	5	261
Development	523	55	578
Metro Workshops	291	11	302
Information	185	64	249
Human Resources	9	3	12
Business Strat & Policy	4	1	5

Organisational Unit	Males	Females	Total
Customer Services:			
Central	2322	283	2605
Northern	978	77	1055
Eastern	501	46	547
Western	855	62	917
Distribution	256	29	285
Energy Services	79	24	103
Home Energy Advisory	15	12	27
Business Perf & Supply	10	2	12
Training	-	2	2
TOTAL	16557	1405	17962

Source: SECV Annual Report 1990, p.130.

Table 12.6
Occupations Employed by ETSA 1989

Excavator Op	40	Tractor	50
Plant Attendant	150	Tne Linesperson	330
Fitter & Turner	90	Elec Fitter	190
Elec Mechanic	50	Elec Special Class	100
Linesperson	10	Linesperson First Class	340
Snr Linesperson	270	Storepersons	170
Mechanical Trades	200	Trades Assistant	30
Rigger	40	Driver	100
Rear Dump Op	120	Carpenter	20
Plumber	10	Painters	30
Motor Mechanic	140	Apprentice	230
Welder	20	Boilermaker	40
Line Clear Off	20	Meter Tester	20
Technician	30	Depot Assistant	10
Garage Attendant	20	Transformer Assembler	20
Technician	30	Other Wages Employees	380
Total	330	Technical Trades	430
Supervisory Gen	490	Surveyor	10
Profess/l Eng	290	General Office	230
Shift Staff	260	Scientific Officer	30
Clerical Admin	760	Executives	40
Graduates	20		
Other Salary	140	Total	2700

Source: Unpublished ETSA data provided to research team

Table 12.4
Age Profile of ETSA Employees
(as at 21 January 1991)

Age	Male	Female	Total
<20	215	68	283
21–25	602	221	823
26–30	728	117	845
31–35	621	62	683
36–40	719	70	789
41–45	765	38	803
46–50	544	28	572
51–55	422	7	429
56–60	299	7	306
61–65	156	1	157
>65	1	0	1

Source: Unpublished ETSA data provided to research team

The relative youth of the employees of these authorities augurs well for the potential success of retraining initiatives, as many believe that younger people are generally more likely to accept change and to make the necessary adjustments to deal with it.

Gender
ETSA also provided a gender breakdown of its employee age data and this is shown in Table 12.4 (above). The SECV produces data on the gender of its employees by organisational unit, and this is reproduced in Table 12.5. In general, electricity, gas and water authorities employ only 0.3 per cent of the women in employment, and women represent only 9.5 per cent of the workforce in these utilities (ABS Cat 6203.0). According to the reports of the electricity authorities the proportion of women in the electricity workforce ranges from 7.3 per cent (W.A.) to 22.8 per cent (ACT) with the average being 10.3 per cent (ESAA, 1989, p.46).

The relatively low proportion of women in the industry is probably due to the nature of traditional power industry work, with its emphasis on construction and maintenance and a preponderance of trades, technical and professional employees. Such jobs are still largely in the male domain. As the nature of the power industry changes — from construction to conservation, and operates with a greater environmental sensitivity — the proportion of women employed in the industry may move closer to the Australian participation rate for women of 40.7 per cent employed (ABS Cat 6203, 1990).

It is an unfortunate fact that the Australian workforce is highly segregated and that there are "men's" jobs and "women's" jobs. While not wishing to further exaggerate this trend, it is true that retraining initiatives for males have more likelihood of acceptance and success if they are in fields related to the original training received. This indicates a need to develop new areas of construction, electrical and trades employment.

Occupation
Employees' occupations in electricity authorities were not generally available. The advent of broadbanding into skill levels during the award restructuring exercise means that occupation is not recorded in a readily accessible format.

ETSA provided occupational groupings which were current in 1989 (see Table 12.6) and stated that "due to award and industry restructuring and the use of a single scale, it is not possible to supply occupational data at this stage". The occupational data provided does not include age, sex or location, but is an indication of the range of trade occupations employed by electricity authorities, and their proportional representations. Unfortunately scientific, technical and administrative positions are not defined by occupation.

There is a severe lack of information collected and/or provided by all authorities.

Changes to the employment profile
Between June 1986 and June 1990, the SECV's workforce was reduced by 18.5 per cent, and a further 20 per cent reduction occurred in 1990 (SECV, 1990, p.130). The effect of these reductions on the types of occupations employed is not known. ETSA has not had such dramatic staffing reductions (ESAA, 1989, p.46), but is currently undergoing a "rightsizing" exercise guided by consultants.

A particular problem which has arisen for rural communities is their dependence on the electricity industry for their economic wellbeing. Mobile occupational groups, such as heavy engineering construction workers, have become settled in rural communities as a result of the ongoing construction work and expectations that such work will be indefinitely available. Decisions by electricity authorities to reduce or defer their construction activities therefore impact on whole communities. The Latrobe Region Commission (LRC) estimated that in 1981 more than 12 per cent of the region's workforce was employed in construction activities. This compared with 5 per cent for Melbourne in the same year (LRC, 1987, p.4). The electricity, gas and water industry accounted for 25.1 per cent of all Latrobe employees. It is important to realise, however, that skilled personnel were also lost from other areas of the SECV's operations.

Employment figures released by electricity authorities do not include contract employees. Because work is contracted out it is difficult to devise accurate figures on the numbers of workers dependent on the electricity authority for employment and the impact upon the community of that work ceasing to be performed. In addition, authorities are contracting out or selling off whole organisational divisions, such as transport, storage, cleaning and maintenance operations.

Information on the range of occupations employed is not of itself useful. It does provide some clues to the probable skills used by these employees, but only for just over half the workforce. As it is not recorded in a format which lists the organisational unit and location of the employees, it is not useful for projections of surplus occupations or skill types, nor for identifying alternative industries which utilise the skill types of existing employees.

The SECV has used a Voluntary Departure Package scheme since late 1989 to retrench staff. The profile of employees who chose a voluntary departure package indicates the level of skill held, and the level of training which may be required in order to ensure ongoing employment. A survey conducted of voluntary departees in 1990 showed that 56.7 per cent of respondents intended to stay in the region. Of these, over a third intended to retire temporarily or permanently, although only 14.1 per cent were aged 60 or over.

The largest group of departees was aged 25–59 years. Of those staying, 7 per cent have a degree or higher qualifications, 11 per cent have a trade qualification, 5 per cent have some other qualification and over 40 per cent have no post secondary qualifications. A large proportion of those intending to stay in the Latrobe region have no formal qualifications (27.3 per cent). This may be because a disproportionate number of the voluntary departees were women — 11 per cent compared with 6.3 per cent in the SECV (LRC, 1990, p.21). Of those who took a package the largest number were plant and machine operators (40.7 per cent); followed by tradespersons (27.7 per cent); labourers 9.9 per cent; managers 6.7 per cent; para professionals 7.6 per cent; and 7.4 per cent were in other occupations. Most of the departees had 6–10 years experience working for the SECV (35.2 per cent).

The large number of semi skilled workers in this group indicates that significant retraining will be required to enable them to obtain future employment.

Before turning to what avenues exist for employment generation, it is worth noting the major conclusions that can be drawn from the above information.

First, there is a clear paucity of employment data collected or made available on which rational and forward thinking plans for the authorities can be based. Second, and as a consequence of this lack, there is no way on knowing whether those who have taken voluntary redundancy packages (or who otherwise have been lost to the authorities) are taking skills with them that the authorities may require to meet their challenges.

This amounts to either a deliberate policy decision by the energy authorities throughout Australia, or it represents an implicit decision to have a non-policy about the planning, forecasting and training of employees coupled with a deliberate decision to not involve employees' representatives in the decision making processes which will eventually affect them. From this it could be inferred that energy authorities are largely indifferent to the fate of their employees.

It could also be inferred that the narrow focus on retrenchment, voluntary retirement and other forms of "downsizing" employment as a means of improving productivity indicates a dearth of real understanding of the direction in which the industry is headed. It implies that there is little capacity to contemplate alternative forms of productivity increase and little creativity available to be applied to the implementation of new strategies. In the context of a developing national perspective for the industry these features must change.

Avenues for employment generation
Introduction
Robyn Williams, Chairman of the Commission for the Future wrote in December 1990 in the foreword to *Toward Toronto: Australia Technical Innovations and Efficient Energy Futures*:

> The report's most interesting conclusion is that the greenhouse cloud has a silver lining. The domestic design and manufacture of efficient and renewable energy equipment and techniques is where the energy efficiency revolution will have its biggest impact on economic growth and new jobs. These gains will greatly exceed those to be obtained merely from microeconomic reform in the energy sector, although these are also needed to foster energy efficiency. But they will be missed altogether if we simply sit back and import the equipment needed to create an energy efficient economy (Saddler, 1990, p.vii).

This is key finding, and suggests that the employment generation strategy we have developed has more than an "outside chance" of success. The commitment to achieving this goal has to be shared by all participants, and it is in our proposed National Electricity Industry Committee that such commitment could be engendered.

Although employment in the energy industry has been declining in the past decade, there are significant opportunities for employment generation in the industry.

Incorporating demand side management and energy efficient programs and technology can increase net employment. A 1987 International Energy Agency report "Energy Conservation in IEA Countries" maintained that job losses do occur in the energy supply industry but studies in Canada, United States, Netherlands, United Kingdom and other EEC countries show that there is an overall increase in employment (quoted in Community Energy Network, 1990, p.4). This increased employment resulted from the enhanced cost-effectiveness of energy supplies and their positive downstream effects in other industries.

Questions do arise concerning the sources of investment capital for the necessary expansion of efficient energy production and utilisation. In this regard, we outline the need for more rational fiscal and monetary policies in Chapter 4. The pusillanimity practised by the federal government in recent years can, and needs to be, reversed.

It also needs to be stressed that the nature of much of the investment in efficiency is quite different from what we have become used to in the energy sector, with our reliance on capital-intensive generating plant:

> Efficiency investments' very high cashflow velocity (short leadtime and fast payback) is especially desirable in this regard because it enables major investment ramp rates to be maintained with only a modest amount of working capital. Equally important is the competitive boost that Australian businesses can get from low energy bills (Lovins, 1990, p.32).

This feature of efficiency investments reduces the stress that energy investments would have on the States' financial resources.

Specific employment generating initiatives within the energy sector are outlined in the following paragraphs.

Energy efficient technologies
Potential for increased employment can be seen in measures designed to reduce consumption of electricity, and in measures designed to develop alternative sources of electricity. Energy efficiency measures include both development of energy saving devices and strategies to educate or impose an energy efficient ethos on domestic and industrial consumers. For the purposes of this section, demand management strategies are included in efficiency strategies.

This perspective on employment generation through energy efficiency implies that the electricity industry will need to change its perspective from being mere suppliers of electricity to a perspective that incorporates a higher priority being given to a new form of customer service i.e. assisting consumers to become more efficient users of electrical energy in their homes and their workplaces

One such area of increasing importance is in assistance with energy audits. Energy audits are already a well established feature in manufacturing industry. Largely conducted by private contractors, they provide industrial users with an understanding of their energy use patterns and the potential to improve the efficiency of their energy use. The SECV is already involved in this area. Energy audits can also be provided for the domestic consumer.

As an example of what can be achieved, it is worthwhile examining the Victorian Government's Home Energy Advisory Service (HEAS) and the Community Home Energy Improvement Scheme (CHEIS).[11] These organisations conducted energy audits and retrofitting for domestic consumers. A study of the projects (Backman, 1985) found that the cost of saving a unit of electricity through the HEAS (0.62c per kWh) compares well with the cost of supplying the same quantity of electricity through the SECV ($1.08).

Furthermore, investment in home energy improvement is almost twice as labour intensive as an equivalent investment in energy supply, while associated employment is more decentralised and can be targeted to areas of high unemployment (Backman, 1990, p.iii). The study found that 138 jobs had been created between 1983 and 1985. The HEAS and CHEIS programs suffered through being short term programs with no certainty of on-going funding and CHEIS collapsed soon after funding ceased.

These initiatives were targeted to low income, high energy user households. Some 10,000 applications were received each year the scheme operated. Backman estimated that there were 240,000 households eligible under the criteria. There are obviously many more dwellings which could benefit from an energy audit and retrofitting activities if the criteria were broadened to include any high energy using household or any dwelling over, say, 20 years old. For example, while we attempted to obtain the data necessary to identify the number of households, occupied by people with disabilities who would be advantaged by having fuse boxes replaced with circuit breakers, this was not available.

Energy auditing seems a job that is peculiarly well suited to employees of electricity authorities. Although Backman considered it a new skill area, many of the skills she lists would be common in some units of electricity authorities. It combines detailed knowledge of household energy use with the ability to diagnose energy problems, use a portable computer and promote energy conservation. Auditors also require good communication skills and the ability to act as on the spot counsellors from time to time.

There is significant potential for employment generation in this area. Small localised business enterprises could be established by energy authorities. The range of skills required are already in existence in the community, and probably fit well with some of the skill areas the electricity authorities are sloughing off. Training requirements are minimal: for the HEAS two weeks training was provided to energy auditors and these were people who had not had experience in the power industry.

As back-up to the provision of energy audits, retrofitting may be required. Retrofitters require a range of "handyperson" skills. These include installing insulation, weatherstripping, installation of flow controls in showers and dampeners in chimneys, double glazing windows, hot water service repairs and pipe lagging, minor carpentry work, appliance servicing, and minor plumbing work. They, and the energy auditors, would also require some knowledge of building construction techniques, heat gain and loss in dwellings, household heating and cooling equipment and electricity pricing and tariff structures.

The trend towards greater energy efficiency has the potential to provide significant opportunities for other industries. Automatic solar controlled external lighting for industry is already available and could be developed for the national (and international) market.

Australia currently lacks a large manufacturing base for energy efficient products, and the costs of imports are high. This has previously been used as an argument against the adoption of energy efficient practices. However, it would be both environmentally and economically more effective to manufacture energy efficient products here. A similar reasoning can be applied to the provision of the expertise necessary to conduct and evaluate energy audits, to design retrofits and to undertake research and development of innovative technology for this expanding field:

For example, building a compact-fluorescent-globe factory costs about 1 per cent as much as building power stations to produce as much electricity as the globes will save. A $10 million superwindow-coating machine saves as much oil and gas as a $400 million off-shore platform extracts (but that kind of oil runs out and pollutes, whilst the first kind doesn't). Whenever we choose the wrong option, we starve the rest of the economy for capital, and hence reduce total employment (Lovins, 1990, p.32).[12]

New technologies such as insulating paint, latent energy storage systems and low energy bricks indicate that there are many innovative solutions in energy efficiency.

Trades skills will not be the only ones likely to be excess to the requirements of electricity authorities in the future. Professional engineering, drafting, design and technical skills will also be excess if some programs are curtailed. This presents an opportunity to use these skills in the design and manufacturing, as well as marketing, sales, fitting and maintenance of energy saving devices.

Construction standards which maximise the potential for improved efficiency of energy use need to be developed. These include insulation standards, passive solar design where practicable, building materials, design of built-in heating and air-conditioning devices etc. Although the potential employment generated from this is very small, the benefits to the community in terms of lower energy use make it worthwhile to include. If there were an emphasis on energy efficiency in construction there would also be an impetus to research and develop energy efficient materials and methods.

By encouraging energy efficient practices and devices, and by investing in cost effective, non polluting, and safe renewable energy source technology, Australia will garner significant economic benefits. First, employment will be created. Second, the skills base of Australia will deepen. Third, there is immense potential for the export of renewable energy technology to other developed countries and to the developing countries of Asia and eastern Europe.

While some would consider such strategies to be "utopian", it is as well to recall that, in order to attain emission targets, the Senate Standing Committee on Industry, Science and Technology (SSCIST) has urged the Federal Government to accelerate the introduction of technologies that improve energy efficiency, given that efficiency improvements currently represent lower cost options than most renewable energy supply options (Mills, 1988, p.125).

In summary, many energy efficiency measures have the potential to be produced or conducted by the public sector, through the creation of new public trading entities or by leasing/contractual arrangements with existing electricity authorities. However, there appears to be a trend to maximising private sector involvement in new initiatives in an "effort to marshal all available expertise and resources (SECV, 1990, p.68) It remains to be seen whether such private sector support will extend to establishing business enterprises that initially are likely to be marginal.

Changes in energy source

The committee rejects the notion suggested by the Department of Primary Industries and Energy that technical limitations prevent Australia from embracing alternative technologies. Australia's role as a world leader in the design and manufacture of solar cells is evidence to the contrary. Rather the committee is of the opinion that Australia currently has both the scientific expertise and the technology to develop renewable energy sources to the point where they can be manufactured locally and exported (SSCIST, 1991, p.131).

The SSCIST has determined that after 2005 "renewable energy options are likely to become much more competitive with energy efficiency and non-renewable supply options" (Mills, 1988, p.125).

Changing the source of power in industrial, commercial and domestic environments also offers some opportunity for employment generation. That should not be taken to mean, however, that the central role of the public sector should be diminished. In fact, as we have suggested in this report, there are compelling reasons why the public sector should retain a strong and vibrant role.

Co-generation has the potential to reduce reliance on the electricity suppliers. In so doing there would be an illusion of less reliance on electricity.

Photovoltaics can be used for co-generation. There are few infrastructure costs associated because photovoltaic generators can be located on the outside of existing buildings. The potential for (limited) employment generation in the short term is in the scientific and research skills areas, as photovoltaics are costly and largely untested at this stage.

In conclusion, as the industry is currently organised, employment generation prospects from co-generation are slim in the public sector. Manufacture of co-generators would be substantially conducted by the private sector, probably using contract labour. This is also true of installation. Design, manufacture and marketing is not an area of rapidly growing employment potential as the technologies are readily available.

Renewable energy sources

Renewable energy sources reduce both energy load and the need for new plant. They are also less environmentally damaging, though few are entirely benign. Alternative energy sources also present the opportunity to manufacture energy producing technologies in Australia, rather than relying on imports, as is the case with current energy producing sources. The viability of alternative energy sources is becoming apparent throughout the electricity industry.

The development of alternative energy sources presents an opportunity to develop new skills for Australia as well as utilising existing skills in research and development. Renewable energy generation is more labour intensive and less capital intensive than conventional energy generation. In the United States, nuclear power requires 100 jobs per thousand giga watt hours a year, geothermal 112 jobs, coal 116 (including mining) jobs, solar 248 jobs and wind 542 jobs (Flavin, 1990, p.43).

Flavin also concluded that:

In the move away from a fossil fuel economy, some of the largest employment opportunities would be in home insulation, carpentry, and sheet metal work. Wind prospectors, photovoltaic engineers and solar architects

are among the new professions that might expand rapidly. Numbering in the thousands today, jobs in these fields may total in the millions within a few decades. Some of the skills now used in a fossil fuel based energy system would still be available. ... most of the jobs in a renewable energy based economy would be cleaner and safer. No one would be required to clean up radioactive spills or decommission "hot" nuclear plants. Nor would workers have to toil deep underground or dispose of toxic ash (Flavin, 1990, p.42).

Diesendorf explains that the main potential for **wind power** is on the coastlines of southern Australia. A small wind farm of six 60kW generators at Esperance in Western Australia is performing well and a wind generator industry has recently been established in Perth. The potential for hundreds of megawatts of wind power generation exists in South Australia, Tasmania, Western Australia and possibly Victoria, without additional storage. Diesendorf goes on to comment that:

If mass-produced in Australia, wind generated electricity may be already economically competitive with new conventional electricity generation in states with high wind energy potential, such as South Australia and Tasmania. With growing interest in wind energy from India, China and the Pacific, it could become an export industry. Two States, Western Australia and Victoria, have recently called for expressions of interest for megawatt-rated wind farms and this will clear the way for local mass production (1990, p.6).

The Electricity Supply Association of Australia has stated that:

it should ...not be forgotten that Australia... has significant wind resources along its southern extremity, good solar radiation intensity over most of the continent and theoretically very large amounts of tidal energy, all of which are largely untapped (ESAA, 1989, p.13).

Wind power has been used to considerable success in Denmark and to a lesser extent in the United States of America. Some small experiments in wind power are being conducted at Breamlea, Victoria and Esperance, Western Australia. The Danish experience with wind energy technology indicates the many positive benefits available. Direct benefits include creating employment, reducing reliance on unemployment benefits, increased taxation revenue and beneficial effects on the balance of payments through export of the technology.

In Denmark there were 3,071 jobs created between 1979 and 1985 in the wind power industry. In 1985 that represented one new job for every aerogenerator produced. The Danish market accounted for only 10.3 per cent of the employment created, with the majority of jobs being in export production (see Table 12.8).

Wind powered generation offers employment generation mainly in the metals fabrication and construction skills areas, although there is a requirement for electrical skills. For instance, the aerogenerators manufactured by Westwind, a Western Australian firm, have an Australian content of about 70 per cent of their capital costs (ATDG, 1985, p.60).

Windfarms require little ongoing maintenance and few operators. The scope for employment in these areas is limited. Windpower is a viable option for connection into the grid because of the short lead times needed for construction which make it "useful for finessing energy supply needs" (Hamlyn-Harris, 1987, p.12).

Solar power is probably the best-known of the renewable energy sources. Solar power can be utilised in two ways: through the introduction of passive solar design (photovoltaics) and through use of solar powered devices such as hot water heaters. Of the two, solar power offers greater opportunities for employment generation. The SSCIST concluded:

> The granting of government contracts to develop these technologies would be extremely beneficial (SSCIST, 1991, p.134).

Solar power is generally used for water heating, either domestic hot water services or commercial and domestic swimming pool heating. It can also be used for industrial purposes where heated water is required.

A 1982 study looked at the job creation potential of the solar water heating industry in Victoria (Andrews, 1982). The report found that imports of solar water heating devices were low and that Australia exported about a quarter of its production. It also found significant variations in take up rates between the States, with Western Australia leading the field with 17 per cent of domestic dwellings fitted with solar water heaters while Victoria had a penetration of less than 0.3 per cent (p.vi). About 900 equivalent full time jobs were in the solar industry Australia wide in 1980–1 (p.xi).

Estimates of the job creation potential of the Victorian solar industry were made, based on three scenarios: the "mini" where Victoria achieved half the penetration of WA in a decade and 100 per cent within two decades; the "midi" where Victoria achieved penetration rates comparable to WA within a decade and half of all water heaters in the state were solar within two decades; and the "maxi" where twice WA's penetration was achieved within a decade and 70 per cent of water heaters sold were solar within two decades.

Each scenario involved ever increasing levels

Table 12.8

The Effect of Windpower Production on Employment in Denmark, 1979–1985

	1979	1980	1981	1982	1983	1984	1985
Production for home market	52	94	131	146	220	273	281
O&M for home market	2	5	8	13	21	29	37
Production for export	-	-	21	47	354	1767	2753
Total employed in wind industry	54	99	160	206	595	2069	3071
Less jobs lost at power plants	-2	-2	-5	-9	-13	-24	-28
Total net employed	52	97	155	197	582	2045	3043

Source: Appropriate Technology Development Group, Inc, 1985, p.59.

of government support in the form of legislation and access to low cost loans for consumers who wished to convert. The number of jobs created in Victoria in the first decade was 404 for the mini, 783 for the midi and 1,652 for the maxi. Within two decades the additional jobs created was expected to be 655 for the mini, 1,229 for the midi and 1,118 for the maxi scenarios (p xxiii).

Unfortunately the report did not study the job types or skill types predominant in the solar industry. It was also probably flawed in having the creation of jobs in Victoria as a focus, yet another example of the parochialism of State-based industries. The industry is already well established in WA and would require less infrastructure expansion, rather than establishing large firms in Victoria. Still, there does appear to be a general potential to generate significant levels of employment from production and installation of solar devices.

As mentioned in Chapter 5, parabolic solar trough concentrators have been installed in California. The Australian National University has developed prototype paraboidal dishes which in theory are more thermally efficient than parabolic troughs, making them cheaper when mass produced. Once this occurs, their potential contribution to grid electricity and remote area power supplies would be enhanced.

A solar steam generator that uses evacuated absorber tubes and low concentration seasonally adjusted parabolic mirrors is capable of generating thermal energy at up to 250 degrees centigrade. This system is "comparatively low-tech, having no moving parts in the collector except a mirror adjusted about once a month" (Mills, 1988, p.5). The collector is currently being demonstrated at Campbelltown District Hospital and is producing steam and hot water at a price which is competitive with electricity. Preliminary calculations suggest that once the system is mass produced "it is likely to become competitive with low-temperature heat from LPG and later, on a larger scale of production, with natural gas" (Diesendorf, 1990, p.5).

Solar thermal collectors have a "multi billion dollar annual potential within Australia alone, and...sixty times that of Australia (in developing countries) by the turn of the century" (SSCIST, 1991, p.134).

Another possible area of employment generation in the alternative energy area comes from **wave power.** Australia is theoretically well placed to take advantage of wave power.

Norway has successfully experimented with integrating wave power into the grid. This involved the development of a new resonating column wave powered electricity turbine (Hamlyn-Harris, 1987, p.13). Employment prospects exist at the design, manufacture and maintenance points (see also Chapter 5).

Local area initiatives

Employment generation schemes need not be confined to the power industry. Localities where there are likely to be significant job losses due to a change in generation methods need to be assessed for their potential to provide alternative employment avenues.

Table 12.9

SECV Employees by Location, June 1990

Location	Male	Female	Total
Head Office Based	3855	502	4357
Latrobe Valley	8046	435	8481
Regions	4656	468	5124
Total	16577	1405	1796

Source: SECV Annual Report 1990, p.130

The large rural communities which depend in large part on the electricity authorities for their economic well being, such as the Hunter Valley in New South Wales, the Latrobe Valley in Victoria and the Collie region in Western Australia are particularly vulnerable (see Table 12.9 for a summary of the Victorian situation). The previously itinerant construction workforce has settled into the communities as a result of the construction emphasis of the past. Related industries, such as engineering, boiler construction, steel fabrication and design and electrical installation also have a tendency to establish in these regions.

Educational institutions have established large campuses in the power generation regions. Major regional hospitals are established. Recreation and entertainment services are well developed and social welfare services established (LRC,1987,p.16).

The regions suitable for large scale, fossil fuel generation are also agricultural or pastoral areas. The combined effects of a decline in the conventional electricity generation area and the rural crisis are devastating to such regions. There are likely to be high levels of unemployment in these areas, and a high emigration rate.

Industry development which would generate employment could be in areas which combine construction skills and agricultural skills. This could mean the development of agricultural machinery or technology, perhaps in alternative crop growing technologies such as hydroponics or in alternative crops such as horticulture. Development of native horticulture as a cash crop is also an option. Horticulture is labour intensive and the jobs generated would be long term, although the initial construction and engineering positions generated would be temporary.

Tourism development is another area for employment generation. The Latrobe Valley, the Hunter Valley and Tasmania have many attractions. Their tourism potential has not yet been fully realised. Employment could be generated in the construction of small holiday hostels, upgrading of access routes, tourism guides and information and the accompanying hospitality industry. However, jobs in the tourism industry would be unlikely to be permanent full time positions. In the initial developmental phases building, road maintenance and marketing positions would be generated. In the longer term positions in the hospitality industry tend to be part time.

The prospects

It bears repeating that there is insufficient data available to make meaningful projections about the potential for employment generation necessary to absorb the workforce currently being retrenched by the electricity authorities throughout Australia.

The inability to provide data about the existing skills of the industry's workforce, the inability or reluctance to provide recent historical data about the skills which have been lost from the power industry in the last two years and the reluctance to detail where the axe will fall in the next twelve months to two years does not present a picture of an industry which is in control of its destiny. There appears to be a gross disinterest in the

welfare of the workforce, and in the welfare of the communities which are so dependent on the presence of large scale generation activities.

The industry strategy we have proposed, with union representation, its strong research base and its access to the full range of State-based data would be able to alleviate many of these problems.

Other aspects

It should not be concluded from the foregoing that an effective industry strategy should concern itself solely with the electricity industry. A consistent strategy also requires an examination of other causes of CO_2 pollution.

Transport

It is as well to recall that transport contributes 26 per cent of CO_2 emissions in Australia — the second largest contribution of this greenhouse gas. This is due to the combination of enormous geographical distances which separate Australia's main centres of population, and traditional urban planning. One thing is clear, more and better roads are not the answer:

> The celebrated sprawl of Australian cities may have been a pardonable luxury when fuel was plentiful and there was little concern for the effects of its use. To continue to plan on the basis of perpetuating the current profligate use of the private car can no longer be justified (Lowe, 1988, p.609).

Strategies for improving energy efficiency within the transport sector include: increasing fuel efficiency via technical improvements; improving public transport to encourage wider use; transferring freight from road to rail; encouraging fuel substitution, and the commercial development of solar powered vehicles. Further information on fuel substitution and solar powered vehicles can be found in "Rescue the Future" (SSCIST, 1990). It should be noted that development of a solar powered vehicle at Sydney University could be accelerated by strategies such as Federal government policy on the incorporation of electric vehicles into their car fleets at the earliest possible date.

Road/rail freight and passenger transfer

The relative costs of providing infrastructure of a sufficiently high standard for an efficient and safe road transport industry and the costs of an equivalent high speed rail link should be compared. (SSCIST, 1991, p.75)

Railways are the most economically efficient means of freight and passenger transport over medium to long distances, particularly in terms of primary energy consumption. Railways carry 35 per cent of Australia's land freight, yet their State funding allocation over the past 20 years or so amounts to a mere 44 per cent of one year's Federal road funding.

Since 1983 the national highway system has received $3,000 million from the Federal government, with only $29 million being spent on national rail main lines. Of this funding $730 million was spent on the Hume Highway. Nothing was spent on the Sydney-Melbourne rail line.

The number of six-axle trucks on the roads has doubled between 1979 and 1985 because of the combination of high investment in national roads and "substantial under-pricing of road damage attributable to heavy vehicles". As the ARU/ACF report states, "these vehicles were responsible for subsidised road damage costs of $828 million ($32,000 per vehicle on average)" (ARU/ACF Executive Summary, p.i). Whilst the requirements of the trucking industry have been accommodated, there would indeed seem to be an overall policy of neglect for the rail system.

As a result, not one feasibility study has been carried out on the possibility of a national rail electrification program. Rail electrification could utilise the over capacity from some of the newer coal-fired power stations which will still be operating for the next 30–40 years. Thus, power station CO_2 emission could at least be offset by the substantial alleviation of CO_2 emissions from the transport sector. The ARU/ACF report succinctly states:

> At a time when the private companies which dominate land transport in Australia are establishing an internationally integrated base, and when European countries are seeking to integrate established national rail operations into a European matrix, the Federal structure of Australia's long distance railway operations appears more perverse and absurd than ever (ARU/ACF, 1990, p.2)

The ARU/ACF has concluded:

> The Federal Government, especially a Federal Labor Government must be prepared to make a comprehensive policy commitment to revitalise, modernise and expand the role of non-urban railways and urban public transport in Australia. Such a commitment would be expected to be achievable by, and approached incrementally to, the year 2000. (ARU/ACF, 1990, p.18)

Other transport

Motor vehicle fuel efficiency has increased gradually over the past 10 years and a 30 per cent improvement is expected between 1990 and 2010. In 1988 the average fuel consumption for cars sold in Australia was reported to be 9.1 litres per 100 kilometres. Several of the large car manufacturers are working on fuel efficiency. For example, Volvo are developing a prototype that uses lightweight components with a fuel consumption of 3.4 litres per 100 kilometres (combined city and highway). Toyota have developed a prototype that consumes 2.4 litres, and Renault has tested a model that uses less than 2 litres per 100 kilometres:

> If both average distances and vehicle numbers continue to grow as projected, an average 40 per cent improvement in fuel efficiency of all vehicles (including trucks) will be required just to maintain current levels of carbon dioxide emissions (Greene, 1990, p.3.24)

Nevertheless:

> It is unreasonable to expect people to reduce car use and use public transport more unless public transport systems are improved significantly (SSCIST, 1991, p.79).

Wider use of public transport "would appear to require a dramatic turnaround from Australian trends, both in funding expansion of public transport networks and in encouraging greater use" (SSCIST, 1991, p.3.25) Since the 1940s, when the basic network structures of public transport systems were established, increasing proportions of State government urban transport budgets have been directed into urban road construction and maintenance.

Since 1960, the combination of road and freeway development, urban sprawl and private vehicle dependence has produced an alarming increase in transport energy consumption per capita in Australian cities. Only Sydney and Melbourne have a markedly slower per capita increase due to "relatively well developed public transport networks based on railways" [ARU/ACF], 1990, p.14).

A significant shift to public transport would not only reduce CO2 emissions — passenger cars consume 54 per cent of all transport fuel consumption, 75 per cent of which is used in urban travel — it would also help conserve dwindling fossil fuel reserves and improve urban air quality (SSCIST, 1991, p.79). This would however require a major change in current attitudes to traffic management which, at the moment, seek to solve traffic problems by building more roads. If buses are to be maintained, then entire fleets should be converted to LPG, and consideration must be given to restricting private vehicle access to all CBDs, as has been successfully done in cities as far apart as Amsterdam and Santiago. Improvements to urban train systems and the replacement of buses by light rail would further reduce emissions and dependence upon private vehicles.

According to one industry participant, making cities "no go areas" for cars is the "only way to reduce traffic chaos and stop pollution choking the environment" (P. Gyllenhammar, Volvo Chief Executive, cited in ARU/ACF, 1990, p.3).

Passive heating and cooling

Urban planning conventions are inhibiting the proliferation of energy efficient passive solar housing. While public housing authorities and several private builders are now constructing passive solar houses which require less cooling in summer, and can reduce the demand for electricity and gas, thereby reducing winter heating costs by 60–90 per cent, local government and the housing industry persistently employ a pattern of street and subdivision orientation that makes it impossible for housing to be correctly orientated.

State governments are also slow to develop and implement energy performance standards for new buildings for both residential and commercial sectors. Most of the commercial sector's energy use is in the heating, cooling and lighting of buildings. Architecture currently relies upon air conditioning to keep buildings comfortable, rather than using orientation and energy efficient design. The principles of energy efficient design are well known and documented in the

commercial sector, as demonstrated by an energy efficiency guide published by the Building Owners and Managers Association of Australia (BOMA). The Australian Construction Service apparently has a "long term commitment to energy efficient design in public buildings", and uses similar principles to the BOMA guide. A further point made by the SSCIST report points out the irony of lost opportunities for exemplary practice:

> The new Parliament House in Canberra is a good example of a modern building constructed without sufficient regard to energy efficiency. Most of its glazed areas face east-west and have no external shading. Consequently the building is subject to excess heating from the sun during the summer months, despite being double-glazed. Additionally, there is no provision for turning off lighting in unoccupied rooms either automatically or from a central switch (SSCIST, 1991, p.99).

A Commonwealth Task Force was established in 1989 to look into establishing energy efficiency in building regulations, but there are as yet no set of uniform building regulations that enforce efficiency standards, although there is a clear need for one if the construction of thermal sieves is to be arrested.

Under current tax provisions which make operating and maintenance costs deductible, commercial space owners tend to opt for least-cost solutions rather than energy efficiency designs. Construction costs can only be amortised over the life of a building. Consequently, whilst regulations can enforce standards, a more comprehensive strategy should employ a carrot as well as a stick and use financial incentives such as Lovins' "feebates", to encourage energy efficient building design and construction (Lovins, 1990).

Remote area power supply

An effective energy strategy would also need to consider issues such as remote area power supply (RAPS). Photovoltaic cells have already found favour as a remote area supply where they are currently the main option for homes, farms, communities, navigation signals and Telecom installations which are isolated from the grid.

Following a study in 1989, SECV has become

the first Australian utility to recognise the financial benefits of encouraging the use of remote area power supplies rather than persistent extension of their grid into uneconomical rural areas. Other utilities are not only content to persist with this costly practice, but also offer subsidies for grid connections to remote homes and farms, although there are signs that ECNSW may eventually follow the SECV's lead.

The SECV noted that where "... connection costs exceed $10,000 (equivalent to four poles or more), under certain circumstances it would be more economic to subsidise people to use a RAPS system rather than to connect them to the grid". RAPS users will be encouraged to install renewable components such as photovoltaics, wind or mini-hydro to "promote the sales of well designed RAPS systems and thus to indirectly assist both the public and solar industry" (SECV/Energy Victoria, 1990, Introduction).

It appears that the Aboriginal and Torres Straight Islander Commission (ATSIC) and Australian Construction Services (ACS) are also open to the possibilities of renewable RAPS, especially when they are "the most politically acceptable alternative to all interested parties and groups". In February this year, ATSIC approved the installation of 13 diesel power stations and a fully operational solar/wind station to provide electricity for 14 Torres Strait communities. ASTIC noted that ACS saw this as "the ideal compromise between the cheapest technical solution using existing diesel generator technology whilst still providing a fully operational solar/wind station on Coconut Island which can be used for monitoring and research on renewable energy sources" (ATSIC, 1991, p.4).

The decision is of particular interest given that diesel generation for remote communities is more expensive than photovoltaics when paybacks are taken into account.

Conclusion

The foregoing discussion of employment opportunities, and other components of an effective, national energy sector strategy, indicate that there are a vast range of issues which would need to be considered.

However, we have also shown that solutions are possible. But they can not be implemented without the wholehearted commitment of the

sector's workforce. For that reason, have undertaken an examination the industrial relations experience of the workforce in various States to ascertain what sort of reforms would be necessary in order to engender this workforce support (Appendix 1).

In light of the information contained in this report, and the suggestions that we have made throughout, as well as the criticisms we have made of the existing industry institutions, we are proposing a radical alternative to the current organisation of the system (see Figure 12.1 and the accompanying notes).

It is necessary, however, before we outline what the institutional arrangements would be for such a strategy, to set the goals of a properly integrated national industry body.

12.5 The National Electricity Industry Committee
Introduction

As we noted above, the issue of an national electricity industry policies must be placed in the context of national integration. But it is as well to recall the conclusions reached in other Chapters which bear on the operation of public sector institutions in general and the electricity industry in particular.

Chapter 9 briefly outlined the reasons for the development of statutory authorities. We showed that the objective of providing ultimate autonomy for public sector management will always be confronted by the reality of political control. The economic conservatives ignore the larger roles of public sector bodies in a parliamentary democracy in the interest of chasing so-called "efficiency gains" which they define from a narrow and erroneous theoretical base

We also dealt with the role that government "interference" has played in ensuring an electricity supply to the bulk of Australian citizens, and we concluded that genuine accountability should be introduced to the management of citizens' assets through more effective representative and participatory structures.

In Chapter 10 we suggested that the enthusiasm of public-sector managers to be allowed to operate through the vehicle of a private sector corporate form, or to emulate private-sector arrangements, may be symptomatic of a desire to avoid both public-service red-tape and demands for financial accountability. It became clear the corporatisation would lead to the reduction or elimination of the safeguards established through financial disclosure and wide-ranging audit of public bodies.

Claims that corporatised bodies will be subject to the discipline of the market were shown to be questionable, based as they are on a "rose tinted" view of private sector operations. We showed that, if public utilities supplying electricity services were to "privatised", one could expect that information about the activities of those bodies would be even less accessible than at present.

There clearly needs to be greater recognition of the principles of public sector performance and accountability by those who are, for a time, responsible for decisions which affect every citizen.

Chapter 11 showed that the privatisation recommendations of the IC and other conservative bodies are likely to retard the positive changes being introduced in the industry, changes that themselves must be supplemented by further measures to reduce the presently wasteful approach to many issues being taken by the industry. It is clear that little positive guidance is likely to be had from the experience so far in either Britain or New Zealand.

The specific conclusions were:
- the need for the development of a wider range of partial production, distribution and end-use measures over time that are accepted across the whole industry is required;
- that there has been a loss of significant human resources reducing the industry's capacity to develop the demand-side of the electricity industry;
- a rejection of further corporatisation of the industry;
- a resistance to the break up of utilities;
- the need for the management of utilities should be made more transparent and participatory. Better management review and accountability procedures should be applied across the whole industry;
- the development of the representative institutions to research, produce information and coordinate the reform in the industry is essential; and
- the need for the provision of information necessary for effective planning, e.g. employment data.

What is required is more effective control of electricity authorities and better production, distribution and end-use information as the basis for making better decisions about them.

Finally, we have shown in Section 12.5 that considerable scope exists for employment generation in the electricity industry.

The goals

The goals which we suggest for the National Electricity Committee are ambitious. However, we believe that the industry is in need of substantial reform, and that the only way this can be achieved is through a process of effective consultation between all industry participants at all levels of operation. We have also concluded that the existing structures are inadequate to achieve these goals.

Simply, we can state the goals in the following way:
- to effectively and realistically analyse the industry within the context of the energy sector, and its role in Australian economy and society;
- on the basis of this analysis, to formulate proposals for each of the independent authorities in the electricity industry to meet the strategic objectives we have outlined in Chapter 3 viz:

  to allow the community to enjoy energy services at a reasonable price, while reflecting, where appropriate, the total cost of providing those services. This would necessitate the inclusion of what have traditionally been seen as externalities;

  to maintain the nation's equity in its resource base, rather than alienating it on the basis of myopic development policies. This would be facilitated by restructuring Australia's national accounts on the basis we have outlined in Chapter 4;

  to recognise that the rights of future generations to resources and an environment providing enjoyment have to be factored into the sector's present operations;

  to facilitate communication and decision-making for the industry among all participants; and

  to recognise and build on the immense human resource the industry holds and to secure its future development.

Within these broad goals, the following are recognised, on the basis of the previous Chapters' conclusions, as matters requiring attention:
- effective integration of the eastern seaboard grid;
- encouragement of the adoption of demand-side management techniques by authorities at all levels, which would have the dual purpose of meeting the environmental imperative and enabling the utilisation of the skills which currently reside in the industry;
- the development of an industry training structure with national skills schedules and standards. As a first step in this process there is a need for the establishment of a national skills register which would facilitate the achievement of all other goals;
- the development of rational plans for capacity expansion (supply-side);
- the preparation of common pricing and accounting principles which can be adopted by each of the independent authorities;
- the encouragement of environmentally conscious proposals for the future of the industry;
- the development of realistic forecasting methodologies;
- development of industry-wide purchasing standards and procedures;
- examination of the community and occupational health and safety issues in the industry, particularly EMR
- coordination with other energy industries, including the encouragement of overarching consultative mechanisms; and
- encouragement of the adoption of progressive industrial relations practices by all independent authorities.

There are a number of related matters which need elucidation.

First, the existing industry body (the Electricity Supply Association of Australia) has clearly outlived any usefulness it may have had. The establishment of the National Committee would signal the demise of the ESAA, while absorbing some of its purely technical functions.

However, there are resources at the command of the ESAA which should be maintained. In particular, we would refer to its technical advisory committees. These committees, in a suitable restructured guise, should provide necessary advice to the National Committee and its Secretariat. Their work could be overseen by the Research Unit.

Second, there should be continual efforts to extend the range of representative organisations with which the industry consults. Priority should be given to establishment of consultation with Aboriginal people, and people with disabilities.

Conclusion

Based on the work of the *Powering the Future* team, we have prepared what is arguably the most comprehensive survey of the electricity industry ever undertaken. The trade unions in the industry are to be commended for their farsightedness and courage in commissioning this body of independent research.

As the reports of the other research projects to which we have referred become available it will be seen that this report encompasses most (if not all) of the issues they raise in a constructive and honest manner.

This approach makes our proposal for a National Electricity Industry Committee not only relevant but possible. It is now up to the industry participants to advance this proposal.

Notes to a National Electricity Industry Committee structure

1. The National Committee would have an advisory role only.
2. The National Secretariat and the Research Unit would be funded by all participants, with governments providing necessary financial assistance to trade union and community representatives.
3. The research unit could be staffed by secondees (selected on merit) from State, federal and local government bodies, and other industry participants.
4. Governments would be represented by Ministers or their nominees.
5. Authorities would be represented by CEOs or their nominees. In the case of non-integrated State electricity supply industries, there would be one from generation/transmission and one to represent distributors.
6. Unions coordinated through the ACTU.
7. The Research Unit could be called on to undertake specific tasks for the National Strategy Committee irregularly.

8. All authorities would guarantee unrestricted access to their own information bases.

9. The Interstate Consultation Sub-committee would have responsibility that initiatives taken by any one authority were communicated throughout the industry.

unfortunately, not confined to the energy sector/electricity industry, but is a trend that can be identified elsewhere.

10. Iceland is not connected due to its geographic isolation.

11. HEAS continues as a unit in the SECV.

12. See above.

Notes

1. The term microeconomic itself has undergone a transformation in meaning throughout the 1980s. The term microeconomic originally referred to the level of the firm. It has come, however, to refer to industry wide, and in some cases economy-wide, matters. For example, achievement of skill based pay systems would have implications economy-wide.

2. The original Accord, what we would now refer to as Accord Mark I, was negotiated between the ACTU and the ALP in Opposition in 1982. For one interpretation which results from this awareness (see Stilwell, 1986).

3. The industry's recent industrial relations record is set out in Appendix 12.1. The record raises serious questions regarding the awareness by industry management and governments of the positive role which unions are prepared to play in initiating microeconomic reform.

4. This listing does not, however, imply that each member of the project team necessarily concurs with each of these initiatives.

5. Some of these other inquiries were conducted by the Senate Standing Committee on Greenhouse Gas Emissions; the production in South Australia of a Green Paper and the work of the Ecologically Sustainable Development Working Party.

6. This difficulty in achieving national coordination extends to fiscal and monetary policy, where the States do have some potential to frustrate federal macro-economic policies (see *Australian Financial Review* leader 3 January 1991)

7. We would be justified in also criticising the Industry Commission's procedures on this ground: electricity authorities (and others) are permitted to nominate sections of their Submissions as "confidential" and the public is not granted access to those sections.

8. See below for our comments regarding the paucity of employment data from the authorities.

9. This characteristic of the means employed by governments to elicit information and formulate policy is,

Figure 12.1

NATIONAL ELECTRICITY INDUSTRY COMMITTEE STRUCTURE

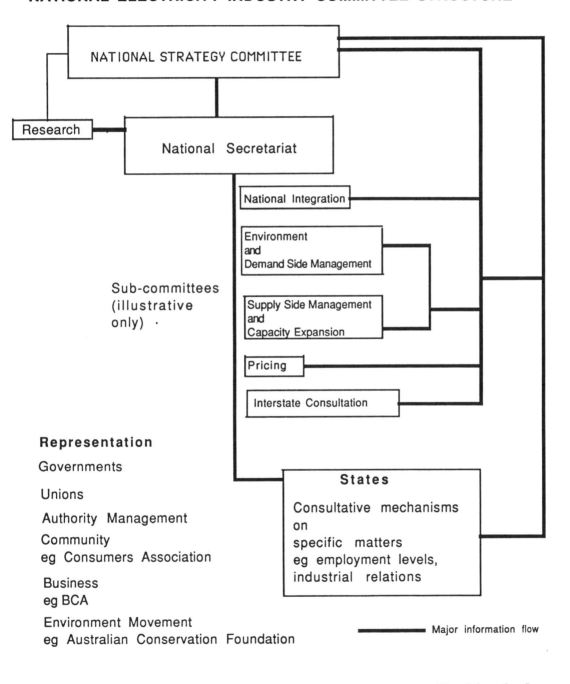

APPENDIX 1

A Perspective on Industrial Relations in the Electricity Industry

In 1990 a number of industrial disputes in the electricity industry focused attention on the exercise of industrial relations in the industry. There are also a number of other developments which we also examine and which bear on the failure of respective statutory authority managements to understand the very real benefits which a more consultative and open decision-making process could deliver to the electricity industry and, ultimately, to the consumers within an overall sector strategy.

Award restructuring

The award restructuring process has occurred within awards on a State-by-State basis. The results to date have accorded with some of the goals of the process identified as essential by the ACTU (for example, the number of awards has been reduced, there has been a consolidation of conditions, and occupation-based classifications have been replaced with broadbanded, generic classifications within a multi-salary point structure).

Nevertheless, the basis for increases awarded under the Structural Efficiency Principle (SEP) has been, in part, the redundancies which have occurred in almost all States. The Industrial Commission of New South Wales has explicitly acknowledged this (Industrial Commission of New South Wales, 1990, p.29).

In respect of the situation in New South Wales, the Commission stated:

The structural efficiency principle is not a "once only" exercise but is an ongoing exercise and must be implemented carefully by all parties so that strategies put in place are not effected hastily as this will only result in further difficulties down the track. If the

ECNSW's submissions were accepted it would mean that all matters put on the table for discussion that were set out in the first instalment application would need to be in place before the granting of the second instalment and that is at the end of the restructuring process. This assumption, in my opinion, is wrong (Industrial Commission of NSW, 1990, pp.30–31).

These and other assessments hardly point to an industry which is plagued by obstructionist unions. In fact, quite the reverse will become clear in the remainder of this section.

Victoria[1]

A perspective on SECV's industrial relations record

We have had reason to criticise the operations of the various authorities in a variety of contexts throughout this report. In respect of the SECV's industrial relations record, criticisms have also been made by Australian Industrial Relations Commissioner Johnson.

Arising out of the application for the second structural efficiency adjustment in 1990, the Commissioner stated in his decision:

... there is some faint evidence in these proceedings that suggests a slow response on the part of the SECV, in some cases, to the setting up of dispute committees. Given the emphasis that I have placed on disputes settlement procedures in the matters now before me, it is imperative, in my opinion, that requests for such committees be met with a prompt, positive response by SECV if employees are to develop the required level of confidence in the procedure and its ability to deal quickly with issues as they arise (Johnson C., 1990, p.11).

The Commissioner was also somewhat critical of the SECV's decision to introduce voluntary departure packages at the same time as the structural adjustment application was being dealt with. He said:

> ... I do question the wisdom of implementing such a decision at the same time as the parties were being required by this Commission to negotiate and settle, amicably, arrangements as complex as structural efficiency. This is especially so in circumstances where the new policy appears, at least on the evidence before me, to have been applied without prior consultation with the unions concerned (Johnson C., 1990, p.11).

It is interesting to note, too, the lengths some SECV managers are willing to go to achieve their targets for "downsizing" (i.e. departures or job losses). A leaked internal memorandum between an SECV manager and his general manager discussed how redundancies could be achieved within a "layered" approach. This layering would consist of classifying employees into three groups: those who are essential to the operations of the division; those who are necessary but are currently in a non-essential area; and those who are in no way essential (*La Trobe Valley Express*, 5 March 1991). To achieve the targeted redundancies, those who are deemed to be non-essential:

> ... are to be collected into one physical area where they would have no meaningful work and limited access to telephones with the objective of demoralising them to the point where the option of the voluntary departure programme is more attractive. Section heads have been clearly directed not to give work to people merely to fill in their time (*La Trobe Valley Express*, 5 March 1991).

At the same time, the memorandum announced that the usual briefings to employees, passing on essential information such as the level of redundancies expected, would not occur.

Fortunately, the SECV's spokesperson stated that the suggested approach had been rejected outright and was not acted on. Nevertheless, the fact that a manager felt comfortable penning such a missive indicates the level of industrial relations expertise (not to mention human compassion) that exists in some areas of the SECV.

Privatisation

Though significant areas of the SECV have been privatised in recent years, the pace of privatisation accelerated considerably in 1990. This culminated in the Victorian government's proposal to privatise the Loy Yang B power station in 1991. The proffered reason for this decision is the large debt carried by the SECV — estimated to have been $7.6 billion in real terms in 1988 (Victorian Economic and Budget Review Committee, 1990, p.61).

Various estimates have been made of the costs associated with the building of the Loy Yang B station. These estimates include the figures $1.4 billion (*The Age*, 17 August 1990, p.6); $1.78 billion (*The Age*, 15 November 1990, p.1); and $1.5 billion (*The Age*, 23 November 1990, p.4).

The link between the debt carried by the SECV and the decision to privatise was made starkly by the Chairman of the SECV:

> Mr Jim Smith, chairman of the SECV ... claimed the ability of the SECV to survive was "seriously threatened" by the project.
> The SECV had pledged to cap its borrowings at $8 billion and could not afford the extra $3 billion of loans needed to complete Loy Yang B. It had to be privatised, he said. If not, electricity prices would have to rise (*The Age*, 28 November 1990, p.13)

This argument is very similar to that advanced by the federal government to justify its proposed sales of, for instance, Qantas and Australian Airlines: that is, that the injections of capital needed to keep the enterprises operating efficiently are not available to the government. The question of whether this is an accurate description of the "dilemma" faced by governments is dealt with in Chapter 4. In addition, and in respect of federal enterprises, this argument has been thoroughly discredited (Evatt, 1988); and a contrary argument at the State level has also been presented (Evatt, 1989). However, it is with the industrial relations implications that we are concerned here.

The press reports concerned with the issue of privatisations (including the sale of Loy Yang B) repeatedly warned that the SECV and the government were faced with the "spectre of a power workers' strike" (*The Age*, 28 November 1990, p.13). It is important to place this spectre in its proper context.

The SECV had already undergone management restructuring, a reduction in so-called "feather bedding" and the introduction of other measures to increase productivity and efficiency. Significant job losses had been borne by the workforce: the workforce had been reduced by over 20 per cent since 1989.

At the same time, there had been industrial disputation concerned with the issue of award restructuring.

The workforce was also concerned with the issues that we have raised in relation to privatisation: the reduction in accountability for the industry's operation being of paramount importance. And the fact that the unopposed privatisation of Loy Yang B would provide tacit support for further privatisations in Victoria (e.g. the Gas and Fuel Corporation).

The proposals to sell Loy Yang B, and the privatisation of the SECV's largest storage depot, were developed without consultation with the unions, and this was one of the major causes of industrial disruption in the La Trobe Valley around Christmas 1990. This lack of consultation led to most unions in the industry concerned that their existing working conditions would be seriously prejudiced under new ownership. When the government finally agreed to meet them, the unions were willing to attend and seek a constructive solution to the problems. The threats to Victoria's power supplies diminished drastically.

Melbourne City Council Electricity Supply Department

We will also examine the unions' position on the proposal to substantially alter the arrangements in the area covered by the City of Melbourne Electricity Supply Authority.

The Melbourne City Council (MCC) is responsible for the distribution of electricity to Melbourne's CBD. It operates 415 volt, 6.6kV and 11kV distribution systems and the 11kV busbars of the zone substations feeding its areas. The Council's Electricity Supply Department is responsible for this function. Thus, the MCC is involved in sub-transmission, primary distribution and secondary distribution. In the case of a high voltage customer, s/he will own and maintain his/her own incoming 11kV or 6.6kV swithchgear and the 11kV/415 volt or 6.6kV/415 volt transformers, obtaining a 4 per cent reduc-

tion on the appropriate tariff.

The MCC's involvement in electricity supply began in 1897. In March 1990 the Victorian government commissioned the Victorian Grants Commission to conduct a "Review of the Financial Arrangements between the State Electricity Commission of Victoria and the Melbourne City Council Electricity Supply Authority". The objectives of the Inquiry were:

- to determine the appropriateness of the MCC's unique costs for inclusion within a revised financial arrangement;
- to express the findings as a set of retail margins which relate the unique circumstances applicable to the MCC and the standards applying within the industry;
- to consider and make recommendations regarding any phasing in arrangements which may be needed to accompany the application of the revised margins; and
- to work closely with the officers of the MCC in the conduct of the work; to consult with all parties with an interest in this matter, including the unions which represent the employees within the industry (Manning et al, 1990, p.1).

The NIEIR, in conjunction with a consulting electrical power and control engineering firm, advised the Grants Commission.

The consulting engineer's report contained the following recommendation:

restriction on the reselling of commercial quality electricity at the same rates as the uniform Victorian tariffs be removed (Manning et al, 1990, Appendix D p.A–31).

In conjunction with this recommendation, it was recommended that the SECV develop a special tariff for resellers of electricity. The reason for this is that, if they were permitted to sell at the current rate, then the cross subsidy (which currently flows to domestic and rural sectors) would flow to the reseller.[2] We will concentrate on the unions' attitude to these recommendations which, if implemented, would significantly alter the institutional arrangements in the MCC's area.

But before progressing to this subject it is worth noting the prime consultant recognised that the reselling recommendation was "not strictly relevant to the present terms of reference", but nevertheless commended it (Manning et al,

1990, p.24).

The submission made by the unions stated:

> In view of the impact that a change in the policy of reselling would have on the ability to cross-subsidise, then any consideration of such change requires far greater analysis than is undertaken by the consultants. Cross-subsidisation is a key issue within many publicly owned utilities, and is a public policy issue.... It is by no means clear that the community would prefer to see a reduction in the level of cross-subsidy which currently exists (Electricity Unions, 1990, p.12).

Given the evidence presented in Chapter 10 regarding the uses (and abuses) to which accounting techniques can be put, we can only agree with the flavour of the unions' statement.

From an industrial relations perspective, the proposal has been a disaster. At the time of writing (April 1991) there has been no resolution of the issue and we understand that bans are in force. The consultants' failure to incorporate the issue of social roles into its recommendation illustrates yet again the limitations of a solely economic or financial perspective on the role of the public sector.

Queensland

In 1990, the Queensland government appointed the merchant bank Jarden Morgan Limited to undertake an audit of that State's electricity supply industry, examining it structure, accountability, financial targets and accountability. On 20 June 1990, the Director-General of the Queensland Minerals and Energy Centre wrote to industry's unions inviting then to make submissions to the audit team. This decision was made on the basis of "fairness".

The President of the Queensland Branch of the Federated Engine Drivers Association of Australasia (FEDFA) in the introductory section of that union's submission made the following points:

> (This union has been) led to the following conclusions:
>
> 1. that the QEC is not running as efficiently as it should be;
> 2. that the people making the policy decisions and recommendations are either unaware of the ramifications of these policies in the long term, or alternatively have been given in-

complete or improper information on which they have based their policies;

> 3. that the people who really know and understand the problems and can find the solutions (the people on the ground floor) are not being given the respect and opportunity needed to solve these very problems; and
> 4. when (3) has been given the opportunity (very infrequently), their recommendations have not been acted upon. Huge savings could have been made in these areas but the recommendations have been totally ignored (FEDFA, 1990, p.1).

Appendix L to that submission is an internal memorandum which contains information related to overhaul of power systems in Queensland. The overhauls referred to were undertaken by contractors, and the memorandum contains the following assessment of the work and operation of the contractors:

> a. standard of tradesmen very poor in most cases
> - little or no industry experience
> - little or no maintenance experience
> b. excessive supervision was required because of (a) above and because of lack of familiarity with the plant
> c. some of the tradesmen exhibited a very poor attitude, showing no pride in their work, and little interest. Those that were enthusiastic tended to suffer greatly from (a) above (FEDFA, 1990).

The President also made the following comment:

> Contractors used for overhauls charge 200–400 per cent of real wage rates. Even allowing 70 per cent on costs they are over charging some 30–70 per cent on what the real costs should be i.e. if our own workforce had been employed (FEDFA, 1990, p.4).

It is the Queensland electricity supply industry which the Industry Commission exhorts the other States to follow in terms of their employment arrangements. The FEDFA's submission bears out our criticisms of the Industry Commission's measures of efficiency and productivity made in Chapter 11.

The attitudes expressed by the union could hardly be described as destructive. In fact, they would more properly be described in the opposite terms: there is a very real concern with the operation of the power industry and a willingness to participate in decision-making designed to overcome any problems which may exist in the industry. As the FEDFA President put it in the conclusion to his union's submission:

I may even be so bold as to advise that this very audit should have expertise from the shop floor involved so that figures quoted could be put in their right perspective (FEDFA, 1990, p.4).

This plea for involvement echoes the ACTU's emphasis on the need for workers and their union representatives to be involved in the management decision making process.

Western Australia

One of the recommendations made by the Western Australian Review Committee chaired by Harman was:

Before any decision in favour of Jurien over Collie for the location of a future coal-fired power station is made, the present value of the net benefit of Jurien over Collie should be determined and this should be used to assess the cost of disturbing the Mt Laseuer area (WA Review Committee, 1990, p.x).

It is worth noting that the Metal Trades Federation of Unions (MTFU) made the following comments in its submission to the Review Committee:

The MTFU believes along with the Department of Conservation and Land Management, the National Parks and Nature Conservation Authority, the Conservation Movement and a great many concerned citizens of Western Australia that the Mt Laseuer area is worthy of National Park status.

Given the unique qualities of the Mt Laseuer area it is inconceivable that a power station and a coal mine should be proposed for this exceptional region (MTFU, 1990, p.3).

Again, it is the unions which have taken the initiative in advancing concerns with the negative impact of a proposed development. It is only through the process of opening up decision-making and allowing the unions to participate that rational decisions, from the strategic to the mundane, can be made.

New South Wales

The proposal for national integration which has been developed in this report refers to the need to ensure that the best working conditions in any State be applied to all States. Why this would be necessary is clearly seen in the case of the efforts made by operators' unions to have 12 hour shifts introduced in the Electricity Commission of New South Wales (ECNSW). It is necessary to note, first, that 12 hour shifts are in operation in the State Electricity Commissions of Victoria and Western Australia.

The requests for the introduction of a 12 hour roster extend back to at least 1988, but it is on the period 1989 to 1990 that we will concentrate.

The reasons the operators give for wanting a 12 hour week include:

- that it provides a better occupational health and safety environment;
- that it is better for family and social life; and
- elimination of day/afternoon shift handovers with a consequent improvement in flow of necessary procedures (FEDFA, 1991).

In January 1989, the FEDFA requested the ECNSW to negotiate, under the structural efficiency principle, on the preparation of a memorandum of understanding for the introduction of a 12 hour shift system. A response from ECNSW was received March 1989 (FEDFA, 1991).

On 6 April 1990, a compulsory conference was held in the New South Wales Industrial Commission between the FEDFA, the ETU, the Australian Institute of Marine and Power Engineers and ECNSW with the express aim of seeking support from the Commission to establish a small group to look at the trial introduction of 12 hour shifts at Munmorah Power Station. While there had been discussions in joint union/management committees ("Specific Functions Groups") going back to the November 1989, ECNSW continued to refuse to entertain the notion of a trial.[3]

The result of the conference was that ECNSW agreed to discuss the issue of 12 hour shifts, and to provide reasons if it was to maintain its objections.

On 13 August 1990, a Memorandum from the Assistant General Manager/Production was distributed. It stated:

... the Electricity Commission is not in a position to introduce a trial at Munmorah using 12 hour shift rosters.

> ... the Commission is prepared to monitor the development of alternative operator work patterns occurring throughout industry and to discuss the merits of such changed work patterns in Committee (FEDFA, 1991).

At the time of writing (April 1991), 12 hour shifts were still not being trialled in ECNSW.

The intransigence of the ECNSW stands in marked contrast to the stated objectives of management as communicated by the Manager/Employee Relations at a Power Industry Conference in March 1991. The synopsis of that presentation notes:

> Workplace change initiatives are currently underway to maximise the potential productivity gains, and to provide employees with more satisfying jobs (Graham, 1991, p.1).

Tasmania

The situation in Tasmania regarding the engagement of contractors illustrates many of the criticisms we have made of electricity industry managements around the country.

In 1987, following opposition from the Electrical Trades Union (ETU), the HEC agreed to undertake a detailed on-the-job comparison of total employment versus contractor's costs. If this comparison of cost showed that employees costs were higher, the ETU agreed that action against such engagement would be curtailed.

To date (April 1991) the union has received no report on the comparison. As one unionist has expressed it:

> Conclusion: Electrical Contractors price must have been higher than total cost of their own personnel.

Notes

1. We are grateful to Ms Yvette Stern, an Honours student at the University of New South Wales for the considerable assistance she provided on this section.

2. It is interesting to note that, when the consultant's report was prepared, the supply authorities in NSW were reluctant to supply resellers precisely because the reseller could "pocket" the cost subsidy which applied there! Reselling was not prohibited in NSW.

3. It should be noted that the operators' proposal does have award implications, but the point remains that ECNSW refused to even discuss how such problems could be overcome.

APPENDIX 2

TABLE 4.1

Development of the Australian Economy 1980/81 - 1989/90

A: AGGREGATE DEMAND COMPONENTS

YEAR	PRIVATE CONSUMPTION	BUSINESS FIXED INVESTMENT	GOVERNMENT SPENDING	INCREASE IN STOCKS	EXPORTS OF GOODS & SERVICES	IMPORTS OF GOODS & SERVICES	GDP
1980/81	92,011	15,973	34,237	508	22,531	25,076	137,539
1981/82	104,482	19,467	39,729	1,568	23,336	29,002	154,988
1982/83	114,779	18,796	45,419	2,403	25,156	28,967	169,921
1983/84	127,404	19,432	49,874	1,393	28,595	31,192	192,276
1984/85	140,635	22,928	55,174	1,072	34,755	38,505	214,735
1985/86	156,967	27,195	62,510	1,466	38,700	46,088	240,082
1986/87	170,142	30,922	67,570	-1,511	43,142	48,015	264,888
1987/88	193,125	36,994	69,941	- 427	50,058	52,599	296,423
1988/89	220,413	42,384	75,060	3,798	53,838	60,783	337,592
1989/90	241,082	43,455	81,197	4,318	58,590	66,025	368,627

Source: RBA Bulletin, December issues

B: SUPPLY SIDE DEVELOPMENTS

YEAR	Population + 15 '000	Participation Rate %	Labour Force '000	Employed Persons '000	Unemployed Persons '000	Unemployment Rate %	Nominal GDP	Real GDP (84/85 Prices)	Nominal GDP % Change	Real GDP % Change	GDP Deflator % Change	Average Earnings % Change	Real Earnings % Change
1980/81	11,027	61.6	6,757	6,361	396	5.8	137,539	192,176	13.6	3.3	10.3	13.4	3.1
1981/82	11,255	61.0	6,863	6,440	423	6.2	154,988	195,677	12.7	1.8	10.9	14.5	3.6
1982/83	11,474	60.6	6,954	6,329	625	9.0	169,921	192,933	09.6	-1.4	11.0	11.4	0.4
1983/84	11,678	60.5	7,069	6,388	681	9.6	192,276	203,149	13.2	5.3	7.9	8.5	0.6
1984/85	11,861	60.6	7,184	6,564	619	8.6	214,735	214,288	11.7	5.5	6.2	6.8	0.6
1985/86	12,070	61.7	7,435	6,847	586	7.9	240,082	223,426	11.8	4.3	7.5	6.4	-1.1
1986/87	12,335	62.0	7,653	7,018	635	8.3	264,888	229,585	10.3	2.8	7.5	6.8	-0.7
1987/88	12,664	62.2	7,876	7,256	610	7.8	296,423	239,198	11.9	4.2	7.7	5.0	-2.7
1988/89	12,914	62.6	8,086	7,551	535	6.6	337,592	248,998	13.9	4.1	9.8	6.8	-3.0
1989/90	13,155	63.5	8,355	7,840	515	6.2	368,627	257,227	09.2	3.3	5.9	6.6	0.7

Source: RBA Bulletin, various issues

TABLE 4.2

The Australia Balance of Payments: 1980/81 - 1989/90

CURRENT ACCOUNT

YEAR	EXPORTS OF GOODS	IMPORTS OF GOODS	TRADE BALANCE	NET SERVICES	NET INCOME	NET TRANSFERS	INVISIBLES BALANCE	CURRENT ACCOUNT BALANCE
1980/81	18,718	19,177	-459	-2,086	-2,759	-140	- 4,985	- 5,444
1981/82	19,080	22,368	-3,228	-2,378	-3,208	-192	- 5,778	- 9,066
1982/83	20,656	21,705	-1,049	-2,762	-2,788	-195	- 5,745	- 6,794
1983/84	23,682	23,497	185	-2,782	-4,883	115	- 7,550	- 7,365
1984/85	29,212	30,093	-881	-3,869	-6,766	198	-10,437	-11,318
1985/86	32,208	5,676	-3,468	-3,920	-8,373	709	-11,584	-15,052
1986/87	35,423	37,159	-1,736	-3,137	-9,391	1,213	-11,315	-13,051
1987/88	40,541	40,386	155	-2,696	-10,204	1,664	-11,236	-11,081
1988/89	43,047	47,032	-3,985	-2,960	-13,013	2,198	-13,775	-17,760
1989/90	47,211	50,990	-3,779	-3,656	-15,773	2,426	-17,003	-20,782

CAPITAL ACCOUNT

OFFICAL	NON-OFFICIAL	NON-OFFICAL	CAPITAL
-1,184	1,875	3,753	4,446
-893	1,674	7,445	8,227
-1,615	488	7,452	6,327
- 1,047	740	6,303	5,723
5,253	872	5,506	11,631
7,551	546	6,187	14,284
2,185	- 182	6,920	8,923
499	- 3,775	12,100	8,824
- 373	4,032	10,796	14,455
136	3,171	11,937	15,212

Source: RBA Bulletin, various issues

TABLE 4.3

AUSTRALIA'S FOREIGN INDEBTNESS 1980/81 - 1989/90

A: GROSS AND NET DEBT

YEAR	Official Gross External Debt	Official Gross External Assets	Total Official Net External Debt	Non-official Gross External Debt	Non-official Gross External Assets	Total Non-official Net External Debt	Total External Gross Debt	Total External Assets	Total Net External Debt
1980/81	4,816	5,727	-911	10,348	939	9,409	15,164	6,666	8,498
1981/82	5,692	6,527	-835	18,487	1,276	17,211	24,179	7,803	16,376
1982/83	7,682	10,755	-3,073	28,209	1,752	26,457	35,891	12,507	23,384
1983/84	8,874	12,420	-3,546	35,228	1,788	33,440	44,101	14,208	29,893
1984/85	14,883	3,623	1,260	52,590	2,641	49,949	67,473	16,256	51,208
1985/86	23,404	13,161	0,248	68,642	3,844	64,798	92,050	17,005	75,045
1986/87	9,857	17,958	11,899	75,049	4,499	70,550	104,906	22,457	82,449
1987/88	32,761	20,831	11,930	84,258	5,899	78,359	117,019	26,730	90,289
1988/89	33,728	21,334	12,394	103,318	7,467	95,851	137,046	28,801	108,244

Source: RBA Bulletin, various issues

B: DEBT RATIOS

YEAR	Official Net Debt as % of GDP	Non-official Net Debt as % of GDP	Total Net Debt as % of GDP	Official Interest Payments	Non-official Interest Payments	Total Interest Payments	Total Debt-Service Ratio
1980/81	-0.6	6.8	6.2	416	801	1,217	5.4
1981/82	-0.5	11.1	10.6	435	1,439	1,874	8.0
1982/83	-1.8	15.6	13.8	596	2,298	2,894	11.5
1983/84	-1.9	17.4	15.5	711	3,075	3,786	13.2
1984/85	0.5	23.3	23.8	964	4,388	5,352	5.4
1985/86	4.3	27.0	31.3	1,612	5,466	7,078	18.3
1986/87	4.5	26.6	31.1	2,626	5,747	8,373	19.4
1987/88	4.1	26.4	30.5	3,360	5,808	9,168	18.3
1988/89	3.7	28.4	32.1	3,463	7,510	10,964	20.4
1989/90	-	-	-	-	-	-	-

TABLE 4.4

AUSTRALIA'S CURRENT ACCOUNT SUSTAINABILITY PROBLEM:

1970 - 1990

THE SUSTAINABILITY CONDITION

$$[TD/Y]^* = [1-r/q][CAD/Y]^*$$

SUSTAINABILITY: 1970 - 1980

$$[1.89]^* = [1-0.00/3.74][1.89]$$

SUSTAINABILITY: 1980 - 1990

$$[-3.70]^* = [1-5.77/3.27][4.84]$$

Notes:

[1]   The actual values of $(T/Y)^*$ during the period 1970-1980 and 1980-1990 are, respectively, -1.9 and -0.73.

[2]   Data for the Table are derived from International Financial Statistics. The real interest rate which is payable on foreign debt (r) is calculated as the US long-term government bond rate less thepercentage change in the US consumer price index.

Source: RBA Bulletin and International Financial Statistics, various issues

TABLE 4.5

FISCAL POLICY SETTINGS 1980/81 - 1989/90

YEAR	Outlays			Revenue		Balance	
	$m	% Real Growth	% of GDP	$m	% of GDP	$m	% of GDP
1980/81	36304	3.3	26.0	35317	25.3	-987	-0.7
1981/82	41515	2.6	26.5	41008	26.2	-507	-0.3
1982/83	49262	7.0	28.9	44750	26.2	-4512	-2.6
1983/84	56950	8.1	29.6	48963	25.4	-7987	-4.1
1984/85	64297	6.7	30.0	57601	26.9	-6696	-3.1
1985/86	70423	2.3	29.6	64787	27.2	-5636	-2.4
1986/87	75471	-0.2	28.8	72989	27.8	-2631	-1.0
1987/88	78740	-2.8	26.6	80800	27.3	2061	0.7
1988/89	82105	-4.4	24.3	87998	26.1	5893	1.7
1989/90	86951	-0.2	23.6	94987	25.8	8036	2.2

Source: Budget Paper No. 1, 1990

TABLE 4.6

Monetary Policy 1980 - 1990

TABLE A

YEAR	Competitiveness		Inflation		Monetary Growth		
	TERMS OF TRADE	TRADE WEIGHTED INDEX	CPI CHANGE %	M1 NOMINAL %	M1 REAL %	M3 NOMINAL %	M3 REAL %
1980/81	87.1	92.9	8.8%	12.0%	3.2%	12.5%	3.7%
1981/82	78.9	88.2	10.9%	0.6%	-10.3%	10.8%	-0.1%
1982/83	86.3	77.7	11.1%	5.9%	-5.2%	12.4%	1.3%
1983/84	87.9	79.2	4.5%	10.7%	6.2%	10.6%	6.1%
1984/85	90.5	65.0	6.6%	14.3%	7.7%	17.4%	10.8%
1985/86	81.1	56.3	8.5%	3.5%	-5.0%	12.5%	4.0%
1986/87	92.3	56.6	9.3%	14.1%	4.8%	12.8%	3.5%
1987/88	96.8	59.8	7.1%	18.1%	11.0%	13.1%	6.0%
1988/89	86.3	59.4	7.6%	8.9%	1.3%	28.0%	20.4%
1989/90	97.1	61.6	7.7%	2.8%	-4.9%	14.2%	6.5%

TABLE B

Interest Rates

YEAR	6 MONTH BAB RATE NOMINAL	6 MONTH BAB RATE REAL	6 MONTH US RATE NOMINAL	NOMINAL DIFFERENTIAL %
1980/81	15.15%	6.35%	15.22%	-0.07%
1981/82	18.35%	7.45%	13.70%	4.56%
1982/83	13.50%	2.40%	9.03%	4.47%
1983/84	12.50%	8.00%	11.23%	1.27%
1984/85	15.50%	8.90%	7.38%	8.12%
1985/86	13.95%	5.45%	6.63%	7.32%
1986/87	13.50%	4.20%	7.00%	6.50%
1987/88	13.15%	6.05%	7.53%	5.62%
1988/89	18.30%	10.70%	8.80%	9.50%
1989/90	15.05%	7.35%	8.06%	6.99%

Source: RBA Bulletin, various issues

TABLE 4.7

Government Expenditure Outlays: 1980-81 to 1989-90

			80/81	81/82	82/83	83/84	84/85	85/86	86/87	87/88	88/89	89/90
1	[A]	CURRENT OUTLAYS										
2		(A1) Final Consumption Expenditure										
3		Budget Sector	6340	7416	8506	9853	11122	12509	13554	14024	14853	15702
4		Non-budget Sector	850	1078	1205	1383	1550	1722	1987	2164	2445	3031
5		Total	7190	8494	9711	11236	12672	14231	15541	16188	17298	18733
6		(A2) Current Transfer Payments										
7		Budget Sector	26893	30631	36249	42196	47850	52527	56686	61088	63290	67808
8		Non-budget Sector	-48	-56	-54	-60	-83	65	42	93	139	53
9		Total	25873	29387	34852	40665	46088	50540	54664	58829	60704	65089
		(A3) TOTAL Current Outlays										
10		Budget Sector	33233	38047	44755	52049	58972	65036	70240	75112	78143	83510
		Non-budget Sector	802	1022	1151	1323	1467	1787	2029	2257	2584	3084
		Total	33063	37881	44563	51901	58760	64771	70205	75017	78002	83822
11	[B]	CAPITAL OUTLAYS										
12		(B1) GROSS Capital Formation										
13		Budget Sector	279	301	446	435	568	603	548	601	532	687
14		Non-budget Sector	150	211	302	298	400	553	710	766	601	238
15		Total	429	512	748	733	968	1156	1258	1367	1133	925
16		B2) CAPITAL TRANSFER Payments										
17		Budget Sector	2000	2187	2729	3380	3938	4091	4232	4051	3736	3926
18		Non-budget Sector	4	28	32	39	50	53	51	54	64	35
19		Total	1788	2009	2500	3157	3601	3628	3604	3440	3478	3857
20		(B3) NET ADVANCES										
21		Budget Sector	960	1007	1362	1135	917	797	529	-665	-205	-1197
22		Non-budget Sector	7	8	13	10	13	19	25	31	32	22
23		Total	967	1015	1375	1145	930	816	554	-634	-173	-1174
24		(B4) TOTAL CAPITAL OUTLAYS										
		Budget Sector	3070	3467	4506	4898	5323	5380	5222	3609	3942	3440
		Non-budget Sector	162	250	346	352	468	646	791	884	756	302
		Total	3016	3511	4591	4988	5404	5510	5334	3828	4376	3639
	[C]	TOTAL OUTLAYS										
		Budget Sector	36303	41514	49261	56947	64295	70416	75462	78721	82085	86951
		Non-budget Sector	964	1272	1497	1675	1935	2433	2820	3141	3340	3386
		Total	36079	41392	49154	56889	64164	70281	75539	78845	82378	87461
25	[D]	TOTAL REVENUE										
26		Budget Sector	35306	41030	44750	48961	57599	64782	72842	80796	88006	94987
27		Non-budget Sector	1135	1326	1518	1676	2036	2455	2693	3112	3383	3277
28		Total										
29	[E]	NET FINANCING REQUIREMENT										
30		Budget Sector	976	455	4474	7966	6581	5481	2347	-2024	-5742	-7943
31		Non-budget Sector	-173	-51	-25	-18	106	-46	74	22	5	-16
32		Total	803	404	4449	7948	6475	5416	2421	-2002	-5737	-7956

Notes to the Table

1.   Source: Statistical appendix of Budget Paper No.1, 1990. Presentation differs and additional information has
      been added.

2.   Row 9 does not equal the sum of rows 7 plus 8 because current grants to the non-budget sector (which
      appears in row 7) must be neeted out in row 9. The same point applies to the relationship between columns
      17-19

TABLE 4.8

Government Expenditure Outlays As A Proportion of Total Outlays.

	80/81	81/82	82/83	83/84	84/85	85/86	86/87	87/88	88/89	89/90
[A] TOTAL CURRENT OUTLAYS										
Budget Sector	91.5	91.6	90.8	91.4	91.7	92.3	93.1	95.4	95.2	96.0
Non-budget Sector	83.2	80.3	76.9	79.0	75.8	73.4	72.0	71.9	77.4	91.1
[B] CAPITAL OUTLAYS										
(B1) GROSS Capital Formative										
Budget Sector	0.8	0.7	0.9	0.8	0.9	0.9	0.7	0.8	0.7	0.8
Non-budget Sector	15.6	16.6	20.2	17.8	20.7	22.8	25.2	24.4	18.0	7.0
(B2) CAPITAL TRANSFER Payments										
Budget Sector	5.5	5.3	5.5	5.9	6.1	5.8	5.6	5.1	4.6	4.5
Non-budget Sector	0.4	2.2	2.1	2.3	2.6	2.2	1.8	1.7	1.9	1.0
(B3) NET ADVANCES										
Budget Sector	2.6	2.4	2.8	2.0	1.4	1.1	0.7	-0.8	-0.2	-1.4
Non-budget Sector	0.7	0.6	0.9	0.7	0.7	0.8	0.9	1.0	1.0	0.6
[C] TOTAL CAPITAL OUTLAYS										
Budget Sector	8.5	8.4	9.2	8.6	8.3	7.7	6.9	4.6	4.8	4.0
Non-budget Sector	16.8	19.7	23.1	21.0	24.2	26.6	28.0	28.1	22.6	8.9
TOTAL	8.4	8.5	9.4	8.8	8.4	7.8	7.1	4.9	5.3	4.2

Source: Budget Paper No. 1 1990, statistical appendix

TABLE 4.9

Government Outlays As a Percent of GDP

	Defence	Education	Health	Social Security and Welfare	Housing and Community Amenities	Fuel and Energy	Transport and Communication	Other	Total
Averages									
1969-70 to 1973-74	2.8	4.2	3.2	4.4	1.8	1.1	4.1	8.7	30.4
1974-75 to 1978-79	2.3	5.8	4.7	7.2	2.2	1.1	4.1	9.5	36.9
1979-80 to 1983-84	2.5	5.5	4.5	8.1	1.6	1.8	4.2	10.8	38.9
1984-85 to 1988-89	2.5	5.2	5.2	8.3	1.5	1.1	4.1	12.5	40.5
1980/81	2.4	5.4	4.4	7.5	1.4	1.5	3.9	9.7	36.1
1981/82	2.5	5.5	4.4	7.8	1.5	2.0	4.1	10.9	38.7
1982/83	2.7	5.7	4.5	8.7	1.7	2.3	4.4	11.4	41.3
1983/84	2.6	5.6	4.8	9.0	1.7	1.7	4.7	12.3	42.3
1984/85	2.6	5.5	5.3	8.8	1.8	1.5	4.3	12.6	42.4
1985/86	2.7	5.4	5.3	8.6	1.7	1.3	4.7	13.0	42.7
1986/87	2.6	5.3	5.4	8.4	1.7	1.2	4.4	13.1	42.2
1987/88	2.3	5.0	5.2	8.2	1.4	0.9	3.7	12.2	38.8
1988/89	2.3	4.8	5.0	7.6	1.1	0.8	3.6	11.6	36.6

Source: Budget Paper No. 1 1990

TABLE 4.10
State Expenditures on New Fixed Assets in Fuel and Energy

	All States		NSW		Victoria		Queensland		S.Australia	
Year	Fuel and Energy	Electr-icity	Fuel and Energy	Electr-icity	Fuel and Energy	Electr-icity	Fuel and Energy	Electr-icity	Fuel and Energy	Electr-icity
1980/81	1982.1	1747.9	705.1	663.1	614.9	472.9	330.0	330.0	114.6	114.6
1981/82	2772.3	2567.3	989.5	948.6	986.9	823.0	396.5	396.5	145.6	145.6
1982/83	3180.1	2971.6	1038.9	964.1	907.3	773.7	638.4	638.3	237.6	237.6
1983/84	2747.5	2553.2	913.4	849.5	699.7	569.3	574.7	574.7	178.4	178.4
1984/85	2426.4	2271.6	692.9	635.6	712.3	628.2	534.7	534.7	122.1	122.1
1985/86	2421.1	2178.0	700.4	582.0	675.5	572.2	541.1	541.1	114.7	114.7
1986/87	2382.4	2193.4	714.1	654.5	570.8	473.4	587.8	587.7	92.0	92.0
1987/88	2027.5	1862.2	391.0	347.2	687.7	603.6	439.4	437.6	145.6	145.6

	All States		W.Australia		Tasmania		N.Territory	
Year	Fuel and Energy	Electr-icity	Fuel and Energy	Electr-icity	Fuel and Energy	Electr-icity	Fuel and Energy	Electr-icity
1980/81	1982.1	1747.9	129.9	129.9	74.1	74.1	5.3	5.3
1981/82	2772.3	2567.3	148.0	148.0	85.8	85.8	13.1	13.1
1982/83	3180.1	2971.6	212.1	212.1	117.1	117.1	28.8	28.7
1983/84	2747.5	2553.2	223.2	223.2	126.9	126.9	31.3	31.3
1984/85	2426.4	2271.6	184.6	171.2	142.9	142.9	37.0	37.0
1985/86	2421.1	2178.0	123.9	162.6	166.1	166.1	99.4	99.4
1986/87	2382.4	2193.4	153.0	121.0	127.7	127.7	136.8	136.8
1987/88	2027.5	1862.2	185.0	149.8	123.1	123.1	55.6	55.6

Source: *ABS State and Local Government and Finance*, Cat. No. 5504

Notes
(1) Fuel and Energy (#09) includes Fuel Affairs and Energy (#091),
Electricity and Other Energy (#092) and Fuel and Energy NEC (#079)
(2) #091 includes coal, petroleum, gas and nuclear.
(3) #092, calles "electricity" in the table, is approx. 99 per cent electricity generation

FIGURE 4.1

Fiscal Policy Settings 1980/81 - 1989/90

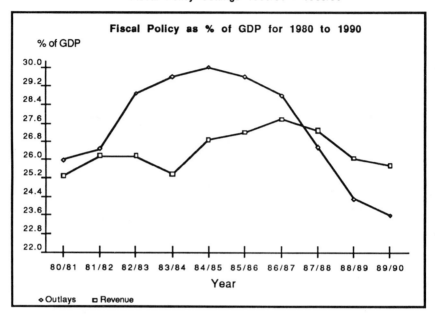

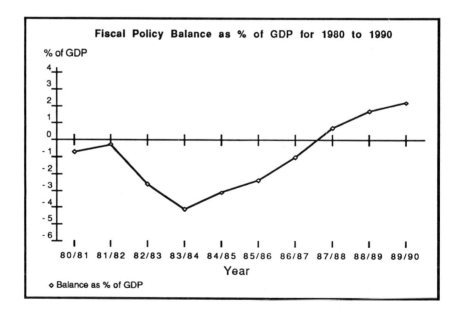

FIGURE 4.2

Monetary Policy Settings: 1980/81 - 1989/90

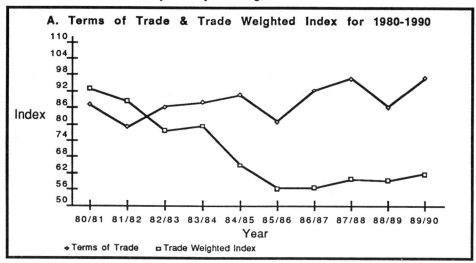

A. Terms of Trade & Trade Weighted Index for 1980-1990

◆ Terms of Trade   □ Trade Weighted Index

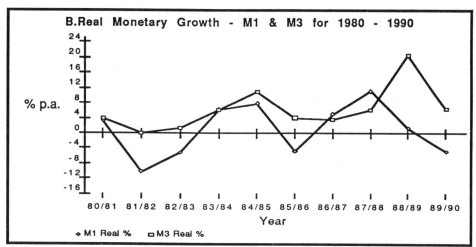

B. Real Monetary Growth - M1 & M3 for 1980 - 1990

◆ M1 Real %   □ M3 Real %

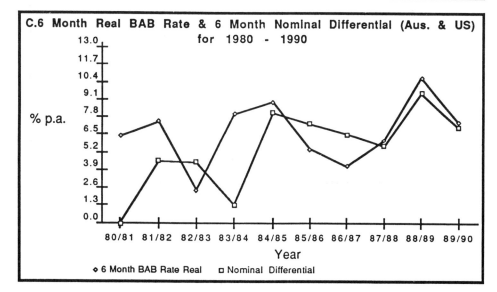

C.6 Month Real BAB Rate & 6 Month Nominal Differential (Aus. & US) for 1980 - 1990

◆ 6 Month BAB Rate Real   □ Nominal Differential

FIGURE 4.3

Structure of the Commonwealth General Government Sector

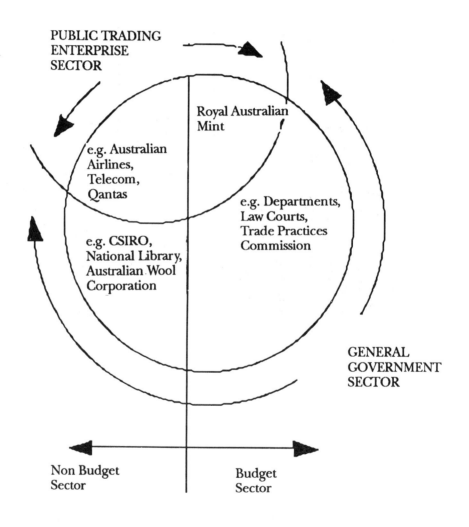

Source: Budget Statement No.1, (1990-91)

Figure 4.4
Public Sector Investment by Economic Programme
1969/70 - 1988/89

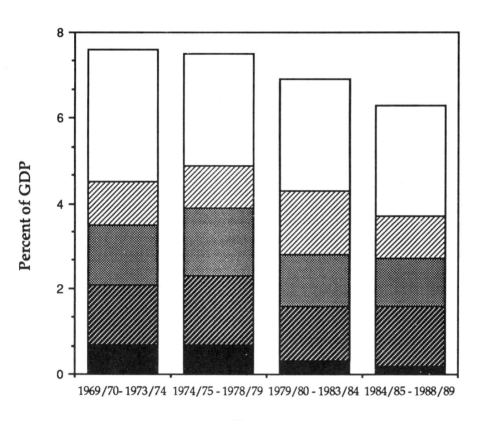

Table 6.1

Projections Of End Use Demand For Electricity (GWh)
(As of 1979-80)

	PUBLIC		PRIVATE		TOTAL	
	Projection	Actual	Projection	Actual	Projection	Actual
1980-81	94810	94750	7246	7612	102056	102362
1981-82	100014	98527	7554	7541	107568	106068
1982-83	105761	99194	7763	7350	113524	106544
1983-84	114969	105070	8285	7684	123254	112754
1984-85	122822	112694	8474	8267	131296	120961
1985-86	130535	118309	8926	8658	139461	126967
1986-87	139194	123698	9081	8971	148265	132669
1987-88	145552	130366	9201	9422	154753	139788
1988-89	152207	137744	9327	10265	161534	148009
1989-90	159773	142399	9454	10643	169227	153042
Average annual growth rate	6.0%	4.6%	3.0%	3.9%	5.8%	4.6%

Source: Department of National Development and Energy
          Australian Bureau of Agricultural and Resource Economics

Table 6.2

Demonstrated Economic Reserves Of
Australian Energy Minerals and Fuels 1989

Mineral	Physical Quantity	Energy Content (PJ)	1989-90 Prod. (PJ)	Reserve: Prod. Ratio
Crude oil[1]	379 giga litres	14 000	1 180	12
LPG	114 giga litres	3 000	100	30
Natural gas[2]	2129 tera litres	80924	800	93
Black coal[2]	51 billion tonnes	1 236 000	4 234	292
Brown coal[2]	42 billion tonnes	410 000	450	910
Uranium	480 000 tonnes U	265 000	1 921	137

1. Includes condensate
2. Recoverable

Source: Bureau of Mineral Resources, Geology and Geophysics

Table 6.3

Industrial Sector Expected Efficiency And Substitution Impacts In Year 2000

ASIC Sector	Description	Efficiency Effect(%)	Substitution Effect(%)	Overall Effect(%)
Div. B	Coal Mining	-6.9	+4.0	-3.2
"	Other Mining	-6.9	+4.0	-3.2
21	Food, Bevges., Tobacco	-9.0	+12.6	+2.5
23 - 24	Textiles, Clothing	-5.4	+3.9	-1.7
25	Wood	-9.4	+29.5	+17.3
26	Paper	-13.7	+30.9	+13.0
27	Chemicals, Petroleum	-2.5	+16.8	+13.9
28	Non-metal Minerals	-10.5	+31.1	+17.3
29	Base Metals	-6.5	+20.8	+12.9
31-34	Engineering	-11.7	+5.3	-7.0

Source: Electricity Commission of New South Wales.

Table 6.4
Load Forecasts

State Date of Forecast		NSW Oct 89	VIC Oct 89	QLD Feb 89	SA Nov 89	WA Sept 89	TAS April 89	NT Feb 89	SMHEA Oct 89
1988/89 Actual	Sys Ave. Load (Min)	+ 5 636	4 144	2 706	1 026		1 018	ø	**
	Sys Peak Load (MW)	+ 9 148	5 858	4 003	* 1 815	1 740	1 452	ø	2 737
	Sys Energy (GWh)	++ 46 809	36 300	+ 23 711	8 988	8 833	8 920	++ 923	4 236
1989/ 1990	Sys Ave Load (MW)	+ 5 793	4 304	2 876	1 057		1 070	ø	
	Sys Peak Load (MW)	+ 9 359	6 300	3 937	* 1 870	1 906	1 483	ø	
	Sys Energy (GWh)	++ 48 100	37 700	+ 25 193	9 255	9 719	9 371	++ 1 048	
1994/ 1995	Sys Ave Load (MW)	+ 6 624	4 646	3 772	1 187		1 217	ø	
	Sys Peak Load (MW)	+ 10 494	7 000	5 056	* 2 130	2 178	1 679	ø	
	Sys Energy (GWh)	++ 55 000	40 700	+ 33 043	10 400	12 386	10 659	++ 1 296	
1999/ 2000	Sys Ave Load (MW)	+ 7 588	5 057	4 729	1 327		1 252	ø	
	Sys Peak Load (MW)	+ 11 778	N/A	6 168	* 2 380	2 628	1 728	ø	
	Sys Energy (GWh)	++ 63 000	44 300	+ 41 427	11 625	14 411	10 966	++ 1 540	
2004/ 2005	Sys Ave Load (MW)	+ 8 542	5 616	5 784	1 461		1 316	ø	
	Sys Peak Load (MW)	+ 13 267	N/A	7 419	* 2 615	3 058	1 814	ø	
	Sys Energy (GWh)	++ 70 930	49 200	+ 50 667	12 800	16 609	11 526	++ 1 859	

NOTES

*	Summer peak adjusted to standard weather conditions and excluding interrupti
**	Not available
ø	Not applicable - isolated systems
	Adjusted for standard weather
+	Generated
++	Sent out

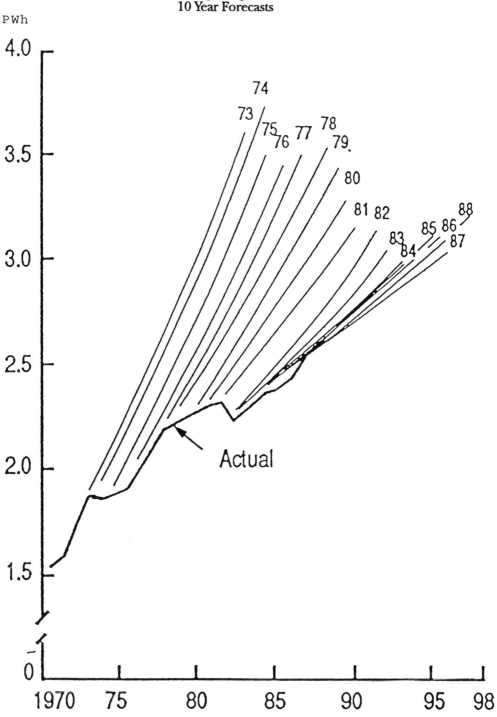

FIGURE 6.1
Energy Requirements (All US Private Utilities)
10 Year Forecasts

Source: National Electricity Reliability Council of the United States

FIGURE 6.2
Total System Energy Sent Out — Forecast v Actual

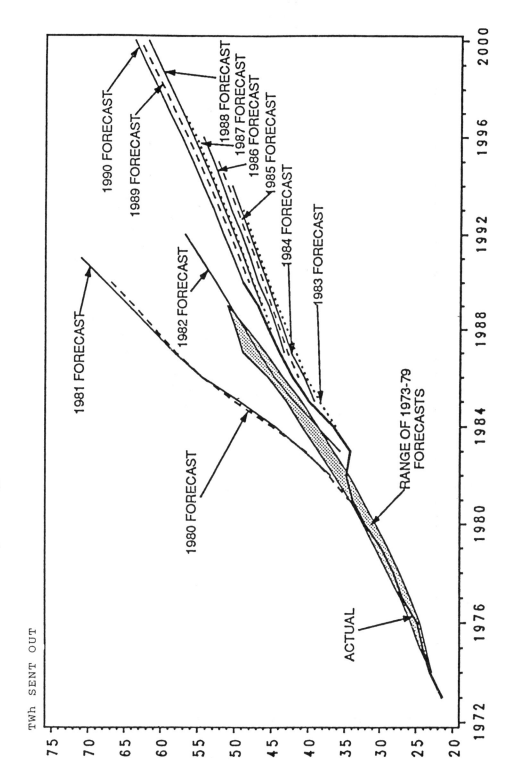

Source: Electricity Commission of New South Wales

FIGURE 6.2
Total System Energy Sent Out — Forecast v Actual

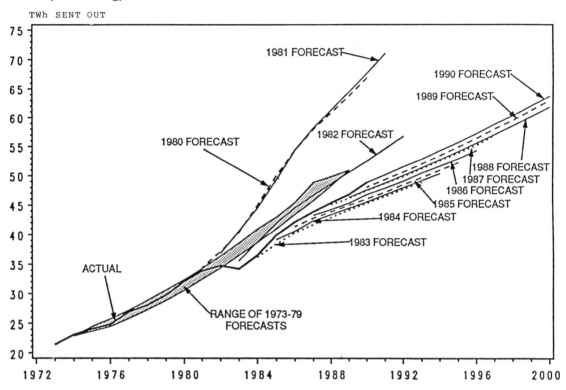

Source: Electricity Commission of New South Wales

FIGURE 6.3
Electricity Consumption by State

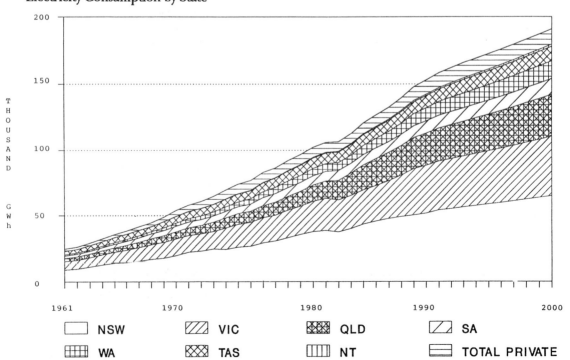

BIBLIOGRAPHY

—— (1987) *Policy Guidelines for Commonwealth Statutory Authorities and Government Business Enterprise*, October.

—— (1990) *Financial Monitoring of Government Business Enterprises: An Economic Framework Treasury Economic Paper No. 14*, Australian Government Publishing Service.

—— (1990) *Independence of the Auditor General and the Office of the Auditor General* Auditor General's Policy Advisory Committee (Western Australia), September.

Aboriginal and Torres Strait Islander Commission (ATSIC) (1991) *Commission Decision: Torres Strait Priority Communities Development Strategy Electricity Project*, February

Alesina, A., Gruen, D.W.R. and Jones, M. (1990) "Fiscal Adjustment, the Real Exchange Rate and Australia's External Imbalance", *Australian National University Centre for Economic Policy Research Discussion Paper No. 233*, May.

Alford, John (1989) "Can Performance Control Promote Public Sector Efficiency, Effectiveness and Quality?", a paper presented to the National Conference on Improving Public Sector Management, Griffith University, Brisbane, 5–7 July.

Allison, K. Hajas, Z. Halyburton, P. and Thomas, M. (1990) *Report of the Inquiry into Electricity Distribution in Broken Hill, Central Darling Shire and the Unincorporated Area*, Report to Neil Pickard, Minister for Minerals and Energy, Sydney.

Andersson, R. and Bohman, M. (1985) "Short- and Long-Run Marginal Cost Pricing — On their Alleged Equivalence," *Energy Economics*, October 7, pp. 279–288.

Andrews, J. (1982) *Solar Jobs in Victoria: The Economic Impact of the Solar Industry — Executive Summary*, Victorian Solar Energy Council, September.

Anon. (1991) "Pickard Postpones ECNSW Transfer of 132kV Assets," *Electricity Week*, Vol. 7, No. 4, March 4, pp. 1–2.

Appropriate Technology Development Group, Inc. (ATDG) (1985) *A Wind Energy Manufacturing industry for Western Australia?*, North Fremantle.

Aschauer, D.A., (1989), "Is Public Expenditure Productive?", *Journal of Monetary Economics*, 23, pp. 177–200.

Australian Bureau of Agricultural and Resource Economics (1989) (ABARE) *Projections of Energy Demand and Supply Australia 1989–90 to 1999–2000*, AGPS, Canberra, October.

Australian Bureau of Agricultural and Resource Economics, (ABARE) (1991) *Energy Demand and Supply Australia 1990–91 to 2004–05*, Australian Government Publishing Service, Canberra.

Australian Bureau of Statistics (ABS) (1990) 'Natural Resource and Environmental Accounting in the National Accounts', in the Australian Bureau of Statistics *Australian National Accounts: National Income and Expenditure*, March Quarter, Cat No. 5206.0.

Australian Bureau of Statistics. (1990) *Catalogue Number 6203.0.*

——————————————————————— *State and Local Government Finance Cat. No. 5504*, various issues

Australian Coal Association (1989) *The Greenhouse Effect, a Position Paper*, November.

Australian Conservation Foundation (1990), *Inquiry into Energy Generation and Distribution*, Submission to Industry Commission, August.

Australian Council of Trade Unions (ACTU) (1987) *Future Strategies for the Trade Union Movement.*

Australian Council of Trade Unions (ACTU) (1990) *Aus-*

tralian Manufacturing and Industry Development: Policies and Prospects for the 1990s and into the 21st Century, September.

Australian Council of Trade Unions, Trade Development Council (ACTU/TDC) (1987) *Australia Reconstructed, ACTU/TDC Mission to Western Europe*, AGPS, Canberra.

Australian Council of Trade Unions (1991) *Press Statement*, 13 March.

Australian Gas Association (1990) *Opportunities for Gas in Electricity Generation*, The AGA, Canberra.

Australian National Audit Office (1990) *Survey of Internal Audit in the Commonwealth Public Service Audit Report No. 6 1990–91*, Australian Government Publishing Service

Australian and New Zealand Solar Energy Society (1990) *Submission to Industry Commission Inquiry into Energy Generation and Distribution,*

Australian Petroleum Exploration Association Limited (1990) *Submission to Industry Commission Inquiry into Energy Generation and Distribution.*

Australian Railways Union/Australian Conservation Foundation (ARU/ACF) (1990) *Mobility in a Clean Environment*, February

Australian Senate Standing Committee on Industry, Science and Technology (1991) *Rescue the Future: Reducing the Impact of the Greenhouse Effect*, Parliament of the Commonwealth of Australia, Canberra.

Australian Society of Accountants (1989) *Long Road to Reform — Privatisation and Corporatisation in Australia* Discussion Paper 1

Australian Stock Exchange (1990) *Improved Reporting by Listed Companies*, ASX Discussion Paper.

Backman, H. and Vivian, H.(1985), *Employment Impacts of Victorian Home Energy Improvement Programs, Department* of Industry, Technology and Resources, Victoria.

Banks, F. E. (1985), *The Political Economy of Coal*, Lexington Books, Lexington

Banks, G. (1990) "Economic Gains from Improved government 'Management' of the Microeconomy", Centre for Australian Public Sector Management Conference: Improving Public Sector Management, Griffith University, Queensland 5–7 July.

Barro, R.J., (1989) "A Cross-Country Study of Growth, Saving and Government", *NBER Working Paper No. 2855.*

Bartels, C, (1990) *Commission — Stage One Situation Analysis,* Report to Tasmanian Government Tariff Steering Committee, Tellus Institute, Boston USA.

Baumol, W.J., Blinder, A.S., Gunther, A.N. and Hicks, R.L. (1988) *Economics: Principles and Policy*, Harcourt Brace Jovanovich, Sydney.

Beatty, B. (1986) NSW Inquiry brings a dozen forgotten gigawatts into focus, *Electrical Engineer*, October, Sydney.

Beatty, B. (1989a) ECNSW blunders in leaving closures out of 30–year plan, *Electricity Week*, July 17, Sydney.

Beatty, B. (1989b) NSW energy policy at sixes and sevens on Greenhouse, *Electricity Week*, August 21, Sydney.

Beazley, The Hon K. (1990) *Speech* 30 August.

Berg, S. V. (1981) "PURPA and Benefit-Cost Analysis of Innovative Rates", *Public Utilities Fortnightly*, Vol. 108, October, pp. 21–30.

BHP Petroleum (1990), *Industry Commission Inquiry into Electricity Generation and Distribution, Submission.*

Blakers, A., Outhred, H. and Diesendorf, M. (1988) "Solar Electricity" in *Prospects for Renewable Energy in Australia*, Australian and New Zealand Solar Energy Society — Status Report.

Bolt, P. F., Butters, J. W. Coulter, C. G., Giddings, A. M and Nicholson, P. T. (1990) *Report of the Inquiry into Electricity Tariffs and Related Matters*, Report to Neil Pickard, NSW Minister for Minerals and Energy, Sydney.

Borthwich, D. (1990) "Funding the Future Infrastructure: A View form the Commonwealth Treasury", paper presented to the 3rd National Infrastructure Conference, September.

Brennan, P. (1990) 'Microeconomic reform" in *Economic Papers*, Vol. 8 No. 4, Economic Society of Australia, pp. 34–50.

Brodeur, Paul (1989) *Currents of Death*, Simon & Schuster, New York.

Bureau of Transport and Communications Economics (BTCE) (1991) 'An Analysis of Total Factor Productivity': With an Application to Australian National',

AGPS, Canberra.

Burke, T., Genn-Bash, A., Haines, B. (1988) *Competition in Theory and Practice*, Croom-Helm, London.

Burke, A. (1990) "Learning to Live Without Nuclear Power", *Current Sweden*, No.372, March, pp. 1–12.

Burt Commission (1989) *Commission on Accountability: Report to Premier*, Western Australian State Government.

Bush, Shane, Jones, Barry, Nguyen-Thuong, Son and Leonard, Michelle (1989) *Projections of Energy Demand and Supply Australia 1989–90 to 1999–2000*, Australian Bureau of Agricultural and Resource Economics, October.

Business Council of Australia (1986) *The Management and Distribution of Productivity*, BCA, Canberra.

Californian Collaborative Process (1990) *An Energy Efficiency Blueprint for California*, Californian Public Utilities Commission, San Francisco.

Caramanis, M.C., Bohn, R.E, and Schweppe, F.C, (1982) "Optimal Spot Pricing: Practice and Theory," *IEEE Trans. on Power Apparatus and Systems*, Vol. PAS–101, September, pp. 3234–3245.

Caygill, Hon David, Minister of Finance, Rodger, Hon Stan, Minister for State Owned Enterprises and Butcher, Hon David, Minister of Commerce (1989) *Press Statement on Reorganisation of the Electricity Industry* September 13.

Chapman, R. (1990) "What Should We Expect of Microeconomic Reform?" *The Economic and Labour Relations Review*, Vol 1, No 2.

Charles River Associates (1990) *Competitive Procurement of Electric Utility Resources*, Report EPRI CU–6898, Electric Power Research Institute, Palo Alto.

Clifton, J.A. (1977) "Competition and the Evolution of the Capitalist Mode of Production" in *Cambridge Journal of Economics*, Vol. 1, No. 2, June

Clower, R.W. (1988) "The Ideas of Economists" in Klamer, R., McCloskey, D.N., Solow, R. (1988) [eds] *The Consequences of Economic Rhetoric*, Cambridge University Press, Cambridge.

———————————— (1983) "Administered Prices in the Context of Capitalist Development" in *Contributions to Political Economy*, Vol. 2, March.

Coates, John (1990) "Government-Owned Companies and Subsidiaries: Issues in Accounting, Auditing and Accountability" in *Australian Journal of Public Administration*, Vol 49, No 1 March, pp. 7–11.

Cohen, S. D, Eto, J. H., Goldman, C. A., Beldock, J. and Grandall, G. (1990), *A Survey of State PUC Activities to Incorporate Environmental Externalities into Electric Utility Planning and Regulation*, Report LBL–28616, Lawrence Berkeley Laboratory, Berkeley.

Commonwealth Parliamentary Accounts Committee (1989) *The Auditor-General: Ally of the People and the Parliament*, AGPS.

Commonwealth-State Relations Secretariat (1990) *Working Group on Electricity Generation, Transmission and Distribution: Terms of Reference*.

Community Energy Network (1990) *Working Papers Based on the Investigations and Findings of the Community Energy Network into the Joint SEC/DITR Demand Management Development Project*.

Conde, H. G. (1957) "The Electricity Commission of New South Wales in *Public Administration (Sydney)* Vol 16, pp. 37–54, pp. 37–54.

Conservation Council of Victoria (1990) *Submission to Industry Commission Inquiry into Energy Generation and Distribution*

Coulter, C. G. (1988) "The greenhouse effect and electricity generation in New South Wales" in *Greenhouse: Planning for Climate Change*, CSIRO, Melbourne.

Crawford, Ian; Page, Denis; Snow, George; White R. J; and Yerbury, D. (1990) *Priorities for Improved Public Sector Management*, Australian Capital Territory Government Priorities Review Board, Canberra,

Curran, C. P, Kennedy, M. W., Kirkwood, J. B. and Shields, R G. (1989) *Future Direction Inquiry Into Sydney County Council*, Report to Neil Pickard, NSW Minister for Minerals and Energy, Sydney.

Curran, C. P; Dominguez, J. T; Nicholls, D. F; and Yonge, J. P. (1988) *Focus on Reform, Report on the State's Finances*, New South Wales Commission of Audit, Sydney.

Dagwell, R., Argus, J. and Lyons, L. (1990) "Presenting Fair Financial Statements — the Case of the Bond Corporation" in *Policy Organisation and Society* No. 1 Winter, pp. 55–58.

Davis, G., Wanna, J., Warhurst, J. and Weller, P. (1988), *Public Policy in Australia*, Allen and Unwin, Sydney, pp. 20–28.

Davis, G. R. (1990) "Energy for Planet Earth" in *Scientific American*, Vol. 263 No.3, September, pp. 20–28.

Deakin, B. M. and Seward, T. (1969) *Productivity in Transport*, Cambridge University Press, Cambridge.

Deane, R. S. (1990) "Deregulation and Reform in the New Zealand Electricity Industry", a paper presented to the IRC Conference on Deregulation and Reform in the Public Sector, 25–26 October, Sydney.

Demsetz, H. (1982) *Economic, Legal, and Political Dimensions of Economics*, North-Holland Publishing Company, Amsterdam.

Dennis, K.G. (1977) *Competition in the History of Economic Thought*, Arno Press, New York.

Department of Finance (1985) *Guidelines for the Form and Standard of Financial Statements of Government Undertakings*, Canberra, *Public Authority Policy and Rate of Return Reporting*.

Department of Management and Budget (Victoria) (1987a) *Rate of Return Reporting*, 2nd ed.

Department of Management and Budget (Victoria) (1987b), *Internal Audit in the Victorian Public Sector: An Introduction to the Function for Management and Staff*.

Department of Minerals and Energy, NSW (1990), *RAPAS: Remote Area Assistance Scheme*, brochure published by NSW Department of Minerals and Energy, August.

Department of Primary Industries and Energy (1988) *Energy 2000: A National Energy Policy Paper*, AGPS, Canberra.

Department of the Treasury (1990) "Financial Monitoring of the Government Business Enterprises — an Economic Framework", *Treasury Economic Paper No. 14*, Australian Government Publishing Service.

———————————————————— (1990) *Budget Paper No. 1*

Dettmer and Littlechild (1990), "Electricity's Conductor", *IEE Review*, London, October pp 343–345.

Devine, K. (1990) "Reform and Privatisation in New Zealand's Electricity Industry", a paper presented to the AIC Conference on Power Generation in the

90s, 8–9 October, Sydney.

Diesendorf, M. (1990), *Australian Energy Options for Slowing the Greenhouse Effect*, Australian Conservation Foundation.

Diesendorf, M & Sonneborn, C (1991) "The Environmental Costs of Electric Power", paper presented at IIR Conference on the future of the power industry in Australia, Sydney, 14–15 March.

Dixon, Peter B.,,Johnson, David T., Marks, Robert E.. McLennan, Peter, Schodde, Richard and Swan, Peter (1989) *The Feasibility and Implications for Australia of the Toronto Proposal for Carbon Dioxide Emissions*, Report to CRA Limited, Melbourne.

Dornbusch, R. (1983) 'Real Interest Rates, Home Goods and Optimal External Borrowing', *Journal of Political Economy, 91, pp. 141–153*.

Edwards, Cecil (1969) *Brown Power: A Jubilee History of the State Electricity Commission of Victoria*, State Electricity Commission of Victoria.

Electoral and Administrative Review Commission (Queensland) (1990) "Review of Public Sector Auditing in Queensland", *Issues Paper No. 9*.

Electricity Commission of New South Wales (Elcom) (1988) *Draft Electricity Development and Fuel Sourcing Plan*, ECNSW, Sydney.

Electricity Commission of New South Wales (Elcom) (1989) *Strategic Plan: Meeting Customer Demands — Electricity Development and Fuel Sourcing Plan*, ECNSW, Sydney.

Electricity Commission of New South Wales (ECNSW) (1990) *Annual Report 1990*, ECNSW, Sydney.

Electricity Commission of New South Wales (Elcom) (1990) *Customer Demand in the 1990s*, February.

Electricity Supply Association of Australia (1989) *Annual Report 1988/89*

Electricity Supply Association of Australia (1990) *Electricity Australia*.

Electricity Supply Association of Australia (1990) *The Electricity Supply Industry in Australia*.

Electricity Supply Association of Australia (1991) *Response: Industry Commission Draft Report on Energy generation and distribution*, March.

Electricity Supply Association of Australia, *Inquiry in Energy*

Generation and Distribution, Submission No 36, to the Industry Commission, ESAA, Melbourne.

Electricity Supply Association of Australia.(1991) *Greenhouse Position Paper.*

Electricity Supply Association of Australia (ESAA) (1991) *Reponse to Industry Commission's Draft Report on Energy Generation and Distribution*, ESAA, Sydney, March.

Electricity Unions [Victoria] (1990) *Electricity Unions Submission to Victorian Grants Commission re. Review of Financial Arrangements Between the State Electricity Commission of Victoria and the Melbourne City Council Electricity Supply Authority* (October)

Electricorp, New Zealand (1988) *Changes to Wholesale Electricity Pricing Structure*, Press Release by Electricorp, Auckland, New Zealand, 4 February.

EPAC (1987) Efficiency in Public Trading Enterprises *Council Paper* No 24.

EPAC (1988) "An Overview of Microeconomic Constraints on Economic Growth", *Council Paper* No 32.

EPAC (1988a), "Economic Infrastructure in Australia", *Economic Planning and Advisory Council Paper* No. 33, Canberra, April.

EPAC (1989) Productivity in Australia: Results of Recent Studies, *Council Paper* No 39.

EPAC (1989) "External Debt: Trends and Issues" *Discussion Paper* No. 89/06

EPAC (1990a) Microeconomic Reform, *Council Paper* No 42

EPAC (1990b) The Size and Efficiency of the Public Sector, *Council Paper* No 44.

Ernst & Young Energy Consulting Group,(1989) *Electricity Industry Reform*, Ernst & Young, Wellington.

Evatt Research Centre (Evatt) (1989) *State of Siege: Renewal or Privatisation for Australian State Public Services?* Evatt Foundation/Pluto Press, Sydney.

Falk, J. and Brownlow, A. (1990) *The Greenhouse Challenge: What's to Be Done?*, Penguin Books, Melbourne.

Federated Engine Drivers and Firemen's Association of Australasia (FEDFA) (1990) *Correspondance, file copy*

Federated Engine Drivers and Firemen's Association of Australasia (FEDFA) (1991) *Correspondance, file copy*

Fine, Ben(1990) "Scaling the Commanding Heights of

Public Enterprise Economics" in *Cambridge Journal of Economics*, Vol.14, No. 2, June.

Fitzgerald, T. (1990) "Economics, broad and narrow" in *Australian Society* December, pp. 21–24.

Flavin, C.. and Lenssen, N.. (1990) *Worldwatch Paper 100– Beyond the Petroleum Age: Designing a Solar Economy.*

Fleming, J. M. (1962) 'Domestic Financial Policies under Fixed and under Floating Exchange Rates', *IMF Staff Papers 9*, pp. 369–379.

Frenkel, J.A. and Razin, A. (1986), 'Fiscal Policies in the World Economy', *Journal of Political Economy*, 94, pp. 564–594.

Frost A (1990) 'Australia's Electricity Beyond 2020', *IEE Review*, London, October, pp..345–351.

Gibbs report, latest study by the Victorian Health Department, US EPA recommendations, US litigation payouts.

Gibbs, H (1991),*Inquiry into Community Needs and High Voltage Transmission Line Development*, New South Wales Government, Sydney.

Gilbert, K. N. (1990), *Land Use and the Environment — an Australian Coal Industry Perspective*, 1990 Australian Coal Conference.

Goldring, John and Wettenhall, Roger (1980) "Three Perspectives on the Responsibility of Statutory Authorities" in Patrick Weller and Dean Jaensch (eds) *Responsible Government in Australia*, Drummond Publishing, Melbourne.

Goodall, K. (1991) *New Zealand Electricity Privatisation: Three Union Responses*, Northern Local Government Officers Union, Auckland, 25 January

Gordon, Ian, Motika, Milena and Nolan, Terry (1990) *Epidemiological Studies of Cancer and Powerline Frequency Electromagnetic Fields: a Meta-analysis*, University of Melbourne Statistical Consulting Centre, Report 242, for Health Department of Victoria, December.

Government Accounting Standards Board (USA) (1987) *Accounting and Financial Reporting for Capital Assets of Governmental Entities.*

Government of Victoria (1990) *Greenhouse: Meeting the Challenge, the Victorian Government's Statement of Action*, October.

P Graham (1991) *Synopsis of Paper presented to "The Impor-*

tance of Leadership in Effectively Managing Organisational Change" Conference, Sydney (15 March)

Green, R. (1990) 'The Impact of Product and Labour Mar-
kets on Workplace Industrial Relations, The
Australian Workplace Industrial Relations Society, Paper
No 2. September.

Greene, D. Consulting Services (1989), Improving Efficiency
of Electricity Use — An Assessment of Potential Resources,
Electricity Commission of New South Wales, Sydney.

——————————————— (1990) Greenhouse Energy
Strategy: Sustainable Energy Development for Australia, a
report prepared fro the Department of Arts, Sports,
the Environment, Tourism and Territories.

Groenewegen, P (1990) "Infrastructure and Asset Disposal:
Some Observations", Policy Paper, Evatt Foundation, October.

Groenewegen, Peter (1988) "New South Wales Commission of Audit: A Critical Review Prepared for the
New South Wales Trades and Labour Council",
mimeo, August.

Groenewegen, Peter (1990a) "Deregulation: Some Reflections on Current Themes" a paper presented at
Deregulation: Issues for the Public Sector Seminar,
23-24 March.

Guthrie, J (1989) "The Adoption of Corporate Forms for
Government Business Undertakings: Critical Issues
and Implications", UNSW Public sector Research
Centre, Discussion Paper No. 5.

Guthrie, J, Parker, L and Shand, D [eds] (1990) The Public
Sector: Contemporary Readings in Accounting and Auditing, Harcourt, Bruce, Javonovich, Australia

Hamlyn-Harris, M.(1987) Alternative Technology Association
Second Submission to the Natural Resources and Environ-
ment Committee Inquiry into Electricity Supply and
Demand Beyond the Mid 1990s Victoria.

Harcourt, G.C. (1972) Some Cambridge Controversies in the
Theory of Capital, Cambridge University Press, Cambridge.

Harden, I (1988) "National Report: United Kingdom" in T
Modeen & A Rosas (eds), in cooperation with the
International Institute of Administrative Sciences
(1988) Indirect Public Administration in Fourteen Coun-

tries, Abo: Abo Academy Press, Finland, pp. 300–
329.

Harman, F. J (1990) "Fuel and Technology Choices in
Electricity Generation", a paper presented to the
Conference of Economists, UNSW September

Heffner G C and Ahlstrand, P T (1987) "System Integration of Real-Time Pricing at PG&E", IEEE
Transactions on Power Systems, PWRS–2, November
1987, pp. 1104–1109

Herzberg, A. (1991) "Directors and Officers Liability for In-
solvent Trading", paper presented at the National
Corporate Law Teachers Workshop, University of
NSW, February.

Hewlett M, (1990) 'Grid Access and Pricing in New Zealand', Workshop on Access and Pricing of Grid Systems,
Britain, April.

Hilmer, F. G. (1991) "Coming to Grips with Competitiveness and Productivity", EPAC Discussion Paper, 19/
01.

Hirst, E., Golmand, C. and Hopkins, M. (1990)'Integrated
Resource Planning for Electric and Gas Utilities',
Proceedings of the ACEEE 1990 Summer Study on Energy
Efficiency in Buildings, American Council for an En-
ergy Efficient Economy, Washington, Vol. 5, pp.
5.95–5.114.

Hocking,, L. (1991) Discussion Paper: Alternative Models for a
National (Eastern Seaboard) Electricity Grid, unpublished.

Hoffman, K. F. (1991) "The Implementation of Demand
Side Management — Problems and Prospects", pa-
per presented at conference March 14–15, The
Future of the Power Industry in Australia, IIR Pty
Ltd, Sydney.

Holdren, J. P. (1990) "Energy in Transition" in Scientific
American, Vol. 263 No.3, September, pp. 10–115.

Holmes, A. (1989) "Electricity Privatisation: the Wakeham
Effect" in Energy Economist No 96, October, pp. 2–6.

Howe, The Hon B. MP (1990) "Towards National Approaches to a National Issue: Infrastructure
Investment in the 1990s", paper presented to the
3rd National Infrastructure Conference, September.

Hydro-Electric Commission of Tasmania (1990) Corporate
Plan 1990, HEC, Hobart.

Industrial Commission of New South Wales (1990) *Judgement Matters No. 257, 309–312, 424, 431, 561, 609 of 1990*.

Industries Assistance Commission (1989) *Government (Non-Tax) Charges: Report No. 422*, AGPS Canberra, September 29.

Industry Commission (1990) *Energy Generation and Distribution*, June.

Industry Commission (1991) *Energy Generation and Distribution*, Draft Report (3 Vols and Attached Report) Industry Commission, Canberra, January.

International Energy Agency (IEA) (1984) *Energy Balances of OECD Countries, 1970/1982*, OECD, Paris.

International Monetary Fund *International Financial Statistics*, various issues.

James Capel & Co (1990), *Reshaping the Electricity Supply Industry in England and Wales*, London.

Jeffery, J (1990) "Dirty Tricks: How the Nuclear Industry Stopped the Development of Wave Power in Britain" in *The Ecologist*, May-June, pp.85–90.

Johnson C. (1990) *Decision — Electrical Power Industry* Decision Print J2497, Melbourne (May)

Johnson, Michael (1990) "Reassessing the economic role of the public sector in Australia", a paper presented to the National Conference on Improving Public Sector Management, Griffith University, Brisbane, 5–7 July.

Joint Committee of Public Accounts (JCPA) (1989) *The Auditor-General: Ally of the Parliament and the People*, Report 296.

Jones, B (19?), *Sleepers Wake!*, Oxford University Press, Melbourne.

Kahn, E. (1988) *Electric Utility Planning and Regulation*, American Council for an Energy-Efficient Economy, Washington D.C. and Berkeley, California.

Kaye, R. J. and Outhred, H. (1990) "Review of Public Participation Practices in Demand Planning: North American Experience", *University of New South Wales, Department of Electric Power Engineering, Report No. DEPE 90.1220*

Kaye, R. J and Outhred, H..R. (1988) "A Theory of Electricity Tariff Design for Optimal Operation and

Investment", *IEEE Trans. on Power Systems*, Vol. 4, May, pp. 606–613.

Kearney, C. (1990) 'Stabilisation Policies with Flexible Exchange Rates', in Llewellyn, D. T. and Milner, C. (eds.), *Current Issues in International Monetary Economics*, Macmillan.

Kewley, T. H. (1957) "Some General Features of the Statutory Corporation in Australia" in *Public Administration (Sydney)* Vol 16., pp. 3–28

Kingston, G. (1991) 'Monetary Policy and Foreign Indebtedness', in Kearney, C. and MacDonald, R. (eds.), *Developments in Australian Monetary Economics*, Longman Cheshire, forthcoming.

Kriesler, P. (1988) "Keynes and Kalecki on Method" University of New South Wales School of Economics Discussion Paper No. 88/14.

Labour Research (1990) "Electricity sale may be trimmed" in *Labour Research*, November.

Landsberg, J. J. (1989) "The Greenhouse Effect: Issues and Directions for Australia", *CSIRO Occasional Paper 4*, Canberra.

Langmore, J. V. MP (1987) *Constructing and Restructuring Australia's Public Infrastructure*, Report of the House of Representatives Standing Committee on Transport, Communications and Infrastructure, AGPS, November.

Latrobe Regional Commission (1990) *SECV Voluntary Departure: Survey in Latrobe Region*, Victoria.

Latrobe Regional Commission.(1987) *Third Submission to the Natural Resources and Environment Committee Inquiry into Electricity Supply and Demand Beyond the Mid 1990s*,Victoria.

Latrobe Valley Wastewater Review (1990) *Final Recommendations*, Government of Victoria.

Lavin, J. (1990) '*The Economy and the Environment.*

Lawrence, D., Swan, P. and Zeitsch, J. (1990) "The Comparative Efficiency of State Electricity Authorities", paper to the 19th Conference of Economists, Sydney.

Lescoeur, B. and Galland, J. (1987) "Tariffs and Load Management: the French Experience", *IEEE Trans. on Power Systems*, PWRS–2, May, pp. 458–464.

Lewis, David (1987) "Statutory Authorities and Constitutional Conventions — the Case of the Reserve Bank in Australia" in *Melbourne University Law Review*, Vol 16, No 2, pp. 348–381.

Lonnroth, Mans (1989) "Private and public provision assessed" a paper presented at the Conference on World Electricity, London, November 16–17.

Lovins, Amory B. (1990) *Report to the Minister for Industry and Economic Planning on Matters Pertaining to Victorian Energy Policy*, Rocky Mountain Institute, Colorado.

Lowe, I. (1988) "The Energy Policy Implications of Climate Change" in *Greenhouse: Planning for Climate Change*, CSIRO, Melbourne.

Manning I & Norman JSP (1990) *Review of the Financial Arrangements between the State Electricity Commission of Victoria and the Melbourne City Council Electricity Supply Authority: Draft Report (with technical appendices by David Sweeting Consulting Services*, (undated)

Maitland, F. W. (1968 reprint) *The Constitutional History of England: A Course of Lectures*, Cambridge University Press (originally published 1908).

McColl, Greg (1976) *The Economics of Electricity Supply in Australia*, Melbourne University Press.

McDonell, G. (1990) 'The Provision of Economic Infrastructure in Australia: Recent Debate and Current Issues', *Evatt Foundation Paper*, September.

McDonell, Gavan (1986) *Commission of Inquiry into Electricity Generation Planning in New South Wales Report*, January.

Metal Trades Federation of Unions (MTFU) (1990) *Submission to Review Committee on Power Options for Western Australia*, January

Mills. D, (1988) "Solar Energy: An Update" paper delivered to 1988 ANZAAS Conference.

Minister for Industry, Technology and Resources. (1985) *Victoria's Energy: Strategy and Policy Options*, Victorian Government Publishing Service.

Moore, B (1990) "Developments in New South Wales Public Administration", in Guthrie, Parker, Shand [eds].

Morgan, R. Research Centre Pty. Ltd. (1989) *Public Perception of and Attitudes Towards the Greenhouse Effect — Including Their Relation to Energy Consumption*, Electricity Commission of New South Wales, Sydney.

Muirden, Bruce (1978) "When Power Went Public, a study in Expediency: the nationalisation of the Adelaide Electricity Supply Company", *APSA Monograph No. 21.*

Mundell, R.A. (1963) 'Capital Mobility and Stabilization Policy Under Fixed and Flexible Exchange Rates', *Canadian Journal of Economic and Political Science*, 29, pp. 475–485.

Municipal Officers' Association (MOA) (1991) "Privatisation UK Style" in *MOA Energy Bulletin* January, pp. 10–13.

Murphy, J. (1987) "Three Paths to the Future", *IEEE Power Engineering Review*, PER-7, November, pp. 3–5.

National Institute of Economic and Industry Research (NIEIR) (1989) *Inquiry into the Local Government Electricity supply Industry*, Report for the Victoria Grants Commission, Melbourne.

National Institute of Economic and Industry Research (NIEIR) (1990) *Efficient Renewable Energy Scenario for Victoria: A study for the Victorian Solar Energy Council*, Victorian Solar Energy Council, May 25.

National Institute of Economic and Industry Research. (1987) *A Study of the Socio-economic Impact of Future Power Project Scenarios — Summary Report*, State Electricity Commission of Victoria.

Natural Resources and Environment Committee (1988) *Report Upon Electricity Supply and Demand Beyond the Mid–1990s*, Parliament of Victoria, Melbourne.

Nevile, J. (1987) "The Macro-Economic Effects of Public Investment", Appendix 5 in Langmore, J.V. MP *Constructing and Restructuring Australia's Public Infrastructure.*

New South Wales Cabinet Committee on Climate Change (1990) *A Greenhouse Strategy for New South Wales: Discussion Paper*, New South Wales Government, Sydney.

New South Wales Commission of Audit (Curran Commission) (1988) *Focus on Reform — Report on the State's Finances.*

New South Wales Electricity Council (1990) *Electricity Supply Industry of NSW — Industry Strategic Plan 1991–1995*, NSW Government, Sydney.

New South Wales Government (1990) *The New South Wales Government Submission to the Industry Commission In-*

quiry Into the Supply and Use of Electricity and Gas in Australia (three volumes).

New South Wales Government Minerals and Energy Committee (1990) *Review of Energy Conservation and Management Policies and Programmes*, Report to the Minister for Minerals and Energy Neil Pickard, Sydney.

New South Wales Public Accounts Committee (NSW PAC) (1989) *The Challenge of Accountability Forty Seventh Report*, October.

New South Wales Steering Committee on Government Trading Enterprises (1988) *A Policy Framework for Improving the Performance of Government Trading Enterprises*, September.

New South Wales Treasury (1989) *Accounting Guidelines for Reporting Physical Assets in the Budget Sector*, November.

New South Wales Treasury (1990a) *Internal Audit — Guidelines for Government Organisations*, May.

New South Wales Treasury (1990b) *Draft Financial Reporting Code on Accrual Accounting for Inner Budget Sector Entities*, November.

New Zealand Electricity Task Force (Task Force) (1989) *Structure, Regulation and Ownership of the Electricity Industry: Report of the Electricity Task Force*, New Zealand Government, Wellington September.

Nordel (1989) *Nordel 1989.*

Offe, Claus (1985) *Disorganised Capitalism: contemporary transformations of work and politics*, Polity Press, Cambridge.

Outhred, H. (1989) Investment Decision Making for the Electricity Industry, Chapter P11, Vol 1, *Lecture Notes for the Residential School in Power System Electrical Engineering*, Department of Electric Power Engineering, University of New South Wales, Sydney.

Outhred, H R (1987) "Report on a Visit to Europe, May–June 1987", University of New South Wales, *Department of Electric Power Engineering Report, DEPE 87.172*, August

Outhred, H. R. (1989) "Forecasting and Demand Side Options" in Outhred H.R. and J. Kaye, *Coordinated Electricity Pricing and Planning*, Department of Electric Power Engineering, University of New South Wales.

Pearman, G. ed (1989) *Greenhouse: Planning for Climate Change*, CSIRO, Melbourne.

Pickard, N. (1991), NSW Initiatives to Improve Power Generation and Distribution Efficiency, paper presented at conference March 14–15, The Future of the Power Industry in Australia, IIR Pty Ltd, Sydney.

Pigott, C. (1989) "Economic Consequences of Continued U.S. External Deficits', *Federal Reserve Bank of New York Quarterly Review*, 13, pp. 4–16.

Pitchford, J. D. (1989) 'Optimum Borrowing and the Current Account when there are Fluctuations in Income', *Journal of International Economics*, 26, pp. 345–358

Power in Europe (1990) "UK Electricity Privatisation: the regulator rides forth" in *Power in Europe*, September 27, pp. 8–9.

Powerline Review Panel (1989) *Final Report to the Victorian Government*, Powerline Review Panel, Melbourne.

Primeaux, W. J. (1985) "Dismantling Competition in a Natural Monopoly" in *Quarterly Review of Economics and Business*, Vol. 25, No. 3, Autumn, pp. 6–21.

Public Accounts Committee, Parliament of NSW (1988). *Report of Proceedings of the Accrual Accounting Seminar*

Public Accounts Committee, Parliament of NSW, (1990) *Report on the New South Wales Auditor-General's Office.*

Public Sector Management Institute (1990) *The Role of the Public Sector in Australia's Economy and Society*, Monash University, December.

Public Sector Research Centre (1990) *Submission Prepared by the Public Sector Research Centre for Trade Unions in the Electricity Industry*, November.

Queensland Electricity Commission (1990) *Sixth Annual Report 1989/90*, QEC, Brisbane

Queensland Treasury (1990) *Government Owned Enterprises*, August.

Rainforest Conservation Society (1990) *Submission to Industry Commission Inquiry into Energy Generation and Distribution*

Repetto, R. *et al* (1989) *Wasting Assets, Natural Resources in the National Income Accounts*, World Resources Institute.

Reserve Bank of Australia *Bulletin*, various issues.

Review Committee on Power Options for Western Australia (WA Review Committee) (1990) *Power Options for Western Australia: Report of the Review Committee*, May.

Rix, S. (1990) "Don't Let the Managers Manage" in *Legal Services Bulletin*, Law Faculty, Monash University, Vol. 15, No. 6, December, p. 264.

_____ (1991) "Lost Authority" in *Australian Left Review*, No. 127, March, pp. 28–29.

Rivers, M. J. (1990) *Restructuring of the Electricity Industry* Rivers Buchan Associates, Wellington, April.

Roads and Traffic Authority of NSW (RTA) (1990) *Annual Report 1989/90*

Robinson, C. (1989) "The Economics of Electricity Privatisation" in *Economics: the journal of the Economics Association*, Vol. XXV Part 3, No. 107, Autumn, pp. 113–116.

Rosas, A. (1988) "Indirect Public Administration: General Comments" in T Modeen & A Rosas (eds), in cooperation with the International Institute of Administrative Sciences *Indirect Public Administration in Fourteen Countries*, Abo: Abo Academy Press, Finland, pp. 31–38.

Rosenthal, Stephen and Russ, Peter (1988) *The Politics of Power: Inside Australia's Electric Utilities* Melbourne University Press, Melbourne.

Rowland, C. and Milne, A. (1990), *Electricity Supply Industry in Scotland*, Barclays de Zoete Wedd, Glasgow.

Rudolph, R. and Ridley, S. (1987) "Power Struggle: Moving Towards Public Ownership of Utilities" in *Dollars and Sense* No. 126, May, pp. 16–18, 22.

Ryland, Michael (1978) *Ministerial Responsibility and Australian Government Administration*, BA Honours Thesis, UNSW.

Sachs, J..D. (1981) 'The Current Account and Macroeconomic Adjustment in the 1970s', *Brookings Papers on Economic Activity* 1, pp. 201–268.

Saddler, H. (1981) *Energy in Australia, Politics and Economics*, George Allen and Unwin Australia, Sydney.

Saddler, H. (1991) *Toward Toronto: Australian Technological Innovations for Efficient Energy Futures*, Commission for the Future Research Paper, December.

Sanghvi, A.P. (1989) "Flexible Strategies for Load/Demand Management using Dynamic Pricing," *IEEE Trans. on Power Systems*, Vol. 4, February, pp. 83–89.

Sawer, G. (1954) "The Public Corporation in Australia" in W Friedmann (ed) *The Public Corporation*.

Scott & Furphy Engineers Pty. Ltd. (1987) *Review of High Voltage ELF Transmission Line Field and Human Health Effects*, Report to the Environmental Protection Authority of Western Australia, Perth.

Senate Standing Committee of Finance and Public Administration (SSFPA) (1987) *List of Commonwealth Bodies* Australian Government Publishing Service, Canberra.

Senate Standing Committee on Finance and Public Administration (SSFPA) (1989) *Government Companies and their Reporting Requirements*, Australian Government Publishing Service, Canberra, November.

Senate Standing Committee on Industry, Science and Technology (1990), *Rescue the Future. Reducing the Impact of the Greenhouse Effect*, Australian Government Publishing Service, Canberra, January.

Sioshansi, Fereidoon P. (1990) *An Energy Efficiency Blueprint for Tasmania*, Report to Tasmanian Department of Resources and Energy, California.

Smisth, N. (1957) "Atomic Energy and Its Importance in Queensland" in *Public Administration (Sydney)* Vol 16, pp. 250–258.

Smith, W.M. (1984) "Utility Routing Perspectives: A Review", IEEE Trans. on Power Systems, Vol. PWRS–4, May 1989, pp. 452–456.

Sorensen, B (1990) "Energy and Greenhouse Strategies in Scandinavia" a paper presented at Energy Research, Development and Information Centre (ERDIC) University of New South Wales workshop *Energy and the Greenhouse Effect: Commercial Opportunities for Research and Development* 3 August

South Australian Government (1991) *Future Directions for the Energy Sector in South Australia: Green Paper*, SA Government, Adelaide.

Special Premiers' Conference (1990) *Communique* 30–31 October.

State Electricity Commission Of Victoria (1987) *Submission to the Natural Resources and Environment Committee Inquiry into Electricity Supply and Demand Beyond the Mid 1990s Part IIb:Scenario Studies*, Victoria.

State Electricity Commission of Victoria (SECV) (1990) *An-*

nual Report 1989–1990, SECV, Melbourne.

State Electricity Commission of Victoria (SECV) (1990) *Submission to Industry Commission Inquiry Into Energy Generation and Distribution*, August.

State Electricity Commission of Victoria and Marsh & McLennan Pty Ltd (1990) *Liability Insurance Underwriting Submission 1990/91*, SECV, Melbourne

State Electricity Commission of Victoria *Annual Report 1989–1990*.

State Electricity Commission of Victoria (SECV) (1991) *Response to Industry Commission Draft Report on Energy Generation and Distribution*, SECV, Melbourne, March.

State Energy Commission of Western Australia (1990) *Corporate Plan 1990–1993*, SECWA, Perth.

Stewart, J. (1989) "Industry policy and Why Australia Needs One", *Canberra Bulletin of Public Administration*, Volume 59, pp. 11–15.

Stilwell, F. (1986) *The Political Economy of the Labour movement: the Accord and Beyond* Pluto Press, Australia.

Sutherland, Lucy S. (1952) *The East India Company in Eighteenth Century Politics*, Clarendon Press, Oxford.

Swan, P. (1989) Corporatisation, Privatisation and the Regulatory Framework for the Electricity Sector, *Economic Papers*, Vol 8, No 3, September.

Sydney County Council (1990) *Annual Report July 1989 – June 1990*, SCC, Sydney.

Tabors, R..D., Schweppe, F..C. and Caramanis, M..C..(1989) "Utility Experience with Real Time Rates," *IEEE Trans. on Power Systems*, Vol. 4, May, pp. 263–471.

The National Grid Company plc (National Grid) (1990) *Annual Report 1989/90* 28 June.

The Pipeline Authority (1990) *Submission to Industry Commission Inquiry on Energy Generation and Distribution.*

Thomas, M., Allison, K., Hajas, Z. and Halyburton, P. (1990), *Report of the Inquiry into Electricity Distribution in Broken Hill, Central Darling Shire and the Unincorporated Area*, New South Wales Government.

Thomis, Malcolm I. (1987) *A History of the Electricity Supply Industry in Queensland Volume 1: 1888–1938*, Boolarong Publications, Brisbane

Thompson, Peter (1981) *Power in Tasmania*, Australian Conservation Foundation.

Thynne, I. (1990) "Transformation of Public Enterprises: Changing Patterns of Ownership, Accountability and Control" for Ng, C. Y. & Wagner, N. (eds) *Marketisation of Public Enterprises*, Institute of Southeast Asian Studies, Singapore (forthcoming).

Tolley, D. (1987) "The Basis for Load Management in England and Wales," *Proceedings of the IEE 1987 MATES Conference*, Paper 1.7.

Trehan, B. and Walsh, C. E. (1988) 'Common Trends, the Government's Budget Constraint and Revenue Smoothing', *Journal of Economic Dynamics and Control*, 12, pp. 425–444.

United Mineworkers' Federation of Australia (1991) "Environment Issues Affecting the Coal Industry", paper for January National Conference.

United Mineworkers' Federation of Australia (1991) *The potential employment impacts within the Australian coal industry of implementing carbon dioxide emission reduction targets*, Sydney.

United States Environmental Protection Agency (1990) *An Evaluation of the Carciogenicity of Electro-magnetic Fields (EMF)*, June

Varian, H. R. (1978) *Microeconomic Analysis*, W.W. Norton & Co. New York and London, (2nd ed.).

Vaughan, K. (1991) "The Queensland Electricity Supply Industry and Corporatisation", paper presented at the conference March 14–15, The Future of the Power Industry in Australia, IIR Pty Ltd, Sydney.

Victorian Department of Industry, Technology and Resources, and the State Electricity Commission of Victoria (SECV/DITR) (1989) "3 Year Demand Management Action Plan:Demand Management Development Project", *Information Paper No. 5*, DITR/SECV, Melbourne.

Victorian Economic and Budget Review Committee (1990) *Twenty Seventh Report to Parliament: Electricity Gas and Water: Limits of Debt*, September.

Victorian Trades Hall Council, Gippsland Trades and Labour Council, Amalgamated Metal Workers' Union, Electrical Trades Union, Federated Engine Drivers' and Firemens' Association, Building Workers' Industrial Union and Federated Iron Workers' Union. (1987) *Submission to Natural Resources and*

Environmental Committee Inquiry Into Electricity Supply and Demand Beyond the Mid 1990s, Victoria.

Walker, I. J. (1990), "Potential to reduce emissions of greenhouse gases in the energy sector" , *EPD Discussion Paper No.1*, Coal Research and Energy Technology Branch, Energy Programs Division, Department of Primary Industries and Energy, Canberra, May.

Walker, R..G. (1987) "Reading between the railways' lines", *Australian Business*, 21 October 1987, p. 21.

Walker, R..G. (1989a) "Governments hide behind exempt status", *New Accountant*, September 7.

Walker, R. G. (1989b) "Should there be common standards for the public and private sectors?", Australian Society of Accountants Research Lecture in Government Accounting.

Walker, Robert (1989a) "NSW jumps the gun on corporatisation" in *New Accountant* 5 October.

Walker, Robert (1989b) "Elcom's smokescreen on revaluations" in *New Accountant* 23 August.

Walsh, P. (1990) "The impact of corporatisation upon industrial relations in New Zealand's state owned enterprises", paper presented to Queensland State government seminar on Corporatisation on Government Owned Enterprises, Brisbane, November 21.

Watson, Graham (1990) Electrical Trades Union, interview, 3 December.

Webb, Beatrice and Sidney (1922) *English Local Government: Statutory Authorities for Special Purposes*, Longmans, Green and Co., England.

Webb, J. (1990) *Seminar on the Industry Commission Inquiry into Energy Generation and Distribution*, University of New South Wales, Sydney.

Weller, Patrick and Jaensch, Dean (eds) (1980) *Responsible Government in Australia*, Drummond Publishing, Melbourne.

Wettenhall, R. L. (1963) "Administrative Boards in Nineteenth Century Australia" in *Public Administration (Sydney)* Vol 22, pp. 255–268.

Wettenhall, R. L. (1985) "Acworth, Attlee and Now: One Hundred Years of Debate About Public Enterprise — Government Relations" in *Political Science (NZ)*, Vol. 37 No. 2, December, pp. 125–139.

Wettenhall, R. L. (1990) "Public Administration Newspeak" in *Current Affairs Bulletin*, Vol. 66, No. 12, May, pp. 13–18.

Wettenhall, Roger (1986) *Organising Government: The Uses of Ministries and Departments*, Croom Helm, Sydney.

Weyman-Jones, T. G. (1989) *Electricity Privatisation* Avebury, UK.

Wicks, John (1990) "Rationalising Services Across States" a paper presented at the Power Generation Reform and Options for the Future Conference, 7–8 October.

Wilkenfeld, G. and Associates (1990) *Greenhouse Gas Emissions from the Australian Energy System: The Impact of Energy Efficiency and Substitution. End of Grant Report 1379 to National Energy Research, Development and Demonstration Programme*

Wilson, D. (1990) "Quantifying and comparing fuel-cycle greenhouse-gas emissions. Coal, oil and natural gas consumption." in *Energy Policy*, July/August, pp. 550–561.

Wood, A..J. Wollenberg, B..F. (1984) *Power Generation, Operation and Control*, J Wiley and Sons, New York.

World Commission on Environment and Development (WCED) (1987) *Our Common Future*, Oxford University Press, New York.

World Resources Institute and The International Institute for Environment and Development (1990), *World Resources 1988–89*, Basic Books Inc., New York.

Worldwatch Institute (1990), *State of the World 1990*, Allen and Unwin, Sydney.

Yeatman, Anna (1990a) *Bureaucrats, Technocrats, Femocrats: Essays on the Contemprary Australian State*, Alllen and Unwin, Sydney.

————————————— (1990b) "Reconstructing Public Bureaucracies: The Residualisation of Equity and Access" in *Australian Journal of Public Administration*, Vol 49, No 1, March, pp. 17–21.